THE CLAY SANSKRIT LIBRARY

FOUNDED BY JOHN & JENNIFER CLAY

WWW.CLAYSANSKRITLIBRARY.ORG
WWW.NYUPRESS.ORG

Artwork by Robert Beer.
Typeset in Adobe Garamond Pro at 10.25 : 12.3+pt.
Editorial input from Dániel Balogh, Adam Bowles,
Ridi Faruque, Chris Gibbons,
Tomoyuki Kono & Eszter Somogyi.
Printed and Bound in Great Britain by
TJ Books Limited, Cornwall on acid free paper

MAHĀBHĀRATA

BOOK TWELVE

PEACE

VOLUME THREE

"THE BOOK OF LIBERATION"

TRANSLATED BY

Alexander Wynne

NEW YORK UNIVERSITY PRESS

JJC FOUNDATION

2009

First Edition 2009

The Clay Sanskrit Library is co-published by
New York University Press
and the JJC Foundation.

Further information about this volume
and the rest of the Clay Sanskrit Library
is available at the end of this book and
on the following websites:
www.claysanskritlibrary.org
www.nyupress.org

ISBN 978-0-8147-9453-1

Library of Congress Cataloging-in-Publication Data
Mahābhārata. Śāntiparva. English & Sanskrit.
Mahābhārata. Book twelve, Peace. -- 1st ed.
p. cm.
Epic Poetry.
In English and Sanskrit (romanized) on facing pages;
includes translation from Sanskrit.
Description based on: v. 3, published in 2009.
ISBN 978-0-8147-9453-1
1. Epic poetry, Sanskrit--Translations into English.
I. Wynne, Alexander, 1974- II. Title. III. Title: Peace.
BL1138.242.S26E5 2009
294.5'92304521--dc22
2008049541

CONTENTS

CSL CONVENTIONS

Sanskrit Alphabetical Order

Vowels:	*a ā i ī u ū ṛ ṝ ḷ ḹ e ai o au ṃ ḥ*
Gutturals:	*k kh g gh ṅ*
Palatals:	*c ch j jh ñ*
Retroflex:	*ṭ ṭh ḍ ḍh ṇ*
Dentals:	*t th d dh n*
Labials:	*p ph b bh m*
Semivowels:	*y r l v*
Spirants:	*ś ṣ s h*

Guide to Sanskrit Pronunciation

a	b*u*t
ā, â	f*a*ther
i	s*i*t
ī, î	f*ee*
u	p*u*t
ū, û	b*oo*
ṛ	vocalic *r*, American p*ur*dy or English p*re*tty
ṝ	lengthened *ṛ*
ḷ	vocalic *l*, ab*le*
e, ê, ē	m*a*de, esp. in Welsh pronunciation
ai	b*i*te
o, ô, ō	r*o*pe, esp. Welsh pronunciation; Italian s*o*lo
au	s*ou*nd
ṃ	*anusvāra* nasalizes the preceding vowel
ḥ	*visarga*, a voiceless aspiration (resembling the English *h*), or like Scottish lo*ch*, or an aspiration with a faint echoing of the last element of the preceding vowel so that *taiḥ* is pronounced *taih*[i]
k	lu*ck*
kh	blo*ckh*ead
g	*g*o
gh	bi*gh*ead
ṅ	a*n*ger
c	*ch*ill
ch	mat*chh*ead
j	*j*og
jh	aspirated *j*, he*dgeh*og
ñ	ca*ny*on
ṭ	retroflex *t*, *t*ry (with the tip of tongue turned up to touch the hard palate)
ṭh	same as the preceding but aspirated
ḍ	retroflex *d* (with the tip

of tongue turned up to touch the hard palate)
ḍh same as the preceding but aspirated
ṇ retroflex *n* (with the tip of tongue turned up to touch the hard palate)
t French *t*out
th ten*t h*ook
d *d*inner
dh guil*dh*all
n *n*ow
p *p*ill
ph u*ph*eaval
b *b*efore
bh a*bh*orrent
m *m*ind
y *y*es
r trilled, resembling the Italian pronunciation of *r*
l *l*inger
v *w*ord
ś *sh*ore
ṣ retroflex *sh* (with the tip of the tongue turned up to touch the hard palate)
s hi*ss*
h *h*ood

CSL Punctuation of English

The acute accent on Sanskrit words when they occur outside of the Sanskrit text itself, marks stress, e.g., Ramáyana. It is not part of traditional Sanskrit orthography, transliteration, or transcription, but we supply it here to guide readers in the pronunciation of these unfamiliar words. Since no Sanskrit word is accented on the last syllable it is not necessary to accent disyllables, e.g., Rama.

The second CSL innovation designed to assist the reader in the pronunciation of lengthy unfamiliar words is to insert an unobtrusive middle dot between semantic word breaks in compound names (provided the word break does not fall on a vowel resulting from the fusion of two vowels), e.g., Maha·bhárata, but Ramáyana (not Rama·áyana). Our dot echoes the punctuating middle dot (·) found in the oldest surviving samples of written Indic, the Ashokan inscriptions of the third century BCE.

The deep layering of Sanskrit narrative has also dictated that we use quotation marks only to announce the beginning and end of every direct speech, and not at the beginning of every paragraph.

CSL Punctuation of Sanskrit

The Sanskrit text is also punctuated, in accordance with the punctuation of the English translation. In mid-verse, the punctuation will not alter the sandhi or the scansion. Proper names are capitalized. Most Sanskrit meters have four "feet" (*pāda*); where possible we print the common *śloka* meter on two lines. The capitalization of verse beginnings makes it easy for the reader to recognize longer meters where it is necessary to print the four metrical feet over four or eight lines. In the Sanskrit text, we use French *Guillemets* (e.g., *«kva saṃcicīrṣuḥ?»*) instead of English quotation marks (e.g., "Where are you off to?") to avoid confusion with the apostrophes used for vowel elision in sandhi.

SANDHI

Sanskrit presents the learner with a challenge: *sandhi* (euphonic combination). Sandhi means that when two words are joined in connected speech or writing (which in Sanskrit reflects speech), the last letter (or even letters) of the first word often changes; compare the way we pronounce "the" in "the beginning" and "the end."

In Sanskrit the first letter of the second word may also change; and if both the last letter of the first word and the first letter of the second are vowels, they may fuse. This has a parallel in English: a nasal consonant is inserted between two vowels that would otherwise coalesce: "a pear" and "an apple." Sanskrit vowel fusion may produce ambiguity.

The charts on the following pages give the full sandhi system.

Fortunately it is not necessary to know these changes in order to start reading Sanskrit. All that is important to know is the form of the second word without sandhi (pre-sandhi), so that it can be recognized or looked up in a dictionary. Therefore we are printing Sanskrit with a system of punctuation that will indicate, unambiguously, the original form of the second word, i.e., the form without sandhi. Such sandhi mostly concerns the fusion of two vowels.

In Sanskrit, vowels may be short or long and are written differently accordingly. We follow the general convention that a vowel with no mark above it is short. Other books mark a long vowel either with a bar called a macron (*ā*) or with a circumflex (*â*). Our system uses the

VOWEL SANDHI

Final vowels:

a	ā	i	ī	u	ū	ṛ	e	ai	o	au	*Initial vowels:*
' â	" â	y a	y a	v a	v a	r a	e '	ā a	o '	āv a	a
' ā	" ā	y ā	y ā	v ā	v ā	r ā	a ā	ā ā	a ā	āv ā	ā
' ê	" ê	' î	" î	v i	v i	r i	a i	ā i	a i	āv i	i
' ē	" ē	' ī	" ī	v ī	v ī	r ī	a ī	ā ī	a ī	āv ī	ī
' ô	" ô	y u	y u	' û	" û	r u	a u	ā u	a u	āv u	u
' ō	" ō	y ū	y ū	' ū	" ū	r ū	a ū	ā ū	a ū	āv ū	ū
a' r	a" r	y ṛ	y ṛ	v ṛ	v ṛ	' ṝ	a ṛ	ā ṛ	a ṛ	āv ṛ	ṛ
' âi	" âi	y e	y e	v e	v e	r e	a e	ā e	a e	āv e	e
' āi	" āi	y ai	y ai	v ai	v ai	r ai	a ai	ā ai	a ai	āv ai	ai
' âu	" âu	y o	y o	v o	v o	r o	a o	ā o	a o	āv o	o
' āu	" āu	y au	y au	v au	v au	r au	a au	ā au	a au	āv au	au

CONSONANT SANDHI

Permitted finals:							(Except āḥ/aḥ)			Initial
k	ṭ	t	p	ṅ	n	m	ḥ/r	āḥ	aḥ	letters:
k	ṭ	t	p	ṅ	n	ṃ	ḥ	āḥ	aḥ	k/kh
g	ḍ	d	b	ṅ	n	ṃ	r	ā	o	g/gh
k	ṭ	c	p	ṅ	ṃś	ṃ	ś	āś	aś	c/ch
g	ḍ	j	b	ṅ	ñ	ṃ	r	ā	o	j/jh
k	ṭ	ṭ	p	ṅ	ṃṣ	ṃ	ṣ	āṣ	aṣ	ṭ/ṭh
g	ḍ	ḍ	b	ṅ	ṇ	ṃ	r	ā	o	ḍ/ḍh
k	ṭ	t	p	ṅ	ṃs	ṃ	s	ās	as	t/th
g	ḍ	d	b	ṅ	n	ṃ	r	ā	o	d/dh
k	ṭ	t	p	ṅ	n	ṃ	ḥ	āḥ	aḥ	p/ph
g	ḍ	d	b	ṅ	n	ṃ	r	ā	o	b/bh
ṅ	ṇ	n	m	ṅ	n	ṃ	r	ā	o	*nasals* (n/m)
g	ḍ	d	b	ṅ	n	ṃ	r	ā	o	y/v
g	ḍ	d	b	ṅ	n	ṃ	*zero*[1]	ā	o	r
g	ḍ	l	b	ṅ	l̃[2]	ṃ	r	ā	o	l
k	ṭ	c ch	p	ṅ	ñ ś/ch	ṃ	ḥ	āḥ	aḥ	ś
k	ṭ	t	p	ṅ	n	ṃ	ḥ	āḥ	aḥ	ṣ/s
gg h	ḍḍ h	dd h	bb h	ṅ	n	ṃ	r	ā	o	h
g	ḍ	d	b	ṅ/ṅṅ[3]	n/nn[3]	m	r	ā	a[4]	*vowels*
k	ṭ	t	p	ṅ	n	m	ḥ	āḥ	aḥ	*zero*

[1]ḥ or r disappears, and if a/i/u precedes, this lengthens to ā/ī/ū. [2]e.g. tān+lokān=tāl̃ lokān.
[3]The doubling occurs if the preceding vowel is short. [4]Except: aḥ+a=o '.

macron, except that for initial vowels in sandhi we use a circumflex to indicate that originally the vowel was short, or the shorter of two possibilities (*e* rather than *ai*, *o* rather than *au*).

When we print initial *â*, before sandhi that vowel was *a*

î or *ê*,	*i*
û or *ô*,	*u*
âi,	*e*
âu,	*o*
ā,	*ā*
ī,	*ī*
ū,	*ū*
ē,	*ī*
ō,	*ū*
ai,	*ai*
āu,	*au*

’, before sandhi there was a vowel *a*

When a final short vowel (*a*, *i*, or *u*) has merged into a following vowel, we print ’ at the end of the word, and when a final long vowel (*ā*, *ī*, or *ū*) has merged into a following vowel we print ” at the end of the word. The vast majority of these cases will concern a final *a* or *ā*. See, for instance, the following examples:

What before sandhi was *atra asti* is represented as *atr’ âsti*

atra āste	*atr’ āste*
kanyā asti	*kany” âsti*
kanyā āste	*kany” āste*
atra iti	*atr’ êti*
kanyā iti	*kany” êti*
kanyā īpsitā	*kany” ēpsitā*

Finally, three other points concerning the initial letter of the second word:

(1) A word that before sandhi begins with *ṛ* (vowel), after sandhi begins with *r* followed by a consonant: *yatha” rtu* represents pre-sandhi *yathā ṛtu*.

(2) When before sandhi the previous word ends in *t* and the following word begins with *ś*, after sandhi the last letter of the previous word is *c*

and the following word begins with *ch*: *syāc chāstravit* represents pre-sandhi *syāt śāstravit*.

(3) Where a word begins with *h* and the previous word ends with a double consonant, this is our simplified spelling to show the pre-sandhi form: *tad hasati* is commonly written as *tad dhasati*, but we write *tadd hasati* so that the original initial letter is obvious.

COMPOUNDS

We also punctuate the division of compounds (*samāsa*), simply by inserting a thin vertical line between words. There are words where the decision whether to regard them as compounds is arbitrary. Our principle has been to try to guide readers to the correct dictionary entries.

Exemplar of CSL Style

Where the Devanagari script reads:

कुम्भस्थली रक्षतु वो विकीर्णसिन्धूररेणुर्द्विरदाननस्य ।
प्रशान्तये विघ्नतमश्छटानां निष्ठ्यूतबालातपपल्लवेव ॥

Others would print:

kumbhasthalī rakṣatu vo vikīrṇasindūrareṇur dviradānanasya /
praśāntaye vighnatamaśchaṭānāṃ niṣṭhyūtabālātapapallaveva //

We print:

kumbha|sthalī rakṣatu vo vikīrṇa|sindūra|reṇur dvirad'|ānanasya
praśāntaye vighna|tamaś|chaṭānāṃ niṣṭhyūta|bāl'|ātapa|pallav" êva.

And in English:

May Ganésha's domed forehead protect you! Streaked with vermilion dust, it seems to be emitting the spreading rays of the rising sun to pacify the teeming darkness of obstructions.

("Nava·sáhasanka and the Serpent Princess" 1.3)

INTRODUCTION

'The Book of Liberation' (*Mokṣadharmaparvan*) is perhaps the most enigmatic philosophical text from ancient India. Although generally believed to contain some of the most important early Hindu teachings, at least one scholar has described it as "for the most part dull and unimportant" (Frauwallner 1973: 80). Both perspectives are valid. In scope, 'Liberation' is unrivaled by any other work of Hindu philosophy. It is much longer and more diverse than the equally elusive early Upanishads that predate it by a few centuries. But this diversity was unintended; 'Liberation' was not an attempt to chronicle the intellectual achievements of a particular age. Compiled in a haphazard manner over several centuries, just like the roughly contemporaneous early Buddhist literature, it is a disordered work, the understanding of which has been further impeded by a deficient textual transmission.

Nevertheless, as the only record of Hindu speculation in the early post-Upanishadic period, 'Liberation' is an invaluable historical source. While lacking the mastery of the great poems of the "Rig Veda," it develops its early speculations in a spirit of earnest enquiry. And while surpassed by the later philosophical texts of the Hindu tradition, it provides the intellectual background to much of what was to follow. But this is not all. 'Liberation' is far more than a useful, if confused, historical witness. It is also a compelling record of a unique period of intellectual endeavor.

Ancient India, in the last few centuries BCE, was a land of great speculative fervor. Its religious culture had exploded into life with a movement of world-renunciation on an unprecedented scale: peripatetic sages meditated under trees, devout ascetics practiced austerities in forest groves, and wandering sophists conducted debates in the towns and cities. There has been nothing comparable before or since—as T.W. RHYS DAVIDS (1908: 247) put it, the religious men (and women) of ancient India enjoyed "the most perfect freedom, both of thought and expression ... a freedom probably unequaled in the history of the world."

The freedom enjoyed by these ancient thinkers was not an end in itself, however, and 'Liberation' is not a record of philosophical speculation for its own sake. Above all it is an animated work of thinkers seeking liberation (*mokṣa*) from a world they believed to be unsatisfactory.

Early Hindu Speculation and Renunciation

From around the middle of the first millennium BCE onwards, the phenomenon of world renunciation transformed India's religion and culture. This new religious order posed a complex problem to the orthodox Brahminic priesthood. The priests made their living by performing rituals and sacrifices, but it was the efficacy of just these rites that the renouncers denied. Unsurprisingly, the renouncers did not share the soteriological goal of the ritualists—a place among their ancestors in heaven after death.

The renouncers believed existence in the world to be bondage, and so proposed various escapes based on the renunciation of normal worldly values. They idealized a new peripatetic "counter-culture" of mendicancy that contrasted sharply with the family-based ritualism of orthodox Brahminism. This posed a threat to the Brahminic order which was about more than simply a matter of religious rivalry. The rubbishing of Brahminic ritualism implicitly denied, or at least challenged, the social order sanctioned by their sacred texts, the Vedas. According to this order, the brahmins occupied the primary position in a hierarchical society of four classes, the other three being, in descending order, the martial class of kshatriyas, the merchant class of vaishyas, and the servile class of shudras.

Although the new renunciant movements posed a subversive threat to orthodox Brahminism, Brahminic schools certainly sprang up among them, and it was within these Brahminic schools that the individual texts of 'Liberation' were composed.[1] Beyond the tensions and rapprochement evident in the extant texts, the relationship between orthodox Brahminism and its renunciant schools is unknown. It seems unlikely, however, that the Brahminic renouncers denied the authority of the Vedas per se, and this probably means that they would not have been disdained in the way that the heterodox schools were. Indeed there are reasons for believing that Brahminic renouncers were deemed to lie within the bounds of acceptability, even if they did not belong to orthodox circles. This follows from the fact that similar speculative and ascetic trends can be traced back to a number of very early Brahminic texts.

The "Rig Veda" contains a number of important speculative texts, at least one of which—the *Nāsadīya Sūkta*—was of particular importance for later Brahminic thought.[2] This mysterious creation poem states that the world was created from "mind" (v. 3: *manas*), the primeval state of consciousness of a divine, nondual deity. It also speaks of seers (*kavi*) who "found the connection of the existent in the nonexistent through inspired thinking." The *Nāsadīya Sūkta* does not mention the meditative and contemplative practices that were of such importance later on. But the peculiar notion of creation emerging from a divine cognition suggests that the "inspired thinking" of its creators was of a mystical kind.[3] The poem certainly influenced later mystical traditions, since its cosmogonic themes provide the theoretical background to much of the thinking recorded in 'Liberation.'

Elsewhere, another Rig Vedic poem speaks of a long-haired sage (*muni*) who wears "dirty red rags" and flies "through the air" (DONIGER 2005: 137–38). The precise meaning of this description is unclear, but the depiction of a class of men who ride "with the rush of the wind" and into whom "the gods enter" shows that there were alternative religious lifestyles and practices even in the late Vedic period. Religious outsiders—holy men, mystics, ascetics and so on—have apparently been important, if marginal, figures in Indian religious life since time immemorial.

There is no reason to believe that such characters were viewed with contempt within ancient Brahminic circles. Even when more radical ideas related to the renunciant movements start to appear in the Brahminic record, it is by no means clear that they posed a cultural threat to orthodox Brahminism. The following passage from the *Chāndogya Upaniṣad* from around the sixth century BCE—mirrored by a similar passage in the contemporaneous *Bṛhadāraṇyaka Upaniṣad*—contains the seeds of the dichotomy in religious values that would emerge, but it was probably the work of a speculative minority:

> "Now, the people who know this, and the people here in the wilderness who venerate thus: "Austerity is faith" —they pass into the flame, from the flame they go into the day, from the day into the fortnight of the waxing moon, from the fortnight of the waxing moon into the six months when the sun moves north, from these months into the year, from the year into the sun, from the sun into the moon, and from the moon into lightning. Then a person who is not human—he leads them to *brahman*. This is the path leading to the gods."
>
> "The people here in villages, on the other hand, who venerate thus: 'Gift-giving is offering to gods and to priests'—they pass into the smoke, from the smoke into the night, from the night into the fortnight of the waning moon, and from the fortnight of the waning moon into the six months when the sun moves south. These do not reach the year but from these months pass into the world of fathers, and from the world of fathers into space, and from space into the moon. This is King Soma, the food of the gods, and the gods eat it. They remain there as long as there is a residue, and then they return by the same path they went—first to space, and from space to the wind. After the wind has formed, it turns into smoke; after the smoke has formed, it turns into a thunder-cloud; after the thunder-cloud has formed, it turns into a

rain-cloud; and after a rain-cloud has formed, it rains down. On earth they spring up as rice and barley, plants and trees, sesame and beans, from which it is extremely difficult to get out. When someone eats that food and deposits the semen, from him one comes into being again."[4]

This passage is certainly obscure, but it explicitly states the idea of reincarnation and the notion of a final release from it for the first time in Indian literature. Those who live in the wilderness are said to have a special knowledge that magically effects their liberation ("Austerity is faith"), whereas ordinary people who follow the ritual religion are reincarnated on earth. The inclusion of such passages in orthodox texts shows that there was room within Brahminism for diverse perspectives and lifestyles. Perhaps if these ideas had remained the concern of a minority of Upanishadic brahmins living at the edge of society, the tension between the lifestyles of the householder and the renouncer could have been avoided.

Such ideas did not remain confined to those living in the wilderness, however, but contributed to the phenomenon of world renunciation. The following passage from the *Muṇḍaka Upaniṣad* seems to show that the anti-ritualistic stream of thought attested in the *Chāndogya Upaniṣad* had developed into a culture of mendicancy:

Deeming sacrifices and gifts as the best,
    the imbeciles know nothing better.
When they have enjoyed their good work,
    atop the firmament,

they return again to this abject world.
But those in the wilderness, calm and wise,
who live a life of penance and faith,
as they beg their food;
Through the sun's door they go, spotless,
to where that immortal Person is,
that immutable self.[5]

Although those who attain liberation are still said to live in the wilderness, the statement that they beg for food and practice a life of "penance" places them within the new culture of mendicancy and world-renunciation. This impression is confirmed by what is said to be the goal of the mendicants: union with an impersonal essence—the immutable self (*ātman*)—rather than the goal of god-like status mentioned in the *Chāndogya Upaniṣad*. Furthermore, the soteriological method of the *Muṇḍaka Upaniṣad* is *yoga* (or *dhyāna*, one-pointed concentration), rather than the magical knowledge of the *Chāndogya Upaniṣad* (*upāsana*, veneration), and its aim is to "perceive" the self through meditation:

Not by sight, not by speech, nor by any other sense;
nor by austerities or rites is he grasped.
Rather the partless one is seen by a man,
as he meditates,
When his being has become pure,
Through the lucidity of knowledge.[6]

It would be simplistic to suppose that the wilderness-dwelling, Upanishadic gnostics of the *Chāndogya* and *Bṛhadāraṇyaka Upaniṣad*s began to practice *yoga* at a later date (perhaps a hundred years or so later).[7] But in the space between the *Chāndogya* and *Muṇḍaka Upaniṣad*s, ideas that had probably been the preserve of a minority of esotericists became the inspiration for world-renunciation. It was the sheer scale of this movement that threatened orthodox Brahminism.[8]

It is difficult to explain the mass appeal of the new renunciant religions. World-renunciation requires a culture of liberty in which men and women think and act for themselves. But a culture of individualism is not so easy to explain in India where group membership (the family, clan, class or caste) dominates, a point well made by V.S. NAIPAUL (1977: 112): "How can anyone used from infancy to the security of the group, and the security of a minutely regulated life, become an individual, a man on his own? He will be drowned in the immensity of the unknown world; he will be lost." These words about India in the twentieth century apply equally to the India of the first millenium BCE. How did renunciant religions—individualistic religions—spring up in a land dominated by the group mentality? It is surely significant that the renunciant religions are associated with an area in the north-east of India termed 'Greater Magadha' by JOHANNES BRONKHORST,[9] and the rise of an urban culture there from around 600 BCE onwards.[10] This change was accompanied by a political transformation from the old order of small fiefdoms and tribal republics to larger monarchies and eventually, by about the mid fifth century BCE, empires. It was a time of great social change and upheaval.

The rise of city life must have brought about greater personal liberty. It would have been possible for individuals to act outside the more restrictive structures of the family/clan as never before. There can be little doubt that this sort of change led to a greater freedom of thought. Indeed it is hardly surprising that the early Buddhist sources depict towns and cities as the centers of intellectual debate and renunciant support. Nor is it a surprise that the early Brahminic texts on law and correct religious conduct (the *Dharmasūtras*) are hostile to cities.[11]

Initially, the diversity and inequality of the new urban environments probably stimulated intellectual enquiry. Since the range of wealth and power in a city is greater than in a village, it is likely that social imbalances were a by-product of the greater freedom of the cities. If so, it is likely that an atmosphere arose in which values were questioned.[12]

Another factor that may well have prompted metaphysical enquiry was the humid and disease-prone climate of the north-east of India. The urban cultivation of the region was preceded by the deforestation of the fertile land around the Ganges. The rapid process of urbanization that followed would have been accompanied by epidemics of disease. The rate of mortality must initially have been unusually high, and such conditions would only have added to the general mood of enquiry in which accepted values were questioned.

An atmosphere of changing values, enquiry and morbidity probably stimulated the new renunciant religions. But this does not explain how they originated. A rise in religious activity is only to be expected in hard times, but adverse circumstances do not normally turn people into wandering mendicants. So why did it happen?

Religious movements depend on compelling figures who act on their own mysterious impulses. The ancient Indian records mention at least one such figure—the Rig Vedic *muni*—and it is likely that there were more, who may even have belonged to non-Vedic milieux. In times of change, enigmatic figures from the religious fringe would have attracted new generations of followers. Perhaps it was thought that they represented an older, quixotic ideal. Inspired by archaic counter-culture figures such as these, the young men of this age may well have been inspired to act upon the adolescent urge to escape civilization. A vivid modern depiction of this urge can be seen in MARK TWAIN's "Adventures of Huckleberry Finn:"

> The Widow Douglas she took me for her son, and allowed she would sivilize me; but it was rough living in the house all the time, considering how dismal regular and decent the widow was in all her ways; and so when I couldn't stand it no longer I lit out. I got into my old rags and my sugar-hogshead again, and was free and satisfied.

The dissatisfaction with civilized life described here touches on what is probably a universal escapist fantasy. Indeed the early Buddhist literature contains a similar account of the reason for becoming a homeless mendicant:

> Life at home is restricted, a path of dust, whereas striving forth is the life of the open air. It is not easy for a

> person living at home to live the holy life that is completely pure and fulfilled, and as perfectly grooved as a conch shell. Why don't I shave off my hair and beard, don a discolored robe and strive forth from home to homelessness? (*Dīgha Nikāya* vol. I: 63)

The sentiment captured by this Buddhist passage is, I think, strikingly similar to that articulated by MARK TWAIN. The Buddhist renouncer is of course motivated by religious ideals, but both he and Huckleberry Finn are drawn towards a life of poverty and liberation from the restrictions of civilization. And what could be more liberating than the peripatetic ways of those adventurers of the mind from ancient India?

Under the right social conditions, and with the appropriate religious background, it is easy to imagine how young men could be drawn to the lifestyle of the ancient Indian wanderers. In ancient India, it so happened that there were compelling social and moral reasons for giving in to the escapist urge to abandon civilization.

Structure

If there had not been sympathy for renouncers and their ideals within orthodox circles, it would be impossible to explain why speculative texts such as the *Muṇḍaka Upaniṣad* were incorporated into the larger Vedic canon. The inclusion of 'Liberation' within a mainstream text like the "Maha·bhárata" seems to confirm this suggestion. By including texts from the renunciant schools of early Brahminism in the "Maha·bhárata," the religion of ascetics and philosophers was officially sanctioned.

This, however, merely begs another question: why was a long book on *mokṣa* included within the "Maha·bhárata" anyway? What possible connection could there be between metaphysical musings and an epic war poem?

'Liberation' is the third and final part of 'Peace,' the twelfth book of the "Maha·bhárata." Within 'Peace,' 'Liberation' follows two other sections: 'Law for kings' (*Rāja-dharma*) and 'Law to be followed in a crisis' (*Āpaddharma*). At the beginning of 'Law for kings,' Yudhi·shthira, the embodiment of dharma, is overcome with sorrow after the carnage of the war with the Káuravas. But instead of taking responsibility for the war, he wishes to renounce the kingdom and retire to the forest. He is therefore acting in accordance with the pacifist ideals of world-renunciation. The first part of 'Peace' consists of the orthodox attempts to cajole Yudhi·shthira to conform to the duties specific to his class, i.e. the kingly duties of ruling and administering justice.

It is important to note that this "persuasion of Yudhi·shthira," as JAMES FITZGERALD (2004: 195) has termed it, is achieved not by conducting a polemic against the renouncers, but by acknowledging the worth of their ideals. FITZGERALD has argued that the authors of 'Peace' attempted to synthesize the newer renunciant values with older Brahminic ones. Their aim was to infuse the religious and social obligations of the martial kshatriya class "with a sense of inner restraint (*niyama*), which—besides having some elements of the obvious about it—was strongly endorsed as dharma by the developing traditions of yoga" (FITZGERALD 2004: 130 n.204).

Ostensibly, 'Liberation' is the conclusion of Bhishma's instructions to Yudhi·shthira on dharma (law, duty, or religion: *dharma* is the most elusive of all Sanskrit terms); its Sanskrit title is indeed *Mokṣadharma*. But 'Liberation' lacks both a central core and a planned structure, and its texts do not obviously synthesize older Brahminic values with newer renunciant ones. Nevertheless, a synthesis of sorts can be seen in 'Liberation,' since some texts seem to juxtapose ideas from the two streams of thought.

A simple synthesis of values can be seen in 'The dialogue between Bhrigu and Bharad·vaja,' an important dialogue found near the beginning of 'Liberation' (cantos 182–192). Its early sections are philosophical and undoubtedly the work of renunciant thinkers. Its later sections, however, offer different perspectives. At 188.6–9, the system of four classes is criticized for ignoring the fact that moral failings are found in all people. This sort of critique is only to be expected from renunciant circles, in which a more universalist ethic prevailed. The response, however, is that a person's class depends upon his good and bad deeds (*karma*). It would appear that the renunciant doctrine of *karma* has been appropriated to justify the Brahminic social order.

Elsewhere in the dialogue renunciant and ritualistic ideals are combined (189.2–4), and the four religious lifestyles (chaste studentship, householdership, forest asceticism and renunciation) are outlined as if all are viable alternatives (191.8–6). In the latter account, a renouncer is even said to internalize the Brahminic fire ritual by offering it "in his mouth." The message seems clear: renunciation is a style of life sanctioned by the Vedas. Otherwise, the passages towards the end of the dialogue frequently state that heaven (*svarga*) is the goal of religious activity (190.1–3 190.12–15; 191.6, 191.9, 191.18). This conflation of different goals—union with *brahman/ātman* is the goal of the earlier parts of the dialogue—looks like an attempt to balance renunciant and orthodox ideals.

A similar tendency to balance renunciant perspectives with orthodox values is seen in the contrast between cantos 194–195 and cantos 196–200. The former contain what are perhaps the most important texts on metaphysics and meditation in the early part of 'Liberation,' but they are immediately followed by a discourse on the more orthodox ideal of intoning the Veda under one's breath (*japa*). Canto 196 explicitly synthesizes renunciant and ritualistic values, by claiming that the practitioner of *japa* should follow the values and practices of *sāṃkhya* and *yoga* (196.9–13), which include concentration, sense-restraint, asceticism, meditation, and, incongruously, tending the sacred fire. The discourse ends with an account of the Vedic reciter's reception by the supreme god Brahma, followed by his absorption into him (200.20–25). It is claimed that this attainment is equivalent, if not marginally superior, to the goal of *yoga*.

This juxtaposition of texts may be accidental, but another important philosophical section, 'The Teachings of Pancha·shikha' (218–219), is also followed by a couple of texts that have little to do with renunciation and liberation. Canto 220 praises the ascetic ideal of restraint (*dama*), and recommends it for all the four religious lifestyles (220.8). While claiming that restraint will lead to meditative results for the brahmin who possesses it (220.14), the goal of the passage is heaven (220.13).

Following this, canto 221 domesticates renunciant values by reinterpreting asceticism (*tapas*) as the ethical qualities of "renunciation" (*tyāga*) and "humility" (*saṃnati*) (221.5), fasting as not eating between meals (221.10), celibacy as engaging in sexual intercourse only when a woman is able to conceive (221.11), and vegetarianism as eating meat that has not been prepared specifically for that purpose (221.12). The goal of this canto is once again heaven (221.14).

'Liberation' does not initially tackle the dichotomy between the values of renunciation and the householder religion head-on; only in some of its later sections does it try to find a credible resolution between the two different value systems. But the alternation between these two in its earlier sections shows how renunciation was integrated with orthodox Brahminism at an earlier stage of development. Although the ultimate aim of most of the texts of 'Liberation' is salvation from the never-ending round of reincarnation, the diversity of its texts shows that such notions were incorporated into a larger Brahminic order.

Date

If 'Peace' was a Brahminic attempt to reconcile renunciation and orthodox Brahminism, FITZGERALD's suggestion that it was composed in the century or so after Ashóka makes good sense. Ashóka (c. 268—235 BCE) was the Mauryan king who ruled over the largest pre-modern Indian empire. He was also a convert to Buddhism who attempted to incorporate renunciant ethics into his rule through a series of edicts on dharma and other measures. According to Fitzgerald, 'Peace' is a Brahminic response to this infusion of renunciant ideals into the sphere of kingship:

> The figure of Yudhiṣṭhira, the new king, being calmed and quieted as he listened to those instructions in the wake of his vigorous efforts to disown the war and the kingship it brought is the epic's answer to the person of Ashóka. (Fitzgerald 2004: 129)

If this is correct it means that 'Liberation' belongs to the post-Ashókan era. But an earlier date for parts of 'Liberation' is possible, since all of its texts pre-existed their inclusion within it. Indeed some of its earliest texts share a number of similarities with the early Buddhist literature,[13] a substantial portion of which must have existed in some form soon after the Buddha's death (c. 404 BCE).[14] It is possible, then, that many of the texts at the beginning of 'Liberation' had been in circulation for some time before their incorporation into the "Maha·bhárata." They may well date to the late fourth/early third century BCE.[15]

It is generally accepted that 'Liberation' was compiled gradually, with new parts being added to the end of a pre-existing collection.[16] While there are many exceptions to this rule, the texts towards the beginning of 'Liberation' are clearly earlier than the texts found towards its end. Some of these later texts probably date to the first century CE, since a cosmogony found in canto 306—mirrored by an account of *yoga* found in canto 310—corresponds to a scheme of thought outlined in Ashva·ghosha's "Life of the Buddha" (*Buddhacarita*).[17] Ashva·ghosha probably flourished in the first century CE. According to E.H. JOHNSTON, ancient fragments of Ashva·ghosha's *Śāriputraprakaraṇa* belong to "the reign of Kaníshka or Huvishka,"[18] which implies that he lived "not later than the time of Kaníshka and may have preceded him" (JOHNSTON 1984, Part II: xvi).

If we follow HARRY FALK in dating the beginning of the Kaníshka era to 127 CE,[19] we can probably agree with JOHNSTON that Ashva·ghosha flourished "between 50 BCE and 100 CE."[20] And since 'Liberation' was compiled gradually, by adding new texts at its end, it would appear that roughly its first two-thirds had been compiled by the first century CE. The final third was probably completed during the first or second century CE.

Important Teachings in the First Volume of 'Liberation'

This first volume of 'Liberation' is dominated by two lengthy philosophical tracts: 'The dialogue between Bhrigu and Bharad·vaja' (cantos 182–192), and 'The Dialogue between Manu and Brihas·pati' (cantos 201–206). The former contains an important cosmogony (182.11–21, 183.8–17) which postulates that world-creation begins with the self-cognition of an unmanifest, nondual deity (called 'pure consciousness,' 182.11, or *brahman*, 182.37). A similar understanding is implied in the dialogue between Manu and Brihas·pati (202.1, 204.10–1), although this text is more interested in the attainment of liberation (*mokṣa*) through meditation (*dhyāna* or *yoga*: 204.5, 205.10–22). Both dialogues probably originated in different but related early Brahminic schools.

The dialogue between Bhrigu and Bharad·vaja is also important for the diverse topics that it covers. As Erich Frauwallner (1973: 98) has pointed out, this text is a rarity in that its interests are "more scientific" than other speculative texts of this period. These interests include passages on the movements of the vital winds (*prāṇa*) within a human being (185), an explanation of cognition according to the doctrine of five elements and their derivatives (184.26ff) and a refutation of the contention that a nondualist doctrine is tantamount to nihilism (186–187).

No less historically important than these dialogues are the two cantos that comprise the teachings of Pancha·shikha (218–219), who is presented as a founding figure of the Samkhya school of thought (218.9, 218.20). Pancha·shikha's teaching features two important subjects of later Samkhya thought: the three psychosomatic states of purity, passion and darkness (*sattva*, *rajas* and *tamas*, 219.24ff), and the method of discrimination of self from not-self (219.15). Unlike the classical Samkhya system of Íshvara·krishna, however, Pancha·shikha does not teach a radical dualism between the two fundamental substances of spirit and matter. His teaching instead conforms to the standard nondualism of early Brahminic thought. Thus the goal taught by his teacher Ásuri is said to have been the "imperishable *brahman*" (218.14), and Pancha·shikha uses the nondualistic metaphor of rivers running into the ocean to describe liberation (219.42).

Perhaps the single most important philosophical text in the present volume of 'Liberation' is canto 194. Its three sections—on the creation of the world through the emanation of a divine being (194.3–14), the three psychosomatic states of being (*bhāva*) and the fundamental duality between spirit and matter (194.22–44), and meditation as the way to attain liberation (194.45ff)—encapsulate the major speculative concerns of this period of early Hinduism.

The most detailed treatment of meditation, an important subject of 'Liberation,' is found in canto 195, which shows a notable influence from early Buddhism. Thus 195.1 mentions the "fourfold discipline of meditation" by which great sages are said to attain Nirvana. A further correspondence is indicated in 195.15, where it is said that the first *dhyāna* contains reflection, investigation and deliberation (*vicāra*, *viveka* and *vitarka*). The goal is again termed Nirvana in 195.22.

This passage seems to have borrowed Buddhist ideas, and not vice versa, because the corresponding ideas form part of a system in the Buddhist scheme of four *jhānas*,[21] whereas in 'Liberation' an attempt is made to describe only the first *dhyāna* after which the similarities disappear. It is also notable that this canto is entirely lacking in the usual metaphysical themes found throughout the rest of 'Liberation,' e.g. the realization of the self, union with *brahman*, the notion of *brahman* as a nondual essence that is the source of the world and so on. Instead, liberation is described in general terms as "accomplishment," (195.1) "gnosis" (195.2) and "freedom from rebirth." (195.3) It is quite possible that the lack of an early Brahminic metaphysic in this text is due to a Buddhist influence, since the Buddhism of this period is notable for its apophatic tendencies. However, the lack of sufficient sources make this contention impossible to prove. Beyond these speculative concerns, 'Liberation' is perhaps most important for its moral vision. Whether in its teachings on yoga or traditional Vedic recitation, or in dialogues between mythical sages or gods, or even in accounts of Vishnu or Brahma as the supreme deity, the ethical point is always the same and constantly reaffirmed: what matters most are personal qualities such as modesty, honesty, humility, sympathy, and so on. It is this ethical core that ties the otherwise disparate components of 'Liberation' together and, more importantly, imagines a religious order around which the various tendencies of the emerging classical Hinduism could be oriented.

The Sanskrit Text of the *Mokṣadharma*

The Sanskrit text followed in this translation of the *Mokṣadharma* is that created and commented on by Nīlakaṇṭha (abbreviated as CSL), a Marathi-speaking brahmin who worked in Benares during the second half of the seventeenth century (Minkowski 2002: 329). This version of the "Maha·bhárata" is variously known as the "Vulgate" or "Bombay edition," the latter because of the location of its first printed editions in the nineteenth century. Although Nīlakaṇṭha selected his readings from a variety of manuscripts, his edition is an idiosyncratic reproduction of the Northern manuscripts of the "Maha·bhárata" (Minkowski 2005: 231–32). Although the most widely disseminated edition of the "Maha·bhárata" ever since Nīlakaṇṭha's time (Minkowski 2005: 241ff.), more recently it has been supplanted by the Critical Edition (CE) published at Poona between 1933 and 1966.

According to FITZGERALD the Critical Edition is a reconstruction of a text of the "Maha·bhárata" originally produced under the Guptas, i.e. during the fourth or fifth century CE.[22] At the current state of research, however, a critical edition of the *Mokṣadharma* is probably not possible, since the period of thought in which its individual texts were composed remains obscure. The religious vocabulary of the *Mokṣadharma* and the philosophical perspective of its authors is hard to pin down.

There are further difficulties with the Sanskrit text. It is often terse and misleading, not because it contains anything esoteric or secret, but probably because its authors deemed a veneer of mystery suitable for such a genre of sacred literature. It is also obvious that the *Mokṣadharma* has suffered excessively from later additions which have altered its meaning; no doubt this was because successive generations of thinkers wished to update the old text to more recent phases of thought. Interpolations from two sources are particularly noteworthy: those from a dualistic tradition of Samkhya thought and those from a Vaishnavite perspective are found throughout the present volume. Even where this is not the case the *Mokṣadharma* has suffered from an unreliable transmission. It is not unusual, for example, for *triṣṭubh* verses to lack the correct number of syllables or to suffer from other metrical mistakes.

These problems cast doubt on the reliability of the Poona edition of the *Mokṣadharma*. While this edition is a valuable work of scholarship—its critical apparatus is indispensable to any study of the Sanskrit text—in places it seems that its editor did not fully understand the historical background to the text. The most obvious example of this is found in the Critical Edition's reading of Mbh XII.211.2 (*bhagavan yad idaṃ na pretya saṃjñā bhavati kasya cit*), a half-verse that is rendered slightly differently in Nīlakaṇṭha's text (219.2*ab*: *bhagavan yadi na pretya saṃjñā bhavati kasya cit*). The verse in the Nīlakaṇṭha edition can be translated as "Perhaps, venerable sir, a person is insentient after death," and is clearly a reference to a famous statement of Yājñavalkya in the *Bṛhadāraṇyaka Upaniṣad* that "after death there is no awareness" (BU II.IV.12, IV.5.13: *na pretya saṃjñāstīty are bravīmi*). But by reading *yad idaṃ* instead of Nīlakaṇṭha's *yadi na*,[23] a reading that in any case makes no sense, this reference to a famous Upanishad is lost in the Critical Edition. This is all the more surprising since later on in the same chapter this statement of Yājñavalkya's is again referred to—219.43*ab* of Nīlakaṇṭha's text asks "how could there be any further consciousness after death?" (*evaṃ sati kutaḥ saṃjñā pretyabhāve punar bhavet*). This failure to recognize a reference to one of the most famous Upanishadic sayings casts doubt over the text reconstructed in the Critical Edition.

I point this out not to denigrate the Critical Edition or exaggerate the worth of Nīlakaṇṭha's text. My point is simply that misunderstandings of the type noted above are inevitable at the current stage of research. As FRAUWALLNER (1973: 80) has noted, "only a careful interpretation of the totality of every text" will bring about a better understanding of the *Mokṣadharma*. In short, the text needs to be reconstructed according to a better historical understanding.[24] Such a textual reconstruction is beyond the aims of the present volume, although I have frequently replaced Nīlakaṇṭha's readings with readings from the Critical Edition or its apparatus. The rational behind these emendations has been to present a more coherent text, according to my understanding of the meaning of individual texts and dialogues. No doubt my criteria for emending Nīlakaṇṭha's text are highly subjective, but it is only through such reconstructions that progress in understanding the *Mokṣadharma* will be made.

A further point to note about the present volume are the notes on the text and translation; these are more copious than those usually found in a Clay Sanskrit Library volume. Many of these notes contain my thoughts on how the Sanskrit text reached its present form, frequently by pointing out what I believe are interpolations. These notes will be most useful to the specialist, but since they help make sense of corrupt passages I hope they will be useful even to a general reader. Any translation of an ancient text is to some degree an interpretation, and this is especially true of the present translation of the *Mokṣadharma*. Although I am aware of the hypothetical nature of much of the present work, I hope that it will provide a basis for further research on this important text.

Concordance of Canto Numbers with the Critical Edition

CSL	CE		
174	168	207	200
175	169	208	201
176	170	209	202
177	171.1–54	210–217	203–210
178	171.55–61	218–219	211–212
179	172	220	213
180	173	221	214
181	174	222	215
182–192	223–225	216–218	
193	186	226	219
194	187	227	220
195	188	228	221
196–200	189–193	229	222
201–206	194–199	230	223

Unless otherwise indicated, all references to the "Maha·bhárata" within this volume indicate the CSL text.

Acknowledgments

I am grateful to Richard Gombrich and Dániel Balogh for their advice on the translation of the Sanskrit text.

Notes

1 There is limited evidence in 'Liberation' for these Brahminic schools; verse 218.11 mentions "the great brotherhood of Kápila" (*Kāpilaṃ maṇḍalaṃ mahat*), but does not give any further details about this important school.

2 The "Rig Veda" is an ancient collection of poems that were recited at Brahminic rituals. Probably composed from the mid second millenium BCE onwards, its late speculative poems probably date to the beginning of the first millenium BCE. See DONIGER (1981).

3 I have discussed this poem at length in WYNNE (2007: 57–64).

4 OLIVELLE's translation (1996: 141–42) of *Chāndogya Upaniṣad* V.10.1–6. See also *Bṛhadāraṇyaka Upaniṣad* VI.2.15–16 (OLIVELLE 1996: 83–84) and the first chapter of the *Kauṣītaki Upaniṣad* (OLIVELLE 1996: 327–33).

5 OLIVELLE's translation (1996: 270) of *Muṇḍaka Upaniṣad* I.2.10–11. For another early Upanishadic reference to the cult of religious mendicancy, see *Bṛhadāraṇyaka Upaniṣad* IV.4.22. OLIVELLE has stated that "a more detailed version of this contrast between people given to rites, who live in villages, and those given to ascetic practices, who live in the wilderness, is given in BU VI.2.15–16 and CU V.10." This is not quite correct, since the *Muṇḍaka Upaniṣad* is not just a simplified version of the passage in the *Chāndogya* and *Bṛhadāraṇyaka Upaniṣad*s. Its religious method is meditation (*yoga*, *dhyāna*) rather than the esoteric knowledge (*upāsana*) of earlier Upanishadic thought.

6 *Muṇḍaka Upaniṣad* III.1.8; OLIVELLE (1996: 275.)

7 The reasons for this change to yogic practice and ideology are obscure. The process must have been complex and multi-faceted.

8 I do not mean to imply that the notion of *karma* and rebirth arose in Brahminic circles and was adopted en masse by heterodox renouncers. The authors of the *Chāndogya* and *Bṛhadāraṇyaka Upaniṣad*s may well have taken this doctrine from a non-Brahminic source and adapted it to their own ends. The important point to note is that at the stage of development depicted by the *Chāndogya* and *Bṛhadāraṇyaka Upaniṣad*s, these new, anti-ritualistic ideas were probably of little concern to orthodox Brahminism. But by the time of the *Muṇḍaka Upaniṣad*, similar ideas

were accepted by groups within and without Brahminism on an unprecedented scale.

9 Greater Magadha, as defined by Bronkhorst, corresponds roughly to modern day Bihar and eastern Uttar Pradesh: "Greater Magadha covers Magadha and its surrounding lands: roughly the geographical area in which the Buddha and Mahāvīra lived and taught. With regard to the Buddha, this area stretched by and large from Śrāvastī, the capital of Kosala, in the north-west to Rājagṛha, the capital of Magadha, in the south-east" (BRONKHORST 2007: 4). Bronkhorst contends that the religious culture of Greater Magadha was distinct from the Vedic society to its West, and remained so until around c. 150 BCE, i.e. "(u)ntil Patañjali's date and perhaps for some time after him" (BRONKHORST 2007: 3). If correct this would mean that the renunciant speculation of the *Mokṣadharma* did not have roots in earlier Brahminic developments, but were inspired by a different, non-Brahminic, religious culture. However, BRONKHORST overlooks the connection between numerous texts of the *Mokṣadharma* and the *Nāsadīya Sūkta*. Moreover, it is hard to believe that a large collection of texts such as the 'Book of Liberation' was a Brahminic reworking of what were originally non-Brahminic texts. Even if the renunciant tradition attested by the 'Book of Liberation' was influenced by the non-Brahminic ideas and practices of "Greater Magadha"—perhaps karmic retribution and/or religious mendicancy among others—it is much more likely that these texts were the work of early Brahminic renouncers who were active in the renunciant culture of Greater Magadha. If so, the opposition noted in ancient Brahminic texts between the land of the "Aryas" (*āryāvarta*: primarily the area between the Ganges and Yámuna rivers) and the "Greater Magadha" of the eastern Ganges Valley (on which see BRONKHORST 2007: 1–4) can be understood as another expression of the schism in early Brahminic ideology: the Vedic traditionalists did not approve of the land and religious culture to the East in which non-conformist brahmins were active participants.

10 An in-depth discussion of the sociological background to world renunciation in ancient India is found in GOMBRICH (1998: 49–59).

11 *Gautama Dharmasūtra* XVI.45, *Baudhāyana Dharmasūtra* II.6.33. See OLIVELLE (2000: 163, 265).

12 I am not suggesting that inequality was a root cause of Indian world-renunciation, as if the unfortunate souls at the bottom decided to call it quits and renounce their measly lot. The available evidence suggests the opposite: it seems that the majority of the early Buddhist community came from elite or privileged backgrounds (GOMBRICH 1988: 55–56). If the predominance of the upper classes in the early Buddhist community (*saṅgha*) had anything to do with the inequality of urban life, it would seem that the more thoughtful among the educated elite were sensitive to the inequalities of their world and rebelled against it (in this connection, it should be noted that the Buddhist *saṅgha* is throroughly egalitarian).

13 See the notes on 174.18, 174.62, 175.9, 175.13 and 178.8 at the end of the volume.

14 I have argued elsewhere that much of the early Buddhist literature predates Ashóka (WYNNE 2005, especially pp. 48–59).

15 ERICH FRAUWALLNER (1973: 76) argued for an early date for the texts contained in the early parts of 'Liberation': "Besides the philosophical texts contained in the Epic are earlier than it was formerly assumed. Thus the texts to be considered here need to be pushed back far into the pre-Christian period."

16 FRAUWALLNER (1973: 79): "We, therefore, find the older texts more towards the beginning and the later texts more towards the end of the collection."

17 "Life of the Buddha," XII.17–20, 27–28, translated for the CSL by OLIVELLE (2008: 332–36). See also JOHNSTON (1984, Part I: 130–31).

18 Johnston (1984, Part ii: xiii), commenting on Heinrich Lüders (ed.), *Bruchstücke buddhistischer Dramen*, Berlin: Druck und Verlag von Georg Reimer, 1911, p. 11.

19 Falk (2001: 130): "If we accept the dropped hundreds then *meṣasaṃkrānti* of 127 AD is the real starting-point of the Kanishka era."

20 Johnston (1984, Part ii: xvii). The upper limit is determined by Johnston on the basis of the Ashóka legend mentioned in the final chapter of the *Buddhacarita*, which means that Ashva·ghosha knew some form of the *Aśokāvadāna*. Based on Przyluski, Johnston asserts (Part ii: xvii) that the *Aśokāvadāna* took shape between 150 and 100 BCE.

21 For a the standard Buddhist description of the four *jhānas*, see *Dīgha Nikāya* vol. i: 73.

22 Fitzgerald (2004: xvi n.2): "Somewhere around the time of the Gupta empire (from Chandragupta I in A.D. 320 through Budhagupta in A.D. 497...), a written Sanskrit text of the Mbh became the basic archetype of all Sanskrit manuscripts of the Mbh throughout India for the next 1,500 years, probably as the result of a major effort of redaction and promulgation, perhaps with direct imperial support. This archetype was approximately recovered in the attempted critical edition of the manuscript tradition carried out by V.S. Sukthankar and others at the Bhandarkar Oriental Research Institute in Pune from the early 1920s to the mid-1960s."

23 The reading *yad idaṃ* is found in a single Śāradā manuscript and a few more Kaśmīri manuscripts. Bronkhorst has noted that "the written signs for na and da are not very different in the Śāradā script" (2007: 322). He concludes that the reading *yadida* probably arose as a scribal error in the Śāradā script. This only goes to show that the reliance the editors of the Critical Edition placed on the Śāradā manuscript Ś1 sometimes impeded a correct appreciation of the Sanskrit text.

24 The manuscript evidence cited in the Critical Edition's apparatus will play a vital role in such studies. As SUKTHANKAR (1933: cii) noted, the Critical Edition should not be understood apart from its apparatus: "To put it in other words, the Mahābhārata is the whole of the epic tradition: the entire Critical Apparatus. Its separation into the constituted text and the critical notes is only a static representation of a constantly changing epic text—a representation made for the purpose of visualizing, studying and analyzing the panorama of the more grand and less thought-movements that have crystallized in the shape of the texts handed down to us in our Mahābhārata manuscripts."

Bibliography

EDITIONS AND MANUSCRIPTS USED

K *The Mahābhārata with the Bharata Bhawadeepa Commentary of Nīlakaṇṭha*. Edited by PANDIT RAMACHANDRASHASTRI KINJAWADEKAR. Poona: Chitrashala Press, 1929–36. [reprint, New Delhi: Oriental Books Reprint Corporation, 1978; 2nd edition. 1979]. Vol 12: Shanti Parva.

B1 *The Mahābhārata with Nīlakaṇṭha's commentary*. Edited by BALAKRISHNA KARBELKAR et al. 1862. 8 vols. Bombay: Bapusadashiva Press.

B2 *The Mahābhārata with Nīlakaṇṭha's commentary*. Edited by A. KHADILKAR. 1862–63. 8 vols. Bombay: Ganapati Krishnaji's Press.

Dn1 Devanāgarī manuscript of the Śāntiparvan with Nīlakaṇṭha's commentary. Bhor, State Library, no.82. Undated.

Dn4 Devanāgarī manuscript of the Mokṣadharma with Nīlakaṇṭha's commentary. Poona, Bombay Govt. Collection (deposited at the Bhandarkar Oriental Research Institute), no. 29c of A 1879 –80. (AD 1758)

CE *The Mahābhārata, Volume 15: The Śāntiparvan, Part III: Mokṣadharma, being the twelfth book of the Mahābhārata, the Great Epic of India*. Edited by SHRIPAD KRISHNA BEVALKAR. Poona: Bhandarkar Oriental Research Institute, 1954.

OTHER TEXTS AND SECONDARY WORKS

BAKKER, HANS and BISSCHOP, PETER. "Mokṣadharma 187 and 239–241 Reconsidered." *Asiatische Studien*, 1999, vol. 3. pp. 459–72.

BRONKHORST, JOHANNES. 2007. *Greater Magadha. Studies in the Culture of Early India.* Leiden, Boston: Brill.

Buddhacarita. See OLIVELLE (2008) and JOHNSTON (1984).

CHERNIAK, ALEX. 2008. *Maha·bhárata VI: Bhishma (volume one of two) Including the Bhagavad Gita in Context*. New York: New York University Press & JJC Foundation.

Dīgha Nikāya vol. I. see RHYS DAVIDS, T.W. and ESTLIN CARPENTER, J. eds. (1995).

DONIGER, WENDY. 2005. *The Rig Veda*, Penguin.

FALK, HARRY. 2001. "The yuga of Sphujiddhvaja and the era of the Kuṣāṇas." *Silk Road Art and Archaeology*, vol. 7, pp. 121–36, Kamakura: The Institute of Silk Road Studies.

FITZGERALD, JAMES L. 2004. *The Mahābhārata* 11. "The Book of the Women" 12. "The Book of Peace, Part One." Chicago, London: University of Chicago Press.

FRAUWALLNER, ERICH. 1973. *History of Indian Philosophy vol. I.* New Delhi: Motilal Banarsidass. [Translation of *Geschichte der indischen Philosophie Band I: Die Philosophie des Veda und des Epos, der Buddha und der Jina, das Sāṃkhya und das Klassische Yogasystem*. Salzburg: O. Müller.]

GANGULY, K.M. 1999. *The Mahabharata of Krishna-Dwaipayana Vyasa, vol. IX: Santi Parva Part II* New Delhi: Munshiram Manoharlal. [The original edition of the translation was published between 1883 and 1896.]

GOMBRICH, RICHARD. 1998. *Theravāda Buddhism. A social history from ancient Benares to modern Colombo*. London and New York: Routledge.

JOHNSTON, E.H. 1984. *Aśvaghoṣa's Buddhacarita, or acts of the Buddha. Complete Sanskrit text with English translation (Parts I–III)*, Calcutta: Baptist Mission Press. First published Lahore, 1936.

MINKOWSKI, CHRISTOPHER. 2002. "Nīlakaṇṭha Caturdhara's Mantrakāśīkhaṇḍa." *Journal of the American Oriental Society*, vol. 122, n. 2, pp. 328–44.

———. 2005. "What Makes a Work 'Traditional'? On the Success of Nīlakaṇṭha's Mahābhārata Commentary." In FEDERICO SQUARCINI (ed.), *Boundaries, Dynamics and Construction of Traditions in South Asia*, Firenze University Press, pp. 225–52. .

MOTEGI, SHUJUN. 1999. "The Teachings of Pañcaśikha in the Mokṣadharma." *Asiatische Studien*, 1999 vol. 3, pp. 513–35.

NAIPAUL, V.S. 1977. *India: A Wounded Civilization*. André Deutsch.

OLIVELLE, PATRICK. 1993. *The Āśrama System*. Oxford, New York: Oxford University Press.

———. 1996. *Upaniṣads*. Oxford, New York: Oxford University Press.

———. 2000. *Dharmasūtras. The Law Codes of Āpastamba, Gautama, Baudhāyana, and Vasiṣṭha*. Delhi: Motilal Banarsidass.

———. 2008. *Life of the Buddha*. New York: New York University Press & JJC Foundation.

RHYS DAVIDS, T.W. 1908. *Early Buddhism*, London: Archibald Constable & Co. Ltd.; reprinted New Delhi: Asian Educational Services (2002).

RHYS DAVIDS, T.W. and ESTLIN CARPENTER, J. (eds). 1995. *The Dīgha Nikāya vol. I*, Oxford: Pali Text Society. Translated by T.W. RHYS DAVIDS as *Sacred Books of the Buddhists vol. II*. (London, 1899). Reprinted as *Dialogues of the Buddha Part I*, (1995, Oxford: Pali Text Society).

VAN BUITENEN, J.A.B. 1956. 'Studies in Sāṃkhya I: An Old Text Reconstituted.' In: *Journal of the American Oriental Society* 76 pp. 153–157. [Also available in *Studies in Indian Literature and Philosophy: Collected Articles of J.A.B. van Buitenen*. 1998, New Delhi: Motilal Banarsidass, pp. 43–52.]

———. 1957. "Studies in Sāṃkhya II: Ahaṃkāra." *Journal of the American Oriental Society*, 77, pp. 15–25. [Also available in *Studies in*

Indian Literature and Philosophy: Collected Articles of J.A.B. van Buitenen. 1998, New Delhi: Motilal Banarsidass, pp. 53–74.]

WYNNE, ALEXANDER. 2005. "The historical authenticity of early Buddhist literature: a critical evaluation." *Wiener Zeitschrift für die Kunde Südasiens*, XLIX, pp. 35–70.

———. 2007. *The Origin of Buddhist Meditation*, Routledge: London and New York.

MAHA·BHÁRATA

BOOK TWELVE

PEACE

VOLUME THREE

"THE BOOK OF LIBERATION"

174

THE DIALOGUE BETWEEN KING SÉNAJIT AND A WANDERING BRAHMIN

YUDHIṢṬHIRA uvāca:

174.1 DHARMĀḤ PITĀ|mahen' ôktā
rāja|dharm'|āśritāḥ śubhāḥ.
dharmam āśramiṇāṃ śreṣṭhaṃ
vaktum arhasi, pārthiva.

BHĪṢMA uvāca:

sarvatra vihito dharmaḥ, saty a|pretya tapaḥ|phalam.
bahu|dvārasya dharmasya n' êh' âsti vi|phalā kriyā.
yasmin yasmiṃs tu viṣaye yo yo yāti viniścayam,
sa tam ev' âbhijānāti, n' ânyaṃ, Bharata|sattama.
yathā yathā ca paryeti loka|tantram a|sāravat,
tathā tathā virāgo 'tra jāyate, n' âtra saṃśayaḥ.
174.5 evaṃ vyavasite loke bahu|doṣe, Yudhiṣṭhira,
ātma|mokṣa|nimittaṃ vai yateta matimān naraḥ.

YUDHIṢṬHIRA uvāca:

naṣṭe dhane vā, dāre vā, putre, pitari vā mṛte,
yayā buddhyā nudec chokaṃ, tan me brūhi, pitā|maha.

BHĪṢMA uvāca:

naṣṭe dhane vā, dāre vā, putre, pitari vā mṛte,
«aho duḥkham!» iti dhyāyan śokasy' âpacitiṃ caret.

YUDHI·SHTHIRA said:

YOU HAVE SPOKEN, grandfather, about the pure laws that govern the duties of kings.* You should also describe the superior law, my Lord, that which is followed by hermits. 174.1

BHISHMA said:

The law of righteousness covers all acts, including the rewards of asceticism that can be attained before death, when a person is still alive. In this world no religious act lacks a reward, for the law of righteousness is multi-faceted.

Despite this, a man can only understand those matters of religion upon which he is firmly resolved, and not any other, exalted Bhárata.

The worldly order lacks any substance; no matter how one contemplates the matter, dispassion for it is bound to
arise. And so when a wise man has determined that the 174.5
world is full of evils, Yudhi·shthira, he should strive for the sake of his own liberation.

YUDHI·SHTHIRA said:

When a man's wealth has been destroyed, when his wife, son or father has died, with what sort of understanding can he overcome sorrow? Please tell me that, grandfather.

BHISHMA said:

When a man's wealth has been destroyed, when his wife, son or father has died, he can limit his sorrow by meditating on the thought "Alas! Suffering!"

atr' âpy udāharant' îmam itihāsaṃ purātanam:
yathā Senajitaṃ vipraḥ kaś cid ety' âbravīt suhṛt.
putra|śok'|âbhisantaptaṃ rājānaṃ śoka|vihvalam
viṣaṇṇa|manasaṃ dṛṣṭvā vipro vacanam abravīt:
174.10 «kiṃ nu muhyasi mūḍhas tvaṃ? śocyaḥ kim anuśocasi?
yadā tvām api śocantaḥ, śocyā yāsyanti tāṃ gatim.
tvaṃ c' âiv' âhaṃ ca, ye c' ânye tvām upāsanti, pārthiva,
sarve tatra gamiṣyāmo yata ev' āgatā vayam.»

SENAJID uvāca:

kā buddhiḥ, kiṃ tapo vipra? kaḥ samādhis, tapo|dhana?
kiṃ jñānaṃ, kiṃ śrutaṃ c' âiva, yat prāpya na viṣīdasi?

BRĀHMAṆA uvāca:

paśya bhūtāni duḥkhena vyatiṣaktāni sarvaśaḥ,
uttam'|âdhama|madhyāni teṣu teṣv iha karmasu.
ātm" âpi c' âyaṃ na mama, sarvā vā pṛthivī mama.
«yathā mama, tath" ânyeṣām» iti cintya na me vyathā.
etāṃ buddhim ahaṃ prāpya na prahṛṣye na ca vyathe.
174.15 yathā kāṣṭhaṃ ca kāṣṭhaṃ ca sameyātāṃ mah"|ôdadhau,
sametya ca vyapeyātāṃ: tadvad bhūta|samāgamaḥ.
evaṃ putrāś ca pautrāś ca, jñātayo, bāndhavās tathā.
teṣāṃ sneho na kartavyo, viprayogo dhruvo hi taiḥ.

On this subject people relate an ancient tradition: the teaching given by a kindly brahmin who had arrived at the court of King Sénajit. King Sénajit was very distressed and tormented by sorrow over the death of his son. Upon seeing that he was depressed, the brahmin said this to him:

"Why are you so bewildered? What are you grieving 174.10
about, you poor man? People will grieve you when you die, and they in turn will die and be grieved. Both you and I, sire, as well as everyone else who waits upon you, we all return to that very source from which we originated."

SÉNAJIT said:

What is your understanding of things, brahmin? What asceticism and concentration have you attained, great ascetic? What is the knowledge and learning that frees you from dejection?

THE BRAHMIN said:

All living beings—be they superior, inferior or mediocre on account of their worldly deeds—are completely enmeshed in suffering. You must see this. Not even this body is mine—or else I would possess the whole earth. I have pondered that this is true of both myself and others, and so feel no anxiety; by virtue of this understanding I experience neither excitement nor anxiety.

The meeting of beings is just like the coming together 174.15
of two pieces of driftwood in a great ocean: they meet, and then drift apart. The same truth applies to one's sons, grandsons, kith and kin. One should not become attached to them, for separation from them is the ordained way of things.

a|darśanād āpatitaḥ punaś c' â|darśanaṃ gataḥ
na tv" âsau veda, na tvaṃ taṃ. kaḥ san kim anuśocasi?
tṛṣṇ"|ārti|prabhavaṃ duḥkhaṃ,
duḥkh'|ārti|prabhavaṃ sukham.
sukhāt sañjāyate duḥkham,
duḥkham evam punaḥ punaḥ.
sukhasy' ânantaraṃ duḥkhaṃ,
duḥkhasy' ânantaraṃ sukham:
sukha|duḥkhe manuṣyāṇāṃ
cakravat parivartataḥ.
174.20 sukhāt tvaṃ duḥkham āpannaḥ. punar āpatsyase sukham.
na nityaṃ labhate duḥkhaṃ, na nityaṃ labhate sukham.
śarīram ev' āyatanaṃ sukhasya,
duḥkhasya c' âpy āyatanaṃ śarīram:
yad yac charīreṇa karoti karma,
ten' âiva dehī samupāśnute tat.
jīvitaṃ ca śarīreṇa ten' âiva saha jāyate;
ubhe saha vivartete, ubhe saha vinaśyataḥ.
sneha|pāśair bahu|vidhair āviṣṭa|viṣayā janāḥ
a|kṛt'|ârthāś ca sīdante, jalaiḥ saikata|setavaḥ.
snehena tilavat sarvaṃ sarga|cakre nipīḍyate,
tila|pīḍair iv' ākramya kleśair ajñāna|sambhavaiḥ.

Your son was struck down by an unknown cause, and has once again passed into the unknown. In reality he does not know you, and you do not know him. So who are you, and what do you lament?

Misery arises from thirst, which is an affliction, and happiness arises from misery, which is also an affliction. Happiness causes misery and so misery is experienced over and over again.

Happiness is quickly followed by misery and misery is
quickly followed by happiness: these two continually alternate in the lives of men, just like a revolving wheel.* You 174.20
have fallen victim to misery because of experiencing happiness. But you will experience happiness once again, for a
person never experiences misery or happiness continually.

The body is the seat of both happiness and suffering: a person experiences the results of his *karma* in the same body in which he commits it,* after the soul has been reborn in that very body. Both become manifest together, and both perish together.*

People are subjected to many different bonds of attachment through their sense faculties. Such people vanish without accomplishing their aims, just like causeways of sand dissolved in water.

Everything is crushed in the wheel of creation, by the defilements caused by ignorance, just as sesame seeds are crushed because of their oil. All is as if attacked by sesamum grinders.*

174.25 sañcinoty a|śubhaṃ karma kalatr'|âpekṣayā naraḥ,
ekaḥ kleśān avāpnoti paratr' êha ca mānavaḥ.
putra|dāra|kuṭumbeṣu prasaktāḥ sarva|mānavāḥ,
śoka|paṅk'|ârṇave magnā jīrṇā vana|gajā iva.
putra|nāśe, vitta|nāśe, jñāti|sambandhinām api,
prāpyate su|mahad duḥkhaṃ dāv'|âgni|pratimaṃ, vibho.
daiv'|āyattam idaṃ sarvaṃ, sukha|duḥkhe, bhav'|âbhavau.
a|suhṛt sa|suhṛc c' âpi, sa|śatrur mitravān api,
sa|prajñaḥ prajñayā hīno, daivena labhate sukham.
n' âlaṃ sukhāya suhṛdo, n' âlaṃ duḥkhāya śatravaḥ.
na ca prajñ" âlam arthānāṃ, na sukhānām alaṃ dhanam.
174.30 na buddhir dhana|lābhāya, na jāḍyam a|samṛddhaye.
loka|paryāya|vṛttāntaṃ prājño jānāti, n' êtaraḥ.
buddhimantaṃ ca, śūraṃ ca,
mūḍhaṃ, bhīruṃ, jaḍaṃ, kavim,
dur|balaṃ, balavantaṃ ca
bhāginaṃ bhajate sukham.
dhenur vatsasya, gopasya, svāminas, taskarasya ca:
payaḥ pibati yas tasyā, dhenus tasy' êti niścayaḥ.
ye ca mūḍhatamā loke, ye ca buddheḥ paraṃ gatāḥ,
te narāḥ sukham edhante; kliśyaty antarito janaḥ.

A man fond of his wife accumulates bad *karma* and he 174.25
alone suffers its afflictions, both here and in the world beyond. All men who are attached to their sons, wives and offspring are immersed in sorrow, just like elderly forest elephants bogged down in a quagmire of mud.

When a person's sons, wealth, kith and kin have been destroyed, the suffering he experiences is terrible—as bad as a forest fire, Mighty King. This whole world—as well as pleasure, pain, existence and non-existence—is ruled by fate.

One's happiness depends upon fate, regardless of whether one has friends or not, or has enemies or allies, or is wise or lacking in wisdom.

Friends and wealth do not lead to happiness, enemies are incapable of causing suffering, wisdom cannot effect one's
aims. Intelligence does not lead to the attainment of wealth, 174.30
and stupidity cannot bring about failure. Only a wise man, and nobody else, understands the events that occur in the course of the world.

Happiness comes to the man who has good fortune, whether he is intelligent, heroic, foolish, cowardly, stupid, wise, weak or strong. In the same way it is accepted that a milch cow belongs to whomever drinks her milk, whether that is her calf, her cowherd, her owner, or a thief.

Men attain bliss when they pass into the stupefaction of dreamless sleep, or when they attain the highest state of consciousness. But the person in between is afflicted with suffering.

antyeṣu remire dhīrā, na te madhyeṣu remire.
antya|prāptiṃ sukhām āhur, duḥkham antaram antyayoḥ.
174.35 ye ca buddhi|sukhaṃ prāptā, dvandv'|âtītā vimatsarāḥ,
tān n' âiv' ârthā na c' ân|arthā vyathayanti kadā cana.
atha ye buddhim a|prāptā, vyatikrāntāś ca mūḍhatām,
te 'tivelaṃ prahṛṣyanti saṃtāpam upayānti ca.
nityaṃ pramuditā mūḍhā, divi deva|gaṇā iva.
avalepena mahatā paribhūtyā vicetasaḥ.
sukhaṃ duḥkh'|ântam. ālasyaṃ†
duḥkhaṃ, dākṣyaṃ sukh'|ôdayam.
bhūtis tv evaṃ śriyā sārdhaṃ
dakṣe vasati, n' âlase.
sukhaṃ vā yadi vā duḥkhaṃ, priyam vā yadi v'' â|priyaṃ,
prāptaṃ prāptam upāsīta hṛdayen' â|parājitaḥ.
174.40 śoka|sthāna|sahasrāṇi bhaya|sthāna|śatāni ca
divase divase mūḍham āviśanti, na paṇḍitam.
buddhimantaṃ, kṛta|prajñaṃ, śuśrūṣum, an|asūyakam,
dāntaṃ, jit'|êndriyaṃ c' âpi śoko na spṛśate naram.
etāṃ buddhiṃ samāsthāya gupta|cittaś cared budhaḥ,
uday'|âstamaya|jñaṃ hi na śokaḥ spraṣṭum arhati.

Wise men find bliss at the extremities of consciousness, but not in the states in between. They say that bliss is to be found at the limits of consciousness, whereas suffering is found in those states in between.

Men who have attained the bliss of consciousness, who 174.35
have transcended duality and are free from envy—they are never perturbed by good fortune or misfortune.

But if they have not attained the highest state of consciousness, or have emerged from the stupefaction of deep sleep, they experience excitement and anguish to an excessive degree.

Fools are always delighted, as if they were the hosts of gods in heaven. They are deluded by their great haughtiness and their superiority.

Happiness ends in misery. Sloth is misery, whereas industry brings about happiness. Prosperity and good fortune are therefore found in the industrious person rather than the idle man.

Whatever a person might encounter in life, be it happiness, misery, pleasure or pain, he should do so with an unconquered heart. Day by day thousands of causes of sorrow 174.40
and hundreds of causes of fear antagonize a fool, but they do not possess the learned man.

Sorrow does not touch the man who is intelligent, wise, obedient, devoid of envy, restrained and a master of his senses. Relying on this understanding, the wise man conducts his life with a guarded mind. Sorrow is incapable of touching the one who knows the origin and end of everything.

yan|nimittaṃ bhavec chokas, tāpo vā, duḥkham eva ca,
āyāso vā, yato|mūlam ek'|âṅgam api tat tyajet.
kiṃ cid eva mamatvena yadā bhavati kalpitam,
tad eva paritāp'|ârthaṃ; sarvaṃ saṃpadyate tathā.
174.45 yad yat tyajati kāmānāṃ, tat sukhasy' âbhipūryate.
kām'|ânusārī puruṣaḥ kāmān anu vinaśyati.
yac ca kāma|sukhaṃ loke, yac ca divyaṃ mahat sukham,
tṛṣṇā|kṣaya|sukhasy' âite n' ârhataḥ ṣoḍaśīṃ kalām.
pūrva|deha|kṛtaṃ karma, śubhaṃ vā yadi v" â|śubham,
prājñaṃ mūḍhaṃ tathā śūraṃ bhajate yādṛśaṃ kṛtam.
evam eva kil' âitāni priyāṇy ev' âpriyāṇi ca
jīveṣu parivartante duḥkhāni ca sukhāni ca.
etāṃ buddhim samāsthāya sukham āste guṇ'|ânvitaḥ.
sarvān kāmāñ jugupseta, kāmān kurvīta pṛṣṭhataḥ.
174.50 vṛtta eṣa hṛdi prauḍho; mṛtyur eṣa mano|bhavaḥ.
krodho nāma śarīra|stho dehināṃ procyate budhaiḥ.
yadā saṃharate kāmān, kūrmo 'ṅgān' îva sarvaśaḥ,
tad" ātma|jyotir ātm" âyam ātmany eva prasīdati.†
na bibheti yadā c' âyaṃ, yadā c' âsmān na bibhyati,
yadā n' êcchati, na dveṣṭi, brahma saṃpadyate tadā.
ubhe saty'|ânṛte tyaktvā, śok'|ānandau, bhay'|âbhaye,
priy'|âpriye parityajya, praśānt'|ātmā bhaviṣyati.

Whatever the characteristic of an experience might be—be it is sorrow, torment, suffering or tribulation—it must be abandoned at its root, even if that is one's own head.

If a person regards anything in a possessive manner, that very thing will torment him; everything turns out in just the same way.

When a person abandons the objects of sensual pleasure, 174.45
they become sources of bliss. But the man who pursues sensual pleasure is destroyed in the course of that pursuit.* The bliss of worldly pleasures and the great bliss of heaven do not amount to one sixteenth of the bliss brought about by the destruction of thirst.

The *karma* committed in a previous life, be it good or bad, finds its way to a wise man, a fool or a hero exactly as it was performed. And so these pleasant and unpleasant things—the sufferings and joys of life—alternate in the lives of living beings. Relying on this understanding, a virtuous person passes his life in bliss.

One should shun all desires, and put them behind oneself. Desire, the mind-born emotion that is deadly, devel- 174.50
ops and becomes strong in the heart. Wise men also say that anger abides in the bodies of men.

When a person curbs his desires, like a tortoise withdrawing its limbs into itself, then the self, which is its own light, becomes tranquil within itself.

When he has no fear and is feared by nobody, when he has no desires and feels no aversion to anything, he attains *brahman*. When he abandons truth, untruth, sorrow, ecstasy, fear, confidence, pleasure and pain, he will find peace.

yadā na kurute dhīraḥ sarva|bhūteṣu pāpakam
karmaṇā, manasā, vācā, brahma saṃpadyate tadā.
174.55 yā dus|tyajā dur|matibhir, yā na jīryati jīryataḥ,
yo 'sau prāṇ'|ântiko rogas, tāṃ tṛṣṇāṃ tyajataḥ sukham.
atra Piṅgalayā gītā gāthāḥ śrūyanti, pārthiva,
yathā sā kṛcchra|kāle 'pi lebhe dharmaṃ sanātanam.
saṃkete Piṅgalā veśyā kānten' âsīd vinā|kṛtā.
atha kṛcchra|gatā śāntāṃ buddhim āsthāpayat tadā.

PIṄGAL" ôvāca:

unmatt" âham anunmattaṃ kāntam anvavasaṃ ciram.
antike ramaṇaṃ santaṃ n' âinam adhyagamaṃ purā.
eka|sthūṇaṃ nava|dvāram apidhāsyāmy agārakam.
kā hi kāntam ih' āyāntam ayaṃ kānt" êti maṃsyate?
174.60 a|kāmāṃ kāma|rūpeṇa dhūrtā naraka|rūpiṇaḥ
na punar vañcayiṣyanti: pratibuddh" âsmi, jāgṛmi.
an|artho hi bhaved artho daivāt pūrva|kṛtena vā.
saṃbuddh" âhaṃ, nir|ākārā, n' âham ady' â|jit'|êndriyā.
sukhaṃ nir|āśaḥ svapiti, nairāśyaṃ paramaṃ sukham.
āśām an|āśāṃ kṛtvā hi, sukhaṃ svapiti Piṅgalā.

When the wise man inflicts no evil on any living creature in deed, thought and word, he attains *brahman.*

It is difficult for the ignorant to abandon thirst, for it does not wither away as a person ages. But if he abandons this fatal disease he will find bliss. 174.55

On this subject, sire, I have heard of the verses sung by Píngala, telling how she realized the eternal truth in a time of great difficulty. Píngala was a courtesan who was stood up by her lover after arranging a tryst. She was overcome with misery, but managed to pacify her mind.

PÍNGALA said:

For so long I lived near to my beloved; I was infatuated with him, but he did not care for me. Though my lover lived close to me, I did not approach him amorously at first.

But when she has closed her body, this house of one pillar and nine doors, what woman would think of her beloved as such even as he approaches her?

Those hellish rogues will not deceive me again, with whatever forms they take at will, for I am without desire: I am awake, and watchful. 174.60

A disappointment can turn into something advantageous, perhaps because of fate or one's past *karma.* But I am now awake and indifferent, and my senses are not uncontrolled.

The person free from desire sleeps blissfully, for desirelessness is the highest bliss. Turning desire into disregard, Píngala sleeps blissfully.*

BHĪṢMA uvāca:

etaiś c' ânyaiś ca viprasya hetumadbhiḥ prabhāṣitaiḥ
paryavasthāpito rājā Senajin mumude sukhī.

BHISHMA said:

Comforted by these and other convincing teachings given by the brahmin, King Sénajit found happiness and rejoiced.

175

THE DIALOGUE BETWEEN A FATHER AND HIS SON

YUDHIṢṬHIRA uvāca:

175.1 ATIKRĀMATI KĀLE 'smin, sarva|bhūta|kṣay'|āvahe,
kiṃ śreyaḥ pratipadyeta? tan me brūhi, pitā|maha.

BHĪṢMA uvāca:

atr' âpy udāharant' îmam itihāsaṃ purātanam,
pituḥ putreṇa saṃvādaṃ. taṃ nibodha Yudhiṣṭhira.
dvijāteḥ kasya cit, Pārtha, svādhyāya|niratasya vai
babhūva putro medhāvī, Medhāvī nāma nāmataḥ.
so 'bravīt pitaraṃ putraḥ svādhyāya|karaṇe ratam
mokṣa|dharm'|ârtha|kuśalo, loka|tattva|vicakṣaṇaḥ.

PUTRA uvāca:

175.5 dhīraḥ kiṃ svit, tāta, kuryāt prajānan?
kṣipraṃ hy āyur bhraśyate mānavānām.
pitas, tad ācakṣva yath"|ârtha|yogaṃ
mam', ānupūrvyā yena dharmaṃ careyam.

PIT" ôvāca:

vedān adhītya brahmacaryeṇa, putra,
putrān† icchet pāvan'|ârthaṃ pitṝṇām.
agnīn ādhāya vidhivac c' êṣṭa|yajño
vanaṃ praviśy' âtha munir bubhūṣet.

YUDHI·SHTHIRA said:

IF TIME PREVAILS over everything and brings about the destruction of all creatures, what is the best thing that a man could do? Please tell me that, grandfather. 175.1

BHISHMA said:

On this subject people relate the ancient tradition of a conversation between a father and his son. Listen to it, Yudhi·shthira.

There was once a son of a certain brahmin, Partha, who was devoted to Vedic recitation. He was a wise man, and was known by the name of Medhávin. Knowledgeable about the purpose of the religion of liberation, and with some understanding of the world's true nature, the son spoke to his father, so devoted to his Vedic recitation, as follows.

THE SON said:

What should a wise and knowledgeable man do, father, 175.5
for the lifespan of men quickly wastes away? Please explain this as it really is, so that in due course I may practice the religious life.

THE FATHER said:

When you have completed your life of Vedic learning as a chaste student, my son, you should seek to obtain offspring so that you may free our ancestors from evil. After you have established the sacred fires according to the rules and performed the Vedic sacrifices, you may then enter the forest and become a silent sage.

PUTRA uvāca:

evam abhyāhate loke samantāt parivārite
a|moghāsu patantīṣu kiṃ dhīra iva bhāṣase?

PIT" ôvāca:

katham abhyāhato lokaḥ? kena vā parivāritaḥ?
a|moghāḥ kāḥ patant' îha? kiṃ nu bhīṣayas' îva mām?

PUTRA uvāca:

mṛtyun" âbhyāhato loko, jarayā parivāritaḥ.
aho|rātrāḥ patanty ete—nanu kasmān na budhyase?
175.10 a|moghā rātrayaś c' âpi, nityam āyānti yānti ca.
yad" âham etaj jānāmi, na mṛtyus tiṣṭhat' îti ha,
so 'haṃ kathaṃ pratīkṣiṣye jñānen' âpihitaś caran?
rātryāṃ rātryāṃ vyatītāyām āyur alpataraṃ yadā,
tad" âiva vandhyaṃ divasam iti vidyād vicakṣaṇaḥ.
gādh'|ôdake matsya iva, sukhaṃ vindeta kas tadā?
an|avāpteṣu kāmeṣu, mṛtyur abhyeti mānavam.
puṣpāṇ' îva vicinvantam anyatra|gata|mānasam,
vṛk" îv' ôraṇam āsādya mṛtyur ādāya gacchati.
ady' âiva kuru yac chreyo—mā tvāṃ kālo 'tyagād ayam,
akṛteṣv eva kāryeṣu, mṛtyur vai saṃprakarṣati.
175.15 śvaḥ|kāryam adya kurvīta, pūrv'|âhṇe c' âparāhṇikam,
na hi pratīkṣate mṛtyuḥ, kṛtam asya na vā kṛtam.

THE SON said:

When the world is wounded and hemmed in on all sides, when unfailing things fall away, why do you speak as if you were a wise man?

THE FATHER said:

How is the world wounded? By what is it hemmed in? And what unfailing things fall away in the world? Why does it seem as if you want to frighten me?

THE SON said:

The world is wounded by death and hemmed in by decrepitude. It is the days and nights that fall away—why are you not aware of this?*

The nights do not fail us, and yet they continually come 175.10
and go. When I know that death waits for nobody, how can
I linger and carry on without being fulfilled by gnosis? Since
his lifespan diminishes with each passing night, a discerning
man should understand that his days are worthless.

Like a fish in shallow water, who is able to find happiness? Death enters a man even before he has attained his desires. When his mind is elsewhere, like that of a man picking flowers, death takes him and departs, just like a she-wolf attacking a sheep.*

On this very day you should do what is best—let not
time overcome you, for death will drag you away before
you have completed your duties. A person should complete 175.15
tomorrow's duties today, and the duties of the evening in
the morning, for death cares not for what a man has done
or not done.

ko hi jānāti, kasy' âdya mṛtyu|kālo bhaviṣyati?
yuv" âiva dharma|śīlaḥ syād, a|nityaṃ khalu jīvitam.
kṛte dharme bhavet kīrtir iha, pretya ca vai sukham.

mohena hi samāviṣṭaḥ, putra|dār'|ârtham udyataḥ
kṛtvā kāryam a|kāryaṃ vā puṣṭim eṣāṃ prayacchati.

taṃ putra|paśu|saṃpannaṃ, vyāsakta|manasaṃ naram
suptaṃ vyāghro mṛgam iva mṛtyur ādāya gacchati.
saṃcinvānakam ev' âinaṃ, kāmānām a|vitṛptakam,
vyāghraḥ paśum iv' ādāya mṛtyur ādāya gacchati.

175.20 «idaṃ kṛtam, idaṃ kāryam, idam anyat kṛt'|âkṛtam,»
evam īhā|sukh'|āsaktaṃ kṛt'|ântaḥ kurute vaśe.

kṛtānāṃ phalam a|prāptaṃ karmaṇāṃ karma|saṃjñitam
kṣetr'|āpaṇa|gṛh'|āsaktaṃ mṛtyur ādāya gacchati.
dur|balaṃ balavantaṃ ca, śūraṃ, bhīruṃ, jaḍaṃ, kavim
a|prāptaṃ sarva|kām'|ârthān mṛtyur ādāya gacchati.

mṛtyur, jarā ca, vyādhiś ca, duḥkhaṃ c' ân|eka|kāraṇam.
anuṣaktaṃ yadā dehe, kiṃ svastha iva tiṣṭhasi?
jātam ev' ântako 'ntāya, jarā c' ânveti dehinam.
anuṣaktā dvayen' âite bhāvāḥ sthāvara|jaṅgamāḥ.

Who knows what person's moment of death will come today? A person should make a habit of righteousness even when he is young, for life is impermanent. If a man's acts are righteous, he attains fame in this world and bliss in the world beyond.

Consumed by delusion, a person exerts himself for the sake of his sons and wives. He brings them prosperity, by doing the things he ought to do as well as the things he should not.

The man who is successful in procuring sons and cattle becomes attached to them. But death takes him and departs, just like a tiger preying on a sleeping deer.* While he is occupied with the search for riches but before he has enjoyed its pleasures, death takes him and departs, just like a tiger preying on cattle.

Karmic destiny controls the person attached to the hap- 175.20
piness that is attained through exertion—the one who thinks "I have done this, I have to do this, I have not finished doing this."

Before a man has attained the rewards of the deeds he has committed—that which is called *karma*—death takes him and departs, regardless of his attachment to his fields, shop or home. Whether he is weak, strong, heroic, cowardly, stupid or intelligent, death takes him and departs, before he has attained all the objects of his desires.

Misery has many causes, such as death, decrepitude and illness. If it clings to your body, why do you carry on as though you are comfortable? Death and decrepitude pursue an embodied being, once he has been born, in order

175.25 mṛtyor vā mukham etad vai, yā grāme vasato ratiḥ.
devānām eṣa vai go|ṣṭho, yad araṇyam, iti śrutiḥ.
nibandhanī rajjur eṣā, yā grāme vasato ratiḥ.
chittv" âitāṃ su|kṛto yānti, n' âināṃ chindanti duṣ|kṛtaḥ.

na hiṃsayati yo jantūn mano|vāk|kāya|hetubhiḥ,
jīvit'|ârth'|âpanayanaiḥ prāṇibhir na sa hiṃsyate.

na mṛtyu|senām āyāntīṃ jātu kaś cit prabādhate,
ṛte satyam. a|sat tyājyaṃ, satye hy a|mṛtam āśritam.
tasmāt satya|vrat'|ācāraḥ, satya|yoga|parāyaṇaḥ,
saty'|āgamaḥ, sadā dāntaḥ, satyen' âiv' ântakaṃ jayet.

175.30 a|mṛtaṃ c' âiva mṛtyuś ca: dvayaṃ dehe pratiṣṭhitam.
mṛtyur āpadyate mohāt, satyen' āpadyate 'mṛtam.

so 'haṃ hy a|hiṃsraḥ, saty'|ârthī,
kāma|krodha|bahiṣkṛtaḥ,
sama|duḥkha|sukhaḥ, kṣemī,
mṛtyuṃ hāsyāmy amartyavat.†

śānti|yajña|rato, dānto, brahma|yajñe sthito muniḥ,
vāṅ|manaḥ|karma|yajñaś ca bhaviṣyāmy udag|āyane.
paśu|yajñaiḥ kathaṃ hiṃsrair mādṛśo yaṣṭum arhati,
antavadbhir iva prājñaḥ kṣatra|yajñaiḥ† piśācavat?

to finish him off. All animate and inanimate creatures are shackled by this pair.

The pleasure a person experiences living in a village is 175.25
the door to death. According to the Vedas, however, the wilderness is the pasture of the gods. The pleasure a person experiences living in a village is a rope that binds him. The virtuous manage to sever it and escape, unlike evil-doers.

The person who does not harm any creature in thought, word or deed is not harmed by the living beings that destroy one's life and property.

Nothing apart from truth can defeat the army of death when it comes. Untruth should be abandoned, for the immortal resides in truth. Therefore one should always practice the vow of truth, be devoted to the discipline of truth, follow the true scriptures and be restrained, for it is by truth alone that one conquers death.

The immortal and death: this pair is rooted in the body. 175.30
Death is brought about by ignorance, whereas the immortal is attained through truth.

I will be nonviolent and pursue truth, driving desire and anger from myself. Indifferent towards pleasure and pain, and peaceful, I will abandon death just like an immortal.

When the sun moves north I will dedicate myself to the sacrifice of peace, and be restrained, a silent sage committed to the sacrifice to *brahman.** I will offer my speech, mind and action as a sacrifice. How could a wise person like me offer a violent animal sacrifice, like a goblin who offers the finite sacrifice of a kshatriya?

yasya vāṅ|manasī syātāṃ samyak praṇihite sadā,
tapas tyāgaś ca satyaṃ ca, sa vai sarvam avāpnuyāt.
175.35 n' âsti vidyā|samaṃ cakṣur, n' âsti satya|samaṃ tapaḥ.
n' âsti rāga|samaṃ duḥkhaṃ, n' âsti tyāga|samaṃ sukham.
ātmany ev' ātmanā jāta, ātma|niṣṭho '|prajo 'pi vā
ātmany eva bhaviṣyāmi: na māṃ tārayati prajā.
n' âitādṛśaṃ brāhmaṇasy' âsti vittaṃ,
yath" âikatā, samatā, satyatā ca,
śīlaṃ, sthitir, daṇḍa|nidhānam, ārjavaṃ,
tatas tataś c' ôparamaḥ kriyābhyaḥ.
kiṃ te dhanair, bāndhavair v" âpi kiṃ te,
kiṃ te dārair, brāhmaṇa, yo mariṣyasi?
ātmānam anviccha guhāṃ praviṣṭaṃ.
pitā|mahās te kva gatāḥ pitā ca?

BHĪṢMA uvāca:

putrasy' âitad vacaḥ śrutvā yath" âkārṣīt pitā, nṛpa,
tathā tvam api vartasva satya|dharma|parāyaṇaḥ.

The person whose speech and mind are always correctly focused, who possesses the qualities of austerity, letting go and truth—he alone attains the whole.

There is no vision equal to knowledge, and no asceticism 175.35
equal to truth. There is no suffering equal to passion, and no bliss equal to letting go.

I have attained an inner transformation by means of the self; I rest in the self even though I have no offspring. I will abide in the self alone: offspring will not save me. Such things as offspring are not a brahmin's wealth, as are solitude, impartiality, truth, virtuous conduct, forbearance, the renunciation of violence, honesty and the avoidance of rituals.

If you are going to die, brahmin, what is the point of your wealth, kinsmen or wives? Search for the self, which lies hidden in the cave of the heart. Where have your grandfathers and your father gone?

BHISHMA said:

The father withdrew upon hearing his son's words, Your Majesty. You too should conduct yourself in this way, being devoted to the religion of truth.

176

THE SONG OF SHAMPÁKA

YUDHIṢṬHIRA uvāca:

176.1 DHANINAŚ C' ÂIDHANĀ ye ca
vartayante sva|tantriṇaḥ,
sukha|duḥkh'|āgamas teṣāṃ
kaḥ, kathaṃ vā, pitā|maha?

BHĪṢMA uvāca:

atr' âpy udāharant' îmam itihāsaṃ purātanam:
Śaṃpāken' êha muktena gītaṃ śānti|gatena ca.
abravīn māṃ purā kaś cid brāhmaṇas tyāgam āśritaḥ,
kliśyamānaḥ ku|dāreṇa ku|cailena bubhukṣayā.

utpannam iha loke vai janma|prabhṛti mānavam,
vividhāny upavartante duḥkhāni ca sukhāni ca.
176.5 tayor ekatare mārge
yad enam abhisaṃnayet,
na sukhaṃ prāpya saṃhṛṣyen,
n' â|sukhaṃ prāpya saṃjvaret.
na vai carasi yac chreya, ātmano vā yad īśiṣe,
a|kām'|ātm" âpi hi sadā, dhuram udyamya c' âiva ha.
a|kiñcanaḥ paripatan sukham āsvādayiṣyasi,
a|kiñcanaḥ sukhaṃ śete, samuttiṣṭhati c' âiva ha.
ākiñcanyaṃ sukhaṃ loke; pathyaṃ, śivam, an|āmayam.
an|amitra|patho hy eṣa: dur|labhaḥ, su|labho mataḥ.

YUDHI·SHTHIRA said:

THE RICH AND the poor are free to live as they please, 176.1
but what is the cause of their pleasure and pain? And how does it come about, grandfather?

BHISHMA said:

On this subject people relate the ancient tradition of a song sung by Shampáka, who had attained liberation and found peace.

Long ago, a brahmin devoted to the practice of renunciation was being harassed by his wicked wife, a poorly-dressed and hungry woman. This is what he said to me:

THE BRAHMIN said:*

From the point a man is born into this world, various
sorts of pleasure and pain come his way. Should something 176.5
lead him down the path to either pleasure or pain, he should not delight when he finds the former or fret when he feels the latter.

You surely do not do what is best or control what you possess, even though you are devoid of desire while undertaking a burdensome task.

But if you follow a peripatetic life devoid of possessions you will experience bliss, for the person without any possessions sleeps and rises in a state of bliss. In this world, freedom from possessions is bliss; it is wholesome, auspicious and free from disease. This is the path that is free from adversaries—it is difficult to find, and yet people think it is a simple matter.

a|kiñcanasya śuddhasya upapannasya sarvataḥ,
avekṣamāṇas trīl lokān na tulyam iha lakṣaye.
176.10 ākiñcanyaṃ ca rājyaṃ ca tulayā samatolayam;
atyaricyata dāridryaṃ rājyād api guṇ'|âdhikam.
ākiñcanye ca rājye ca viśeṣaḥ su|mahān ayam:
nity'|ôdvigno hi dhanavān, mṛtyor āsya|gato yathā.
n' âiv' âsy' âgnir, na c' âriṣṭo, na mṛtyur, na ca dasyavaḥ
prabhavanti dhana|tyāgād vimuktasya nir|āśiṣaḥ.
taṃ vai sadā kāma|caram an|upastīrṇa|śāyinam,
bāh'|ûpadhānaṃ śāmyantaṃ praśaṃsanti div'|âukasaḥ.
dhanavān krodha|lobhābhyām āviṣṭo, naṣṭa|cetanaḥ,
tiryag|īkṣaḥ, śuṣka|mukhaḥ, pāpako, bhru|kuṭī|mukhaḥ.
176.15 nirdaśann adhar'|ôṣṭhaṃ ca, kruddho dāruṇa|bhāṣitā.
kas tam icchet paridraṣṭuṃ, dātum icchati cen mahīm?
śriyā hy abhīkṣṇaṃ saṃvāso mohayaty a|vicakṣaṇam.
sā tasya cittaṃ harati, śārad'|âbhram iv' ânilaḥ.
ath' âinaṃ rūpa|mānaś ca dhana|mānaś ca vindati,
«abhijāto 'smi, siddho 'smi, n' âsmi kevala|mānuṣaḥ.»
ity ebhiḥ kāraṇais tasya tribhiś cittaṃ pramādyati.
saṃprasakta|manā bhogān visṛjya pitṛ|saṃcitān
parikṣīṇaḥ para|svānām ādānaṃ sādhu manyate.
tam atikrānta|maryādam, ādadānaṃ tatas tataḥ,
pratiṣedhanti rājāno, lubdhā mṛgam iv' êṣubhiḥ.

Surveying the three worlds, I see no equal to the one who has no possessions, the pure man who is completely perfected. I weighed possessionlessness and kingship in the 176.10
balance and found that poverty is superior, for it has more virtues than kingship.

There is a vast difference between possessionless and kingship, since a rich man is always agitated as if sitting in the jaws of death. Neither fire, misfortune, death nor the *dasyus** can overpower the one who is liberated and free from desire, for he has abandoned wealth. The gods praise him, the calm man who always moves freely, sleeping on the bare ground with his arm as a pillow.

The rich man is possessed by anger and greed, his thoughts are corrupt. Squinting out of the corners of his eyes, with his mouth parched, this wicked man knits his eye-brows. Biting down on his lower lip, when angered he 176.15
speaks dreadful words. Who would want to look at such a person, even if he wishes to give away the earth?

Continual association with splendrous things deludes an ignorant man. It takes away his mind, like the wind blowing away autumnal clouds. If the person obsessed by beauty and wealth finds them, he thinks that he is handsome, accomplished, and not a mere man.

Thus it is that his mind becomes intoxicated by these three motives.* With an infatuated mind, he relinquishes the possessions accumulated by his forefathers, and when he is ruined he thinks it is right to take the possessions of another. Surpassing his limits, stealing from here and there, kings must drive him away like hunters with arrows chasing a deer.

176.20 evam etāni duḥkhāni tāni tān' îha mānavam
vividhāny upapadyante; gātra|saṃsparśa|jāny api.
teṣāṃ parama|duḥkhānāṃ buddhyā bhaiṣajyam ācaret,
loka|dharmam avajñāya dhruvāṇām a|dhruvaiḥ saha.
n' â|tyaktvā sukham āpnoti, n' âtyaktvā vindate param;
n' âtyaktvā c' âbhayaḥ śete. tyaktvā sarvaṃ sukhī bhava!

ity etadd Hāstinapure brāhmaṇen' ôpavarṇitam
Śaṃpākena purā mahyaṃ. tasmāt tyāgaḥ paro mataḥ.

Therefore these sufferings and various others afflict a man 176.20
in this world, but they are caused by sense perception. To these most severe sufferings he should apply a cure, with his intelligence, once he has no regard for the worldly nature of intransient and transient things.

One cannot attain bliss or find the transcendent without renunciation; without renunciation one cannot sleep free from fear. Abandon all and find bliss!

BHISHMA said:

This is the exalted speech that the brahmin Shampáka delivered unto me long ago in the city of Hástina·pura. Therefore I have the highest regard for renunciation.

177

THE SONG OF MANKI

YUDHIṢṬHIRA uvāca:

177.1 ĪHAMĀNAḤ SAMĀRAMBHĀN
yadi n' āsādayed dhanam,
dhana|tṛṣṇ"|âbhibhūtaś ca,
kiṃ kurvan sukham āpnuyāt?

BHĪṢMA uvāca:

sarva|sāmyam an|āyāsaḥ,† satya|vākyaṃ ca Bhārata,
nirvedaś c' â|vidhitsā ca yasya syāt, sa sukhī naraḥ.
etāny eva padāny āhuḥ pañca vṛddhāḥ praśāntaye,
eṣa: svargaś ca dharmaś ca sukhaṃ c' ânuttamaṃ matam.
atr' âpy udāharant' îmam itihāsaṃ purātanam
nirvedān Maṅkinā gītaṃ. tan nibodha, Yudhiṣṭhira.
177.5 īhamāno dhanaṃ Maṅkir, bhagn'|ēhaś ca punaḥ punaḥ,
kena cid dhana|śeṣeṇa krītavān damya|go|yugam.
su|saṃbaddhau tu tau damyau damanāy' âbhiniḥsṛtau,
āsīnam uṣṭraṃ madhyena sahas" âiv' âbhyadhāvatām.
tayoḥ saṃprāptayor uṣṭraḥ skandha|deśam a|marṣaṇaḥ
utthāy', ôtkṣipya tau damyau prasasāra mahā|javaḥ.
hriyamāṇau tu tau damyau ten' ôṣṭreṇa pramāthinā,
mriyamāṇau ca saṃprekṣya, Maṅkis tatr' âbravīd idam:

YUDHI·SHTHIRA said:

IF THE PERSON WHO pursues various undertakings does not obtain wealth, since he is overwhelmed by the thirst for wealth how might he attain bliss? 177.1

BHISHMA said:

The man who is impartial towards everything, free from toil, true to his word, completely indifferent and without any purpose—he might attain bliss, Bhárata.

The elders taught that only these five words conduce to the attainment of peace. That is: "heaven," "righteousness" and the "highest imaginable bliss."

On this subject people relate the ancient tradition of a song sung by Manki, who had become completely indifferent. Listen to it, Yudhi·shthira.

In the search for wealth, Manki's endeavors came to 177.5
nothing over and over again; with what little capital he had left, he bought a pair of untrained bullocks. But when Manki was leading the bullocks out for training, although they were well bound they suddenly bolted towards a camel sitting in the middle of their path.

When the bullocks reached its shoulders the camel impatiently stood up, lifted them off the ground and ran off at great speed. As the bullocks were being carried away by that manic camel, thinking that they were at the point of death Manki spoke this.

na c' âiv' â|vihitaṃ śakyaṃ dakṣeṇ' âp' īhituṃ dhanam,
yuktena śraddhayā, samyag īhāṃ samanutiṣṭhatā.

177.10 kṛtasya pūrvaṃ c' ân|arthair, yuktasy' âpy anutiṣṭhataḥ,
imaṃ paśyata saṃgatyā mama daivam upaplavam.

udyamy' ôdyamya me damyau viṣameṇ' âiva gacchataḥ.
utkṣipya kāka|tālīyam, utpathen' âiva dhāvataḥ.
maṇ" îv' ôṣṭrasya lambete priyau vatsatarau mama!
śuddhaṃ hi daivam ev' êdaṃ.

haṭhen' âiv' âsti pauruṣam.
yadi v" âpy upapadyeta† pauruṣaṃ nāma karhi cit,
anviṣyamāṇaṃ tad api daivam ev' âvatiṣṭhate.
tasmān nirveda ev' êha gantavyaḥ sukham icchatā;
sukhaṃ svapiti nirviṇṇo, nir|āśaś c' ârtha|sādhane.

177.15 «aho samyak!» Śuken' ôktaṃ sarvataḥ parimucyatā,
pratiṣṭhatā mah"|âraṇyaṃ Janakasya niveśanāt.

yaḥ kāmān āpnuyāt sarvān, yaś c' âitān kevalāṃs tyajet;
prāpaṇāt sarva|kāmānāṃ parityāgo viśiṣyate.
n' ântaṃ sarva|vidhitsānāṃ gata|pūrvo 'sti kaś cana:
śarīre jīvite c' âiva tṛṣṇā mandasya vardhate.

MANKI said:

A clever man cannot accumulate wealth if it is not ordained, even if he applies himself to his endeavors diligently, confidently and correctly. Despite the failures of my 177.10
former deeds I have exerted myself diligently, and yet look
at this misfortune that has come to me by chance. It is fate!

Being lifted by the camel again and again, my bullocks are running around in a disjointed fashion. They rush off with the stray camel, and are thrown about like the crow that was accidentally killed by a falling palm fruit. My beloved young bullocks dangle from the camel like a pair of jewels! This must be fate, which is irreproachable.

Human agency can only be exerted through force. If, however, anybody should come to possess what is referred to as "human agency," once investigated it will be found to be nothing but fate. Therefore the one who desires bliss should surrender himself to complete indifference, for the indifferent man sleeps blissfully, being free from the desire to attain wealth.

When Shuka renounced everything and left Jánaka's 177.15
palace to set off for the great forest, he said "Aha! This is
right!"

Someone might obtain all his desires and another might renounce them, but of the two renunciation is better. Nobody has ever fulfilled all his wishes, for a dullard's thirst grows in his body and soul.

nivartasva vidhitsābhyaḥ, śāmya nirvidya, Kāmuka.
a|sakṛc c' âsi nikṛto, na ca nirvidyase tataḥ.
yadi n' âhaṃ vināśyas te, yady evaṃ ramase mayā,
mā māṃ yojaya lobhena vṛthā tvaṃ, vitta|kāmuka.
177.20 sañcitaṃ sañcitaṃ dravyaṃ, naṣṭaṃ tava punaḥ punaḥ.
kadā cin mokṣyase, mūḍha, dhan'|ēhāṃ, dhana|kāmuka.

aho nu mama bāliśyaṃ, yo 'haṃ krīḍanakas tava!
kiṃ n' âivaṃ jātu puruṣaḥ pareṣāṃ preṣyatām iyāt?
na pūrve n' âpare jātu kāmānām antam āpnuvan;
tyaktvā sarva|samārambhān pratibuddho 'smi, jāgṛmi.
nūnaṃ te hṛdayaṃ, Kāma, vajra|sāra|mayaṃ dṛdham?
yad an|artha|śat'|āviṣṭaṃ śatadhā na vidīryate.†
jānāmi, Kāma, tvāṃ c' âiva, yac ca kiṃ cit priyaṃ tava.
tav' âhaṃ priyam anvicchann ātmany upalabhe sukham.
177.25 Kāma, jānāmi te mūlaṃ: saṃkalpāt kila jāyase.
na tvāṃ saṃkalpayiṣyāmi, sa|mūlo na bhaviṣyasi.
īhā dhanasya na sukhā, labdhvā cintā ca bhūyasī.
labdha|nāśe yathā mṛtyur; labdhaṃ bhavati vā na vā.

DESIRE said:*

Turn away from your wishes, lustful one, be indifferent and find peace. You have been repeatedly deceived, but still you do not become indifferent. If you do not destroy me, but continue to find your pleasure in me, at least you should not engage me greedily or frivolously, you who lusts after
wealth. Whatever possessions you pile up, they will be de- 177.20
stroyed over and over again. You fool who lusts after wealth! At some point you will have to relinquish your desire for it.

MANKI said:

Alas my foolishness, I who am your toy! Might a man ever not be a servant to others in this way? I did not fulfill all my desires in the past, and will not fulfill them in the future; but since I have abandoned all undertakings, I am awake and watchful.

O Desire, is not your heart adamantine and firm? Although it is filled by hundreds of disappointments, it cannot be split into a hundred pieces. I know you, Desire, and what you hold dear. But while I was searching for that which you hold dear, I found bliss within.

I know your source, Desire: verily you arise from the 177.25
imagination. But I will not ponder you, and so you, along with your source, will not come into being. The endeavor for wealth is not pleasurable, and when wealth is obtained one's worries multiply. Once wealth is lost it feels like death, and the attainment of wealth comes and goes.

parityāge na labhate. tato duḥkhataraṃ nu kim?
na ca tuṣyati labdhena, bhūya eva† ca mārgati.
anutarṣula ev' ârthaḥ, svādu Gāṅgam iv' ôdakam.
mad|vilāpanam etat tu, pratibuddho 'smi, saṃtyaja!

ya imaṃ māmakaṃ dehaṃ bhūta|grāmaḥ samāśritaḥ:
sa yātv ito yathā|kāmaṃ, vasatāṃ vā yathā|sukham.
177.30 na yuṣmāsv iha me prītiḥ kāma|lobh'|ânusāriṣu.
tasmād utsṛjya kāmān vai sattvam ev' āśrayāmy aham.

sarva|bhūtāny ahaṃ dehe paśyan manasi c' ātmanaḥ,
yoge buddhiṃ, śrute sattvaṃ, mano brahmaṇi dhārayan.
vihariṣyāmy an|āsaktaḥ, sukhī, lokān nir|āmayaḥ,
yathā māṃ tvaṃ punar n' âivaṃ duḥkheṣu praṇidhāsyasi.
tvayā hi me praṇunnasya gatir anyā na vidyate.
tṛṣṇā|śoka|śramāṇāṃ hi tvaṃ kāma|prabhavaḥ sadā.

dhana|nāśe 'dhikaṃ duḥkhaṃ manye sarva|mahattaram,
jñātayo hy avamanyante mitrāṇi ca dhanāc cyutam.
177.35 avajñāna|sahasrais tu doṣāḥ kaṣṭatarā dhane;
dhane sukha|kalā yā tu, s" âpi duḥkhair vidhīyate.
dhanam asy' êti, puruṣaṃ puro nighnanti dasyavaḥ.
kliśyanti vividhair daṇḍair, nityam udvejayanti ca.

When one is separated from wealth one gains nothing. Is there a greater suffering than this? A person is never satiated with the wealth he gains, and looks for it in even greater measure. Wealth causes desire, just like the sweet water of the Ganges. This has been the cause of my lamentation, but I am now awake, so leave me!

Let the collection of elements that abides in this body of
mine leave this place whenever it wants, or abide wherever
it wishes; I do not find my delight among you, O elements, 177.30
for you conform to the greed for sensual pleasure. Therefore
I will relinquish desires and rest in purity alone.

Seeing all living beings in my body and mind, I will focus my awareness in yogic discipline, my essence in sacred knowledge and my mind in *brahman*. I will abide free from attachment, experiencing bliss and, without the illness found in the world, so that you will never again mire me in such sufferings. For you have driven me away, and I now have no other destiny. You will always be a source of desire, thirst, sorrow and toil.

I think that the greatest, most excessive suffering of all
comes about when one's wealth is destroyed, for even kinsmen and friends despise the person who has lost his wealth.
The evils of wealth are more terrible than being disrespected 177.35
a thousand times; even a small amount of the happiness
wealth brings is riddled with suffering. Barbarians kill the
man in front of them if they think he possesses wealth—they
torment him with different kinds of punishment and ter-
rify him without relent.

artha|lolupatā duḥkham, iti buddhaṃ cirān mayā.
yad yad ālambase, Kāma,† tat tad ev' ânurudhyase.
a|tattva|jño 'si, bālaś ca,
dus|toṣo, '|pūraṇo 'nalaḥ;
n' âiva tvaṃ vettha su|labhaṃ,
n' âiva tvaṃ vettha dur|labham.
Pātāla iva duṣ|pūro, māṃ duḥkhair yoktum icchasi.
n' âham adya samāveṣṭuṃ śakyaḥ, Kāma, punas tvayā.
177.40 nirvedam aham āsādya dravya|nāśād yadṛcchayā,
nivṛttiṃ paramāṃ prāpya n' âdya kāmān vicintaye.
atikleśān sahām' îha, n' âhaṃ budhyāmy a|buddhimān.
nikṛto dhana|nāśena śaye sarv'|âṅga|vijvaraḥ.
parityajāmi, Kāma, tvāṃ hitvā sarva|manogatīḥ.
na tvaṃ mayā punaḥ, Kāma, vatsyase na ca raṃsyase.
kṣamiṣye kṣipamāṇānāṃ; na hiṃsiṣye vihiṃsitaḥ.
dveṣya|yuktaḥ priyaṃ vakṣyāmy an|ādṛtya tad apriyam.
tṛptaḥ, sva|sth'|êndriyo nityaṃ, yathā|labdhena vartayan
na sa|kāmaṃ kariṣyāmi tvām ahaṃ śatrum ātmanaḥ.
177.45 nirvedaṃ, nirvṛtiṃ, tṛptiṃ,
śāntiṃ, satyaṃ, damaṃ, kṣamām,
sarva|bhūta|dayāṃ c' âiva
viddhi māṃ samupāgatam!
tasmāt kāmaś ca, lobhaś ca,
tṛṣṇā, kārpaṇyam eva ca
tyajantu māṃ pratiṣṭhantaṃ,
sattva|stho hy asmi sāṃpratam.

At last I have realized that lusting after wealth is misery. O Desire, you cling to whatever object you lay hold of. You are an ignorant fool, a primeval fire that brings no satisfaction for you know neither what is easy or difficult to attain.

You would like to shackle me with sufferings, just like
the insatiable Patála hell.* But now, Desire, it will be impossible for you to enter me again. With the destruction of 177.40
my property, by chance I have reached a state of complete
indifference. Having attained the supreme state of inaction,
I now have no thought for desires.

I can endure the world's troubles for I no longer think of myself as a fool. Humbled by the destruction of my wealth, I rest with my body completely free from the fever of desire. I abandon you, Desire, by putting aside all my wishes. O Desire, never again will you abide in me or take your pleasure with me.

I will defer to those who abuse me; even if harmed I will not harm others. In the presence of enemies I will speak pleasant words, ignoring that which is unpleasant. I shall be content, my senses continually fixed within, subsisting on whatever I find. But I will not make you and your desirable objects into my enemy.

Know that I have attained a state of complete indiffer- 177.45
ence, bliss, contentment, peace, truth, restraint, forbearance and compassion to all living beings! Therefore let my
desire, greed, thirst and niggardliness leave me, for I now
stand firm and abide in purity.

prahāya kāmaṃ lobhaṃ ca,
sukhaṃ prāpto 'smi sāṃpratam.
n' âdya lobha|vaśaṃ prāpto
duḥkhaṃ prāpsyāmy an|ātmavān.
yad yat tyajati kāmānāṃ, tat sukhasy' âbhipūryate.
kāmasya vaśago nityaṃ duḥkham eva prapadyate.
kām'|ānubandhaṃ nudate yat kiṃ cit puruṣo rajaḥ,
kāma|krodh'|ôdbhavaṃ duḥkham, a|hrīr, a|ratir eva ca.
177.50 eṣa brahma|pratiṣṭho 'haṃ, grīṣme śītam iva hradam.
śāmyāmi, parinirvāmi; sukham mām eti kevalam.
yac ca kāma|sukhaṃ loke, yac ca divyaṃ mahat sukham,
tṛṣṇā|kṣaya|sukhasy' âite n' ârhataḥ ṣoḍaśīṃ kalām.
ātmanā saptamaṃ kāmaṃ
hatvā, śatrum iv' ôttamam,
prāpy' â|vadhyaṃ brahma|puraṃ,
rāj" êva syām ahaṃ sukhī.

etāṃ buddhiṃ samāsthāya Maṅkir nirvedam āgataḥ;
sarvān kāmān parityajya, prāpya brahma mahat sukham.
damya|nāśa|kṛte Maṅkir amṛtatvaṃ kil' âgamat.
acchinat kāma|mūlaṃ sa, tena prāpa mahat sukham.

Abandoning desire and greed, I have now attained bliss. I am no longer controlled by greed, and will not experience the suffering of a person who lacks self-control. When a person abandons the objects of sensual pleasure they become sources of bliss. But the person who is continually controlled by desire will find nothing but suffering.* A man should dispel those passions that bind him to desire, for desire and anger cause misery, shamelessness and discontent.

Just like a cool lake in summer, I am firmly established 177.50
in *brahman*. Being tranquil, and completely quenched, I experience nothing but bliss.

The bliss of sensual pleasures as well as the great bliss of heaven do not amount to one sixteenth of the bliss brought about by the destruction of thirst.* Through slaying desire—the "seventh"—all by myself, as if it were my principal enemy, I have reached the unconquered city of *brahman* and like a king experience bliss.

BHISHMA said:

Relying on this understanding, Manki attained complete indifference; he abandoned all his desires and attained the great bliss of *brahman*.

Manki certainly attained immortality on account of the fact that his bullocks were killed. He severed the very root of desire, and because of that attained great bliss.

178

THE SONG OF BODHYA

BHĪṢMA uvāca:

178.1 ATR' ÂPY UDĀHARANT' îmam itihāsaṃ purātanam
gītaṃ Videha|rājena Janakena praśāmyatā.
«an|antam iva me vittaṃ, yasya me n' âsti kiṃ cana.
Mithilāyāṃ pradīptāyāṃ na me dahyati kiṃ cana.»
atr' âiv' ôdāharant' îmaṃ Bodhyasya pada|saṃcayam
nirvedaṃ prati vinyastaṃ. taṃ nibodha Yudhiṣṭhira.
Bodhyaṃ śāntam ṛṣiṃ rājā Nāhuṣaḥ paryapṛcchata
nirvedāc chāntim āpannaṃ, śāstra|prajñāna|tarpitam:
178.5 «upadeśaṃ, mahā|prājña, śamasy' ôpadiśasva me.
kāṃ buddhiṃ samanudhyāya śāntaś carasi nirvṛtaḥ?»

BODHYA uvāca:

upadeśena vartāmi, n' ânuśāsm' îha kaṃ cana.
lakṣaṇaṃ tasya vakṣye 'haṃ; tat svayaṃ parimṛśyatām.
Piṅgalā, kuraraḥ, sarpaḥ, sāraṅg'|ânveṣaṇaṃ vane,
iṣu|kāraḥ, Kumārī ca: ṣaḍ ete guravo mama.

BHIṢMA uvāca:

āśā balavatī, rājan; nairāśyaṃ paramaṃ sukham.
āśāṃ nir|āśāṃ kṛtvā tu sukhaṃ svapiti Piṅgalā.

BHISHMA said:

ON THIS SUBJECT people relate the ancient tradition of 178.1
a verse sung by Jánaka, the king of Vidéha, when he had attained peace:*

"Although my wealth is virtually limitless, I possess nothing. Even when Míthila was set on fire, nothing belonging to me was burnt."*

On the same subject people also relate the stanzas on complete indifference composed by Bodhya. Listen to them, Yudhi·shthira. Bodhya was a quietist and a seer who became satiated through an understanding of the treatises, and attained peace by means of complete indifference. He was questioned by King Náhusha as follows:

"Advise me on peace, wise man. What is the object of 178.5
your contemplation through which you are quenched and live in peace?"

BODHYA said:

I follow a teaching and do not instruct anyone else. But I will give you an indication of the teaching that I follow, and you should reflect on this yourself. Píngala the courtesan, the osprey, the snake, the searching of the speckled peacock in the forest, the fletcher and the Kumári river: these six are my teachers.

BHISHMA said:

Desire is very powerful, Your Majesty, but freedom from it is the highest bliss. Turning desire into disregard, Píngala sleeps happily.*

s'|āmiṣaṃ kuraraṃ dṛṣṭvā vadhyamānaṃ nir|āmiṣaiḥ
āmiṣasya parityāgāt kuraraḥ sukham edhate.
178.10 gṛh'|ārambho hi duḥkhāya, na sukhāya kadā cana.
sarpaḥ para|kṛtaṃ veśma praviśya sukham edhate.
sukhaṃ jīvanti munayo bhaikṣya|vṛttiṃ samāśritāḥ,
a|droheṇ' âiva bhūtānāṃ, sāraṅgā iva pakṣiṇaḥ.
iṣu|kāro naraḥ kaś cid iṣāv āsakta|mānasaḥ
samīpen' âpi gacchantaṃ rājānaṃ n' âvabuddhavān.
bahūnāṃ kalaho nityaṃ,
dvayoḥ saṃkathanaṃ dhruvam.
ekākī vicariṣyāmi,
Kumārī|śaṅkhako yathā.

An osprey that had caught its quarry was slain by other ospreys who had none. Upon seeing this, another osprey abandoned its prey and found bliss.

Building a home leads to misery and never to happiness. 178.10
But a snake found bliss by entering the home built by another creature.

Resorting to the practice of mendicancy, silent sages pass their lives in bliss. Like speckled peacocks, they do not injure any other creature.

A certain fletcher was so engrossed by the arrow he was making that he did not notice a king traveling through his neighborhood.

There will always be conflict within a group, for conversation between two people is inevitable. Therefore I will rove alone, just like a conch-shell of the Kumári river.

179

THE DIALOGUE BETWEEN AJA·GARA AND PRAHRÁDA

YUDHIṢṬHIRA uvāca:

179.1 KENA VṚTTENA, VṚTTA|jña, vīta|śokaś caren mahīm?
kiṃ ca kurvan naro loke prāpnoti gatim uttamām?

BHĪṢMA uvāca:

atr' âpy udāharant' îmam itihāsaṃ purātanam:
Prahrādasya ca saṃvādaṃ muner Ājagarasya ca.
carantaṃ brāhmaṇaṃ kaṃ cit kalpa|cittam, an|āmayam
papraccha rājā Prahrādo buddhimān buddhi|saṃmataṃ.

PRAHRĀDA uvāca:

sva|sthaḥ, śakto, mṛdur, dānto, nir|vidhitso, 'n|asūyakaḥ,
su|vāk, pragalbho, medhāvī, prājñaś carasi bālavat!
179.5 n' âiva prārthayase lābhaṃ, n' â|lābheṣv anuśocasi.
nitya|tṛpta iva, brahman, na kiṃ cid iva manyase.
srotasā hriyamāṇāsu prajāsv a|vimanā† iva,
dharma|kām'|ârtha|kāryeṣu kūṭa|stha iva lakṣyase.
n' ânutiṣṭhasi dharm'|ârthau, na kāme c' âpi vartase.
indriy'|ârthān an|ādṛtya muktaś carasi sākṣivat.
kā nu prajñā, śrutaṃ vā kiṃ, vṛttir vā kā nu te, mune?
kṣipram ācakṣva me, brahmañ, śreyo yad iha manyase.

YUDHI·SHTHIRA said:

HOW SHOULD A man conduct himself so that he might wander the earth free from sorrow, O master of conduct? Through what worldly deed does a man attain the highest destiny? 179.1

BHISHMA said:

On this subject people relate the ancient tradition of a dialogue between Prahráda and the sage Aja·gara.* The wise King Prahráda put the following questions to a certain wandering brahmin, who was able minded and healthy, and considered by all to be intelligent.

PRAHRÁDA said:

Being content, accomplished, gentle, restrained, free from desire and envy, eloquent, confident, learned and
wise, you live like a child! You do not hanker after acquisi- 179.5
tions and you do not lament your losses. You always seem to be satisfied, brahmin, as if you were thinking about nothing at all. Although creatures are carried away in the torrent of life, you do not seem to be troubled. In matters of religion, pleasure and material gain, you appear to be as immovable as a mountain peak.*

You take no notice of religion or material gain, and do not incline towards pleasure. Forsaking the objects of the senses, you wander about in a state of release, just like a detached witness. What is your wisdom, learning and conduct, silent sage? Tell me immediately, brahmin, that which you consider supreme in this world.

BHĪṢMA uvāca:

anuyuktaḥ sa medhāvī loka|dharma|vidhāna|vit,
uvāca ślakṣṇayā vācā Prahrādam an|apārthayā.

179.10 paśya, Prahrāda, bhūtānām utpattim a|nimittataḥ.
hrāsaṃ, vṛddhiṃ, vināśaṃ ca na prahṛṣye na ca vyathe.
sva|bhāvād eva saṃdṛśyā vartamānāḥ pravṛttayaḥ.
sva|bhāva|niratāḥ sarvāḥ, parituṣyen na kena cit.
paśya, Prahrāda, saṃyogān viprayoga|parāyaṇān,
saṃcayāṃś ca vināś'|ântān; na kva cid vidadhe manaḥ.
antavanti ca bhūtāni guṇa|yuktāni paśyataḥ,
utpatti|nidhana|jñasya, kiṃ kāryam avaśiṣyate?
jala|jānām api hy antaṃ paryāyeṇ' ôpalakṣaye,
mahatām api kāyānāṃ, sūkṣmāṇāṃ ca mah"|ôdadhau.
179.15 jaṅgama|sthāvarāṇāṃ ca bhūtānām, asur'|âdhipa,
pārthivānām api vyaktaṃ mṛtyuṃ paśyāmi sarvaśaḥ.
antarikṣa|carāṇāṃ ca, Dānav'|ôttama, pakṣiṇām,
uttiṣṭhate yathā|kālaṃ mṛtyur balavatām api.
divi saṃcaramāṇāni hrasvāni ca mahānti ca
jyotīṃṣy api yathā|kālaṃ patamānāni lakṣaye.

BHISHMA said:

Upon being questioned the learned Aja·gara, who understood the religious order of the world, replied in eloquent, meaningful words to Prahráda.

AJA·GARA said:

You must see, Prahráda, that there is no cause for the origination of living beings. Their growth, deterioration and destruction neither pleases me nor cause me anxiety. Consider that all things that come into existence and persist are caused by their inherent nature. Because all living beings are bound to their inherent nature, one should not delight in anything. 179.10

Understand, Prahráda, that I let my mind rest nowhere since union ends up in separation and accumulation ends up in annihilation. All living things are finite and burdened with qualities. For the person who sees this, who understands their origination and destruction, what remains to be done? I know that even aquatic creatures, those massive in body as well as the minute, will eventually meet their end in the great ocean.

I see death manifest all around, *ásura* king, for all the an- 179.15
imate and inanimate creatures of the earth. In due course death will come to the birds flying about in the sky, supreme *dánava*, even if they are mighty. The celestial lights that traverse the heavens above include those that are minute and vast, but I believe that even they will disappear in due course.

iti bhūtāni saṃpaśyann anuṣaktāni mṛtyunā,
sarva|sāmānya|go, vidvān, kṛta|kṛtyaḥ sukhaṃ svape.
su|mahāntam api grāsaṃ grase labdhaṃ yadṛcchayā,
śaye punar a|bhuñjāno divasāni bahūny api.
179.20 āśayanty api mām annaṃ punar bahu|guṇaṃ bahu,
punar alpaṃ, punaḥ stokaṃ, punar n' âiv' ôpapadyate.
kaṇaṃ kadā cit khādāmi, piṇyākam api ca grase,
bhakṣaye śāli|māṃsāni, bhakṣāṃś c' ôcc'|âvacān punaḥ.
śaye kadā cit paryaṅke, bhūmāv api punaḥ śaye,
prāsāde c' âpi me śayyā kadā cid upapadyate.
dhārayāmi ca cīrāṇi śāṇa|kṣaum'|âjināni ca;
mah"|ârhāṇi ca vāsāṃsi dhārayāmy aham ekadā.
na saṃnipatitaṃ dharmyam upabhogaṃ yadṛcchayā
pratyācakṣe, na c' âpy enam anurudhye su|dur|labham.
179.25 a|calam, a|nidhanaṃ, śivaṃ, vi|śokaṃ,
śucim, a|tulaṃ, viduṣāṃ mate praviṣṭam,
an|abhimatam, a|sevitaṃ vimūḍhair
vratam idam Ājagaraṃ śuciś carāmi.
a|calita|matir, a|cyutaḥ sva|dharmāt,
parimita|saṃsaraṇaḥ, par'|âvara|jñaḥ,
vigata|bhaya|kaṣāya|lobha|moho
vratam idam Ājagaraṃ śuciś carāmi.
a|niyata|phala|bhakṣya|bhojya|peyaṃ,
vidhi|pariṇāma|vibhakta|deśa|kālam,
hṛdaya|sukham, a|sevitaṃ kadaryair
vratam idam Ājagaraṃ śuciś carāmi.

Thus seeing living beings shackled by death, and gaining understanding from the contemplation that everything else is no different, I sleep blissfully, having done what had to be done.

I swallow what food I get by chance, even if it is a great feast, but sometimes I rest for many days without eating anything. Sometimes people offer me excellent food in 179.20
abundance, sometimes they feed me a little or an insignificant amount, and sometimes I get nothing at all. Sometimes I eat a single grain of corn or even an oil cake. I eat rice and meat, and meals that are both excellent and disgusting.

Sometimes I rest in a palanquin, sometimes I lie on the ground and occasionally I am offered a bed on a terrace. I wear garments made from tree-bark, hemp, linen or antelope hide, and sometimes I wear very expensive clothes. I do not reject a suitable pleasure that falls to me by chance, but I do not cling to it even if it is very difficult to obtain.

Being pure, I follow this vow of Aja·gara, which is un- 179.25
shakeable, indestructible, auspicious, free from sorrow, pure and unequaled. It abides in the thoughts of the wise, but fools do not approve of or practice it. My mind is unshakeable, I am unfailing in my duties, I regulate my movements, and I understand what is superior and inferior. Being pure and devoid of fear, defilement, greed and delusion, I follow this vow of Aja·gara.

Being pure, I follow this vow of Aja·gara which possesses an inner bliss that cannot be experienced by misers. According to this vow fruit, drink and all kinds of food are taken irregularly, for time and place are left to the workings of fate.

idam idam iti tṛṣṇay" âbhibhūtaṃ
janam an|avāpta|dhanaṃ viṣīdamānam
nipuṇam anuniśamya, tattva|buddhyā,
vratam idam Ājagaraṃ śuciś carāmi.
bahu|vidham anudṛśya c' ârtha|hetoḥ
kṛpaṇam ih' āryam an|āryam āśrayantam,
upaśama|rucir, ātmavān, praśānto
vratam idam Ājagaraṃ śuciś carāmi.
179.30 sukham, a|sukham, a|lābham, artha|lābhaṃ,
ratim, a|ratiṃ, maraṇaṃ ca jīvitaṃ ca
vidhi|niyatam avekṣya tattvato 'haṃ
vratam idam Ājagaraṃ śuciś carāmi.
apagata|bhaya|rāga|moha|darpo,
dhṛti|mati|buddhi|samanvitaḥ, praśāntaḥ
upagata|phala|bhogino niśamya
vratam idam Ājagaraṃ śuciś carāmi.
a|niyata|śayan'|āsanaḥ prakṛtyā,
dama|niyama|vrata|satya|śauca|yuktaḥ,
apagata|phala|saṃcayaḥ, prahṛṣṭo
vratam idam Ājagaraṃ śuciś carāmi.
apagatam a|sukh'|ârtham īhan"|ârthair
upagata|buddhir avekṣya c' ātma|saṃstham,
tṛṣitam a|niyataṃ mano niyantuṃ
vratam idam Ājagaraṃ śuciś carāmi.
hṛdayam anurudhya, vāṅ|mano vā,
priya|sukha|dur|labhatām a|nityatāṃ ca,
tad ubhayam upalakṣayann iv' âhaṃ
vratam idam Ājagaraṃ śuciś carāmi.
179.35 bahu kathitam idaṃ hi buddhimadbhiḥ
kavibhir api prathayadbhir ātma|kīrtim;

A person overcome with thirst for different things becomes depressed when he does not obtain wealth. Considering this carefully, and understanding the way things really are, I am pure and follow this vow of Aja·gara.

I have seen that all kinds of wretches approach honorable and dishonorable men to obtain money, and so have lost my appetite for things. Being self-controlled, peaceful and pure, I follow this vow of Aja·gara.

All is determined by fate: pleasure and pain, gain and 179.30
loss, joy and misery, life and death. Contemplating this as
it really is, and being pure, I follow this vow of Aja·gara.

I am devoid of fear, passion, delusion and pride, but am peaceful, being endowed with resolve, wisdom and intelligence. Observing that snakes eat only what comes by,* and being pure, I follow this vow of Aja·gara.

I am of the habit of taking no fixed lodging, being endowed with restraint, control, religious vows, truth and purity. Delighting in the fact that I have no hoard of fruit, and being pure, I follow this vow of Aja·gara.

Endowed with intelligence, I have contemplated that the cause of my pain has vanished through my own exertion. Being pure, I follow this vow of Aja·gara in order to control the thirsty and uncontrolled mind that rests in the body.

Curbing my heart, speech and mind, I perceive that joy and pleasure are difficult to attain and transitory to boot; being pure, I follow this vow of Aja·gara.

This much has been proclaimed by the wise seers who 179.35
spread their fame far and wide; although they held different

idam idam iti tatra tatra, hanta,
    sva|para|matair gahanaṃ pratarkayadbhiḥ.
tad idam anuniśamya, viprapātaṃ
    pṛthag abhipannam ih' â|budhair manuṣyaiḥ
an|avasitam an|anta|doṣa|pāraṃ,
    nṛṣu viharāmi vinīta|doṣa|tṛṣṇaḥ.

BHĪṢMA uvāca:

Ajagara|caritaṃ vrataṃ mah"|ātmā
    ya iha naro 'nucared vinīta|rāgaḥ
apagata|bhaya|lobha|moha|manyuḥ
    sa khalu sukhī vihared imaṃ vihāram.

opinions on various subjects, they investigated profound matters through their own and opposing views. In consideration of this foolish men withdraw to mountain cliffs by themselves, but have not passed over to the far shore beyond endless evil. I, on the other hand, live among men but am devoid of evil and thirst.

BHISHMA said:

Free from passion, fear, greed, delusion and anger, a holy man should practice the vow undertaken by Aja·gara. If he follows this way of life, he will indeed attain bliss.

180

THE DIALOGUE BETWEEN KÁSHYAPA AND A JACKAL

YUDHIṢṬHIRA uvāca:

180.1 BĀNDHAVĀḤ, KARMA, vittaṃ vā,
prajñā v" êha, pitā|maha—
narasya kā pratiṣṭhā syād?
etat pṛṣṭo vadasva me.

BHĪṢMA uvāca:

prajñā pratiṣṭhā bhūtānāṃ; prajñā lābhaḥ paro mataḥ.
prajñā niḥśreyasī loke: prajñā svargo mataḥ satām.
prajñayā prāpit'|ârtho hi Balir aiśvarya|saṃkṣaye,
Prahrādo, Namucir, Maṅkis. tasyāḥ kiṃ vidyate param?
atr' âpy udāharant' îmam itihāsaṃ purātanam:
Indra|Kāśyapa|saṃvādaṃ. tan nibodha, Yudhiṣṭhira.
180.5 vaiśyaḥ kaś cid ṛṣi|sutaṃ Kāśyapaṃ saṃśita|vratam
rathena pātayām āsa śrīmān, dṛptas tapasvinam.
ārtaḥ sa patitaḥ, kruddhas, tyaktv"† ātmānam ath' âbravīt:
«mariṣyāmy! a|dhanasy' êha jīvit'|ârtho na vidyate.»
tathā mumūrṣum āsīnam, a|kūjantam, a|cetasam
Indraḥ sṛgāla|rūpeṇa babhāṣe lubdha|mānasam:

manuṣya|yonim icchanti sarva|bhūtāni sarvaśaḥ,
manuṣyatve ca vipratvaṃ sarva ev' âbhinandati.
manuṣyo brāhmaṇaś c' âsi, śrotriyaś c' âsi, Kāśyapa.
su|dur|labham avāpy' âitan, na doṣān martum arhasi.

YUDHI·SHTHIRA said:

O GRANDFATHER, WHAT is a man's foundation in this world? Is it his kinsmen, deeds, wealth or wisdom? Please give me an answer to this question. 180.1

BHISHMA said:

Wisdom is the foundation of living beings, it is thought to be the highest acquisition. Wisdom is the most splendid thing in the world: virtuous men consider it to be heaven. When Bali had become powerless he obtained his goal through wisdom, and the same is true of Prahráda, Námuchi and Manki.* What could be better than wisdom?

On this subject people relate the ancient tradition of a dialogue between Indra and Káshyapa. Listen to it, Yudhi·shthira.

Káshyapa was the son of a seer, an ascetic who was ar- 180.5
dent in his vows. But he was knocked over by the chariot of a handsome and arrogant vaishya. Wounded by his fall, Káshyapa became angry and lost his self-control, saying: "I will die! In this world a destitute man's life is meaningless." And so he lay there whimpering, barely conscious and wanting to die. But then Indra took the form of a jackal, and said this to the bewildered man.

THE JACKAL said:

All living beings desire a human birth, and all esteem Brahminhood the most among humankind. You are both a man and a brahmin, Káshyapa, and a learned one at that. You have attained that which is very difficult to find, and
will not die because of your present misfortune. All acqui- 180.10

180.10 sarve lābhāḥ s'|âbhimānā: iti satyavatī śrutiḥ.
saṃtoṣaṇīya|rūpo 'si, lobhād yad abhimanyase.
aho! siddh'|ârthatā teṣāṃ yeṣāṃ sant' îha pāṇayaḥ.
atīva spṛhaye teṣāṃ yeṣāṃ sant' îha pāṇayaḥ!
pāṇimadbhyaḥ spṛh" âsmākaṃ yathā tava dhanasya vai:
na pāṇi|lābhād adhiko lābhaḥ kaś cana vidyate.
a|pāṇitvād vayaṃ brahman, kaṇṭakaṃ n' ôddharāmahe,
jantūn ucc'|âvacān aṅge daśato na kaṣāma vā.
atha yeṣāṃ punaḥ pāṇī deva|dattau daś'|âṅgulī,
uddharanti kṛmīn aṅgād, daśato nikaṣanti ca.
180.15 varṣā|him'|ātapānāṃ ca paritrāṇāni kurvate.
cailam, annaṃ, sukhaṃ śayyāṃ, ni|vātaṃ c' ôpabhuñjate.
adhiṣṭhāya ca gāṃ loke bhuñjate vāhayanti ca;
upāyair bahubhiś c' âiva vaśyān ātmani kurvate.
ye khalv a|jihvāḥ kṛpaṇā alpa|prāṇā, a|pāṇayaḥ,
sahante tāni duḥkhāni. diṣṭyā tvaṃ na tathā, mune!
diṣṭyā tvaṃ na sṛgālo vai, na kṛmir, na ca mūṣakaḥ,
na sarpo, na ca maṇḍūko, na c' ânyaḥ pāpa|yoni|jaḥ!
etāvat" âpi lābhena toṣṭum arhasi, Kāśyapa,
kiṃ punar yo 'si sattvānāṃ sarveṣāṃ, brāhmaṇ', ôttamaḥ?
180.20 ime māṃ kṛmayo 'danti, yeṣām uddharaṇāya vai
n' âsti śaktir a|pāṇitvāt. paśy' âvasthām imāṃ mama!
a|kāryam iti c' âiv' êmaṃ n' ātmānaṃ saṃtyajāmy aham,
n' âtaḥ pāpīyasīṃ yoniṃ pateyam aparām iti.
madhye vai pāpa|yonīnāṃ sārgālīṃ yām ahaṃ gataḥ,
pāpīyasyo bahu|tarā ito 'nyāḥ pāpa|yonayaḥ.

sitions are bound up in conceit: this is the true word of the Veda. You have a charming appearance, but covet it out of greed.

Alas! Only those who possess hands succeed in their worldly aims. How I long to be counted among the world's dextrous! We desire hands just as you desire wealth: no acquisition is more valuable than that of hands. Because we do not have any hands, brahmin, we cannot remove thorns from our bodies and we cannot scratch off the different creatures that bite us. But those to whom the gods give two hands and ten fingers, they can remove worms from their bodies and can scratch off biting creatures.

They can build refuges from the rain, snow and sun; they 180.15
can enjoy fine clothes, food, a pleasant bed and a shelter from the wind. In this world they can herd cattle, enjoy their products and make them carry loads; they can exert their control over them in all sorts of ways. But those wheezing wretches without tongues or hands endure terrible sufferings. Thank heaven you are not like them, silent sage!

Thank heaven that you are not a jackal, worm, mouse, snake, frog or any other creature of beastly origin. You should be content with what you have, Káshyapa—how much more so since you are the best of all creatures, O brahmin.

These worms devour me but because I have no hands 180.20
I am incapable of removing them. Look at my condition! And yet I do not renounce my body, which I consider improper, and so I will not fall to another state even more beastly than this. Among evil births, there are many other states more beastly than that of a jackal, which is my lot.

jāty" âiv' âike sukhi|tarāḥ, santy anye bhṛśa|duḥkhitāḥ.
n' âikāntaṃ sukham ev' êha kva cit paśyāmi kasya cit.
manuṣyā hy āḍhyatāṃ prāpya
rājyam icchanty an|antaram.
rājyād devatvam icchanti,
devatvād Indratām api.
180.25 bhaves tvaṃ yady api tv āḍhyo, na rājā na ca daivatam.
devatvaṃ prāpya c' Êndratvaṃ, n' âiva tuṣyes tathā sati.
na tṛptiḥ priya|lābhe 'sti, tṛṣṇā n' âdbhiḥ praśāmyati:
saṃprajvalati sā bhūyaḥ samidbhir iva pāvakaḥ
asty eva tvayi śoko 'pi, harṣaś c' âpi tathā tvayi,
sukha|duḥkhe tathā c' ôbhe. tatra kā paridevanā?
paricchidy' âiva kāmānāṃ sarveṣāṃ c' âiva karmaṇām,
mūlaṃ rundh' îndriya|grāmaṃ,† śakuntān iva pañjare.
na dvitīyasya śirasaś chedanaṃ vidyate kva cit,
na ca pāṇes tṛtīyasya: yan n' âsti, na tato bhayam.
180.30 na khalv apy a|rasa|jñasya kāmaḥ kva cana jāyate,
saṃsparśād, darśanād v" âpi, śravaṇād v" âpi jāyate.
na tvaṃ smarasi Vāruṇyā Laṭvākānāṃ ca pakṣiṇām,
tābhyāṃ c' âbhyadhiko bhakṣyo na kaś cid vidyate kva cit.
yāni c' ânyāni bhūteṣu bhakṣya|jātāni kasya cit,
yeṣām a|bhukta|pūrvāṇi, teṣām a|smṛtir eva te.
a|prāśanam, a|saṃsparśam, a|saṃdarśanam eva ca,
puruṣasy' âiṣa niyamo, manye, śreyo na saṃśayaḥ.

Some creatures experience bliss by virtue of their birth, whereas others suffer excessively. But I do not see that any creature enjoys complete bliss anywhere in the world.

Once human beings have attained riches they yearn for kingship, when they have attained that they yearn to become gods, and after that they hanker after the status of Indra. You might become rich without becoming a king or a 180.25
god, but even if you were to attain the status of a god or of Indra, you would still not be happy in that state.

There is no satisfaction in attaining those things that you hold dear, just as thirst is not satiated by water: it only burns to an even greater degree, like a fire being fed more fuel.

You experience sorrow as well as joy, pleasure and pain. Why should you lament this fact? You should cut off the root of all your desires and action, and confine your sense faculties like birds in a cage.

Nowhere is there found any such thing as cutting off one's second head or one's third hand: fear cannot arise from that which does not exist. Desire for a thing cannot 180.30
arise for a person who does not know its pleasure, be it incited by touch, sight or sound.

You have no knowledge of the Váruni wine or the *latváka* bird, but no superior meal is to be found anywhere. And whatever other meals a person may make of creatures, if people have not previously eaten them they can have no knowledge of them. I certainly believe that a man's best form of restraint consists of desisting from eating, touching and seeing.

pāṇimanto balavanto, dhanavanto, na saṃśayaḥ.
manuṣyā mānuṣair eva dāsatvam upapāditāḥ.
180.35 vadha|bandha|parikleśaiḥ kliśyante ca punaḥ punaḥ,
te khalv api ramante ca, modante ca, hasanti ca.
apare bāhu|balinaḥ, kṛta|vidyā, manasvinaḥ,
jugupsitāṃ ca kṛpaṇāṃ pāpa|vṛttim upāsate.
utsahante ca te vṛttim anyām apy upasevitum,
sva|karmaṇā tu niyataṃ bhavitavyaṃ tu tat tathā.

na pulkaso na cāṇḍāla ātmānaṃ tyaktum icchati,
tayā tuṣṭaḥ svayā yonyā. māyāṃ paśyasva yādṛśīm!
dṛṣṭvā kuṇīn, pakṣa|hatān manuṣyān āmayāvinaḥ;
su|saṃpūrṇaḥ svayā yonyā: labdha|lābho 'si, Kāśyapa.
180.40 yadi, brāhmaṇa, dehas te nir|ātaṅko, nir|āmayaḥ,
aṅgāni ca samagrāṇi, na ca lokeṣu dhik|kṛtaḥ.

na kena cit pravādena satyen' âiv' âpahāriṇā,
dharmāy' ôttiṣṭha, vipra'|rṣe, n' ātmānaṃ tyaktum arhasi.
yadi, brahman, śṛṇoṣy etac, chraddadhāsi ca me vacaḥ,
ved'|ôktasy' âiva dharmasya phalaṃ mukhyam avāpsyasi.
sv'|âdhyāyam, agni|saṃskāram a|pramatto 'nupālaya,
satyaṃ, damaṃ ca, dānaṃ ca; spardhiṣṭhā mā ca kena cit.

ye ke cana sv|adhyayanāḥ prāptā yajana|yājanam,
kathaṃ te c' ânuśoceyur, dhyāyeyur v" âpy a|śobhanam?
180.45 icchantas te vihārāya, sukhaṃ mahad avāpnuyuḥ.
uta jātāḥ su|nakṣatre, su|tithau, su|muhūrta|jāḥ

Those who possess hands are strong and undoubtedly gain wealth. Some men, however, are forced into servitude
by others. Again and again they are afflicted by the hard- 180.35
ship of being beaten or bound, but even they can enjoy themselves, rejoice and laugh. Other men, although strong-armed, learned and intelligent, are drawn to evil forms of conduct that are disgusting and wretched. Even if they are able to pursue another way of life, what eventually comes about is fixed by their *karma*.

A low caste *púlkasa* or *chandála* would not wish to abandon his own body, for he is content with his station in life. Consider what self-deception this is! You have seen diseased people with withered arms and partial paralysis, and so should be content with your own station: the advantage
is yours, Káshyapa. O brahmin, if your body was free from 180.40
pain and illness, and if you were to possess a full set of limbs, people would not deride you.

You should strive for righteousness, Brahminic seer, and should not abandon your body, not even if some slander about you were true and forced you into exile. If, brahmin, you hear these words of mine and have faith in them, you will attain what the Veda states to be the highest reward of righteousness. Being diligent, cherish your Vedic recitation, the fire rituals, truth, restraint and charity; do not try to emulate anybody else.

How could those who are skilled in Vedic recitation and offer sacrifices regret anything or contemplate that which is
impure? If they desire pleasure they will attain great bliss. 180.45
Failing that, born at a favorable moment of an auspicious lunar day, under an auspicious constellation, they exert

yajña|dāna|praj"|ēhāyāṃ yatante śakti|pūrvakam.
nakṣatreṣv āsureṣv anye dus|tithau dur|muhūrta|jāḥ
saṃpatanty āsurīṃ yoniṃ yajña|prasava|varjitāḥ.
aham āsaṃ paṇḍitako haituko veda|nindakaḥ;
ānvīkṣikīṃ tarka|vidyām anurakto nir|arthikām.
hetu|vādān pravaditā, vaktā saṃsatsu hetumat,
ākroṣṭā c' âbhivaktā ca brahma|vākyeṣu ca dvijān.
nāstikaḥ sarva|śaṅkī ca, mūrkhaḥ paṇḍita|mānikaḥ.
tasy' êyaṃ phala|nirvṛttiḥ sṛgālatvaṃ mama, dvija.
180.50 api jātu tathā tasmād aho|rātra|śatair api,
yad ahaṃ mānuṣīṃ yoniṃ sṛgālaḥ prāpnuyāṃ punaḥ.
saṃtuṣṭaś c' â|pramattaś ca, yajña|dāna|tapo|ratiḥ,
jñeya|jñātā bhaveyaṃ vai, varjya|varjayitā tathā.

tataḥ sa munir utthāya Kāśyapas tam uvāca ha:
«aho bat'! âsi kuśalo buddhimāṃś c'!» êti vismitaḥ.
samavaikṣata taṃ vipro jñāna|dīrgheṇa cakṣuṣā,
dadarśa c' âinaṃ devānām devam Indraṃ Śacī|patim.
tataḥ saṃpūjayām āsa Kāśyapo Harivāhanam,
anujñātas tu ten' âtha praviveśa svam ālayam.

themselves in acts of sacrifice, charity and procreation, as long as they are able to. Others are born under demonic constellations of the southern hemisphere, at an unfavorable moment of an inauspicious lunar day. They ignore the Vedic sacrifices and procreation, and fall to a demonic station.

I used to be a learned skeptic who scorned the Vedas; I was devoted to logic and the science of debate, both of which are pointless. I formulated arguments based on reason and proffered rational statements in assemblies, abusing and denouncing brahmins over their sacred works. The heretic doubts everything—he is a fool who fancies himself learned. As a result of his *karma*, brahmin, he will become a jackal just like me.*

Maybe I will once again attain the human station, per- 180.50
haps even within a few hundred days and nights. If I am content and diligent, and dedicated to sacrifice, charity and asceticism, I may understand what I ought to understand, and avoid what I ought to avoid.

BHISHMA said:

After that speech the sage Káshyapa was astonished. He got up, and to the jackal said: "My word! How clever and intelligent you are!"

The brahmin looked at the jackal with his discerning eyes, and then recognized that he was Indra, Lord of the gods and husband of Shachi. Thereupon Káshyapa honored Indra, and upon being granted permission to leave he returned to his own home.

181

TEACHINGS ON KARMA

YUDHIṢṬHIRA uvāca:*

181.1 YADY ASTI DATTAM, iṣṭaṃ vā, tapas taptaṃ tath" âiva ca,
gurūṇāṃ v" âpi śuśrūṣā? tan me brūhi, pitā|maha.

BHĪṢMA uvāca:

ātman" ân|artha|yuktena pāpe niviśate manaḥ;
sva|karma kaluṣaṃ kṛtvā kṛcchre loke vidhīyate.
dur|bhikṣād eva dur|bhikṣaṃ,
kleśāt kleśaṃ, bhayād bhayam,
mṛtebhyaḥ pramṛtaṃ yānti
daridrāḥ pāpa|kāriṇaḥ.
utsavād utsavaṃ yānti, svargāt svargaṃ, sukhāt sukham
śraddadhānāś ca dāntāś ca dhan|āḍhyāḥ śubha|kāriṇaḥ.
181.5 vyāla|kuñjara|durgeṣu sarpa|cora|bhayeṣu ca
hastād vāmena* gacchanti nāstikāḥ. kim ataḥ param?
priya|dev'|ātitheyāś ca, vadānyāḥ, priya|sādhavaḥ,
kṣemyam ātmavatāṃ mārgam āsthitā hasta|dakṣiṇam.
pulākā iva dhānyeṣu, puttikā iva pakṣiṣu,
tad|vidhās te manuṣyāṇāṃ, yeṣāṃ dharmo na kāraṇam.
su|śīghram api dhāvantaṃ vidhānam anudhāvati;
śete saha śayānena, yena yena yathā kṛtam.
upatiṣṭhati tiṣṭhantaṃ, gacchantam anugacchati:
karoti kurvataḥ karma, chāy" êv' ânuvidhīyate.
181.10 yena yena yathā yad yat purā karma samācitam,†
tat tad ekataro bhuṅkte. nityaṃ vihitam ātmanā.
sva|karma|phala|nikṣepaṃ vidhāna|parirakṣitam
bhūta|grāmam imaṃ kālaḥ samantāt parikarṣati.

YUDHI·SHTHIRA said:

TELL ME, GRANDFATHER, are donations, sacrifices, severe austerities and obedience to one's elders efficacious? 181.1

BHISHMA said:

If a person occupies himself with worthless things his mind will be drawn towards evil; by polluting his own duties, he is destined for a world of pain. Destitute, evil men will suffer from famine, distress, danger and death over and over again. But people who are faithful, restrained, wealthy and perform good deeds will likewise experience joy, heaven and bliss.

Heretics travel along the deviant left-hand path, in per- 181.5
ilous areas full of vicious elephants and dangers such as snakes and thieves. What could be worse? But those who are munificent and devoted to the gods, their guests and mendicants, they follow the peaceful, right-hand path of holy men. Those men who are not motivated by religion are like rotten pieces of grain, or gnats among birds.

A person's karmic destiny pursues him even if he runs off at great pace; even as he lies down to sleep, a deed lingers in a person just as he committed it. It is near him when he stands still, it follows him when he walks: *karma* acts on the person who performs it and follows him like a shadow.

Whoever has accumulated *karma* in the past experiences 181.10
its result, no matter how it was done. One ordains it oneself: this fact never changes. All living beings are flung down by the results of their own *karma*, but their karmic destiny also protects them; time drags them away in all sorts of direction.

a|codyamānāni yathā puṣpāṇi ca phalāni ca
svaṃ kālaṃ n' âtivartante, tathā karma purā kṛtam.
saṃmānaś c' âvamānaś ca, lābh'|âlābhau, kṣay'|ôdayam
pravṛttāni vivartante vidhān'|ânte punaḥ punaḥ.

ātmanā vihitaṃ duḥkham, ātmanā vihitaṃ sukham;
garbha|śayyām upādāya bhujyate paurvadehikam.
181.15 bālo, yuvā ca, vṛddhaś ca yat karoti śubh'|âśubham,
tasyāṃ tasyām avasthāyāṃ tat phalaṃ pratipadyate.
yathā dhenu|sahasreṣu vatso vindati mātaram,
tathā pūrva|kṛtaṃ karma kartāram anugacchati.

samunnam agrato vastraṃ paścāc chudhyati karmaṇā.
upavāsaiḥ prataptānāṃ dīrghaṃ sukham anantakam.
dīrgha|kālena tapasā sevitena tapo|vane
dharma|nirdhūta|pāpānāṃ saṃpadyante mano|rathāḥ.

śakunānām iv' ākāśe, matsyānām iva c' ôdake
padaṃ yathā na dṛśyeta, tathā jñāna|vidāṃ gatiḥ.
181.20 alam anyair upālambhaiḥ kīrtitaiś ca vyatikramaiḥ!
peśalaṃ c' ânurūpaṃ ca kartavyaṃ hitam ātmanaḥ.

The *karma* committed by a person in the past develops just like flowers and fruits; it cannot be hurried up, and does not exceed its ordained time. Once committed *karma* manifests itself, over and over again, at the end of the period ordained. That is why a person experiences respect and contempt, gain and loss, and disintegration and growth.

A person ordains his own suffering and happiness; he grasps hold of an embryo and reaps the *karma* sown in a
past existence. He receives the retribution of the good and 181.15
bad deeds performed as a child, a youth or an elderly person in the same circumstances in the following incarnation. The *karma* committed in the past follows its agent just as a young calf finds its mother among thousands of milch-cows.

After a cloth has been soaked right through it can be cleaned by one's own endeavors. In the same way, those who practice asceticism by fasting will attain limitless bliss for a lengthy period of time. By practicing asceticism for a long time in an ascetic's grove, a person's evil deeds can be expunged by righteousness and his heart's desires obtained.

One cannot see the path of those who have attained gnosis, just as one cannot see the path of birds in the sky, or fish in the water.

But enough of outlining transgressions and any other 181.20
censures! One should do that which is pleasant, suitable and beneficial to oneself.

182–192

THE DIALOGUE BETWEEN BHRIGU AND BHARAD·VAJA

YUDHIṢṬHIRA uvāca:

182.1 KUTAḤ SṚṢṬAM IDAṂ viśvaṃ jagat sthāvara|jaṅgamam?
pralaye ca kam abhyeti? tan me brūhi, pitā|maha.
sa|sāgaraḥ, sa|gaganaḥ, sa|śailaḥ, sa|balāhakaḥ,
sa|bhūmiḥ, s'|âgni|pavano loko 'yaṃ kena nirmitaḥ?
kathaṃ sṛṣṭāni bhūtāni?
kathaṃ varṇa|vibhaktayaḥ?
śauc'|âśaucaṃ kathaṃ teṣāṃ?
dharm'|âdharma|vidhiḥ katham?
kīdṛśo jīvatāṃ jīvaḥ? kva vā gacchanti ye mṛtāḥ?
asmāl lokād amuṃ lokaṃ, sarvaṃ śaṃsatu no bhavān.

BHĪṢMA uvāca:

182.5 atr' âpy udāharant' îmam itihāsaṃ purātanam:
Bhṛguṇ" âbhihitaṃ śāstraṃ Bharadvājāya pṛcchate.
Kailāsa|śikhare dṛṣṭvā dīpyamānam mah"|âujasam
Bhṛguṃ maha"|rṣim āsīnaṃ Bharadvājo 'nvapṛcchata
«sa|sāgaraḥ, sa|gaganaḥ, sa|śailaḥ, sa|balāhakaḥ,
sa|bhūmiḥ, s'|âgni|pavano loko 'yaṃ kena nirmitaḥ?
kathaṃ sṛṣṭāni bhūtāni?
kathaṃ varṇa|vibhaktayaḥ?
śauc'|âśaucaṃ kathaṃ teṣāṃ?
dharm'|âdharma|vidhiḥ katham?
kīdṛśo jīvatāṃ jīvaḥ? kva vā gacchanti ye mṛtāḥ?
para|lokam imaṃ c' âpi, sarvaṃ śaṃsitum arhasi.»

YUDHI·SHTHIRA said:

WHAT IS THE SOURCE of the universe, this world of animate and inanimate things? And to what does it return during a period of cosmic dissolution? Please tell me this, grandfather. Who fashioned this world of oceans, sky, mountains, clouds, earth, fire and wind? 182.1

How were the different creatures created, and how were they divided into different classes? How did they become pure and impure? How did the order of right and wrong come about?

What is the nature of the soul that abides within living beings? And where do the dead go? Please explain all this to me, from this world to the world beyond.

BHISHMA said:

On this subject people relate an ancient tradition: the in- 182.5
struction imparted to the enquiring Bharad·vaja by Bhrigu.*

The great seer Bhrigu was seated on the peak of Mount Kailása, glowing with great energy. Upon seeing him, Bharad·vaja asked these questions: "Who fashioned this world of oceans, sky, mountains, clouds, earth, fire and wind?

How were the different creatures created, and how were they divided into different classes? How did they become pure and impure? How did the order of right and wrong come about?

What is the nature of the soul that abides within living beings, and what happens to people when they die? Please tell me everything about this world and the world beyond."

182.10 evaṃ sa bhagavān pṛṣṭo Bharadvājena saṃśayam,
brahma'|ṛṣir Brahma|saṃkāśaḥ sarvaṃ tasmai tato 'bravīt.

BHṚGUR uvāca:

«mānaso» nāma yaḥ pūrvo viśruto vai maha"|ṛṣibhiḥ
an|ādi|nidhano devas, tath" â|bhedyo '|jarā|maraḥ.
«avyakta» iti vikhyātaḥ, śāśvato 'th' â|kṣayo '|vyayaḥ.
yataḥ sṛṣṭāni bhūtāni, jāyante ca mriyanti ca.

so 'sṛjat prathamaṃ devo «mahāntaṃ» nāma nāmataḥ.
mahān sasarj' âhaṃ|kāraṃ; sa c' âpi bhagavān atha.
«ākāśam» iti vikhyātaṃ sarva|bhūta|dharaḥ prabhuḥ;
ākāśād abhavad vāri, salilād agni|mārutau,
agni|māruta|saṃyogāt tataḥ samabhavan mahī.

182.15 tatas tejo|mayaṃ divyaṃ padmaṃ sṛṣṭaṃ svayaṃ|bhuvā.
tasmāt padmāt samabhavad Brahmā veda|mayo nidhiḥ.
«ahaṃ|kāra» iti khyātaḥ, sarva|bhūt'|ātma|bhūta|kṛt.
Brahmā vai sa mahā|tejā, ya ete pañca dhātavaḥ.

śailās tasy' âsthi|saṃjñās tu, medo māṃsaṃ ca medinī,
samudrās tasya rudhiram, ākāśam udaraṃ tathā.
pavanaś c' âiva niḥśvāsas, tejo 'gnir, nimnagāḥ sirāḥ.
agnī|ṣomau tu candr'|ârkau nayane tasya viśrute.
nabhaś c' ōrdhvaṃ śiras tasya, kṣitiḥ pādau; bhujau diśaḥ.

Thus questioned on these perplexing matters by Bharad- 182.10
vaja, the blessed Bhrigu, a Brahminic seer who looked just like the god Brahma himself, explained everything to him.

BHRIGU said:

The great seers used the expression "pure consciousness" to eulogize the ancient deity, which is indivisible, without beginning or end, and beyond decrepitude and death. It is eternal, unfailing and immutable, and also called the "unmanifest." All creatures which are born and then die are its creation.

In the beginning this deity emitted a substance called "the absolute," and this ejaculated the utterance "I!"; this utterance was the blessed Lord.* The Lord, upholder of the world, created that which is called "space"; water came into being from space. Fire and wind came into being from the water, and the contact between them produced the earth.

After the creation of the five elements, *brahman*, the self- 182.15
existent absolute created a divine lotus of lustrous light. From that lotus emerged the lord Brahma; the Vedas are his substance, and he is the source of everything. He is both the soul of all beings and their creator, and is known by the name "the utterance I!"* Brahma is brilliantly lustrous, and comprises the five elements.

The mountains are said to be his bones, the earth is his bone marrow and flesh, the oceans are his blood and space is his belly. The wind is his breath, fire is his energy and the rivers are his veins. The sun and moon, *agni* and *soma*, are said, in eulogies, to be his eyes. The sky above is his head, the earth below is his feet; the directions are his arms. Even the

dur|vijñeyo hy a|cinty'|ātmā siddhair api, na saṃśayaḥ.
182.20 sa eva bhagavān Viṣṇur, «an|anta» iti viśrutaḥ.
sarva|bhūt'|ātma|bhūta|stho, dur|vijñeyo '|kṛt'|ātmabhiḥ.
ahaṃ|kārasya yaḥ sraṣṭā sarva|bhūta|bhavāya vai,
yataḥ samabhavad viśvaṃ—pṛṣṭo 'haṃ yad iha tvayā.

BHARADVĀJA uvāca:

gaganasya, diśāṃ c' âiva, bhū|talasy', ânilasya vā
kāny atra parimāṇāni? saṃśayaṃ chinddhi tattvataḥ.

BHṚGUR uvāca:

an|antam etad ākāśaṃ, siddha|daivata|sevitam,
ramyaṃ, nān"|āśray'|ākīrṇaṃ, yasy' ânto n' âdhigamyate.
ūrdhvaṃ gater adhastāt tu candr'|ādityau na dṛśyataḥ,
tatra devāḥ svayaṃ|dīptā bhāsvar'|ābh"|âgni|varcasaḥ.
182.25 te c' âpy antaṃ na paśyanti nabhasaḥ prathit'|âujasaḥ
durgamatvād anantatvād: iti me viddhi, mānada.
upariṣṭ'|ôpariṣṭāt tu prajvaladbhiḥ svayaṃ|prabhaiḥ
niruddham etad ākāśam a|prameyaṃ surair api.
pṛthivy|ante samudrās tu, samudr'|ânte tamaḥ smṛtam.
tamaso 'nte jalaṃ prāhur, jalasy' ânte 'gnir eva ca.
Rasātal'|ânte salilaṃ, jal'|ânte pannag'|âdhipaḥ.
tad|ante punar ākāśam, ākāś'|ânte punar jalam.

Siddhas find it hard to perceive him, undoubtedly, because his essence is unthinkable.

He is the blessed lord Vishnu, who is eulogized as "the limitless." Incomplete men cannot perceive him, the one who abides within as the soul of all beings. 182.20

He is the one you asked me about—the source of the universe, the one who ejaculated the utterance "I!" in order to bring all creatures into existence.

BHARAD·VAJA said:

What is the extent of the sky, the cardinal directions, the earth and the wind? Please dispel my doubts, in accordance with the true nature of things.

BHRIGU said:

This space here is infinite, a realm of pleasure frequented by Siddhas and gods. It contains dominions of all kinds, but no end to it is found. The self-lustrous gods, resplendent and as brilliant as fire, are to be found where the sun and moon cannot be seen, being beyond their range.

Although the gods have power in abundance, even they cannot perceive an end to the sky. This is because it is infinite and impassable: understand that this is my opinion, courteous one. This region of space cannot be measured by the blazing, self-luminous gods, since it comes to an end beyond them. 182.25

It is held that there are oceans at the end of the earth, and darkness after that. Beyond the darkness there is more water, so they say, after which there is the fire of the Rasátala hell. Beyond this hell there is water, and after that the Lord

evam antaṃ Bhagavataḥ, pramāṇaṃ salilasya ca,
agni|māruta|toyebhyo, dur|jñeyaṃ daivatair api.
182.30 agni|māruta|toyānāṃ varṇāḥ kṣiti|talasya ca
ākāśād avagṛhyante; bhidyante tattva|darśanāt.
paṭhanti c' âiva munayaḥ śāstreṣu vividheṣu ca,
Trailokya|sāgare c' âiva pramāṇaṃ vihitaṃ yathā.
a|dṛśyāya tv a|gamyāya kaḥ pramāṇam udāharet?
siddhānāṃ devatānāṃ ca yadā parimitā gatiḥ,
tadā gauṇam an|antasya nām' «ân|ant'» êti viśrutam
nāmadhey'|ânurūpasya mānasasya mah"|ātmanaḥ.
yadā tu divyaṃ yad rūpaṃ
hrasate vardhate punaḥ,
ko 'nyas tad vedituṃ śakyo?
yo 'pi syāt tad|vidho 'paraḥ.
182.35 tataḥ puṣkarataḥ sṛṣṭaḥ sarva|jño mūrtimān prabhuḥ
Brahmā dharma|mayaḥ pūrvaḥ prajā|patir an|uttamaḥ.

BHARADVĀJA uvāca:

puṣkarād yadi saṃbhūto, jyeṣṭhaṃ bhavati puṣkaram.
Brahmāṇaṃ pūrva|jaṃ c' āha bhavān; saṃdeha eva me.

of serpent demons has his lair. Then there is more space, after which there is water once again.

And so even the gods cannot fathom the limit of the Blessed One, and the extent of water, fire and wind.

The nature of fire, wind, water and the ground is different 182.30
from that of space; they are distinguished from each other when a person sees the truth.

The silent sages pronounce the extent of the world in various treatises, just as it has been laid down in the "Ocean of the triple world." But who can declare the extent of that which cannot be seen or traversed? Since the movement of even the Siddhas and gods is circumscribed, the term "infinite," which is pronounced of the infinite, macrocosmic "pure consciousness" which fits this description, is but a figurative designation.

When the divine form of *brahman* contracts and expands over and over again, who else is able to know him? Such a
person would have to be of a similar nature. It is for this 182.35
reason that the all-knowing Lord emerged from a lotus in an embodied form. This is the personal god Brahma, the ancient, incomparable Lord of creatures whose substance is the religious order.

BHARAD·VAJA said:

If Brahma was born from a lotus, then the lotus must be older than him. I am confused, because you say that Brahma was born first.

BHṚGUR uvāca:

mānasasy' êha yā mūrtir brahmatvaṃ samupāgatā,
tasy' āsana|vidhān'|ârthaṃ pṛthivī padmam ucyate.
karṇikā tasya padmasya Merur gaganam ucchritaḥ.
tasya madhye sthito lokān sṛjate jagataḥ prabhuḥ.

BHARADVĀJA uvāca:

183.1 PRAJĀ|VISARGAṂ vividhaṃ kathaṃ sa sṛjate prabhuḥ
Meru|madhye sthito Brahmā? tad brūhi, dvija|sattama.

BHṚGUR uvāca:

prajā|visargaṃ vividhaṃ mānaso manas" âsṛjat.
saṃrakṣaṇ'|ârthaṃ bhūtānāṃ sṛṣṭaṃ prathamato jalam,
yat prāṇāḥ sarva|bhūtānāṃ, vardhante yena ca prajāḥ,
parityaktāś ca naśyanti—ten' êdaṃ sarvam āvṛtam.
pṛthivī, parvatā, meghā, mūrtimantaś ca ye pare,
sarvaṃ tad vāruṇaṃ jñeyam, āpas tastambhire yataḥ.

BHARADVĀJA uvāca:

183.5 kathaṃ salilam utpannaṃ? kathaṃ c' âiv' âgni|mārutau?
kathaṃ ca medinī sṛṣṭ"? êty atra me saṃśayo mahān.

BHṚGUR uvāca:

brahma|kalpe purā, brahman, brahma'|rṣīṇāṃ samāgame
loka|saṃbhava|saṃdehaḥ samutpanno mah"|ātmanām.
te 'tiṣṭhan dhyānam ālambya, maunam āsthāya niścalāḥ,
tyakt'|āhārāḥ, pavana|pā, divyaṃ varṣa|śataṃ dvijāḥ.

BHRIGU said:

The material form of pure consciousness is endowed with its divine essence, whereas the earth is called a lotus because it provides a seat for Brahma. The pericarp of that lotus towers up into the sky as Mount Meru. Abiding at its center, the Lord of the world creates all the worlds.

BHARAD·VAJA said:

HOW DID THE LORD Brahma bring about the numerous 183.1
emanations of different creatures while abiding at the center of Mount Meru? Tell me that, exalted brahmin.

BHRIGU said:

Pure consciousness created all the different creatures through mind. First of all, in order to protect living beings it created water, because water is the breath of all beings and that through which creatures flourish. Water envelops the entire world—without it everything would be destroyed. The earth, mountains, clouds and anything of a corporeal nature should be understood as forms of water, for it was the waters themselves that became solid.

BHARAD·VAJA said:

How did water come into being? And what about fire 183.5
and wind? How was the earth created? I am very confused about this.

BHRIGU said:

Long ago, brahmin, in the Brahma aeon, a doubt about the origin of the world arose during a council of holy Brahminic seers. These brahmins remained in meditation for a hundred celestial years, during which they practiced silence

teṣāṃ dharma|mayī vāṇī sarveṣāṃ śrotram āgamat,
divyā Sarasvatī tatra saṃbabhūva nabhas|talāt.

purā stimitam ākāśam an|antam, a|cal'|ôpamam,
naṣṭa|candr'|ârka|pavanaṃ; prasuptam iva saṃbabhau.
183.10 tataḥ salilam utpannaṃ, tamas' îv' âparaṃ tamaḥ.
tasmāc ca salil'|ôtpīḍād udatiṣṭhata mārutaḥ.

yathā bhājanam a|cchidraṃ niḥ|śabdam iva lakṣyate;
tac c' âmbhasā pūryamāṇaṃ sa|śabdaṃ kurute 'nilaḥ.
tathā salila|saṃruddhe nabhaso 'nte nir|antare
bhittv" ârṇava|talaṃ vāyuḥ samutpatati ghoṣavān,
sa eṣa carate vāyur arṇav'|ôtpīḍa|saṃbhavaḥ:
ākāśa|sthānam āsādya praśāntiṃ n' âdhigacchati.

tasmin vāyv|ambu|saṃgharṣe dīpta|tejā mahā|balaḥ
prādur abhūd ūrdhva|śikhaḥ, kṛtvā nis|timiraṃ nabhaḥ.
183.15 agniḥ pavana|saṃyuktaḥ khaṃ samākṣipate jalam.
so 'gnir māruta|saṃyogād ghanatvam upapadyate.
tasy' ākāśe† nipatitaḥ snehas tiṣṭhati yo 'paraḥ,
sa saṃghātatvam āpanno bhūmitvam anugacchati.

rasānāṃ, sarva|gandhānāṃ, snehānāṃ prāṇināṃ tathā
bhūmir yonir iha jñeyā; yasyāṃ sarvaṃ prasūyate.

and were motionless, shunning all food and drinking the wind. And then they heard the sound of religious order, as the celestial Sarásvati river burst forth from the roof of space.

Before that the infinity of space had been calm, and seemingly motionless, for it was devoid of sun, moon and wind; it was as if it had been sunk in a deep sleep. But then water sprang forth, like another great darkness within the gloom. The pressure within it produced wind.

It is just like a pot that, if it is not cleft, is seen to be virtually noiseless. But when it is filled with water the air in it makes a noise. So it was when the interior of space, which really has no interior, was immersed in water: wind pierced the surface of this foaming mass of water and rose up in a thunder. That wind, produced by the pressure within the water, is the same wind that still blows here: when it escaped into space, it could not be stilled.

In the friction between wind and water a powerful, radiant flame arose. With its crest rising up this fire lit up space, and when it came into contact with the wind it forced space and water together, but because of its contact with wind, some of the fire congealed. This viscous part of fire stood apart descended within space. In the process it was compressed, and so it turned into earth.

This earth should be known as the source of all tastes, smells, fluids and sentient beings; everything is generated within it.

BHARADVĀJA uvāca:

184.1 TA ETE DHĀTAVAḤ pañca, Brahmā yān asṛjat purā,
āvṛtā yair ime lokā mahā|bhūt'|âbhisaṃjñitaiḥ.
yad" âsṛjat sahasrāṇi bhūtānāṃ sa mahā|matiḥ,
pañcānām eva bhūtatvaṃ kathaṃ samupapadyate?

BHṚGUR uvāca:

a|mitānāṃ mahā|śabdo; yānti bhūtāni saṃbhavam.
tatas teṣāṃ mahā|bhūta|śabdo 'yam upapadyate.
ceṣṭā vāyuḥ, kham ākāśam, ūṣm" âgniḥ, salilaṃ dravaḥ,
pṛthivī c' âtra saṃghātaḥ; śarīraṃ pāñcabhautikam.
184.5 ity etaiḥ pañcabhir bhūtair yuktaṃ sthāvara|jaṅgamam,
śrotraṃ, ghrāṇaṃ, rasaḥ, sparśo, dṛṣṭiś c' êndriya|saṃjñitāḥ.

BHARADVĀJA uvāca:

pañcabhir yadi bhūtais tu yuktāḥ sthāvara|jaṅgamāḥ,
sthāvarāṇāṃ na dṛśyante śarīre pañca dhātavaḥ.
an|ūṣmaṇām, a|ceṣṭānāṃ, ghanānāṃ c' âiva tattvataḥ,
vṛkṣāṇāṃ n' ôpalabhyante śarīre pañca dhātavaḥ.

na śṛṇvanti, na paśyanti, na gandha|rasa|vedinaḥ,
na ca sparśaṃ vijānanti. te kathaṃ pāñcabhautikāḥ?
a|dravatvād, an|agnitvād, a|bhūmitvād, a|vāyutaḥ,
ākāśasy' â|prameyatvād vṛkṣāṇāṃ n' âsti bhautikam.

BHARAD·VAJA said:

IN THE BEGINNING Brahma created five cosmic strata that encompass these worlds and are called "great beings." If the lofty-minded Brahma created thousands of livings beings, how is it that the five strata are also called "beings?" 184.1

BHRIGU said:

The word "great" is applied to things that cannot be measured, whereas "beings" are things that come into existence. Therefore the term "great being" was applied to the five strata of the cosmos. The body is made of these five "beings" or "elements." Its movement is caused by wind, its apertures consist of space, its heat is really fire, its fluid is
water and its solid parts are made of earth. All animate and 184.5
inanimate things are bound by these five elements, as are the things called "powers:" the auditory, olfactory, gustatory, tactile and visual faculties.

BHARAD·VAJA said:

Perhaps animate and inanimate things are bound by these five elements, but they cannot be seen in the bodies of inanimate things. The five elements are not found in the bodies of trees, which lack heat and movement, and are really nothing but solid substances.

Trees cannot hear or see and cannot perceive smells or tastes; they cannot cognize physical sensations. So how can they be made of the five elements? Since trees lack water, fire, earth and wind, and because space is immeasurable, they cannot be made out of all the elements.

BHṚGUR uvāca:

184.10 ghanānām api vṛkṣāṇām ākāśo 'sti, na saṃśayaḥ.
teṣāṃ puṣpa|phala|vyaktir nityaṃ samupapadyate.
ūṣmato mlāyate varṇaṃ, tvak, phalaṃ, puṣpam eva ca
mlāyate śīryate c' âpi; sparśas ten' âtra vidyate.
vāyv|agny|aśani|nirghośaiḥ phalaṃ puṣpaṃ viśīryate.
śrotreṇa gṛhyate śabdas, tasmāc chṛṇvanti pādapāḥ.
vallī veṣṭayate vṛkṣaṃ, sarvataś c' âiva gacchati.
na hy adṛṣṭeś ca mārgo 'sti, tasmāt paśyanti pādapāḥ.
puṇy'|âpuṇyais tathā gandhair, dhūpaiś ca vividhair api,
a|rogāḥ puṣpitāḥ santi, tasmāj jighranti pādapāḥ.
184.15 pādaiḥ salila|pānāc ca, vyādhīnām api darśanāt,
vyādhi|pratikriyatvāc ca vidyate rasanaṃ drume.
vaktreṇ' ôtpala|nālena yath" ôrdhvaṃ jalam ādadet,
tathā pavana|saṃyuktaḥ pādaiḥ pibati pāda|paḥ.
sukha|duḥkhayoś ca grahaṇāc, chinnasya ca virohaṇāt
jīvaṃ paśyāmi vṛkṣāṇām: a|caitanyaṃ na vidyate.
tena taj jalam ādattaṃ jarayaty agni|mārutau,
āhāra|pariṇāmāc ca sneho vṛddhiś ca jāyate.

BHRIGU said:

There is no doubt that space is found in trees, even 184.10
though they are solid, for they never fail to flower or bear fruit.

Their color, bark, fruit and flowers wither away in the heat: they wither away and decay, proving that they feel physical sensations.

The fruits and flowers of a tree are damaged by the roaring sound made by wind, fire and bolts of lightning. Because a sound is perceived by the ear, trees must be able to hear.

The creepers of a tree envelop it and move in all directions. This must mean that trees can see, since a thing cannot move along a path without seeing.

Because trees bloom and are maintained in good health through fragrant and foul smells, and by various sorts of incense, it means that they can smell.

It is evident that diseased trees receive their remedies by 184.15
absorbing water through their roots, which must mean that they have the faculty of taste. Just as a person can suck water upwards through the stalk of a blue lotus, so too can a tree, when aided by the wind, drink through its roots.

Trees can experience pleasure and pain, and will sprout again after being cut down. I believe that trees possess a soul: they are not insentient. The water that a tree draws up consumes the fire and wind within it. When this sustenance is digested, sap is produced and the tree grows.

jaṅgamānāṃ ca sarveṣāṃ śarīre pañca dhātavaḥ
pratyekaśaḥ prabhidyante, yaiḥ śarīraṃ viceṣṭate.
184.20 tvak ca, māṃsaṃ, tath" âsthīni,
majjā, snāyuś ca pañcamam:
ity etad iha saṃghātaṃ
śarīre pṛthivī|mayam.
tejo hy agnis, tathā krodhaś, cakṣur, ūṣmā tath" âiva ca,
agnir jarayate yac ca. pañc'|āgneyāḥ śarīriṇaḥ.
śrotraṃ, ghrāṇam, tath" āsyaṃ ca,
hṛdayaṃ, koṣṭham eva ca:
ākāśāt prāṇinām ete
śarīre pañca dhātavaḥ.
śleṣmā, pittam, atha svedo, vasā, śoṇitam eva ca:
ity āpaḥ pañcadhā dehe bhavanti prāṇināṃ sadā.
prāṇāt praṇīyate prāṇī, vyānād vyāyacchate tathā.
gacchaty apāno 'dhaś c' âiva; samāno hṛdy avasthitaḥ.
184.25 udānād ucchvasiti ca, pratibhedāc ca bhāṣate.
ity ete vāyavaḥ pañca ceṣṭayant' îha dehinam.
bhūmer gandha|guṇān vetti, rasaṃ c' âdbhyaḥ śarīravān.
jyotiṣā cakṣuṣā rūpaṃ, sparśaṃ vetti ca vāhinā.
gandhaḥ, sparśo, raso, rūpaṃ, śabdaś c' âtra guṇāḥ smṛtāḥ.
tasya gandhasya vakṣyāmi vistar'|âbhihitān guṇān.

The five elements are found in the bodies of all animate creatures.* One by one they are divided up and enable the body to move.

The solid substances of the body—skin, flesh, bones, 184.20
bone marrow and sinew—are made of earth.

The fire element is found in energy, anger, the faculty of vision and heat, as well as the internal fire that digests food. These are the five forms of fire found in an embodied creature.

The apertures within the ears, nose, mouth, heart and stomach are the five parts of a sentient creature's body that are derived from space.

The five derivatives of water, which are always found in a sentient creature's body, are phlegm, bile, sweat, fat and blood.

A sentient creature breathes in by means of the in-breath, the *prana*, and exerts himself by means of the breath that is diffused throughout the body, the *vyana*. The *apána* is the breath that moves down, whereas the *samána* is the breath
that is fixed in the heart. A person breathes out by means 184.25
of the breath that moves upwards, the *udána*, and speaks when this is temporarily interrupted. Thus these five winds impel a man.

It is because of the earth that a person perceives different sorts of smell, whereas the perception of taste is due to water. The perception of a visible form is due to fire and the faculty of vision, whereas a person feels a physical sensation by means of the wafting wind. It is held that there are different sorts of smell, touch, taste, visible form and sound. I will now describe the different sorts of smell in full.

iṣṭaś c' ân|iṣṭa|gandhaś ca, madhuraḥ, kaṭur eva ca,
nirhārī, saṃhataḥ, snigdho, rūkṣo, viśada eva ca.
evaṃ nava|vidho jñeyaḥ pārthivo gandha|vistaraḥ.
jyotiḥ paśyati cakṣurbhyāṃ, sparśaṃ vetti ca vāyunā.
184.30 śabdaḥ, sparśaś ca, rūpaṃ ca, rasaś c' âpi guṇāḥ smṛtāḥ.
rasa|jñānaṃ tu vakṣyāmi; tan me nigadataḥ śṛṇu.

raso bahu|vidhaḥ prokta ṛṣibhiḥ prathit'|ātmabhiḥ,
madhuro, lavaṇas, tiktaḥ, kaṣāyo, 'mlaḥ, kaṭus tathā.
eṣa ṣaḍ|vidha|vistāro raso vāri|mayaḥ smṛtaḥ.
śabdaḥ sparśaś ca rūpaṃ ca: tri|guṇaṃ jyotir ucyate.

jyotiḥ paśyati rūpāṇi, rūpaṃ ca bahudhā smṛtam:
hrasvo, dīrghas, tathā sthūlaś, catur|asro, 'ṇu, vṛttavān,
śuklaḥ, kṛṣṇas, tathā raktaḥ, pīto, nīl'|âruṇas tathā,
kaṭhinaś, cikkaṇaḥ, ślakṣṇaḥ, picchilo, mṛdu|dāruṇaḥ.
184.35 evaṃ ṣodaśa|vistāro jyotī rūpa|guṇaḥ smṛtaḥ.
śabda|sparśau ca vijñeyau, dvi|guṇo vāyur ity uta.

vāyavyas tu guṇaḥ sparśaḥ, sparśaś ca bahudhā smṛtaḥ:
uṣṇaḥ, śītaḥ, sukho, duḥkhaḥ, snigdho, viśada eva ca,
tathā kharo, mṛdū, rūkṣo, laghur, gurutaro 'pi ca.
evam ekādaśa|vidho† vāyavyo guṇa ucyate.

They are: pleasant, unpleasant, sweet, acrid, fragrant, intense, mild, pungent and pure. Therefore smell, when fully enumerated, is ninefold and ought to be understood as a derivative of earth. A person sees light by means of the two eyes, and feels a physical sensation by means of wind.*

Different sorts of sound, touch, visible form and taste 184.30
are also taught. I will now describe the cognition of taste; please listen as I speak.

The famous seers have said that taste has many varieties, such as sweet, salty, bitter, astringent, sour and acrid. In full there are six sorts of taste, which are thought to be forms of water. It is said that fire has three perceptible qualities: sound, touch and visible form.*

It is fire that sees visible forms, of which many kinds are taught: small, extended, bulky, quadrangular, tiny, round, white, black, red, yellow, iridescent blue,* hard, slippery, smooth, slimy, soft and rough.

Thus the different sorts of visible form, which are thought 184.35
to be fire, are sixteen in total.* Wind has two perceptible qualities, sound and touch, and these must also be understood.

Touch, which is the perceptible quality of wind, is thought to have many different kinds: hot, cold, pleasant, unpleasant, unctuous, pure, hard, soft, rough, light or heavy. Thus touch, which is said to be a perceptible quality of wind, is elevenfold.

tatr' âika|guṇam ākāśaṃ, śabda ity eva tat smṛtam.
tasya śabdasya vakṣyāmi vistaraṃ vividh'|ātmakam.
ṣaḍja, ṛṣabha|gāndhārau, madhyamo, dhaivatas tathā,
pañcamaś c' âpi vijñeyas, tathā c' âpi niṣādavān.
184.40 eṣa sapta|vidhaḥ prokto guṇa ākāśa|saṃbhavaḥ.
aiśvaryeṇa tu sarvatra, sthito 'pi paṭah'|ādiṣu.

mṛdaṅga|bherī|śaṅkhānāṃ, stanayitno, rathasya ca
yaḥ kaś cic chrūyate śabdaḥ, prāṇino '|prāṇino 'pi vā,
eteṣām eva sarveṣāṃ viṣaye saṃprakīrtitaḥ.
evaṃ bahu|vidh'|ākāraḥ śabda, ākāśa|saṃbhavaḥ.
ākāśa|jaṃ śabdam āhur ebhir vāyu|guṇaiḥ saha.

a|vyāhataiś cetayate, na vetti viṣama|sthitaiḥ.
āpyāyante ca te nityaṃ dhātavas tais tu dhātubhiḥ.
āpo, 'gnir, mārutaś c' âiva nityaṃ jāgrati dehiṣu:
mūlam ete śarīrasya, vyāpya prāṇān iha sthitāḥ.

BHARADVĀJA uvāca:

185.1 PĀRTHIVAṂ DHĀTUM āsādya śārīro 'gniḥ kathaṃ, prabho?
avakāśa|viśeṣeṇa kathaṃ vartayate 'nilaḥ?

BHṚGUR uvāca:

vāyor gatim ahaṃ, brahman, kathayiṣyāmi te, 'n|agha,
prāṇinām anilo dehān yathā ceṣṭayate balī.

Space has only one perceptible quality, which is thought to be sound. I will now describe the various sorts of sound in detail. They are *shadja*, *ríshabha*, *gandhára*, *mádhyama*, *dhávata*, *pánchama* and *nishháda*.* Thus sound is a percep- 184.40
tible quality derived from space, and is said to have seven different kinds. Because it is the sovereign perceptible quality it is omnipresent, although it is also found in war drums and other things.

Whatever sound is heard, whether it arises from an animate or inanimate thing, such as a tabor, kettledrum, conch, thunder or a chariot, it is said to fall within the range of the seven sorts of sound. Therefore sound has many varieties, and is derived from space. Sound, along with the derivatives of wind, is born from space, so they say.

A person is fully conscious when the five elements are not impeded, but is not when they are not equally configured. It is through the five elements that the different parts of the body continually find their nourishment. Water, fire and wind always watch over living beings: they are the source of the body, and become established in the world by pervading all sentient beings.

BHARAD·VAJA said:

MY LORD, HOW does the bodily fire settle down in the 185.1
earth element within the body? And how does wind move though the space remaining?

BHRIGU said:

I will explain the internal movement of wind to you, faultless brahmin, and show how it has the power to move the bodies of sentient beings.

śrito mūrdhānam agnis tu śarīraṃ paripālayan.
prāṇo mūrdhani c' âgnau ca vartamāno viceṣṭate.

sa jantuḥ sarva|bhūt'|ātmā, puruṣaḥ sa sanātanaḥ:
mano, buddhir, ahaṃ|kāro, bhūtāni viṣayāś ca saḥ.

185.5 evaṃ tv iha sa sarvatra prāṇena paricālyate.
pṛṣṭhatas tu samānena, svāṃ svāṃ gatim upāśritaḥ.
basti|mūlaṃ gudaṃ c' âiva pāvakaṃ samupāśritaḥ,
vahan mūtraṃ purīṣaṃ c' âpy apānaḥ parivartate.

prayatne, karmaṇi, bale ya ekas triṣu vartate,
udāna iti taṃ prāhur adhyātma|viduṣo janāḥ.
saṃdhiṣv api ca sarveṣu saṃniviṣṭas tath" ânilaḥ
śarīreṣu manuṣyāṇāṃ vyāna ity upadiśyate.

dhātuṣv agnis tu vitataḥ samānena samīritaḥ;
rasān dhātūṃś ca doṣāṃś ca vartayann avatiṣṭhate.
185.10 apāna|prāṇayor madhye prāṇ'|âpāna|samāhitaḥ,
samanvitas tv adhiṣṭhānaṃ samyak pacati pāvakaḥ.

āsyaṃ hi pāyu|paryantam ante syād guda†|saṃjñitam
srotas. tasmāt prajāyante sarva|srotāṃsi dehinām.
prāṇānāṃ saṃnipātāc ca saṃnipātaḥ prajāyate,
ūṣmā c' âgnir iti jñeyo, yo 'nnaṃ pacati dehinām.

Fire nourishes the body from its station in the head. The vital breath—the *prana*—circulates within this cranial fire, and it is this that spreads around the body.

That entity is the world self, the primeval person that comprises everything: mind, intelligence, self-consciousness, the elements and the sense faculties.*

And so fire is circulated to all parts of the body by means 185.5
of the *prana*. By means of the *samána*, the breath stationed in the upper part of the body, each of the breaths is made to reside in their specific areas. The *apána*—the breath that goes down—abides in the fire that is found in the bladder and the anus. It circulates there and empties the body of urine and excrement.

According to those who know the supreme self, the single breath that operates when a person exerts himself, performs any deed or makes a show of strength is the *udána*—the breath that moves upwards. The wind found in all the joints of the bodies of men is said to be the *vyana*, or diffused breath.

The *samána* circulates the fire that is diffused in all the constituent parts of the body; it continually moves fluids,
juices and humors around. Situated between the *apána* and 185.10
prana, and joined to both of them, this fire is found in the navel and digests food thoroughly.

There is a channel that begins in the mouth and leads down to the anus—that which is called the anus being found at its end. All the channels of a person's body arise from this central channel. When all the different breaths meet they mix together and heat is produced. This heat

agni|vega|vahaḥ prāṇo gud'|ânte pratihanyate†
sa ūrdhvam āgamya punaḥ samutkṣipati pāvakam.
pakv'|āśayas tv adho nābhyām, ūrdhvam ām'|āśayaḥ sthitaḥ.
nābhi|madhye śarīrasya sarve prāṇāś ca saṃsthitāḥ.

185.15 prasthitā hṛdayāt sarve tiryag, ūrdhvam, adhas tathā,
vahanty anna|rasān nāḍyo daśa prāṇa|pracoditāḥ.
eṣa mārgo 'tha yogānāṃ, yena gacchanti tat padam
jita|klamāḥ, samā, dhīrā, mūrdhany ātmānam ādadhan.

evaṃ sarveṣu vihitaḥ prāṇ'|âpāneṣu dehinām:
tasmin samidhyate nityam agniḥ, sthālyām iv' āhitaḥ.

BHARADVĀJA uvāca:

186.1 YADI PRĀṆAYATE vāyur, vāyur eva viceṣṭate,
śvasity ābhāṣate c' âiva, tasmāj jīvo nir|arthakaḥ.
yad ūṣma|bhāva āgneyo, vahninā pacyate yadi,
agnir jarayate c' âiva,† tasmāj jīvo nir|arthakaḥ.

jantoḥ pramīyamāṇasya jīvo n' âiv' ôpalabhyate.
vāyur eva jahāty enam, ūṣma|bhāvaś ca naśyati.

should be known as the fire that digests the food within a person's body.

The *prana* conveys currents of fire around the body. After it has been pressed down to the anus, it moves upwards and once again distributes fire throughout the body. The part of the stomach which contains digested food is situated below the navel, whereas the food to be digested is found above the navel. All the breaths in the body meet at the very center of the navel.

Ten channels lead out from the heart; they go sideways, 185.15
upwards and down. These channels carry chyle around the body, and are impelled by the *prana*. The central channel is the path of yogins, by which they attain the supreme place. Overcoming fatigue, these wise, equanimous men focus the self in the head.

Thus fire is diffused in a person's in- and out-breaths: it is always burning within the breath, like a fire placed in a cauldron.

BHARAD·VAJA said:

IF IT IS WIND that animates a person, and wind which 186.1
moves him, breathes and speaks, then the soul serves no purpose. If a creature's bodily warmth is derived from fire, and if it is fire that digests and causes a person to age, then the soul serves no purpose.

When a person dies no soul can be found. At death his internal wind abandons him and his bodily warmth is destroyed.

yadi vāyu|mayo jīvaḥ, saṃśleṣo yadi vāyunā,
vāyu|maṇḍalavad dṛśyo, gacchet saha Marud|gaṇaiḥ.
186.5 saṃśleṣo yadi vātena. yadi, tasmāt praṇaśyati,
mah"|ârṇava|vimuktatvād anyat salila|bhājanam.
kūpe vā salilaṃ dadyāt, pradīpaṃ vā hut'|âśane,
kṣipraṃ praviśya naśyeta. yathā naśyaty asau tathā.
pañca|dhāraṇake hy asmiñ śarīre jīvitaṃ kutaḥ?
yeṣām anyatar'|âbhāvāc caturṇāṃ n' âsti saṃśayaḥ
naśyanty āpo hy an|āhārād, vāyur ucchvāsa|nigrahāt.
naśyate koṣṭha|bhedāt kham, agnir naśyaty a|bhojanāt.
vyādhi|vraṇa|parikleśair† medinī c' âiva śīryate.
pīḍite 'nyatare hy eṣāṃ saṃghāto yāti pañcadhā.
186.10 tasmin pañcatvam āpanne jīvaḥ kim anudhāvati?
kiṃ vedayati vā jīvaḥ? kiṃ śṛṇoti bravīti ca?
«eṣā gauḥ para|loka|sthaṃ tārayiṣyati mām» iti
yo dattvā mriyate jantuḥ, sā gauḥ kaṃ tārayiṣyati?
gauś ca pratigrahītā ca dātā c' âiva samaṃ yadā
ih' âiva vilayaṃ yānti, kutas teṣāṃ samāgamaḥ?

If, however, there is a soul that consists of wind, or is closely connected to the wind, then at death it should be visible, like a whirlwind is, for it would depart the body in a swirl of wind.

Perhaps the soul is closely connected to wind. If so, it 186.5
must be destroyed at death, for it would become something different, like a small portion of water released into a great ocean. If one were to put water into a well, or the flame of a lamp into fire, they would be destroyed as soon as they were absorbed into the water or fire. In just the same way, if the soul were wind, it would be absorbed into wind at death and so destroyed.

How can there be a soul in this body made of five elements? There is no doubt that if one of those elements disappears, then so do the other four.

Water is destroyed when no sustenance is taken, whereas wind is destroyed when a person's respiration is suppressed. Space disappears when the internal spaces in the body are destroyed, and fire is destroyed when a person does not eat. Earth is broken up by the afflictions of disease and wounds. When one of the five elements in the body is destroyed, the collection of five is also destroyed.

When a person has died, what happens to the soul? What 186.10
does it feel? What does it hear or say?

I believe that this cow will help me cross over to the next world. But if the person who gives the cow dies after donating it, whom does the cow help to cross over? If the cow, its recipient and the person who donates it all die in this world, how can they meet again?

vihagair upayuktasya, śail'|âgrāt patitasya ca,
agninā c' ôpayuktasya kutaḥ saṃjīvanaṃ punaḥ?
chinnasya yadi vṛkṣasya na mūlaṃ pratirohati,
bījāny asya pravartante, mṛtaḥ kva punar eṣyati?
186.15 bīja|mātraṃ purā sṛṣṭaṃ, yad etat parivartate.
mṛtā mṛtāḥ praṇaśyanti, bījād bījaṃ pravartate.

BHṚGUR uvāca:

187.1 NA PRAṆĀŚO 'STI jīvānāṃ, dattasya ca kṛtasya ca.
yāti deh'|ântaraṃ prāṇī, śarīraṃ tu viśīryate.
na śarīr'|āśrito jīvas tasmin naṣṭe praṇaśyati.
samidhām iva dagdhānāṃ yath" âgnir dṛśyate, tathā.

BHARADVĀJA uvāca:

agner yathā, tathā tasya: yadi nāśo na vidyate.
indhanasy' ôpayog'|ânte, sa c' âgnir n' ôpalabhyate.
naśyat', îty eva jānāmi śāntam agnim an|indhanam,
gatir yasya, pramāṇaṃ vā, saṃsthānaṃ vā na vidyate.

BHṚGUR uvāca:

187.5 samidhām upayog'|ânte yath" âgnir n' ôpalabhyate
ākāś'|ânugatatvādd hi, dur|grāhyo hi nir|āśrayaḥ.
tathā śarīra|saṃtyāge jīvo hy ākāśavat sthitaḥ.
na gṛhyate tu sūkṣmatvād, yathā jyotir, na saṃśayaḥ.

How does a person come to live again after being eaten up by birds, or after falling from a mountain top or being consumed by fire? If the stump of a tree that has been felled does not grow again, and only its seeds sprout into life, where does a person go when he dies? In the beginning 186.15
only seeds were created, and it is these that continue in existence. Successive generations die and are annihilated, but from their seeds other seeds sprout into life.

BHRIGU said:

NEITHER THE SOUL nor the merit resulting from a per- 187.1
son's donations or deeds is destroyed. The soul enters another body at death, but the body itself disintegrates. The soul which abides in the body does not perish when the body is destroyed. Just like fire is thought to exist even when its kindling wood has been burned, so too is the soul thought to exist.*

BHARAD·VAJA said:

As it is for fire, so it is for the soul: perhaps it is not destroyed. However, when the kindling wood has been fully consumed, fire is not perceived. When a fire has been extinguished, and has no more kindling wood, I think that it is destroyed for it has no movement, dimension or shape.

BHRIGU said:

Fire is not perceived when its kindling wood has been 187.5
consumed because it has entered into space, and being without a physical locus it is impossible to perceive. In much the same way, when the soul has abandoned the body its existence is just like that of space. It is because of its sub-

prāṇān dhārayate hy agniḥ, sa jīva upadhāryatām.
vāyu|saṃdhāraṇo hy agnir, naśyaty ucchvāsa|nigrahāt.
tasmin naṣṭe śarīr'|âgnau, tato deham a|cetanam
patitaṃ yāti bhūmitvam, ayanaṃ tasya hi kṣitiḥ.

jaṅgamānāṃ hi sarveṣāṃ sthāvarāṇāṃ tath" âiva ca
ākāśaṃ pavano 'nveti, jyotis tam anugacchati,
teṣāṃ trayāṇām ekatvād. dvayaṃ bhūmau pratiṣṭhitam.
187.10 yatra khaṃ tatra pavanas, tatr' âgnir yatra mārutaḥ.
a|mūrtayas te vijñeyā, mūrtimantaḥ śarīriṇām.

BHARADVĀJA uvāca:

yady agni|mārutau, bhūmiḥ, kham, āpaś ca śarīriṣu,
jīvaḥ kiṃ|lakṣaṇas tatr'? êty etad ācakṣva me, 'n|agha.
pañc'|ātmake, pañca|ratau, pañca|vijñāna|cetane
śarīre prāṇināṃ jīvaṃ: vettum icchāmi yādṛśam.

māṃsa|śoṇita|saṃghāte, medaḥ|snāyv|asthi|saṃcaye
bhidyamāne śarīre tu jīvo n' âiv' ôpalabhyate.
yady a|jīvaṃ śarīraṃ tu pañca|bhūta|samanvitam,
śārīre mānase duḥkhe kas tāṃ vedayate rujam?

tlety, undoubtedly, that it cannot be perceived—just like fire.

The fire that upholds the vital breaths in the body ought to be thought of as the soul. For fire is supported by the wind found in the body, but disappears when a person restrains his breathing. When the fire in the body disappears, the body becomes insentient. It falls down and devolves into earth, for the earth is its final resting place.

The wind found in all animate and inanimate beings enters into space, and fire follows it, because of the essential unity of these three things. But the pair remaining—water
and earth—are rooted in the earth. Where there is space 187.10
there is wind, and where there is wind there is fire. One should understand that these things are formless, and only assume a form within embodied creatures.

BHARAD·VAJA said:

If embodied creatures contain fire, wind, earth, space and water, please explain to me what characterizes the soul therein, faultless one. The body of sentient beings consists of five elements; it has five sorts of enjoyment and five forms of cognition and sentience. Hidden within it is a soul: I would like to know its nature.

The body is an aggregate of flesh and blood, a mass of fat, sinew and bone. When it is split up at death, the soul cannot be perceived. If the body has no soul and consists of the five elements, who is it that feels the pain of physical or mental suffering?

187.15 śṛṇoti kathitaṃ jīvaḥ karṇābhyāṃ; na śṛṇoti tat,
maha"|rṣe, manasi vyagre. tasmāj jīvo nir|arthakaḥ.
sarvaṃ paśyati yad dṛśyaṃ mano|yuktena cakṣuṣā.
manasi vyākule, cakṣuḥ paśyann api na paśyati.
na paśyati, na c' āghrāti, na śṛṇoti, na bhāṣate,
na ca sparśa|rasau vetti nidrā|vaśa|gataḥ punaḥ.
hṛṣyati krudhyate ko 'tra? śocaty udvijate ca kaḥ?
icchati, dhyāyati, dveṣṭi, vācam īrayate ca kaḥ?

BHṚGUR uvāca:

na pañca|sādhāraṇam atra kiṃ cic
charīram, eko vahate 'ntar|ātmā.
sa vetti gandhāṃś ca, rasāñ, śrutiṃ ca,
sparśaṃ ca, rūpaṃ ca, guṇāś ca ye 'nye.
187.20 pañc'|ātmake pañca|guṇa|pradarśī
sa sarva|gātr'|ânugato 'ntar'|ātmā.
sa vetti duḥkhāni sukhāni c' âtra,
tad|viprayogāt tu na vetti dehaḥ.
yadā na rūpaṃ na sparśo, n' ūṣma|bhāvaś ca pāvake,
tadā śānte śarīr'|âgnau deha|tyāgena naśyati.
āpo|mayam idaṃ sarvam; āpo mūrtiḥ śarīriṇām.
tatr' ātmā mānaso brahmā sarva|bhūteṣu loka|kṛt.
ātmā «kśetra|jña» ity uktaḥ saṃyuktaḥ prākṛtair guṇair.
tair eva tu vinirmuktaḥ «param'|ātm"» êty udāhṛtaḥ.

The soul hears what is said by means of the ears, but does 187.15
not hear anything if the mind is not focused, great seer. The inevitable conclusion of this is that the soul has no function.

A person sees everything that is visible through the faculty of vision functioning in connection with the mind. But when the mind is distracted, although the eye sees it does not in fact see an object. In the same way a person does not see, smell, hear, speak or perceive a physical sensation or taste when he is overcome with sleep.

Who is it that becomes excited or angry? Who is it that grieves and trembles? Who is it that desires, contemplates things, feels aversion and utters speech?

BHRIGU said:

The physical body is individualized by the five elements within it, and supported by the inner self alone. The self perceives smells, tastes, sound, physical sensation, visible
form and other sense objects. The inner self pervades the en- 187.20
tire body, and perceives the five sense objects from within. It knows sorrows and joys, but the body becomes insentient when the self is separated from it. When a person does not perceive a visible form or a physical sensation, and when no heat is found in the fire within, it means that the bodily fire has been extinguished. When the self abandons the body, the body is destroyed.

This whole world consists of water; water is the form of all embodied creatures. Within it is found the self, which is the pure consciousness identical to *brahman*, the world creator hidden within all beings. When the individual self is connected to the evolvents of primeval matter, it is called

ātmānaṃ taṃ vijānīhi sarva|loka|hit'|ātmakam.
tasmin yaḥ saṃśrito dehe hy, ab|bindur iva puṣkare.
187.25 kṣetra|jñaṃ taṃ vijānīhi nityaṃ loka|hit'|ātmakam.
tamo rajaś ca sattvaṃ ca, viddhi jīva|guṇān imān.
sa|cetanaṃ jīva|guṇaṃ vadanti;
sa ceṣṭate ceṣṭayate ca sarvam.
ataḥ paraṃ kṣetra|vido vadanti
prāvartayad yo bhuvanāni sapta.
na jīva|nāśo 'sti hi deha|bhede;
mithy" âitad āhur mṛta ity a|buddhāḥ.
jīvas tu deh'|ântaritaḥ prayāti;
daś'|ârdhat" âiv' âsya śarīra|bhedaḥ.
evaṃ sarveṣu bhūteṣu gūḍhaś carati saṃvṛtaḥ.
dṛśyate tv agryayā buddhyā sūkṣmayā tattva|darśibhiḥ.
taṃ pūrv'|âpara|rātreṣu yuñjānaḥ satataṃ budhaḥ,
laghv|āhāro, viśuddh'|ātmā, paśyaty ātmānam ātmani.
187.30 cittasya hi prasādena hitvā karma śubh'|âśubham,
prasann'|âtm" ātmani sthitvā sukham ānantyam aśnute.
mānaso 'gniḥ śarīreṣu jīva ity abhidhīyate.
sṛṣṭiḥ Prajāpater eṣā, bhūt'|âdhyātma|viniścaye.

the "field-knower." But when it is completely freed from them, it is called the "supreme self."*

Know that the self is essentially beneficial to the whole world. It abides in the body, like a drop of water on a blue lotus-flower.

Know that the welfare of the whole world is always the 187.25
essence of the field-knower, and that darkness, passion and purity are the three states of the soul. They say that the field-knower is sentient, and that the soul is its derivative. It moves and causes everything else to move, hence those that know the "field" say that it created the seven worlds.

The soul is not destroyed when the body breaks up; it is ignorant men who claim, falsely, that it perishes. The soul moves on and finds another body; a person's death is simply the dissolution of the body. And so it is hidden within all living beings, but its movements are concealed. But those who see the truth can perceive it by means of a refined, subtle intelligence.*

The wise man who constantly disciplines himself in the earlier and latter periods of the night, who takes little food
and remains pure—he see the self within. Through the 187.30
calming of the mind he abandons his good and bad *karma*. Being calm, and established in the self, he attains endless bliss.

The fire of consciousness found within all bodies is called the soul. According to this enquiry into the supreme self of a living being, it is the creation of Praja·pati, the Lord of creatures.

BHṚGUR uvāca:

188.1 ASṚJAD BRĀHMAṆĀN eva pūrvaṃ Brahmā prajā|patīn
ātma|tejo|'bhinirvṛttān, bhāskar'|âgni|sama|prabhān.
tataḥ satyaṃ ca, dharmaṃ ca, tapo, brahma ca śāśvatam,
ācāraṃ c' âiva, śaucaṃ ca svargāya vidadhe prabhuḥ.
deva|Dānava|gandharvā, Daity|āsura|mah"|ôragāḥ,
yakṣa|rākṣasa|nāgāś ca, piśācā manujās tathā.
brāhmaṇāḥ, kṣatriyā, vaiśyāḥ, śūdrāś ca, dvija|sattama,
ye c' ânye bhūta|saṃghānāṃ varṇās, tāṃś c' âpi nirmame.
188.5 brāhmaṇānāṃ sito varṇaḥ, kṣatriyāṇāṃ tu lohitaḥ,
vaiśyānāṃ pītako varṇaḥ, śūdrāṇām a|sitas tathā.

BHARADVĀJA uvāca:

cāturvarṇyasya varṇena yadi varṇo vibhajyate,
sarveṣāṃ khalu varṇānāṃ dṛśyate varṇa|saṃkaraḥ.
kāmaḥ, krodho, bhayaṃ, lobhaḥ,
śokaś, cintā, kṣudhā, śramaḥ
sarveṣāṃ naḥ prabhavati;
kasmād varṇo vibhajyate?
sveda|mūtra|purīṣāṇi, śleṣmā, pittaṃ sa|śoṇitam
tanuḥ kṣarati sarveṣāṃ, kasmād varṇo vibhajyate?
jaṅgamānām a|saṃkhyeyāḥ sthāvarāṇāṃ ca jātayaḥ
teṣāṃ vividha|varṇānāṃ kuto varṇa|viniścayaḥ?

BHṚGUR uvāca:

188.10 na viśeṣo 'sti varṇānāṃ, sarvaṃ brāhmam idaṃ jagat.
Brahmaṇā pūrva|sṛṣṭaṃ hi karmabhir varṇatāṃ gatam.

BHRIGU said:

IN THE BEGINNING Brahma only created the Brahminic patriarchs; he produced them from his intrinsic luster, and they were as luminous as the fire of the sun. The Lord then ordained that truth, righteousness, asceticism, the eternal Veda, good conduct and purity would lead to heaven. 188.1

After that he created the gods, *dánava*s, *gandhárva*s, *daitya*s, *ásura*s, great serpents, *yaksha*s, evil spirits, serpent demons, goblins and men. Brahma created brahmins, kshatriyas, vaishyas and shudras, most excellent brahmin, as well as the other classes that are found within different species
of living beings. The color of brahmins is white, kshatriyas 188.5
are red, vaishyas are yellowish and shudras are black.

BHARAD·VAJA said:

Perhaps class is distinguished from class in the system of four classes, but it appears that the classes are all mixed up. If lust, anger, fear, greed, sorrow, anxiety, hunger and fatigue overpower all of us, why is class distinguished?

If all bodies leak sweat, urine, excrement, phlegm, bile and blood, why is class distinguished? Given that there are incalculable species of animate and inanimate creatures, and that these creatures are themselves so diverse, how is class determined?

BHRIGU said:

In so far as the entire world has the nature of *brahman*, 188.10
there is no distinction between the classes. However, the creatures Brahma created in the beginning assume a particular class because of their deeds.

kāma|bhoga|priyās, tīkṣṇāḥ, krodhanāḥ, priya|sāhasāḥ,
tyakta|sva|dharmā, rakt'|âṅgās: te dvijāḥ kṣatratāṃ gatāḥ.
gobhyo vṛttiṃ samādhāya pītāḥ, kṛṣy|upajīvinaḥ
sva|dharmaṃ n' ânutiṣṭhanti: te dvijā vaiśyatāṃ gatāḥ.

hiṃs"|ânṛta|priyā, lubdhāḥ, sarva|karm'|ôpajīvinaḥ,
kṛṣṇāḥ, śauca|paribhraṣṭās: te dvijāḥ śūdratāṃ gatāḥ.
ity etaiḥ karmabhir vyastā dvijā varṇ|ântaraṃ gatāḥ.
dharmo yajña|kriyā teṣāṃ nityaṃ na pratiṣidhyate

188.15 ity ete caturo varṇā, yeṣāṃ brāhmī sarasvatī
vihitā Brahmaṇā pūrvaṃ, lobhāt tv a|jñānatāṃ gatāḥ.
brāhmaṇā brahma|tantra|sthās, tapas teṣāṃ na naśyati
brahma dhārayatāṃ nityaṃ, vratāni niyamāṃs tathā.

brahma c' âiva purā† sṛṣṭaṃ: ye na jānanti te '|dvi|jāḥ.
teṣāṃ bahu|vidhās tv anyās tatra tatra hi jātayaḥ:
piśācā, rākṣasāḥ, pretā, vividhā mleccha|jātayaḥ,
pranaṣṭa|jñāna|vijñānāḥ, sva|cchand|ācāra|ceṣṭitāḥ.

prajā brāhmaṇa|saṃskārāḥ sva|karma|kṛta|niścayāḥ
ṛṣibhiḥ svena tapasā sṛjyante c'; âpare 'paraiḥ.

Brahmins become kshatriyas through addiction to the enjoyment of pleasure, or if they are cutting, wrathful, foolhardy and negligent of their duties so that their bodies become red. Brahmins who do not carry out their duties, who turn yellow while herding cows and making their living from agriculture, they become vaishyas.

Brahmins become shudras through addiction to violence and lying, through hunting and making their living in all sorts of ways, thus becoming black and losing their purity. Differentiated by these deeds, brahmins assume different classes. But the religious law and its sacrificial rites are never prohibited for any of them.

Therefore these four classes, who possess the sacred words 188.15
of the Veda, were created by Brahma in the beginning, but then some of them became ignorant because of greed. The brahmins who abide by the Vedic teachings never lose their ascetic power. They should always uphold the Veda, as well as their religious vows and observances.

The Veda was created in the beginning: those who do not know it are not counted among the twice-born. There are diverse classes of these other beings, which are found here and there, such as goblins, evil spirits, the ghosts of the dead and various classes of barbarians. All these suffer from defective forms of knowledge and cognition, and are frivolous in their deeds and gestures.

The resolve of people who undergo the Brahminic ceremonies is fashioned by their own deeds. They were created by the seers through their ascetic power; other creatures are created by others.

188.20 ādi|deva|samudbhūtā brahma|mūl'|âkṣay'|âvyayā
sā sṛṣṭir mānasī nāma dharma|tantra|parāyaṇā.

BHARADVĀJA uvāca:

189.1 BRĀHMAṆAḤ KENA bhavati, kṣatriyo vā, dvij'|ôttama?
vaiśyaḥ śūdraś ca, vipra'|rṣe? tad brūhi, vadatāṃ vara.

BHṚGUR uvāca:

jāta|karm'|ādibhir yas tu saṃskāraiḥ saṃskṛtaḥ, śuciḥ,
ved'|âdhyayana|saṃpannaḥ, ṣaṭsu karmasv avasthitaḥ,
śauc'|ācāra|sthitaḥ samyag, vighas'|āśī, guru|priyaḥ,
nitya|vratī, satya|paraḥ; sa vai brāhmaṇa ucyate.
satyaṃ, dānaṃ, ath' â|droha, ānṛśaṃsyaṃ, trapā, ghṛṇā,
tapaś ca dṛśyate yatra, sa brāhmaṇa iti smṛtaḥ.
189.5 kṣatra|jaṃ sevate karma, ved'|âdhyayana|saṃgataḥ,
dān'|ādāna|ratir yas tu, sa vai kṣatriya ucyate.
vāṇijyā† paśu|rakṣā ca, kṛṣy|ādāna|ratiḥ, śuciḥ,
ved'|âdhyayana|saṃpannaḥ, sa vaiśya iti saṃjñitaḥ.
sarva|bhakṣa|ratir nityaṃ, sarva|karma|karo '|śuciḥ,
tyakta|vedas tv an|ācāraḥ, sa vai śūdra iti smṛtaḥ.
śūdre c' âitad bhavel lakṣyaṃ, dvije tac ca na vidyate.

This unfailing, immutable creation that is rooted in *brahman* was created by the primeval deity. Its nature is pure consciousness and its essence is the religious order. 188.20

BHARAD·VAJA said:

WHAT MAKES A man a brahmin or a kshatriya, most excellent brahmin? And how, Brahminic seer, does a man become a vaishya or a shudra? Please tell me that, most eloquent one. 189.1

BHRIGU said:

The one who has been consecrated and purified by the sacraments beginning with the birth ceremony, who is accomplished in Vedic recitation, practices the six acts,* adheres to pure conduct in the proper manner, eats only the remains of oblations, is devoted to his teacher, unfailing in his religious vows and intent on truth—he alone is called a brahmin. The person in whom truth, charity, non-violence, benevolence, bashfulness, tenderness and austerity are seen is held to be a brahmin.

The person who deals with acts of governance, who is well-versed in Vedic recitation and is dedicated to appropriating wealth and offering gifts, he is said to be a kshatriya. 189.5

The person occupied with trade and cattle herding, who is pure, dedicated to appropriating wealth by means of agriculture and accomplished in Vedic recitation, he is called a vaishya.

The person who will habitually eat anything and commit any deed, thereby becoming impure, who disregards the Vedas and ignores the code of conduct, he is held to be a shudra. This behavior might be observable in a shudra,

na vai śūdro bhavec chūdro, brāhmaṇo na ca brāhmaṇaḥ.

sarv'|ôpāyais tu, lobhasya krodhasya ca vinigrahaḥ,
etat pavitraṃ jñānānāṃ, tathā c' âiv' ātma|saṃyamaḥ.
189.10 vāryau sarv'|ātmanā, tau hi śreyo|ghāt'|ârtham ucchritau.
nityaṃ krodhāc chriyaṃ rakṣet, tapo rakṣec ca matsarāt,
vidyāṃ mān'|âpamānābhyām, ātmānaṃ tu pramādataḥ.

yasya sarve samārambhā nirāśīr|bandhanā, dvija,
tyāge yasya hutaṃ sarvaṃ, sa tyāgī, sa ca† buddhimān.
a|hiṃsraḥ sarva|bhūtānāṃ, maitrāyaṇa|gataś caret.
parigrahān parityajya, bhaved buddhyā jit'|êndriyaḥ.
a|śokaṃ sthānam ātiṣṭhed, iha c' âmutra c' â|bhayam.

tapo|nityena, dāntena muninā saṃyat'|ātmanā,
a|jitaṃ jetu|kāmena bhāvyaṃ, saṅgeṣv a|saṅginā.
189.15 indriyair gṛhyate yad yat, tat tad «vyaktam» iti sthitiḥ.
«a|vyaktam» iti vijñeyaṃ liṅga|grāhyam at'|îndriyam.

a|visrambhe na gantavyaṃ, visrambhe dhārayen manaḥ.
manaḥ prāṇe nigṛhṇīyāt, prāṇaṃ brahmaṇi dhārayet.

but is not found in a brahmin. Otherwise, a shudra would not be a shudra and a brahmin would not be a brahmin.

Subduing greed and anger by all possible methods is the means of purifying one's knowledge and attaining self-
control. These two must be warded off with one's entire be- 189.10
ing, for when they arise within they have the effect of destroying one's luster. One should always guard one's luster against anger, austerity against envy, knowledge against conceit and disrespect, and oneself against carelessness.

The person whose only attachment to his undertakings is indifference, O brahmin, who offers everything in the act of renunciation—he is a renouncer, and a wise man. Such a person should wander in a spirit of non-violence towards all beings, and be full of benevolence. Abandoning all his possessions, he should control his sense faculties through his intelligence. If he focuses on the state that is free from sorrow, he will attain freedom from fear in this world and the world beyond.

Unfailing in his asceticism, restrained, self-controlled and wishing to conquer the unconquered, the silent sage should free himself from attachment to all objects.

Whatever the sense faculties grasp is held to be the man- 189.15
ifest. That which is beyond the sense faculties, but can be grasped by its characteristic mark, should be understood as the unmanifest.

One should hold the mind in that which inspires confidence, and not that which does not. One should fix the mind in the *prana*, and then focus that in *brahman*.

nirvedād eva nirvāṇaṃ: na ca kiṃ cid vicintayet.
sukhaṃ vai brāhmaṇo brahma nirveden' âdhigacchati.
śaucena satataṃ yuktaḥ, sad|ācāra|samanvitaḥ,
s'|ânukrośaś ca bhūteṣu; tad dvi|jātiṣu lakṣaṇam.

BHṚGUR uvāca:

190.1 SATYAṂ BRAHMA, tapaḥ satyaṃ,; satyaṃ visṛjati prajāḥ.
satyena dhāryate lokaḥ, svargaṃ satyena gacchati.
an|ṛtaṃ tamaso rūpaṃ; tamasā nīyate hy adhaḥ.
tamo|grastā na paśyanti prakāśaṃ tamas" āvṛtāḥ.
«svargaḥ prakāśa» ity āhur, narakaṃ tama eva ca.
saty'|ânṛtaṃ tad ubhayaṃ prāpyate jagatī|caraiḥ.
tatr' âpy evaṃ|vidhā loke
vṛttiḥ: saty'|ânṛte bhavet,
dharm'|âdharmau, prakāśaś ca
tamo, duḥkhaṃ sukhaṃ tathā.

190.5 tatra yat satyaṃ sa dharmo, yo dharmaḥ sa prakāśo, yaḥ
prakāśas tat sukham iti. tatra yad an|ṛtaṃ so '|dharmo yo
'|dharmas tat tamo, yat tamas tad duḥkham iti. atr' ôcyate:
śārīrair mānasair duḥkhaiḥ, sukhaiś c' âpy a|sukh'|ôdayaiḥ
loka|sṛṣṭiṃ prapaśyanto na muhyanti vicakṣaṇāḥ.
tatra, duḥkha|vimokṣ'|ârthaṃ prayateta vicakṣaṇaḥ,
sukhaṃ hy a|nityaṃ bhūtānām, iha|loke paratra ca.

Nirvana is attained through complete indifference: one must not think about anything at all. By means of indifference a brahmin attains *brahman* quite easily.

Always possessing purity, endowed with good conduct and full of compassion to all living beings: this is characteristic of brahmins.

BHRIGU said:

TRUTH IS *brahman*, and asceticism is truth; it is truth 190.1
that creates all creatures. The world is maintained by truth, and it is through truth that one attains heaven. Untruth is a form of darkness, through which one is dragged down. Consumed and hemmed in by darkness, people cannot see the light of truth. They say that heaven is light, and that hell is nothing but darkness. The creatures who roam the earth meet with both truth and untruth.

In this world a person's conduct is also of this kind: it can be either truthful or untruthful, righteous or unrighteous, light or dark, pleasant or painful.

Among these, truth is righteousness, which is light, and 190.5
light is bliss. On the other hand untruth is unrighteousness, which is darkness, and darkness is suffering. On this point, the following verses have been uttered:

Seeing that the creation of the world necessitates physical and mental misery, and that its pleasures lead to pain, discerning men are not deceived. This being the case, the discerning man should strive for the sake of his own liberation from misery, for the happiness that living beings experience is impermanent, both in this world and the world beyond.

Rāhu|grastasya somasya yathā jyotsnā na bhāsate, tathā tamo|'bhibhūtānāṃ bhūtānāṃ naśyate sukham.

tat khalu dvi|vidhaṃ sukham ucyate: śārīraṃ mānasaṃ ca. iha khalv amuṣmiṃś ca loke vastu|pravṛttayaḥ sukh'|ârtham abhidhīyante. na hy ataḥ paraṃ tri|varga|phalaṃ viśiṣṭataram asti: sa eva kāmyo guṇa|viśeṣo, dharm'|ârtha|guṇ'|ārambhas tadd|hetur. asy' ôtpattiḥ sukha|prayojan'|ârtha āraṃbhaḥ.

BHARADVĀJA uvāca:

190.10 yad etad bhavat" âbhihitaṃ sukhānāṃ paramā sthitir iti, na tad upagṛhṇīmo. na hy eṣām ṛṣīṇāṃ mahati sthitānām a|prāpya eṣa kāmyo guṇa|viśeṣo, na c' âinam abhilaṣanti ca. tapasi, śrūyate, tri|loka|kṛd Brahmā prabhur ekākī tiṣṭhati. brahma|cārī na kāma|sukheṣv ātmānam avadadhāti. api ca bhagavān viśv'|êśvara Umā|patiḥ kāmam abhivartamānam an|aṅgatvena śamam anayat.

tasmād brūmo, na mah"|ātmabhir ayaṃ pratigṛhīto. na tv eṣāṃ tāvad viśiṣṭo guṇa|viśeṣa, iti n' âitad bhagavataḥ pratyemi. bhagavatā t' ûktaṃ, sukhān na param ast' îti. loka|pravādo hi dvi|vidhaḥ phal'|ôdayaḥ: su|kṛtāt sukham avāpyate duṣ|kṛtād duḥkham iti.

Moonlight does not shine forth when the moon is swallowed by Rahu.* In just the same way, bliss disappears when living beings are overwhelmed by darkness.

Bliss is said to be twofold: physical and mental. In this world and the world beyond, the endeavor to obtain objects is said to lead to bliss. The supreme reward of the three aims of life is no different from this: that bliss is the only particular object that one desires, and striving after the goals of religion and material gain is motivated by it. Striving is the source of that, the purpose of which is the effecting of bliss.

BHARAD·VAJA said:

We do not understand what you have said about the highest of all states of bliss. For this superior object—that is, sexual pleasure—is not outside the reach of sages who have attained the absolute, but they do not desire it. Moreover, we have heard that the Lord Brahma, creator of the triple world, remains in solitude while practicing asceticism. And a celibate student does not subject himself to the bliss of sexual pleasure. Furthermore, Shiva, the blessed Lord of the cosmos and husband of Uma, obliterated the love god Kama by depriving him of a body when he approached.* 190.10

Therefore we say that holy men do not indulge in sexual pleasure. These seers did not enjoy the highest sexual pleasure, which is why I do not accept your position. However, you have said that there is nothing beyond this bliss. It is a common saying that karmic retribution comes about in two ways: either one attains happiness, because of one's good deeds, or one attains misery, because of one's bad deeds.

BHṚGUR uvāca:

atr’ ôcyatām. an|ṛtāt khalu tamaḥ prādurbhūtaṃ. tatas tamo|grastā a|dharmam ev’ ânuvartante na dharmam. krodha|lobha|hiṃs”|ânṛt’|ādibhir avacchannā na khalv asmil̃ loke n’ âmutra sukham āpnuvanti. vividha|vyādhi|ruj”|ôpatāpair avakīryante, vadha|bandhana|parikleś’|ādibhiś ca kṣut|pipāsā|śrama|kṛtair upatāpair upatapyante. varṣa|vāt’|âtyuṣṇ’|âtiśīta|kṛtaiś ca pratibhayaiḥ śārīrair duḥkhair upatapyante. bandhu|dhana|vināśa|viprayoga|kṛtaiś ca mānasaiḥ śokair abhibhūyante, jarā|mṛtyu|kṛtaiś c’ ânyair iti.

yas tv etaiḥ śārīra|mānasair duḥkhair na saṃspṛśyate, sa sukhaṃ veda. na c’ âite doṣāḥ svarge prādur bhavanti. tatra khalu bhavanti:

su|sukhaḥ pavanaḥ svarge, gandhaś ca surabhis tathā.
kṣut|pipāsā|śramo n’ âsti; na jarā na ca pāpakam.
nityam eva sukhaṃ svarge; sukhaṃ duḥkham ih’ ôbhayam.
narake duḥkham ev’ āhuḥ, sukhaṃ tat paramaṃ padam.

190.15 pṛthivī sarva|bhūtānāṃ janitrī; tad|vidhāḥ striyaḥ.
pumān prajā|patis tatra, śukraṃ tejo|mayaṃ viduḥ.

BHRIGU said:

On this matter, you should listen to the following. Darkness arose from untruth. Hence those consumed by darkness follow unrighteousness rather than righteousness. Overcome by anger, greed, violence and untruth, they do not attain bliss in this world or the world beyond. They are subjected to various sorts of illness, sickness and disease and are tormented by such sufferings as beatings, imprisonment and pain, as well as those caused by hunger, thirst and fatigue. Furthermore, they are tormented by the dangers and physical sufferings of rain, wind, excessive heat and cold. They are overwhelmed by the mental sorrow caused by the destruction of their kinsmen and wealth, or else the separation from them, as well as by other sufferings caused by decrepitude and death.

The person who is not touched by these physical and mental sufferings finds bliss, and these evils do not appear in heaven. On this subject there are these verses:

In heaven the breeze is very pleasant and there is a fragrant scent. There is no hunger, thirst, fatigue, decrepitude or evil. The happiness experienced in heaven is continual, whereas both happiness and misery are found in this world. In hell there is nothing but misery, so they say; the bliss of heaven is the highest state.

Earth is the mother of all living beings, and the model 190.15
for all women. They know that Praja·pati is the man, and that his semen consists of light.

ity etal loka|nirmāṇaṃ Brahmaṇā vihitaṃ purā
prajā samanuvartante, svaiḥ svaiḥ karmabhir āvṛtāḥ.

BHARADVĀJA uvāca:

191.1 DĀNASYA KIṂ PHALAṂ prāhur, dharmasya caritasya ca,
tapasaś ca su|taptasya, sv'|âdhyāyasya, hutasya ca?

BHṚGUR uvāca:

hutena śāmyate pāpaṃ, sv'|âdhyāyaiḥ śāntir uttamā.
dānena bhogān, ity āhus, tapasā svargam āpnuyāt.
dānaṃ tu dvi|vidhaṃ prāhuḥ: paratr'|ârtham ih' âiva ca.
sadbhyo yad dīyate kiṃ cit, tat paratr' ôpatiṣṭhate.
a|sadbhyo dīyate yat tu tad dānam iha bhujyate.
yādṛśaṃ dīyate dānaṃ, tādṛśaṃ phalam aśnute.

BHARADVĀJA uvāca:

191.5 kiṃ kasya dharm'|ācaraṇaṃ?
kiṃ vā dharmasya lakṣaṇam?
dharmaḥ kati|vidho v" âpi?
tad bhavān vaktum arhati.

BHṚGUR uvāca:

sva|dharm'|ācaraṇe yuktā ye bhavanti manīṣiṇaḥ,
teṣāṃ svarga|phal'|âvāptir. yo 'nyathā, sa vimuhyate.

Thus Brahma ordained the creation of the world in the beginning. The creatures followed afterwards, each one of them constrained by their own *karma*.

BHARAD·VAJA said:

WHAT REWARDS, DO they say, can be achieved through 191.1
charity, righteousness, good conduct, severe asceticism, Vedic recitation and ritual offerings?

BHRIGU said:

Evil is pacified through ritual offerings, whereas Vedic recitation leads to the highest peace. They say that physical pleasures are attained through charity, whereas heaven is attained by means of asceticism.

Charity is twofold, so they say: that which pertains to this world and that which pertains to the world beyond. Whatever is given to virtuous men is received by the donor in the world beyond. A person enjoys the reward of the gift offered to unworthy recipients in this world. The particular result conferred by giving is determined by the nature of the gift.

BHARAD·VAJA said:

What is righteous conduct and who ought to observe 191.5
it? What is the characteristic of righteousness? How many facets does righteousness have? Please tell me this.

BHRIGU said:

Heaven is the reward received by wise men for their commitment to performing their duties. The man who deviates from his duty becomes bewildered.

BHARADVĀJA uvāca:

yad etac cāturāśramyaṃ brahma'|rṣi|vihitaṃ purā,
teṣāṃ sve sve samācārās, tān me vaktum ih' ârhasi.

BHṚGUR uvāca:

pūrvam eva bhagavatā Brahmaṇā loka|hitam anutiṣṭhatā dharma|saṃrakṣaṇ'|ârtham āśramāś catvāro 'bhinirdiṣṭāḥ. tatra guru|kula|vāsam eva prathamam āśramam udāharanti. samyag yatra śauca|saṃskāra|niyama|vrata|viniyat'|ātmā ubhe saṃdhye bhāskar'|âgni|daivatāny upasthāya, vihāya tandry|ālasye, guror abhivādana|ved'|âbhyāsa|śravaṇa|pavitrīkṛt'|ântar|ātmā, tri|ṣavaṇam upaspṛśya, brahma|cary'|âgni|paricaraṇa|guru|śuśrūṣā|nitya|bhikṣā|bhaikṣy'|ādi|sarva|nivedit'|ântar|ātmā, guru|vacana|nirdeś'|ânuṣṭhān'|âpratikūlo, guru|prasāda|labdha|svādhyāya|tatparaḥ syāt. bhavati c' âtra ślokaḥ:

gurum yas tu samārādhya dvijo vedam avāpnuyāt,
tasya svarga|phal'|âvāptiḥ, sidhyate c' âsya mānasam.

BHARAD·VAJA said:

Please tell me about the system of four religious paths ordained by the Brahminic seers long ago, and the practices that pertain to each stage of life.

BHRIGU said:*

In ancient times when the Blessed Lord Brahma was attending to the welfare of the world, he appointed four religious paths in order to safeguard righteousness. Among these paths, they say that living in the teacher's house is the first. While there the student should discipline himself properly in the ceremonies, religious observance and vows that confer purity. At dawn and dusk he should rid himself of lassitude and sloth, and worship the sun, the sacred fire and the deities. Making himself pure within in order to salute his teacher, and to listen to and reflect upon the Veda, he should anoint himself with water at dawn, noon and dusk, and then report everything about his inner life concerning such things as his celibacy, the tending of the sacred fire, obedience to his teacher and his usual practice of begging for alms. He should not be averse to putting the words and instruction of his teacher into practice, and should be dedicated to the Vedic recitation that depends on his teacher's kindness. On this subject there is a verse:

The brahmin who satisfies his teacher will master the Vedas. He will attain heaven, and accomplish his heart's desires.

191.10 gārhasthyaṃ khalu dvitīyam āśramaṃ vadanti. tasya sam udācāra|lakṣaṇaṃ sarvam anuvyākhyāsyāmaḥ. samāvṛttā nāṃ sad|ācārāṇāṃ† saha|dharma|carya|phal'|ârthināṃ gṛh'|āśramo vidhīyate. dharm'|ârtha|kām'|âvāptir hy atra tri|varga|sādhanam apekṣy', â|garhitena karmaṇā dhanāny ādāya. sv'|âdhyāy'|ôpalabdha|prakarṣena vā, brahma'|rṣi nirmitena vā, adri|sāra|gatena vā, havya|kavya|niyam' âbhyāsa|daivata|prasād'|ôpalabdhena vā dhanena gṛha stho gārhasthyaṃ vartayet. tadd hi sarv'|āśramāṇāṃ mūlam udāharanti: guru|kula|nivāsinaḥ parivrājakā ye c' anye saṃkalpita|vrata|niyama|dharm'|ânuṣṭhāyinas teṣām apy ata eva bhikṣā|bali|saṃvibhāgāḥ pravartante.

vānaprasthānāṃ ca dravy'|ôpaskāra iti prāyaśaḥ khalv ete sādhavaḥ sādhu|pathy'|âudanāḥ, sv'|ādhyāya|prasaṅginas tīrth'|âbhigamana|deśa|darśan'|ārthaṃ pṛthivīṃ paryaṭanti. teṣāṃ pratyutthān'|âbhigaman'|âbhivādan'|ânasūyā|vāk pradāna|sukha|śakty|āsana|sukha|śayan'|âbhyavahāra|sat kriyā c' êti. bhavati c' âtra ślokaḥ:

They say that the second religious path is that of the 191.10
householder. We will now explain all the salient features of the correct conduct expected of him. The householder's path is specified for those who have returned from the teacher's house, whose conduct is virtuous and who desire the rewards of performing the customary religious duties. Hoping to succeed in the three aims of life—religion, wealth and sensual pleasure—he will obtain them through blameless action. By means of the eminence attained through Vedic recitation, or through the ceremonies performed for the Brahminic seers, or through working with iron, or through the wealth obtained by offering oblations to the gods and his ancestors, or through religious observances, study and faith in the gods, he should maintain the status of a householder. For they say that the householder is the root of all religious paths: alms and oblations come from the householder alone, and these are distributed among students living in a teacher's house, wandering mendicants and everyone else following the religious life of resolute vows and observances.

Forest dwellers are generally allowed additional possessions. These holy men subsist on the wholesome oatmeal that is their staple and are devoted to Vedic recitation. They wander the earth so that they can visit places of pilgrimage and see foreign lands. They should be honored by rising to greet them, by paying visits to them, saluting them, speaking to them with kind words and offering them gifts, pleasant seats, pleasant beds and food. On this subject there is a verse:

«atithir yasya bhagn'|āśo gṛhāt pratinivartate,
sa dattvā duṣ|kṛtaṃ tasmai puṇyam ādāya gacchati»

api c' âtra yajña|kriyābhir devatāḥ prīyante, nivāpena pitaro, vidy"|âbhyāsa|śravaṇa|dhāraṇena ṛṣayaḥ, apaty'|ôtpādanena Prajāpatir iti. ślokau c' âtra bhavataḥ:

«vātsalyāt sarva|bhūtebhyo vācyāḥ śrotra|sukhā giraḥ.
paritāp'|ôpaghātaś ca, pāruṣyaṃ c' âtra garhitam.
191.15 avajñānam, ahaṃ|kāro, dambhaś c' âiva vigarhitaḥ.
a|hiṃsā, satyam, a|krodhaḥ sarv'|āśrama|gataṃ tapaḥ.»

api c' âtra māly'|ābharaṇa|vastr'|âbhyaṅga|niyat'|ôpabhoga|nṛtya|gīta|vāditra|śruti|sukha|nayan'|âbhirāma|darśanānāṃ prāptir, bhakṣya|bhojya|lehya|peya|coṣyāṇām abhyavahāryāṇāṃ vividhānām upabhogaḥ, sva|vihāra|saṃtoṣaḥ, kāma|sukh'|âvāptir iti.

tri|varga|guṇa|nirvṛttir yasya nityaṃ gṛh'|āśrame,
sa sukhāny anubhūy' êha śiṣṭānāṃ gatim āpnuyāt.

uñcha|vṛttir gṛha|stho yaḥ sva|dharm'|ācaraṇe rataḥ,
tyakta|kāma|sukh'|ārambhaḥ, svargas tasya na dur|labhaḥ.

"Should a guest be turned away from a home without receiving food, he gives his bad deeds to the householder and takes his merit with him as he goes."

Furthermore, the deities are satisfied by various sacrifices and rituals, the ancestors are satisfied by the oblations made to them and the seers are satisfied by the maintenance of Vedic study and learning. Praja·pati, the Lord of creatures, is satisfied by the procreation of offspring. On this subject there are two verses:

"Motivated by affection for all living beings, one should
utter words that are pleasing to the ear. Striking in order to
cause pain and rough language are censured, as are disre- 191.15
spect, egotism and hypocrisy. Non-violence, truth, the sup-
pression of anger and asceticism are recommended for all
religious paths."

In addition to the above rules, householders can enjoy the use of garlands, ornaments, clothes, ointments, food at any time, dancing, listening to singing and music, and they can enjoy delightful sights that lead to bliss. They can enjoy various types of food, both hard and soft, as well as things that can be licked, drunk or sucked. In this way the householder finds satisfaction in his own station and obtains sensual pleasure.

The householder who enjoys the objects of the three aims of life without interruption experiences bliss in this world, and will obtain a destiny among exalted beings in the next.

The householder who subsists on gleanings, who is dedicated to the performance of his duties and abandons the endeavor for sensual pleasure—he does not find it difficult to attain heaven.

BHṚGUR uvāca:

192.1 VĀNAPRASTHĀḤ KHALV api dharmam anusarantaḥ, puṇyāni tīrthāni nadī|prasravaṇāni su|vivikteṣv araṇyeṣu mṛga|mahiṣa|varāha|vana|gaj'|ākīrṇeṣu tapasyanto 'nusaṃcaranti. tyakta|grāmya|vastr'|âbhyavahār'|ôpabhogā, vany'|âuṣadhi|phala|mūla|parṇa|parimita|vicitra|niyat'|āhārāḥ, sthān'|āsanino, bhūmi|pāṣāṇa|sikatā|śarkarā|vālukā|bhasma|śāyinaḥ, kāśa|kuśa|carma|valkala|saṃvṛt'|âṅgāḥ, keśa|śmaśru|nakha|roma|dhāriṇo, niyata|kāl'|ôpasparśanā, a|skandita|kāla|bali|hom'|ânuṣṭhāyinaḥ, samit|kuśa|kusum'|âpahāra|saṃmārjana|labdha|viśrāmāḥ, śīt'|ôṣṇa|varṣa|pavana|viṣṭambha|vibhinna|sarva|tvaco, vividha|niyam'|ôpayoga|cary"|ânuṣṭhāna|vihita|pariśuṣka|māṃsa|śoṇita|tvag|asthi|bhūtā, dhṛti|parāḥ sattva|yogāc charīrāṇy udvahanti.

yas tv etāṃ niyataś caryāṃ brahma'|rṣi|vihitāṃ caret,
sa dahed agnivad doṣāñ, jayel lokāṃś ca dur|jayān.

parivrājakānāṃ punar ācāraḥ. tad yathā: vimucy' âgni|dhana|kalatra|paribarhaṇaṃ, saṅgeṣv ātmanaḥ sneha|pāśān avadhūya parivrajanti. sama|loṣṭ'|âśma|kāñcanās, tri|varga|pravṛtteṣv a|sakta|buddhayo, 'ri|mitr'|ôdāsīnānāṃ tulya|darśanāḥ, sthāvara|jarāyuj'|âṇḍaja|svedaj'|ôdbhijjānāṃ

BHRIGU said:

FOREST DWELLERS ALSO follow the religious life, visiting 192.1
holy bathing spots and river springs, and practicing asceticism in isolated areas of the wilderness full of deer, buffalo, wild boar and forest elephants. Abandoning the use of village clothing and meals, they are abstemious in their food, which is limited to the various sorts of herbs, fruits, roots and leaves found in the woods. They should remain standing or else lie down on the bare ground, stones, sand, pebbles, gravel or ash. They dress themselves in *kásha* or *kusha* grass, or in animal skins or tree-bark, and do not cut their hair, beards, nails and bodily hair. They bathe at fixed times, and offer *bali* oblations at the designated moments.* They rest only after sweeping out their abodes and after gathering firewood, *kusha* grass and flowers. Their skin is cracked all over from enduring the cold, heat, rain and wind. Although their flesh, blood, skin and bones shrivel up because they have become accomplished through following their practices and applying themselves to various restraints, they remain dedicated to their ascetic resolve, and bear their bodies by means of their pure discipline.

The person who is committed to following the practice prescribed by the Brahminic seers burns away his evils, just like a fire, and conquers worlds that are difficult to conquer.

The code of conduct adopted by wandering ascetics is as follows. Leaving behind their fire, wealth and retinue of wives, shaking off their bonds of affection to the objects of their attachment, they wander forth. They regard a clod of earth, a stone and a piece of gold as the same; their thoughts are not attached to the undertakings that lead to the objects

bhūtānāṃ vāṅ|manaḥ|karmabhir an|abhidrohiṇo, '|niketāḥ parvata|pulina|vṛkṣa|mūla|devat"|āyatanāny anucaranto, vās'|ârtham upeyur nagaraṃ grāmaṃ vā. nagare pañca|rātrikā, grāme c' âika|rātrikāḥ. praviśya ca prāṇa|dhāraṇ'|ârthaṃ dvi|jātīnāṃ bhavanāny a|saṃkīrṇa|karmaṇām upatiṣṭheyuḥ. pātra|patit'|āyācita|bhaikṣyāḥ, kāma|krodha|darpa|lobha|moha|kārpaṇya|dambha|parivād'|âbhimāna|hiṃs"|nivṛttā iti. bhavanti c' âtra ślokāḥ:

«a|bhayaṃ sarva|bhūtebhyo dattvā yaś carate muniḥ,
na tasya sarva|bhūtebhyo bhayam utpadyate kva cit.

192.5 kṛtv" âgni|hotraṃ sva|śarīra|saṃsthaṃ,
śārīram agniṃ sva|mukhe juhoti.
vipras tu bhaikṣy'|ôpagatair havirbhiś
cit'|âgnināṃ sa vrajate hi lokam.»

mokṣ'|āśramaṃ yaś carate yath"|ôktaṃ
śuciḥ, su|saṃkalpita|mukta|buddhiḥ,
an|indhanaṃ jyotir iva praśāntaṃ,
sa brahma|lokaṃ śrayate manuṣyaḥ.

of the three aims of life. They view enemies, friends and neutrals in the same way and do not harm living beings in word, thought or deed, be they inanimate, viviparous, egg-born, moisture-born or plants. Being homeless, they seek out mountains, sandbanks, the roots of trees and temples, but may enter a town or village in order to find a dwelling place. They may spend up to five nights in a town, but only a single night in a village. Once they have entered a town or village to find sustenance, they should approach the house of a brahmin whose deeds are pure. The alms they request is thrown into their bowls upon request, and they desist from sensual pleasure, anger, pride, greed, delusion, niggardliness, hypocrisy, abuse, conceit and violence. On this subject there are these verses:

"Presenting no danger to all living beings as he wanders the earth, the silent sage is in turn not endangered by any living being wherever he goes.

Internalizing the fire offering within his own body, he 192.5
offers the bodily fire in his mouth. With the burned oblations of funeral pyres as his alms food, the brahmin wanders the world."

The person who follows this religious path as described, the goal of which is liberation, becomes pure and attains a resolute and liberated state of consciousness. He attains the world of *brahman*, just as a fire without any fuel is extinguished.*

BHARADVĀJA uvāca:

asmāl lokāt paro lokaḥ śrūyate, n' ôpalabhyate.
tam ahaṃ jñātum icchāmi; tad bhavān vaktum arhati.

BHṚGUR uvāca:

uttare Himavat|pārśve puṇye sarva|guṇ'|ânvite
puṇyaḥ kṣemyaś ca kāmyaś ca, sa paro loka ucyate.
tatra hy a|pāpa|karmāṇaḥ, śucayo, 'tyanta|nirmalāḥ,
lobha|moha|parityaktā mānavā, nir|upadravāḥ.
192.10 sa svarga|sadṛśo deśas, tatra hy uktāḥ śubhā guṇāḥ.
kāle mṛtyuḥ prabhavati, spṛśanti vyādhayo na ca.
na lobhaḥ para|dāreṣu, sva|dāra|nirato janaḥ.
n' ânyonyaṃ badhyate tatra, dravyeṣu ca na vismayaḥ,
paro hy a|dharmo n' âiv' âsti, saṃdeho n' âpi jāyate.
kṛtasya tu phalaṃ tatra pratyakṣam upalabhyate,
pān'|āsan'|âśan'|ôpetāḥ prāsāda|bhavan'|āśrayāḥ.
sarva|kāmair vṛtāḥ ke cidd, hem'|ābharaṇa|bhūṣitāḥ.
prāṇa|dhāraṇa|mātraṃ tu keṣāṃ cid upapadyate.
śrameṇa mahatā ke cit kurvanti prāṇa|dhāraṇam.
iha dharma|parāḥ ke cit, ke cin naikṛtikā narāḥ.
sukhitā duḥkhitāḥ ke cin, nir|dhanā dhanino 'pare.

BHARAD·VAJA said:

I have heard about another world beyond this one, but not perceived it. I would like to know about that; please tell me about it.

BHRIGU said:

The northern slopes of the Himalayas is an auspicious place full of all good things. Auspicious, peaceful and lovely, it is said to be a world beyond. The people there are free from evil *karma*; they are pure and completely undefiled. They have left greed and delusion behind and are free from misfortune. That place is just like heaven, for it is said 192.10
to contain only pure qualities. And when death in due course overpowers a person who abides there, he remains untouched by illness.

Because they are satisfied with their own wives, men do not lust after the wives of others. The people are not attached to each other there, do not covet another's possessions, and since no other person is unrighteous, suspicion does not arise. The rewards of a person's former deeds are clearly visible there, and the people enjoy fine food, drink and seats, living in palaces and mansions.

Some people are surrounded with every pleasure and adorn themselves with golden ornaments. But some get barely enough to sustain their lives, and others eke out a living with a great effort.

In this world some men are dedicated to religion, whereas others are dishonest. Some men are happy, others suffer. Some men are poor, others are rich.

192.15 iha śramo, bhayaṃ, mohaḥ, kṣudhā tīvrā ca jāyate,
lobhaś c' ârtha|kṛto nṝṇāṃ, yena muhyanty a|paṇḍitāḥ.
iha vārtā bahu|vidhā dharm'|âdharmasya kāriṇaḥ,
yas tad ved' ôbhayaṃ prājñaḥ, pāpmanā na sa lipyate.

sopadhaṃ, nikṛti|steyaṃ, parivādo hy, asūyitā,
par'|ôpaghāto, hiṃsā ca, paiśunyam, an|ṛtaṃ tathā;
etān āsevate yas tu, tapas tasya prahīyate.
yas tv etān n' ācared vidvāṃs, tapas tasya pravardhate.

iha cintā bahu|vidhā dharm'|âdharmasya karmaṇaḥ,
karma|bhūmir iyaṃ. loke iha kṛtvā śubh'|âśubham,
śubhaiḥ śubham avāpnoti, tath" â|śubham ath' ânyathā.
192.20 iha Prajāpatiḥ pūrvaṃ, devāḥ sa'|rṣi|gaṇās tathā,
iṣṭv" êṣṭa|tapasaḥ, pūtā Brahma|lokam upāśritāḥ.

uttaraḥ pṛthivī|bhāgaḥ sarva|puṇyatamaḥ, śubhaḥ.
iha|sthās tatra jāyante ye vai puṇya|kṛto janāḥ.
yadi sat|kāram ṛcchanti, tiryag|yoniṣu c' âpare.
kṣīṇ'|āyuṣas tathā c' ânye naśyanti pṛthivī|tale.

anyonya|bhakṣaṇ'|āsaktā, lobha|moha|samanvitāḥ
ih' âiva parivartante, na te yānty uttarāṃ diśam.
ye gurūn paryupāsante niyatā brahma|cāriṇaḥ,
panthānaṃ sarva|lokānāṃ vijānanti manīṣiṇaḥ.

In this world there is toil, fear, delusion and intense 192.15
hunger. Men are greedy for wealth, and this deludes the ignorant. In this world one hears all sorts of things about people doing lawful and unlawful things, but the wise man who understands the danger in wealth is not tainted by evil.

Fraudulence, dishonesty, theft, abuse, envy, harming others, violence, calumny and untruth: the ascetic power of a person who succumbs to these dwindles. But the ascetic power of a learned man who does not yield to them increases.

In this world people worry about doing good and bad in all sorts of ways, for this is the realm of *karma*: by performing good and bad deeds here, in this world, a person will receive good through good deeds and bad through bad deeds.
It was here that Praja·pati, in the beginning, along with the 192.20
gods and legions of seers, performed sacrifices and offered their asceticism as a form of sacrifice. Thus they were purified and reached the world of Brahma.

The northern region of the earth is pure, the most auspicious of all places. The people of this world are reborn there if they perform good deeds. If people achieve respect, they are reborn among the animals there. But there are others who disappear on the surface of the earth when their lifespan is exhausted.

Those beings who are addicted to feasting upon each other and are full of greed and delusion—they will remain in this very world, and will not go to the northern region. Wise men who remain celibate and venerate their teachers know the path to all worlds.

192.25 ity ukto 'yaṃ mayā dharmaḥ
saṃksipto brahma|nirmitaḥ.
dharm'|âdharmau hi lokasya
yo vai vetti, sa buddhimān.

BHĪṢMA uvāca:

ity ukto Bhṛguṇā, rājan, Bharadvājaḥ pratāpavān,
Bhṛguṃ parama|dharm'|ātmā vismitaḥ pratyapūjayat.
eṣa te prasavo, rājañ, jagataḥ saṃprakīrtitaḥ
nikhilena. mahā|prājña, kiṃ bhūyaḥ śrotum icchasi?

Brahma created this religion that I have explained in brief. The one who knows what is righteous and unrighteous in this world is truly wise. 192.25

BHISHMA said:

Once the powerful Bharad·vaja had been addressed, Your Majesty, being assured of the highest religion and filled with astonishment, he revered Bhrigu. This account of the world has been declared to you in full, Your Majesty. What else do you wish to know, wise man?

193
A DISCOURSE ON THE BRAHMINIC RULES OF CONDUCT

YUDHIṢṬHIRA uvāca:

193.1 ĀCĀRASYA VIDHIṂ, tāta,
procyamānaṃ tvay", ân|agha,
śrotum icchāmi, dharma|jña,
sarva|jño hy asi me mataḥ.

BHĪṢMA uvāca:

dur|ācārā, dur|viceṣṭā, duṣ|prajñāḥ, priya|sāhasāḥ,
a|santas tv iti vikhyātāḥ; santaś c' ācāra|lakṣaṇāḥ.
purīṣaṃ yadi vā mūtraṃ ye na kurvanti mānavāḥ
rāja|mārge, gavāṃ madhye, dhānya|madhye ca, te śubhāḥ.
śaucam āvaśyakaṃ kṛtvā, devatānāṃ ca tarpaṇam—
dharmam āhur manuṣyāṇām—upaspṛśya nadīṃ taret.
193.5 sūryaṃ sad" ôpatiṣṭheta, na ca sūry'|ôdaye svapet.
sāyaṃ|prātar japet saṃdhyāṃ tiṣṭhan pūrvāṃ, tath" êtarām.
pañc'|ārdro bhojanaṃ bhuñjyāt
prāṅ|mukho, maunam āsthitaḥ.
na nindyād anna|bhakṣyāṃś ca,
svādu svādu ca bhakṣayet.
ārdra|pāṇiḥ samuttiṣṭhen; n' ārdra|pādaḥ svapen niśi.
deva'|rṣir Nāradaḥ prāha etad ācāra|lakṣaṇam.
śuciṃ deśam, anaḍvāhaṃ,
deva|goṣṭhaṃ, catuṣ|patham,
brāhmaṇaṃ dhārmikaṃ, caityaṃ
nityaṃ kuryāt pradakṣiṇam.

YUDHI·SHTHIRA said:

BLAMELESS FATHER, master of righteousness, I would like to hear you explain the rule of conduct, for I consider you to be all-knowing. 193.1

BHISHMA said:

Men whose conduct and behavior is evil, who are stupid and steadfast in their recklessness—they are said to be wicked, whereas virtuous men are characterized by correct conduct. If men do not defecate or urinate along a highroad or among cows or grain, they are pure.

They have outlined the religious law of men as follows: once a man has attended to the call of nature in a pure fashion and offered libations to the gods, he should touch
himself with water and then get out of the river. He should 193.5
always worship the sun, and not sleep when it starts to rise. In the morning and evening, at dawn and dusk, he should stand facing first the East and then the West, and intone his Vedic prayers.

When he has washed his hands, feet and face, he should sit facing the East and silently eat his meal. He should not be disgusted by his food, but instead eat dishes that are palatable. Once he has washed his hands he should get up; at night he should not sleep with wet feet. The celestial seer Nárada said that this is characteristic of correct conduct.

A person should always circumambulate a pure place, a bull, a temple, a cross-roads, a righteous brahmin and a sacred tree in a clockwise direction.

atithīnāṃ ca sarveṣāṃ, preṣyāṇāṃ, sva|janasya ca
sāmānyaṃ bhojanaṃ bhṛtyaiḥ puruṣasya praśasyate.
193.10 sāyaṃ|prātar manuṣyāṇām aśanaṃ Veda|nirmitam.
n' ântarā bhojanaṃ dṛṣṭam; upavāsī tathā bhavet.

homa|kāle tathā juhvann, ṛtu|kāle tathā vrajan,
an|anya|strī|janaḥ prājño brahma|cārī tathā bhavet.

amṛtaṃ brāhmaṇ'|ôcchiṣṭaṃ jananyā hṛdayaṃ|kṛtam.
taj janāḥ paryupāsante; satyaṃ santaḥ samāsate.

loṣṭa|mardī, tṛṇa|cchedī, nakha|khādī tu yo naraḥ,
nity'|ôcchiṣṭaḥ, śaṅkuśuko* n' êh' āyur vindate mahat.

Yajuṣā saṃskṛtaṃ māṃsaṃ nivṛtto māṃsa|bhakṣaṇāt.
na bhakṣayed vṛthā|māṃsaṃ, pṛṣṭha|māṃsaṃ ca varjayet.
193.15 sva|deśe para|deśe vā atithiṃ n' ôpavāsayet.
kāmya|karma|phalaṃ labdhvā gurūṇām upapādayet.
gurubhya āsanaṃ deyaṃ, kartavyaṃ c' âbhivādanam.
gurūn abhyarcya yujyante āyuṣā, yaśasā, śriyā.

n' ēkṣet' ādityam udyantaṃ, na ca nagnāṃ para|striyam.
maithunaṃ satataṃ dharmyaṃ, guhye c' âiva samācaret.

The man who gives the same food to all his guests, slaves, kinsmen and servants is praised. The Vedas prescribe that 193.10
men should eat in the evening and morning. Eating between these times is not allowed; that way a person effectively observes a fast.

The wise man who does not frolic with another man's wife but approaches his own only when she is in season, after making a burned offering at the correct time, he effectively follows the life of a celibate student.

The remains of a brahmin's food are like nectar from the bosom of one's mother. People venerate that; virtuous men revere it as truth.

Crushing clods of earth, cutting grass, eating with his nails and always living off the remains of food, the fickle man does not achieve a long lifespan in this world

The person who has stopped eating flesh can eat the flesh consecrated by Yajus formulas. He should also avoid eating flesh that is intended only for himself as well as the flesh of an animal's hind.

A person should not enforce a fast upon a guest, regard- 193.15
less of whether he resides in his own country or a foreign land. When he attains the reward of an optional deed, he should offer it to his teachers. The teachers should be offered seats and greeted respectfully. If he worships his teachers he will enjoy a long lifespan, fame and good fortune.

He should not look at the sun as it rises, nor at another man's naked wife. When he has sexual intercourse it should always be in accordance with religious law, and in private.

tīrthānāṃ hṛdayaṃ tīrthaṃ, śucīnāṃ hṛdayaṃ śuciḥ.
sarvam ārya|kṛtaṃ caukṣyaṃ, vāla|saṃsparśanāni ca.
darśane darśane nityaṃ sukha|praśnam udāharet;
sāyaṃ|prātaś ca viprāṇāṃ pradiṣṭam abhivādanam.
193.20 dev'|āgāre, gavāṃ madhye, brāhmaṇānāṃ kriyā|pathe,
sv'|âdhyāye, bhojane c' âiva dakṣiṇaṃ pāṇim uddharet.
sāyaṃ|prātaś ca viprāṇāṃ pūjanaṃ ca yathā|vidhi.
paṇyānāṃ śobhate paṇyaṃ, kṛṣīṇāṃ bādyate kṛṣiḥ.
bahu|kāraṃ ca sasyānāṃ, vāhye vāho, gavāṃ tathā.
saṃpannaṃ bhojane nityaṃ, pānīye tarpaṇaṃ tathā;
su|śṛtaṃ pāyase brūyād, yavāgvāṃ, kṛsare tathā.
śmaśru|karmaṇi saṃprāpte, kṣute, snāne, 'tha bhojane,
vyādhitānāṃ ca sarveṣām āyuṣyam abhinandanam.
praty|ādityaṃ na meheta, na paśyed ātmanaḥ śakṛt,
saha striy" âtha śayanaṃ saha|bhojyaṃ ca varjayet.
193.25 tvaṃ|kāraṃ nāmadheyaṃ ca jyeṣṭhānāṃ parivarjayet,
avarāṇāṃ samānānām ubhayeṣāṃ na duṣyati.

One's preceptor is the heart of all sacred places; fire is the heart of all pure things. Everything that a nobleman does is pure, as is the touch of a horse's hair.

One should always make pleasant enquiries whenever one sees someone; brahmins should make respectful greetings both in the evening and morning. One should raise 193.20
one's right hand in a temple, among cows, in the area where brahmins perform religious rites, and when engaged in Vedic recitation or eating.

One should pay homage to brahmins in the correct manner, both in the evening and morning. In doing this one's trade in commodities prospers and the harvest of farming is made steady. One also attains an abundance of grains and gains oxen and the use of cows as draft animals.

Food should always be palatable, drinks should be refreshing; when feeding someone with rice-pudding, rice gruel or spiced rice and peas, one should mention that it has been well cooked.

When a person cuts his beard, sneezes, bathes and eats, the longevity of all diseased people should be praised.

One should not urinate when facing the sun nor look at one's own excrement, and one should avoid sleeping and eating with one's wife.

One should avoid using the names of one's elders and 193.25
addressing them in the second person, but this is not wrong when speaking to one's inferiors or equals.

hṛdayaṃ pāpa|vṛttānāṃ pāpam ākhyāti vai kṛtam,
jñāna|pūrvaṃ vinaśyanti gūhamānā mahā|jane.
jñāna|pūrva|kṛtaṃ pāpaṃ chādayanty† a|bahu|śrutāḥ;
n' âinaṃ manuṣyāḥ paśyanti, paśyanty eva div'|âukasaḥ.
pāpen' âpihitaṃ pāpaṃ, pāpam ev' ânuvartate.
dharmen' âpihito dharmo, dharmam ev' ânuvartate:
dhārmikeṇa kṛto dharmo dharmam ev' ânuvartate.
pāpaṃ kṛtaṃ na smarat' îha mūḍho,
vivartamānasya tad eti kartuḥ.
Rāhur yathā candram upaiti c' âpi,
tath" a|budhaṃ pāpam upaiti karma.
193.30 āśayā saṃcitaṃ dravyaṃ duḥkhen' âiv' ôpabhujyate.
tad budhā na praśaṃsanti, maraṇaṃ na pratīkṣate.
mānasaṃ sarva|bhūtānāṃ dharmam āhur manīṣiṇaḥ.
tasmāt sarveṣu bhūteṣu manasā śivam ācaret.
eka eva cared dharmaṃ, n' âsti dharme sahāyatā.
kevalaṃ vidhim āsādya sahāyaḥ kiṃ kariṣyati?
dharmo yonir manuṣyāṇāṃ, devānām amṛtaṃ divi;
pretya|bhāve sukhaṃ dharmāc chaśvat tair upabhujyate.

The heart of men whose conduct is evil betrays the evil they have committed. If they conceal the intentional evil they have done from society at large, they will perish. Unlearned men conceal an intentional evil—although people do not see this, the gods do.

Evil is eclipsed by evil, and succeeds evil alone, but righteousness is eclipsed by righteousness, and succeeds righteousness alone: a righteous deed committed by a righteous person follows nothing but righteousness. The fool does not remember the evil he commits in this world, but it finds its agent despite his transformations. An ignorant man's evil *karma* will find him just as Rahu approaches and covers the moon.

The possessions that a person accumulates out of desire 193.30
are consumed by suffering. The wise do not recommend that, for death waits for nobody.

Wise men say that the consciousness within all beings is righteousness. Therefore a person should make a conscious effort to act benevolently towards all living beings. As an individual he should follow righteousness, for in righteousness there is no companionship. If he conforms to this rule of conduct in its entirety, what can a friend do?

Righteousness is the source of all mankind, it is the heavenly nectar of the gods through which people experience perpetual bliss in the state after death.

194

A DISCOURSE ON THE SUPREME SELF

YUDHIṢṬHIRA uvāca:

194.1 ADHYĀTMAM NĀMA yad idaṃ
puruṣasy' êha cintyate,
yad adhyātmaṃ, yathā c' âitat,
tan me brūhi, pitā|maha.
kutaḥ sṛṣṭam idaṃ viśvaṃ,
brahman, sthāvara|jaṅgamam?
pralaye katham abhyeti?
tan me vaktum ih' ârhasi.

BHĪṢMA uvāca:

adhyātmam iti māṃ, Pārtha, yad etad anupṛcchasi,
tad vyākhyāsyāmi te, tāta, śreyaskaratamaṃ sukham
sṛṣṭi|pralaya|saṃyuktam, ācāryaiḥ paridarśitam,
yaj jñātvā puruṣo loke prītiṃ saukhyaṃ ca vindati,
phala|lābhaś ca tasya syāt, sarva|bhūta|hitaṃ ca tat.
194.5 pṛthivī, vāyur, ākāśam, āpo, jyotiś ca pañcamam:
mahā|bhūtāni bhūtānāṃ sarveṣāṃ prabhav'|âpyayau.
yataḥ sṛṣṭāni, tatr' âiva tāni yānti punaḥ punaḥ:
mahā|bhūtāni bhūtebhyaḥ sāgarasy' ōrmayo yathā.
prasārya ca yath" âṅgāni kūrmaḥ saṃharate punaḥ,
tadvad bhūtāni bhūt'|ātmā sṛṣṭāni harate punaḥ.
mahā|bhūtāni pañc' âiva sarva|bhūteṣu. bhūta|kṛt
akarot teṣu vaiṣamyaṃ, tat tu jīvo na paśyati.
śabdaḥ, śrotraṃ, tathā khāni: trayam ākāśa|yoni|jam.
vāyoḥ sparśas, tathā ceṣṭā, tvak c' âiva tritayaṃ smṛtam.
194.10 rūpaṃ, cakṣus, tathā pākas: tri|vidhaṃ teja ucyate.
rasaḥ, kledaś ca, jihvā ca trayo jala|guṇāḥ smṛtāḥ.

YUDHI·SHTHIRA said:

PLEASE TELL ME, grandfather, about that which is thought to be the supreme self of a man in this world—what it is, and what its mode of existence is. 194.1

What is the source of this universe of animate and inanimate creatures, brahmin? And what happens to it during a period of cosmic dissolution? Please tell me this.

BHISHMA said:

Since you ask me about the supreme self, Partha, I will explain it to you—that bliss which is the ultimate cause of a man's felicity, my son. Teachers claim that it is the cause of creation and dissolution. When a man knows it he finds joy and bliss in this world, and the reward he attains benefits all living beings.

Earth, wind, space, water and fire, the fifth: these great 194.5
elements are the origin and end of all things. The great elements are the source of all living beings, just as waves belong to the ocean, and return to that same source of their creation over and over again.

Just as a tortoise extends its limbs and withdraws them once again, so the world self withdraws the elements into himself each time he creates them.* The five great elements are found in all living beings. The creator fashioned the diversity among them, but no creature perceives him.

The three things that originated from space are sound, the faculty of hearing and the cavities within the body. It is held that the triad of touch, movement and skin emerged
from the wind. Fire is said to be threefold: visible form, the 194.10

ghreyaṃ, ghrāṇaṃ, śarīraṃ ca, ete bhūmi|guṇās trayaḥ.
mahā|bhūtāni pañc' âiva; ṣaṣṭhaṃ ca mana ucyate.
indriyāṇi manaś c' âiva vijñānāny asya, Bhārata.
saptamī buddhir ity āhuḥ, kṣetra|jñaḥ punar aṣṭamaḥ.

cakṣur ālocanāy' âiva, saṃśayaṃ kurute manaḥ.
buddhir adhyavasānāya, kṣetra|jñaḥ sākṣivat sthitaḥ.
ūrdhvaṃ pāda|talābhyāṃ yad; arvāk c' ôrdhvaṃ ca paśyati.
etena sarvam ev' êdaṃ viddhy abhivyāptam antaram.

194.15 puruṣair indriyāṇ' îha veditavyāni kṛtsnaśaḥ.
tamo rajaś ca sattvaṃ ca, te 'pi bhāvās tad|āśritāḥ.

etāṃ buddhvā naro buddhyā bhūtānām āgatiṃ gatim,
samavekṣya śanaiś c' âiva, labhate śamam uttamam.

guṇān† nenīyate buddhir, buddhir ev' êndriyāṇy api
manaḥ|ṣaṣṭhāni, bhūtāni. tad|abhāve kuto guṇāḥ?
iti tan|mayam ev' âitat sarvaṃ sthāvara|jaṅgamam.
pralīyate c' ôdbhavati tasmān, nirdiśyate tathā.

faculty of vision and digestion. The three evolvents of water are said to be taste, moisture and the tongue.

The three evolvents of earth are odor, the faculty of smell and the body. These, then, are the five great elements; the mind is said to be the sixth. The sense faculties and the mind are a man's means of cognition, Bhárata. They say that the faculty of intelligence is the seventh, and that the field-knower is the eighth.

The eye's only function is seeing, whereas the mind ponders things. The faculty of intelligence is for determining things, whereas the field-knower stands apart, like a witness. The field-knower sees what is above the soles of his feet; he sees what is below his head and above his feet. Know that he pervades the whole world from within.

The men of this world should have a comprehensive 194.15
knowledge of the sense faculties. The three psychosomatic states of darkness, passion and purity abide within the sense faculties.

When a man quietly contemplates the birth and death of living beings, and gains knowledge of them by means of his understanding, he attains sublime peace.*

The faculty of intelligence governs the three psychosomatic states, as well as the sense faculties, mind—the sixth sense faculty—and the elements. If the faculty of intelligence did not exist, how could the psychosomatic states come into being? Therefore this entire world, which comprises both animate and inanimate things, consists of intelligence. It arises from it and is dissolved into it, so it is proclaimed.

yena paśyati, tac cakṣuḥ; śṛṇoti, śrotram ucyate.
jighrati, ghrāṇam ity āhū; rasaṃ jānāti jihvayā,
194.20 tvacā sparśayate sparśaṃ: buddhir vikriyate '|sakṛt.
yena prārthayate kiñ cit, tadā bhavati tan manaḥ.

adhiṣṭhānāni buddher hi pṛthag arthāni pañcadhā;
indriyāṇ' îti yāny āhus, tāny a|dṛśyo 'dhitiṣṭhati.

puruṣe tiṣṭhatī buddhis triṣu bhāveṣu vartate.
kadā cil labhate prītiṃ, kadā cid anuśocati,
na sukhena na duḥkhena kadā cid api vartate.
evaṃ narāṇāṃ manasi triṣu bhāveṣv avasthitā.

s" êyaṃ bhāv'|ātmikā bhāvāṃs trīn etān ativartate,
saritāṃ sāgaro bhartā mahā|velām iv' ôrmimān.
194.25 ati|bhāva|gatā buddhir bhāve manasi vartate.
pravartamānaṃ tu rajas, tad bhāvam anuvartate,
indriyāṇi hi sarvāṇi pravartayati sā tadā.
tataḥ sattvaṃ, tamo|bhāvaḥ prīti|yogāt pravartate.
prītiḥ sattvaṃ, rajaḥ śokas, tamo mohas; tu te trayaḥ.
ye ye ca bhāvā loke 'smin, sarveṣv eteṣu vai triṣu.

iti buddhi|gatiḥ sarvā vyākhyātā tava, Bhārata.
indriyāṇi ca sarvāṇi vijetavyāni dhīmatā.

By which one sees, that is the eye; when one hears, it is
said to be the ear. They say it is the nose that smells, whereas
one perceives tastes by means of the tongue and sensation 194.20
by means of the skin. Thus is the faculty of intelligence
repeatedly modified—when a person desires something, it
becomes the mind.*

The places in which the faculty of intelligence settles are the five different sense objects; the unseeable self presides over the sense faculties, so they say.

The intelligence that abides in a man exists in three different states. Sometimes it experiences joy, sometimes it experiences lamentation, and sometimes it experiences neither pleasure nor pain. Thus the faculty of intelligence abides in the minds of men in three states.

The faculty of intelligence is the essence of these three states, although it also transcends them, just as the billowy ocean—the lord of rivers—encompasses the shore.

In its transcendent condition, the faculty of intelligence 194.25
abides within the mind. But when passion is aroused it succeeds that transcendent state, at which point the faculty of intelligence impels all the sense faculties into operation. Therefore, first there is a state of purity, and then a darkness, which results from a person's contact with joy. Purity is joy, passion is sorrow, and darkness is delusion; these are the three states. Whatever psychosomatic states are found in the world are subsumed within these three.

Thus I have explained all the modifications of the intelligence to you, Bhárata. A wise man should master all his sense faculties.

sattvaṃ, rajas, tamaś c' âiva prāṇināṃ saṃśritāḥ sadā,
tri|vidhā vedanā c' âiva sarva|sattveṣu dṛśyate:
194.30 sāttvikī rājasī c' âiva, tāmasī c' êti, Bhārata.
sukha|sparśaḥ sattva|guṇo, duḥkha|sparśo rajo|guṇaḥ.
tamo|guṇena saṃyuktau bhavato '|vyāvahārikau.

tatra yat prīti|saṃyuktaṃ kāye manasi vā bhavet,
«vartate sāttviko bhāva» ity ācakṣīta tat tathā.
atha yad duḥkha|saṃyuktam a|prīti|karam ātmanaḥ,
«pravṛttaṃ raja» ity eva tan na saṃrabhya cintayet.
atha yan moha|saṃyuktam, avyakta|viṣayam bhavet,
a|pratarkyam, a|vijñeyaṃ, tamas tad upadhārayet.

praharṣaḥ, prītir, ānandaḥ, sukhaṃ, saṃśānta|cittatā
kathaṃ cid abhivartanta; ity ete sāttvikā guṇāḥ.
194.35 a|tuṣṭiḥ, paritāpaś ca, śoko, lobhas, tath" â|kṣamā
liṅgāni rajasas tāni; dṛśyante hetv|a|hetubhiḥ.
avamānas, tathā mohaḥ, pramādaḥ, svapna|tandritā
kathaṃ cid abhivartante: vividhās tāmasā guṇāḥ.

dūra|gaṃ, bahudhā|gāmi, prārthanā|saṃśay'|ātmakam
manaḥ; su|niyataṃ yasya sa sukhī pretya c' êha ca.

Purity, passion and darkness are always found within sentient creatures, in whom three similar kinds of sensation
can be seen: those that are either pure, passionate or im- 194.30
bued with darkness, Bhárata. A pleasant physical sensation
is a sort of purity, whereas an unpleasant physical sensation
is a sort of passion. When purity and passion are joined by
any kind of darkness, the two become indistinct.

As regards the sensations, that which is imbued with joy can arise in body or mind. One should regard that as a pure state of being that has come into being.* That which is imbued with suffering causes a person's pain. One should not be affected by such an experience, but merely note that passion has been impelled into being. What is imbued with delusion, whose object may be unmanifest and incapable of being comprehended or cognized, should be regarded as darkness.

Rapture, joy, bliss, happiness and mental serenity come
about in all sorts of way: they are the different forms of
purity. Displeasure, torment, sorrow, greed and impatience 194.35
are the characteristics of passion; they are seen to result from
causes, but sometimes this is not so. Contempt, delusion,
carelessness, sleep and lassitude come about in all sorts of
ways: they are the various forms of darkness.

The mind travels far and moves in various directions; its essence is desire and doubt. But the person whose mind is well controlled experiences bliss both in this world and the world beyond.

sattva|kṣetrajñayor etad antaraṃ paśya sūkṣmayoḥ:
sṛjate tu guṇān eka, eko na sṛjate guṇān.
maśak'|ôdumbarau v" âpi saṃprayuktau yathā sadā,
anyonyam etau syātāṃ ca, saṃprayogas tathā tayoḥ.
194.40 pṛthag|bhūtau prakṛtyā tau, saṃprayuktau ca sarvadā,
yathā matsyo† jalaṃ c' âiva saṃprayuktau tath" âiva tau.
na guṇā vidur ātmānaṃ, sa guṇān vetti sarvaśaḥ.
paridraṣṭā guṇānāṃ tu saṃsṛṣṭān manyate tathā.
indriyais tu pradīp'|ârthaṃ kurute buddhi|saptamaiḥ
nir|viceṣṭair a|jānadbhiḥ, param'|ātmā pradīpavat.
sṛjate hi guṇān sattvaṃ, kṣetra|jñaḥ paripaśyati.
saṃprayogas tayor eṣa sattva|kṣetrajñayor dhruvaḥ.
āśrayo n' âsti sattvasya kṣetra|jñasya ca kaś cana;
sattvaṃ manaḥ saṃsṛjate, na guṇān vai kadā cana.
194.45 raśmīṃs teṣāṃ sa manasā yadā samyaṅ niyacchati,
tadā prakāśate 'sy' ātmā, ghaṭe dīpo jvalann iva.
tyaktvā yaḥ prākṛtaṃ karma nityam ātma|ratir muniḥ,
sarva|bhūt'|ātma|bhūs tasmāt sa gacched uttamāṃ gatim.
yathā vāri|caraḥ pakṣī salilena na lipyate,
evam eva kṛta|prajño bhūteṣu parivartate.
evaṃ sva|bhāvam ev' âitat sva|buddhyā viharen naraḥ,
a|śocann a|prahṛṣyaṃś ca, samo, vigata|matsaraḥ.

One must see this difference between substance and the field-knower, those subtle entities: one creates the material evolvents, whereas the other one does not. The connection between these two is just like that between a gnat and an *udúmbara* tree, which are always mutually connected.

The two are fundamentally distinct, but always con- 194.40
nected, just like the connection between a fish and water. The evolvents of matter do not know the self, but the self knows them thoroughly. The self is the witness of the evolvents, but thinks that they are connected to him.

When a person practices meditation for the sake of illumination, with the sense faculties and the faculty of intelligence—the seventh—motionless and insentient, then the supreme self becomes like a lamp within.

Substance emits the evolvents, the field-knower looks on—this connection between the two is fixed. Both lack a material substratum, and although substance is connected to the mind, it is never connected to the material evolvents.

When a man correctly controls the rays of the senses* 194.45
with his mind, then his self shines forth like a light burning in a jar. By abandoning his wicked *karma* and continually finding joy in the self, the silent sage thereby becomes the self of all living beings and attains the supreme destiny.

Just as a bird moves around on the water but is not tainted by it, so does the wise man move among living beings.

Therefore a man should abide in his own inherent state by means of his intelligence, not feeling sorrow or joy, but being equanimous and free from envy.

sva|bhāva|yuktyā yuktas tu sa nityaṃ sṛjate guṇān,
ūrṇa|nābhir yathā sūtraṃ, vijñeyās tantuvad guṇāḥ.
194.50 pradhvastā na nivartante, nivṛttir n' ôpalabhyate.
pratyakṣeṇa parokṣaṃ tad, anumānena sidhyati.
evam eke 'dhyavasyanti; nivṛttir iti c' âpare.
ubhayaṃ saṃpradhāry' âitad vyavasyeta yathā|mati.
it' îmaṃ hṛdaya|granthiṃ buddhi|bheda|mayaṃ dṛḍham
vimucya, sukham āsīta. na śocec chinna|saṃśayaḥ.
malināḥ prāpnuyuḥ śuddhiṃ†
yathā pūrṇāṃ nadīṃ narāḥ
avagāhya su|vidvāṃso;
viddhi jñānam idaṃ tathā.
mahā|nadyā hi pāra|jñas tapyate; na tad anyathā.
na tu tapyati tattva|jñaḥ: phale jñāte taraty uta.
194.55 evaṃ ye vidur ādhyātmaṃ, kevalaṃ jñānam uttamam.
etāṃ buddhvā naraḥ sarvāṃ, bhūtānām āgatiṃ gatim
avekṣya ca śanair buddhyā, labhate śamanaṃ tataḥ.
tri|vargo yasya viditaḥ, prekṣya yaś ca vimuñcati,
anviṣya manasā yuktas, tattva|darśī nir|utsukaḥ.

Connected to its inherent state, the self always creates the naterial evolvents. One should understand that the mateial evolvents are just like the thread emitted by a spider.

When people die they do not cease to exist; there is no 194.50
uch thing as the cessation of existence. This matter is beond direct experience, but is established by inference. Thus lo some men resolve the matter; others claim that there is cessation of existence. Having considered both possibiliies, one should resolve the matter according to one's own udgment.

The knot in a person's heart is firmly fixed and destroys is intelligence. Once it has been released, a person experinces bliss. With his doubts cut away he would not feel any orrow.

Just as dirty men become pure by plunging into a full iver, so you should understand this knowledge that wise nen attain. A person who knows of the far shore of a great iver is tormented; his knowledge can never have any other ffect. But a person who knows the way things truly are is
ot tormented: once he knows his goal, he crosses over. It 194.55
s just so for those people who know the supreme self, that bsolute and sublime state of awareness.

When a man quietly contemplates the birth and death of living beings by means of his understanding, and undertands everything, he attains peace.

The diligent man who inquires with his mind, who unlerstands the set of three and lets go of them through his relections, he sees the way things really are and is freed from nxiety.

na c' ātmā śakyate draṣṭum indriyaiś ca vibhāgaśaḥ,
tatra tatra visṛṣṭaiś ca, dur|vāryaiś c' â|kṛt'|ātmabhiḥ.
etad buddhvā bhaved† buddhaḥ.
kim anyad buddha|lakṣaṇam?
vijñāya tadd hi manyante
kṛta|kṛtyā manīṣiṇaḥ.
194.60 na bhavati viduṣāṃ† tato bhayaṃ,
yad a|viduṣāṃ su|mahad bhayaṃ bhavet.
na hi gatir adhik" âsti kasya cit:
sati hi guṇe pravadanty a|tulyatām.
yaḥ karoty an|abhisaṃdhi|pūrvakaṃ,
tac ca nirṇudati yat purā kṛtam,
n' â|priyaṃ tad ubhayaṃ, kutaḥ priyaṃ,
tasya taj janayat' îha sarvataḥ.
lokam āturam asūyate janas,
tasya taj janayat' îha sarvataḥ.
loka ātura|janān nir|āviśaṃs†
tat tad eva bahu paśya śocataḥ!
tatra paśya kuśalān a|śocato,
ye vidus tad ubhayaṃ padaṃ satāṃ.

It is impossible to perceive the self by means of the individual sense faculties, for they are released on different sort of objects and hard for incomplete men to restrain.

When he has understood this he becomes a wise man. What else could a wise man be characterized by? Once the wise have understood it, they are thought to have done what they had to do.

Therefore these men of knowledge do not feel fear, the 194.60
very great fear that the ignorant might suffer. For there is no further rebirth for any such person: once he has attained this quality of understanding, they say that he has no equal.

The person who acts without any prior intention, and who wards off the deeds committed in the past, does not generate what is unpleasant or a mixture of pleasure and pain—let alone what is pleasant—for himself anywhere in this world.

A person finds no contentment with this world of affliction, and generates these three different experiences for himself everywhere in this world.

Without becoming involved with the afflicted people of this world, look at how much they grieve over different things! But look at the skillful men who do not grieve, those who know both states of the virtuous.

195

A DISCOURSE ON THE DISCIPLINE OF MEDITATION

BHĪṢMA uvāca:

195.1 HANTA, VAKṢYĀMI TE, Pārtha,
dhyāna|yogaṃ catur|vidham.
yaṃ jñātvā śāśvatīṃ siddhiṃ
gacchant' îha maha"|rṣayaḥ.

yathā sv|anuṣṭhitaṃ dhyānaṃ, tathā kurvanti yoginaḥ.
maha"|rṣayo jñāna|tṛptā, Nirvāṇa|gata|mānasāḥ.
n' āvartante punaḥ, Pārtha, muktāḥ saṃsāra|doṣataḥ;
janma|doṣa|parikṣīṇāḥ, sva|bhāve paryavasthitāḥ.
nir|dvaṃdvā, nitya|sattva|sthā, vimuktā, niyama|sthitāḥ,
a|saṅgāny a|vivādīni manaḥ|śānti|karāṇi ca.
195.5 tatra dhyānena saṃśliṣṭam ek'|âgraṃ dhārayen manaḥ,
piṇḍī|kṛty' êndriya|grāmam āsīnaḥ kāṣṭhavan muniḥ.
śabdaṃ na vindec chrotreṇa, sparśaṃ tvacā na vedayet;
rūpaṃ na cakṣuṣā vidyāj, jihvayā na rasāṃs tathā.
ghreyāṇy api ca sarvāṇi jahyād dhyānena yoga|vit;
pañca|varga|pramāthīni n' êcchec c' âitāni vīryavān.
tato manasi saṃgṛhya pañca|vargaṃ vicakṣaṇaḥ,
samādadhyān mano bhrāntam, indriyaiḥ saha pañcabhiḥ.

BHISHMA said:

NOW THEN, PARTHA, I will describe the fourfold disci- 195.1
pline of meditation to you. Once they understand this, great seers attain eternal perfection in this world.

The followers of *yoga* discipline themselves so that they become accomplished in meditation. These great seers are satiated by gnosis; their minds established in Nirvana.

They do not return to this world again, Partha, but attain release from the evils of transmigration. They bypass the evils of birth, being firmly rooted in their true state.

Beyond duality, always abiding in purity, released and committed to their religious observances, they dwell in places conducive to mental peace, where there is neither attachment nor conflict.

In those places, the silent sage should sit as still as a piece 195.5
of wood and bring his sense faculties together. Then he should keep his mind one-pointed, and steeped in meditation.

He should not perceive a sound with his ears or feel any physical sensation with his skin; he should not perceive a visible object with the eye or flavors with the tongue. Through meditation the practitioner of *yoga* should abandon all smells; the vigorous one should not hanker after the objects that disturb the five sense faculties.

The wise man should then gather his five sense faculties within the mind, and keep both focused when the latter wanders.

visaṃcāri, nir|ālambaṃ, pañca|dvāraṃ, cal'|âcalam
pūrve dhyāna|pathe dhīraḥ samādadhyān mano 'ntarā.

195.10 indriyāṇi manaś c' âiva yadā piṇḍī|karoty ayam,
eṣa dhyāna|pathaḥ pūrvo mayā samanuvarṇitaḥ.

tasya tat pūrva|saṃruddham ātmanaḥ ṣaṣṭham āntaram
sphuriṣyati, samudbhrāntā vidyud ambu|dhare yathā.

jala|bindur yathā lolaḥ parṇa|sthaḥ sarvataś calaḥ,
evam ev' âsya cittaṃ ca bhavati dhyāna|vartmani.

samāhitaṃ kṣaṇaṃ kiṃ cid dhyāna|vartmani tiṣṭhati.
punar vāyu|pathaṃ bhrāntaṃ, mano bhavati vāyuvat.

a|nirvedo, gata|kleśo, gata|tandrīr, a|matsarī
samādadhyāt punaś ceto dhyānena dhyāna|yoga|vit.

195.15 vicāraś ca, vivekaś ca, vitarkaś c' ôpajāyate,
muneḥ samādadhānasya prathamaṃ dhyānam āditaḥ.

manasā kliśyamānas tu samādhānaṃ ca kārayet.
na nirvedaṃ munir gacchet, kuryād ev' ātmano hitam.

In the first stage of meditation the wise man should focus the mind within, for it moves hither and thither and has no foundation; with the five senses as its outlets, it is very unsteady.

When a person brings the sense faculties and the mind 195.10
together, this is the first stage of meditation, as I have explained.

Even when a person has managed to hold his mind firm within, when excited it will burst forth, just like lightning in a cloud.

The mind of a person who follows the path of meditation is like a drop of water which rolls about on a leaf, moving in all directions.

On the path of meditation the mind remains focused for a few moments. But just like the wind it will be shaken, for the mind follows the path of wind.

Without becoming despondent, anguished, lethargic or exhilarated, the person who understands the discipline of meditation should once again focus the mind by means of meditative practice.

At the beginning, when the silent sage practicing inner 195.15
concentration attains the first stage of meditation, reflection, investigation and deliberation arise.

When the activity of his mind torments him, he should once again bring about inner concentration. The silent sage should not become despondent, but should do that which benefits him.

pāṃsu|bhasma|karīṣāṇāṃ yathā vai rāśayaś citāḥ
sahasā vāriṇā siktā na yānti paribhāvanam,
kiṃ cit snigdhaṃ yathā ca syāc chuṣka|cūrṇam a|bhāvitam,
kramaśas tu śanair gacchet sarvaṃ tat paribhāvanam.
evam ev' êndriya|grāmaṃ śanaiḥ saṃparibhāvayet.
saṃharet kramaśaś c' âiva, sa samyak praśamiṣyati.
195.20 svayam eva manaś c' âiva, pañca|vargaṃ ca, Bhārata,
pūrvaṃ dhyāna|pathe sthāpya nitya|yogena śāmyati.
na tat puruṣa|kāreṇa, na ca daivena kena cit
sukham eṣyati tat tasya, yad evaṃ saṃyat'|ātmanaḥ.
sukhena tena saṃyukto raṃsyate dhyāna|karmaṇi.
gacchanti yogino hy evaṃ Nirvāṇaṃ, tan nir|āmayam.

Piled up heaps of soil, ash and dung do not become saturated even when forcibly sprinkled with water, although dry powder that is slightly damp, but not saturated, will slowly but surely become soaked through. The yogin should gently unite his sense faculties in just the same way. If he brings them together gradually, he will find complete peace.

Once he has established his mind and five sense faculties 195.20
in the preliminary stages of meditation, Bhárata, with his discipline constant, he experiences peace.

Not by normal human effort or by fate can a person attain that bliss which the person of inner control experiences.

When he has encountered that bliss he will find pleasure in the practice of meditation. Thus the practitioners of *yoga* attain Nirvana, the state free from disease.

196–200

A DISCOURSE ON THE PRACTICE OF QUIET RECITATION

YUDHIṢṬHIRA uvāca:

196.1 CĀTURĀŚRAMYAM UKTAṂ te, rāja|dharmās tath" âiva ca,
nān"|āśrayāś ca bahava itihāsāḥ pṛthag|vidhāḥ.
śrutās tvattaḥ kathāś c' âiva dharma|yuktā, mahā|mate.
saṃdeho 'sti tu kaś cin me, tad bhavān vaktum arhati.
jāpakānāṃ phal'|âvāptiṃ śrotum icchāmi, Bhārata.
kiṃ phalaṃ japatām uktaṃ? kva vā tiṣṭhanti jāpakāḥ?
japyasya ca vidhiṃ kṛtsnaṃ vaktum arhasi me, 'n|agha.
«jāpakā» iti kiṃ c' âitat? Sāṃkhya|Yoga|kriyā|vidhiḥ?
196.5 kiṃ yajña|vidhir ev' âiṣa? kim etaj japyam ucyate?
etan me sarvam ācakṣva, sarva|jño hy asi me mataḥ.

BHĪṢMA uvāca:

atr' âpy udāharant' îmam itihāsaṃ purātanam,
Yamasya yat purā vṛttaṃ, Kālasya brāhmaṇasya ca.
Sāṃkhya|Yogau tu yāv uktau munibhir mokṣa|darśibhiḥ
saṃnyāsa eva Vedānte, vartate japanaṃ prati.
Veda|vādāś ca nirvṛttāḥ śāntā brahmaṇy avasthitāḥ.
sāṃkhya|yogau tu yāv uktau munibhiḥ sama|darśibhiḥ.
mārgau tāv apy ubhāv etau saṃśritau, na ca saṃśrutau.

YUDHI·SHTHIRA said:

YOU HAVE OUTLINED the system of four religious paths, 196.1
as well as the duties of a king and many different traditions on all sorts of subjects. I have heard you narrate stories on righteousness, great thinker, but I still have some doubt, which you should resolve.

I would like to hear how quiet reciters obtain their goal, Bhárata. What reward are they said to attain by practicing quiet recitation? And where do they abide? You should explain to me the entire method of quiet recitation, faultless one. What is meant by the word "reciter?" Is this method equivalent to the practice of Samkhya and Yoga followers?

What is the sacrificial method? What is quiet recitation 196.5
said to be? You should explain all this to me, for I consider you to be all-knowing.

BHISHMA said:

On this subject people relate the ancient tradition of what happened long ago between Yama, Time, and a brahmin.*

However, the silent sages who witness liberation directly speak of two spiritual methods: Samkhya and Yoga. Only renunciation is taught in the Vedanta,* but it is connected to quiet recitation. Vedic learning arises, ceases and is rooted in *brahman*.

The silent sages who see things impartially speak of two spiritual methods: Samkhya and Yoga. These two paths are connected, but are not well understood.

yathā saṃśrūyate rājan, kāraṇaṃ c' âtra vakṣyate.
manaḥ|samādhir atr' âpi, tath" êndriya|jayaḥ smṛtaḥ.
196.10 satyam, agni|parīcāro, viviktānāṃ ca sevanam,
dhyānaṃ, tapo, damaḥ, kṣāntir, an|asūyā, mit'|âśanam,
viṣaya|pratisaṃhāro, mita|jalpas, tathā śamaḥ:
eṣa pravartako yajño. nivartakam atho śṛṇu.
yathā nivartate karma japato brahma|cāriṇaḥ,
etat sarvam a|śeṣeṇa yath"|ôktaṃ parivartayet.
nivṛttaṃ mārgam āsādya vyakt'|âvyaktam an|āśrayam.
kuś'|ôccaya|niṣaṇṇaḥ san, kuśa|hastaḥ, kuśaiḥ śikhī,
kuśaiḥ parivṛtas tasmin, madhye channaḥ kuśais tathā,
196.15 viṣayebhyo namas|kuryād, viṣayān na ca bhāvayet.
sāmyam utpādya manasā manasy eva mano dadhat.
tad dhiyā dhyāyati brahma japan vai saṃhitāṃ hitām.
saṃnyasyaty atha vā tāṃ vai samādhau paryavasthitaḥ.
dhyānam utpādayaty atra saṃhitā|bala|saṃśrayāt
śuddh'|ātmā, tapasā dānto, nivṛtta|dveṣa|kāmavān.

I will describe their foundation, Your Majesty, as it is generally understood. Concentration of the mind and mastery of the senses are taught in connection with them.

Truth, tending the sacred fire, living in isolated places, 196.10
meditation, asceticism, restraint, forbearance, freedom from spite, moderation in eating, withdrawal of the senses from their objects, controlled speech and peace: this is the sacrifice that produces results in the world. Now listen to the one which stops them.

The celibate student practicing quiet recitation should follow all of this, just as he has been taught it and without omitting anything, so that his *karma* will cease. He should aspire to the path of cessation, which comprises both the manifest and unmanifest and is without substratum.

Sitting on a heap of *kusha* grass, with *kusha* grass in his hands and topknot, surrounded by *kusha* grass and with
kusha grass around his loins, he ought to pay homage to 196.15
his sense faculties, but should not cherish them. Bringing about a state of equanimity, he should hold the mind within itself.

In his thought he should meditate on *brahman* by quietly reciting the Vedas, which are suitable for this purpose. Alternatively, if he is well established in concentration, he can renounce them. By resorting to the power of the Vedas, he brings about a state of meditation. Being internally pure through his asceticism, and restrained, he desists from aversion and desire.

a|rāga|moho, nir|dvaṃdvo: na śocati na sajjate,
na kartā kāraṇānāṃ ca, na kāryāṇām, iti sthitiḥ.
na c' âhaṃkāra|yogena manaḥ prasthāpayet kva cit.
na c' ârtha|grahaṇe yukto, n' âvamānī na c' â|kriyaḥ.

196.20 dhyāna|kriyā|paro, yukto, dhyānavān, dhyāna|niścayaḥ,
dhyāne samādhim utpādya tad api tyajati kramāt.

sa vai tasyām avasthāyāṃ sarva|tyāga|kṛtaḥ sukham:
nir|icchas tyajati prāṇān, brāhmīṃ saṃviśate tanum.
atha vā n' êcchate tatra brahma|kāya|niṣevaṇam,
utkrāmati ca mārga|stho, n' âiva kva cana jāyate.

ātma|buddhyā samāsthāya śāntī|bhūto, nir|āmayaḥ,
a|mṛtaṃ, vi|rajaḥ, śuddham ātmānaṃ pratipadyate.

YUDHIṢṬHIRA uvāca:

197.1 GATĪNĀM UTTAMA|prāptiḥ kathitā jāpakeṣv iha.
ek" âiv' âiṣā gatis teṣām, uta yānty aparām api?

BHĪṢMA uvāca:

śṛṇuṣv' âvahito, rājañ, jāpakānāṃ gatiṃ, vibho,
yathā gacchanti nirayān an|ekān, puruṣa'|rṣabha.

He is free from passion and delusion, and beyond duality: he feels no sorrow, has no attachment and carries out no acts or duties, so we believe. When caught in a state of self-consciousness he should not fix his mind on anything. He should not be given to grasping after sense objects, and should not be contemptuous or inactive.

Intent on the practice of meditation and resolved on 196.20
meditation alone, the disciplined meditator should gradually abandon even the states of concentration he attains in meditation.

In that state of meditation he lets go of everything quite easily: being without desire he relinquishes his breaths and enters into a divine body. Alternatively, if the wayfarer has no such desire to inhabit a divine body, he rises up and is not reborn anywhere.

Once he had accomplished his practice through self-understanding, so becoming peaceful and free from disease, he attains the self, which is immortal, spotless and pure.

YUDHI·SHTHIRA said:

YOU HAVE DESCRIBED how quiet reciters attain the high- 197.1
est of all destinies in this world. But is this the only destiny they achieve, or do they find any other?

BHISHMA said:

Listen attentively, Mighty King, to the destiny that quiet reciters attain, and how they end up in many different sorts of hell, bullish man.

yath"|ôkta|pūrvaṃ pūrvaṃ yo n' ânutiṣṭhati jāpakaḥ,
eka|deśa|kriyaś c' âtra, nirayaṃ sa ca gacchati.
avamānena kurute, na prīyati na hṛṣyati,
īdṛśo jāpako yāti nirayaṃ, n' âtra saṃśayaḥ.
197.5 ahaṃ|kāra|kṛtaś c' âiva sarve niraya|gāminaḥ,
par'|âvamānī puruṣo bhavitā niray'|ôpagaḥ.
abhidhyā|pūrvakaṃ japyaṃ kurute yaś ca mohitaḥ,
yatr' âsya rāgaḥ patati tatra tatr' ôpapadyate.
ath' âiśvarya|pravṛtteṣu jāpakas tatra rajyate,
sa eva nirayas tasya, n' âsau tasmāt pramucyate.
rāgeṇa jāpako japyaṃ kurute tatra mohitaḥ,
yatr' âsya rāgaḥ patati, tatra tatr' ôpapadyate.
dur|buddhir a|kṛta|prajñaś cale manasi tiṣṭhati,
calām eva gatiṃ yāti, nirayaṃ vā niyacchati.
197.10 a|kṛta|prajñako bālo mohaṃ gacchati jāpakaḥ.
sa mohān nirayaṃ yāti, tatra gatv" ânuśocati.
dṛḍha|grāhī «karom'» îti, japyaṃ japati jāpakaḥ,
na sampūrṇo na saṃyukto, nirayaṃ so 'nugacchati.

YUDHIṢṬHIRA uvāca:

a|nivṛttaṃ paraṃ yat tad a|vyaktaṃ brahmaṇi sthitam,
tad|bhūto jāpakaḥ kasmāt sa śarīram ih' āviśet?

The quiet reciter who does not follow the practice in the fashion already outlined, who only follows one aspect of the practice, he goes to hell.

The quiet reciter who acts out of contempt, who finds no joy or rapture in his practice, he undoubtedly goes to hell. All those who act out of self-consciousness go to hell, 197.5
as will the man who holds another person in contempt.

The person who practices quiet recitation and yet is infatuated by an ulterior motive, he will be reborn wherever his passion directs him.

The quiet reciter who is motivated by the rewards of superhuman powers will end up in hell and not be released from it.

The person who practices quiet recitation and yet is infatuated by passion, he will be reborn wherever his passion directs him.

If his mind remains unstable, this stupid dullard attains an unstable destiny or else is bound to hell.

The foolish dullard who practices quiet reciter will be- 197.10
come deluded. Because of his delusion he goes to hell, and once there he will lament.

If the quiet reciter practices quiet recitation based on the rigid notion that he is acting, he will find no completion or inner absorption, and will go to hell.

YUDHI·SHTHIRA said:

If a quiet reciter attains that transcendent, unmanifest state which is rooted in *brahman* and from which there is no return, why does he enter another body in this world?

BHĪṢMA uvāca:
duṣ|prajñānena nirayā bahavaḥ samudāhṛtāḥ.
praśastaṃ jāpakatvaṃ ca, doṣāś c' âite tad|ātmakāḥ.

YUDHIṢṬHIRA uvāca:
198.1 KĪDṚŚAṂ NIRAYAṂ yāti jāpako? varṇayasva me.
kautūhalaṃ hi, rājan, me, tad bhavān vaktum arhati.

BHĪṢMA uvāca:
Dharmasy' âṃśa|prasūto 'si, dharmiṣṭho 'si sva|bhāvataḥ.
dharma|mūl'|āśrayaṃ vākyaṃ śṛṇuṣv' âvahito, 'n|agha.
amūni yāni sthānāni devānāṃ param'|ātmanām,
nānā|saṃsthāna|varṇāni, nānā|rūpa|phalāni ca.
divyāni kāma|cāriṇi vimānāni, sabhās tathā,
ākrīḍā vividhā, rājan, padminyaś c' âiva kāñcanāḥ:
198.5 caturṇāṃ loka|pālānāṃ, Śukrasy', âtha Bṛhaspateḥ
Marutāṃ, Viśvadevānāṃ, Sādhyānām, Aśvinor api,
Rudr'|Āditya|Vasūnāṃ ca, tath" ânyeṣāṃ div'|âukasām.
ete vai nirayās, tāta, sthānasya param'|ātmanaḥ.
a|bhayaṃ c' â|nimittaṃ ca;
na tat kleśa|samāvṛtam.
dvābhyāṃ muktaṃ, tribhir muktam,
aṣṭābhis tribhir eva ca.
catur|lakṣaṇa|varjaṃ tu, catuṣ|kāraṇa|varjitam,
a|praharṣam, an|ānandam, a|śokaṃ, vigata|klamam.
kālaḥ saṃpadyate tatra, kālas tatra na vai prabhuḥ,
sa kālasya prabhū, rājan, svargasy' âpi tath" ēśvaraḥ.
198.10 ātma|kevalatāṃ prāptas tatra gatvā na śocati.

BHISHMA said:

It has been stated that ignorance leads to many sorts of hell. Although the practice of quiet recitation is commended, these are the faults that are found in it.

YUDHI·SHTHIRA said:

198.1
TELL ME, WHAT sort of hell does a quiet reciter end up in? Please explain this curiosity of mine, Your Majesty.

BHISHMA said:

You were born from a portion of the god Dharma, and are naturally righteous in the extreme. Listen attentively, faultless one, to this account on the source of righteousness.

Those abodes of the highest gods are varied in appearance and splendor, and confer different sorts of rewards.

Divine chariots that go where one wants, assembly halls as well as various pleasure gardens and lotus ponds made of
gold, Your Majesty: these are enjoyed by the four protec- 198.5
tors of the world, and by Shukra, Brihas·pati,* the *maruts*, Vishva·devas, Sadhyas, Ashvins, *rudras*, Adítyas, Vasus as well as other divinities. And these are mere hells, my child, in comparison with the condition of the transcendent self.

That condition is free from fear and any characteristic sign; it is not beset by afflictions. It is free from the two, the three, the eight and the three again.* It is devoid of the four characteristics and the four causes, and is beyond rapture, bliss, sorrow and fatigue.

Time dominates there—in the world—but has no power there—the domain of the self—for the self is the master of
time, Your Majesty, and the Lord of heaven too. Once a 198.10
person attains the absolute state of the self and identifies

īdṛśaṃ paramaṃ sthānaṃ, nirayās te ca tādṛśāḥ.
ete te nirayāḥ proktāḥ sarva eva yathā|tatham:
tasya sthāna|varasy' êha sarve niraya|saṃjñitāḥ.

YUDHIṢṬHIRA uvāca:

199.1 KĀLA|MṚTYU|Yamānāṃ te, Ikśvākor brāhmaṇasya ca
vivādo vyāhṛtaḥ pūrvaṃ. tad bhavān vaktum arhati.

BHĪṢMA uvāca:

atr' âpy udāharant' îmam itihāsaṃ purātanam:
Ikṣvākoḥ sūrya|putrasya yad vṛttaṃ brāhmaṇasya ca,
Kālasya Mṛtyoś ca tathā: yad vṛttaṃ tan nibodha me,
yathā† sa teṣāṃ saṃvādo, yasmin sthāne 'pi c' âbhavat.
brāhmaṇo jāpakaḥ kaś cid dharma|vṛtto mahā|yaśāḥ
ṣaḍ|aṅga|vin, mahā|prājñaḥ, Paippalādiḥ sa Kauśikaḥ.
199.5 tasy' â|parokṣaṃ vijñānaṃ ṣaḍ|aṅgeṣu babhūva ha,
Vedeṣu c' âiva niṣṇāto, Himavat|pāda|saṃśrayaḥ.
so 'dyaṃ brāhmaṃ tapas tepe saṃhitāṃ saṃyato japan;
tasya varṣa|sahasraṃ tu niyamena tathā gatam.
sa devyā darśitaḥ sākṣāt, «prīt" âsm'!» îti tadā kila.
japyam āvartayaṃs tūṣṇīṃ, na sa tāṃ kiṃ cid abravīt.

with it, he does not grieve. Such is that transcendent condition: those other states are but hells in comparison.

All these hells have been described to you as they really are: everything in this world is called a hell in comparison to that supreme condition.

YUDHI·SHTHIRA said:

EARLIER ON YOU mentioned a dispute between Time, 199.1
Death, Yama, Ikshváku and a brahmin. Please tell me about that.*

BHISHMA said:

On this subject people relate an ancient tradition: the episode involving Ikshváku,* scion of the Sun, and a brahmin. It also involved Time and Death as well—listen to my account of what happened and the course of their dialogue on that occasion.

There was once a particular brahmin of immense wisdom. He was a descendent of Kúshika* and the son of Pippaláda, a famed practitioner of quiet recitation who was righteous in conduct and a master of the six Vedic disciplines. Living in a shelter at the foot of the Himalayas, he 199.5
was deeply versed in the Vedas—indeed his grasp of the six Vedic disciplines was clear to all.*

He lived a life of self-control, practicing a Vedic form of asceticism and quietly reciting the Veda. A thousand years passed while he was engaged in this religious observance, after which the goddess Sávitri appeared before his eyes. She exclaimed "I am delighted!" but he continued his practice of quiet recitation in silence and did not say anything to her.

tasy' ânukampayā devī prītā samabhavat tadā
veda|mātā, tatas tasya taj japyaṃ samapūjayat.
samāpta|japyas t' ûtthāya śirasā pādayos tathā
papāta devyā dharm'|ātmā, vacanaṃ c' êdam abravīt:
199.10 «diṣṭyā, devi, prasannā tvaṃ, darśanaṃ c' âgatā mama.
yadi c' âpi prasann' âsi, japye me ramatāṃ manaḥ.»

SĀVITRY uvāca:

kiṃ prārthayasi, vipra'|rṣe? kiṃ c' êṣṭaṃ karavāṇi te?
prabrūhi, japatāṃ śreṣṭha, sarvaṃ tat te bhaviṣyati!

BHĪṢMA uvāca:

ity uktaḥ sa tadā devyā
vipraḥ provāca dharma|vit:
«japyaṃ prati mam' êcch" êyaṃ:
vardhatv!» iti punaḥ punaḥ.
«manasaś ca samādhir me vardhet' âhar ahaḥ, śubhe.»
«tat tath"!» êti tato devī madhuraṃ pratyabhāṣata.
idaṃ c' âiv' âparaṃ prāha devī tat|priya|kāmyayā:
«nirayaṃ n' âiva yātā tvaṃ, yatra yātā dvija'|rṣabhāḥ.
199.15 yāsyasi brahmaṇaḥ sthānam a|nimittam a|ninditam.
sādhaye bhavitā c' âitad yat tvay" âham ih' ârthitā.
niyato japa c' âik'|âgro, Dharmas tvāṃ samupaiṣyati;
Kālo, Mṛtyur Yamaś c' âiva samāyāsyanti te 'ntikaṃ.
bhavitā ca vivādo 'tra tava teṣāṃ ca dharmataḥ.»

The goddess Sávitri, mother of the Veda, was overjoyed with the compassion she felt for him, and payed homage to his practice of quiet recitation. Having completed his practice, the righteous brahmin stood up and prostrated himself with his head at the goddess's feet, speaking these words to her:

"It is remarkable, goddess, that you are pleased and have 199.10
come to see me. If you really are pleased with me, let it be that my mind finds pleasure in quiet recitation alone."

SÁVITRI said:

What do you long for, Brahminic seer? What wish can I grant you? Tell me everything you would like, supreme reciter!

BHISHMA said:

Upon being addressed by the goddess, the Brahminic master of religion repeatedly said: "My only wish concerns the practice of quiet recitation: may it increase! Let my mental absorption increase day by day, auspicious one." The goddess replied, in sweet words, "Let it be so!"

But wanting the best for him she granted this wish and others: "You will not go to hell, where even bullish brahmins end up. You will attain the condition of *brahman*, 199.15
which has no characteristic sign and is irreproachable. I will become manifest and do whatever you want, if you need me here. If you practice quiet recitation and remain self-controlled and one-pointed, Dharma will approach you. Time, Death and Yama will also appear at your death. But there will be a dispute in this place between you and them, over righteousness itself."

BHĪṢMA uvāca:

evam uktvā bhagavatī jagāma bhavanaṃ svakam.
brāhmaṇo 'pi japann āste divyaṃ varṣa|śataṃ tathā;
sadā dānto, jita|krodhaḥ, satya|sandho, 'n|asūyakaḥ.
samāpte niyame tasminn atha viprasya dhīmataḥ
sākṣāt prītas tadā Dharmo darśayām āsa taṃ dvijam.

DHARMA uvāca:

199.20 dvi|jāte, paśya māṃ Dharmam!
aham tvāṃ draṣṭum āgataḥ.
japyasy' âsya phalaṃ yat tat
saṃprāptaṃ, tac ca me śṛṇu.
jitā lokās tvayā sarve, ye divyā ye ca mānuṣāḥ;
devānāṃ nilayān, sādho, sarvān utkramya yāsyasi.
prāṇa|tyāgaṃ kuru, mune, gaccha lokān yath"|epsitān,
tyaktv" âtmanaḥ śarīraṃ ca tato lokān avāpsyasi!

BRĀHMAṆA uvāca:

kiṃ nu lokair hi me, Dharma?
gaccha tvaṃ ca yathā|sukham.
bahu|duḥkha|sukhaṃ dehaṃ
n' ôtsṛjeyam ahaṃ, vibho.

DHARMA uvāca:

a|vaśyaṃ, bhoḥ, śarīraṃ te tyaktavyaṃ, muni|puṃgava!
svarga āroha, bho vipra! kiṃ vā vai rocate, 'n|agha?

BHISHMA said:

After speaking this to him the Blessed goddess went off o her own abode. As for the brahmin, he remained seated nd practiced quiet recitation for a hundred celestial years; e remained continually restrained, in control of his anger, ruthful and free from envy. When the wise brahmin had ompleted that religious observance, the god Dharma was vidently delighted and revealed himself to him.

DHARMA said:

O brahmin, look at me—Dharma! I have come to see 199.20
ou. Now hear from me the rewards you have attained
hrough quiet recitation. You have conquered all the worlds,
oth divine and human; you will go up and reach all the
bodes of the gods, holy man. Let go of your life-breath,
ilent sage, and go to the worlds of your desire, for you can
nly attain these worlds when you have given up your body!

THE BRAHMIN said:

What purpose have I with worlds, Dharma? Please leave n your own time. I will not relinquish this body, mighty od, even though it is the cause of much pleasure and pain.

DHARMA said:

It is an inescapable fact, venerable sir, that even a bullish age like you must abandon your body! Go to heaven, venrable brahmin! What else could possibly appeal to you, aultless man?

BRĀHMAṆA uvāca:

199.25 na rocaye svarga|vāsaṃ
vinā deham ahaṃ, vibho.
gaccha, Dharma, na me śraddhā
svargaṃ gantuṃ vin" ātmanā.

DHARMA uvāca:

alaṃ dehe manaḥ kṛtvā! tyaktvā dehaṃ sukhī bhava.
gaccha lokān a|rajaso yatra gatvā na śocasi.

BRĀHMAṆA uvāca:

rame japan, mahā|bhāga. kiṃ nu lokaiḥ sanātanaiḥ?
sa|śarīreṇa gantavyaṃ mayā svargaṃ, na vā, vibho.

DHARMA uvāca:

yadi tvaṃ n' êcchase tyaktuṃ śarīraṃ, paśya vai, dvija:
eṣa Kālas tathā Mṛtyur, Yamaś ca tvām upāgatāḥ!

BHĪṢMA uvāca:

atha Vaivasvataḥ, Kālo, Mṛtyuś ca tritayaṃ, vibho,
brāhmaṇaṃ taṃ mahā|bhāgam upagamy' êdam abruvan.

YAMA uvāca:

199.30 tapaso 'sya su|taptasya tathā su|caritasya ca
phala|prāptis tava śreṣṭhā, Yamo 'haṃ tvām upabruve.

KĀLA uvāca:

yathāvad asya japyasya phalaṃ prāptam an|uttamam:
kālas te svargam āroḍhuṃ. Kālo 'haṃ tvām upāgataḥ!

THE BRAHMIN said:

I am not interested in dwelling in heaven without my body, mighty god. So leave me, Dharma, for I do not have the confidence to go to heaven without my body. 199.25

DHARMA said:

Enough of this concern for the body! Let go of it and attain bliss. Travel to these undefiled worlds where you will be free from sorrow.

THE BRAHMIN said:

I find pleasure in quiet recitation, auspicious god. What is the point in worlds that go on for ever? Let me go to heaven in this body, or else not at all, mighty god.

DHARMA said:

If you do not wish to let go of your body, look yonder, brahmin: here are Time, Death and Yama coming to you!

BHISHMA said:

And then, Mighty King, Yama, Time and Death approached that fortunate brahmin and spoke this to him.

YAMA said:

I am Yama, and I say to you that you have attained a most splendid reward for practicing such vigorous asceticism. 199.30

TIME said:

I am Time, who has come to you! It is only right to attain an incomparable reward for this practice of quiet recitation. Now is the time for you to ascend to heaven.

MṚTYUR uvāca:

Mṛtyuṃ mā viddhi, dharma|jña,
rūpiṇaṃ svayam āgatam.
kālena codito, vipra,
tvām ito netum adya vai.

BRĀHMAṆA uvāca:

svāgataṃ Sūrya|putrāya, Kālāya ca mah"|ātmane,
Mṛtyave c', âtha Dharmāya! kiṃ kāryaṃ karavāṇi vaḥ?

BHĪṢMA uvāca:

arghyaṃ pādyaṃ ca dattvā sa tebhyas, tatra samāgame
abravīt parama|prītaḥ: «sva|śaktyā kiṃ karomi vaḥ?»
199.35 tasminn ev' âtha kāle tu tīrtha|yātrām upāgataḥ
Ikṣvākur agamat tatra, sametā yatra te, vibho.
sarvān eva tu rāja'|rṣiḥ saṃpūjy' âtha praṇamya ca,
kuśala|praśnam akarot sarveṣāṃ rāja|sattamaḥ.
tasmai so 'th' āsanaṃ dattvā,
pādyam arghyaṃ tath" âiva ca,
abravīd brāhmaṇo vākyaṃ,
kṛtvā kuśala|saṃvidam:
«svāgataṃ te mahā|rāja! brūhi yad yad ih' êcchasi.
sva|śaktyā kiṃ karom' îha? tad bhavān prabravītu mām.»

RĀJ" ôvāca:

rāj" āhaṃ, brāhmaṇaś ca tvaṃ yadā ṣaṭ|karma|saṃsthita
dadāni vasu kiṃ cit te: prathitaṃ tad vadasva me.

DEATH said:

O master of righteousness, recognize me as Death, who has come here himself in an embodied form. Time has implored me to lead you away from here right now, brahmin.

THE BRAHMIN said:

Welcome to you, Yama, offspring of the Sun, and also to Time, who is so lofty in spirit, as well as to Death and Dharma! What may I do for you?

BHISHMA said:

The brahmin made the offering of water for guests and gave them water for their feet. Being filled with great joy at that meeting, he asked: "What, within my power, can I do for you?"

At that very moment Ikshváku, on a pilgrimage to a sa- 199.35
cred spot, arrived where the gods had gathered, Mighty King. That royal seer, a most exalted king, bowed down and payed homage to the gods before enquiring about their good health.

The brahmin offered a seat to the king, as well as water for his feet and the offering of water for a guest. He then said this, after enquiring about his good health:

"Welcome to you, great king! Please tell me what you seek here. What, within my power, can I do? Please tell me that."

THE KING said:

Since I am a king and you are a brahmin who observes the six duties of a brahmin,* I will give you some money: tell me what you want.

BRĀHMAṆA uvāca:

199.40 dvi|vidhā brāhmaṇā, rājan,
dharmaś ca dvi|vidhaḥ smṛtaḥ:
pravṛttāś ca nivṛttāś ca.
nivṛtto 'haṃ pratigrahāt.
tebhyaḥ prayaccha dānāni ye pravṛttā, nar'|âdhipa,
ahaṃ na pratigṛhṇāmi. kim iṣṭaṃ? kiṃ dadāmi te?
brūhi tvaṃ, nṛpati|śreṣṭha: tapasā sādhayāmi kim?

RĀJ" ôvāca:

kṣatriyo 'haṃ; na jānāmi «deh'!» îti vacanaṃ kva cit.
«prayaccha yuddham!» ity evaṃ|vādinaḥ smo, dvij'|ôttama.

BRĀHMAṆA uvāca:

tuṣyasi tvaṃ sva|dharmeṇa, tathā tuṣṭā vayaṃ, nṛpa.
anyonyasy' ântaraṃ n' âsti; yad iṣṭaṃ tat samācara.

RĀJ" ôvāca:

«sva|śakty" âhaṃ dadān'» îti tvayā pūrvam udāhṛtam.
yāce tvāṃ, dīyatāṃ mahyaṃ japyasy' âsya phalaṃ, dvija.

BRĀHMAṆA uvāca:

199.45 «yuddhaṃ mama sadā vāṇī yācat'» îti vikatthase,
na ca yuddhaṃ mayā sārdhaṃ kim|arthaṃ yācase punaḥ?

THE BRAHMIN said:

It is held that there are two types of brahmin, O King, as 199.40
well as two sorts of religion: that which is involved in the world and that which is uninvolved. I belong to the latter group: I have ceased accepting gifts. Give gifts to those who are involved in the world, ruler of men, for I do not accept them. What do you desire? And what can I give to you? Speak, exalted King! What can I win for you through my asceticism?

THE KING said:

I am a kshatriya, and do not recollect using the command "give!" on any occasion. We only speak thus when we say "Give us battle!," supreme brahmin.

THE BRAHMIN said:

You find contentment in your own duties, and so do I, Your Majesty. There is no difference between us, so do as you please.

THE KING said:

Earlier on you said that you would give, should it be within your power to do so. So I ask you, brahmin, to give away the valuable reward of your quiet recitation.

THE BRAHMIN said:

You boast that your words only ever request battle, so 199.45
why do you not request battle with me?

RĀJ" ôvāca:

vāg|vajrā brāhmaṇāḥ proktāḥ; kṣatriyā bāhu|jīvinaḥ.
vāg|yuddhaṃ tad idaṃ tīvraṃ mama, vipra, tvayā saha.

BRĀHMAṆA uvāca:

s" âiv' âdy' âpi pratijñā me: «sva|śaktyā kiṃ pradīyatām?»
brūhi, dāsyāmi, rāj'|êndra, vibhave sati. mā ciram!

RĀJ" ôvāca:

yat tad varṣa|śataṃ pūrṇaṃ japyaṃ vai japatā tvayā
phalaṃ prāptaṃ, tat prayaccha mama, ditsur bhavān yadi.

BRĀHMAṆA uvāca:

paramaṃ gṛhyatāṃ tasya phalaṃ, yaj japitaṃ mayā.
ardhaṃ tvam a|vicāreṇa phalaṃ tasya hy avāpnuhi.
199.50 atha vā sarvam ev' êha māmakaṃ jāpakaṃ phalam,
rājan: prāpnuhi kāmaṃ tvaṃ, yadi sarvam ih' êcchasi.

RĀJ" ôvāca:

kṛtaṃ sarveṇa, bhadraṃ te! japyaṃ yad yācitaṃ mayā.
svasti te 'stu, gamiṣyāmi. kiṃ ca tasya phalaṃ? vada.

BRĀHMAṆA uvāca:

phala|prāptiṃ na jānāmi dattaṃ yaj japitaṃ mayā,
ayaṃ Dharmaś ca, Kālaś ca, Yamo, Mṛtyuś ca sākṣiṇaḥ.

THE KING said:

A brahmin's thunderbolt is speech, so it is said; kshatriyas make their living in diverse ways. My battle of speech with you is intense, brahmin.

THE BRAHMIN said:

On this very day I have made a promise: "What, within my power, should I give?" Just say the word and I will give, lord of kings, if I have enough power. Do not delay!

THE KING said:

Give me the reward you have attained by practicing quiet recitation for a total of a hundred celestial years, if you so wish.

THE BRAHMIN said:

Accept the highest reward of my practice of quiet recitation. You must accept half of it without hesitation. Alterna- 199.50
tively, Your Majesty, take the entire fruit of my quiet recitation: receive it willingly, if you want it all.

THE KING said:

Homage to you! I have no need for the entire fruit of the quiet recitation that I have inquired about. May you be prosperous, and I will go. Please tell me, however—what is the reward of this practice?

THE BRAHMIN said:

I do not know the reward on offer, which I have attained through quiet recitation. But Dharma, Time, Yama and Death are witnesses to this.

RĀJ" ôvāca:

a|jñātam asya dharmasya phalaṃ kiṃ me kariṣyati?
phalaṃ bravīṣi dharmasya na cej japya|kṛtasya mām,
prāpnotu tat phalaṃ vipro, n' âham icche sa|saṃśayam.

BRĀHMAṆA uvāca:

n' ādade 'para|vaktavyaṃ: dattaṃ c' âsya phalaṃ mayā.
vākyaṃ pramāṇaṃ, rāja'|rṣe, mam' âdya tava c' âiva hi.
199.55 n' âbhisaṃdhir mayā japye kṛta|pūrvaḥ kadā cana,
japyasya, rāja|śārdūla, kathaṃ vetsyāmy ahaṃ phalam?
«dadasv'» êti tvayā c' ôktaṃ, «dadān'» îti mayā tathā!
na vācaṃ dūṣayiṣyāmi; satyaṃ rakṣa, sthiro bhava.
ath' âivaṃ vadato me 'dya vacanaṃ na kariṣyasi,
mahān a|dharmo bhavitā tava, rājan, mṛṣā|kṛtaḥ.
na yuktaṃ tu mṛṣā|vāṇī tvayā vaktum, ariṃ|dama,
tathā may" âpy abhihitaṃ mithyā kartuṃ na śakyate.
saṃśrutaṃ ca mayā pūrvaṃ, «dadān'!» îty a|vicāritam.
tad gṛhṇīṣv' â|vicāreṇa, yadi satye sthito bhavān.
199.60 ih' āgamya hi māṃ, rājañ, jāpyaṃ phalam ayācathāḥ.
tan me nisṛṣṭaṃ gṛhṇīṣva; bhava satye sthiro 'pi ca!
n' âyaṃ loko 'sti, na paro, na ca pūrvān sa tārayet,
kuta eva janiṣyāṃs tu mṛṣā|vāda|parāyaṇaḥ?
na yajña|phala|dānāni, niyamās tārayanti hi:
yathā satyaṃ pare loke tath" êha, puruṣa'|rṣabha.
tapāṃsi yāni cīrṇāni, cariṣyanti ca yat tapaḥ

THE KING said:

What effect will the unknown reward of this religious practice have on me? If you do not tell me the reward of the merit created through quiet recitation, let a brahmin obtain it, for I do not wish for a dubious reward.

THE BRAHMIN said:

I will not accept anything else that you have to say: I have given you the reward of my practice. Speech is the measure
of both you and I, royal seer, on this very day. I have never 199.55
had any ulterior motive for practicing quiet recitation, so how can I know its reward, tigerish king? You tell me to give and I respond that I will! I will not violate my word, so respect the truth and stand firm.

If you do not act on the words I speak today, great unrighteousness will be yours, Your Majesty, since you act untruthfully. It is not right that you should utter untruths, vanquisher of foes, just as it is not possible that I could falsify what I have said.

Earlier on I did not hesitate to promise: "I will give!" Accept that without vacillation, if you are committed to
truth. You have come here, Your Majesty, and asked me for 199.60
the reward I have gained through quiet recitation. Take that which I have bestowed upon you, and stand firm in the truth!

If a person is addicted to lying, he has neither this world nor the world beyond and does not save his departed ancestors. How will he be able to beget offspring? The rewards of sacrifice, as well as gifts and religious observances do not save a person: truth applies in the world beyond, just

sataiḥ śata|sahasraiś ca, taiḥ satyān na viśiṣyate.

satyam ek'|â|kṣaraṃ brahma, satyam ek'|â|kṣaraṃ tapaḥ,
satyam ek'|â|kṣaro yajñaḥ, satyam ek'|â|kṣaraṃ śrutam.
199.65 satyaṃ vedeṣu jāgarti, phalaṃ satye paraṃ smṛtam.
satyād dharmo damaś c' âiva: sarvaṃ satye pratiṣṭhitam.

satyaṃ vedās tath" âṅgāni; satyaṃ vidyās tathā vidhiḥ,
vrata|caryā tathā satyam, oṃ|kāraḥ satyam eva ca.
prāṇināṃ jananaṃ satyaṃ, satyaṃ saṃtatir eva ca;
satyena vāyur abhyeti, satyena tapate raviḥ.

satyena c' âgnir dahati, svargaḥ satye pratiṣṭhitaḥ.
satyaṃ yajñas, tapo, vedāḥ, stobhā, mantrāḥ, Sarasvatī.
tulām āropito dharmaḥ satyaṃ c' âiv', êti naḥ śrutam.
sama|kakṣāṃ tulayato yataḥ satyaṃ tato 'dhikam.

199.70 yato dharmas tataḥ satyaṃ; sarvaṃ satyena vardhate.
kim|artham an|ṛtaṃ karma kartuṃ, rājaṃs, tvam icchasi?
satye kuru sthiraṃ bhāvaṃ, mā, rājann, an|ṛtaṃ kṛthāḥ.
kasmāt tvam an|ṛtaṃ vākyaṃ «deh'!» îti kuruṣe '|śubham?

as it does in this one, bullish man. The ascetic practices I have undertaken, and the asceticism others will practice for hundreds of years and even hundreds of thousands of years henceforth, are not superior to truth.

Truth is the single, imperishable *brahman*, the single, imperishable asceticism, the single, imperishable sacrifice and the single, imperishable learning. Truth watches over the 199.65
Vedas, and is held to confer a supreme reward. Righteousness and restraint spring from truth: everything is established in truth.

Truth is the Vedas and its auxiliary branches of learning; it is knowledge, religious custom, the practice of religious vows and the sacred syllable "OM." Truth is the begetting of offspring and the continuation of one's lineage; the wind blows and the sun blazes because of truth.

Fire burns because of truth, and even heaven is established in truth. Truth is the sacrifice, asceticism, the Vedas, their chants and the sacred formulae; it is Sarásvati.* We have heard that righteousness and truth were once weighed in the balance. But when the two were balanced against each other, truth was found to be heavier.

When there is righteousness, there is truth; everything 199.70
increases through truth. So why do you wish to commit an untruth, Your Majesty? Stand firm in truth, Your Majesty, and do not commit any untruth. Why did you address me with the untrue and inauspicious word "Give!?"

yadi japya|phalaṃ dattaṃ mayā n' āiṣiṣyase, nṛpa,
dharmebhyaḥ saṃparibhraṣṭo lokān anucariṣyasi.
saṃśrutya yo na ditseta, yācitvā yaś ca n' êcchati:
ubhāv ānṛtikāv etau na mṛṣā kartum arhasi.

RĀJ" ôvāca:

yoddhavyaṃ rakṣitavyaṃ ca: kṣatra|dharmaḥ kila, dvija.
dātāraḥ kṣatriyāḥ proktā, gṛhṇīyāṃ bhavataḥ katham?

BRĀHMAṆA uvāca:

199.75 na cchandayāmi te, rājan, n' âpi te gṛham āvrajam.
ih' āgamya tu yācitvā na gṛhṇīṣe punaḥ katham?

DHARMA uvāca:

a|vivādo 'stu yuvayor: vittaṃ māṃ Dharmam āgatam.
dvijo dāna|phalair yukto, rājā satya|phalena ca.

SVARGA uvāca:

Svargaṃ māṃ viddhi, rāj'|êndra,
rūpiṇaṃ svayam āgatam.
a|vivādo 'stu yuvayor:
ubhau tulya|phalau yuvām.

RĀJ" ôvāca:

kṛtaṃ svargeṇa me kāryaṃ, gaccha, Svarga, yath"|āgatam
vipro yad' îcchate gantuṃ, cīrṇaṃ gṛhṇātu me phalam.

If you will not seek the reward of quiet recitation that I give to you, Your Majesty, you will fall away from righteousness and wander the worlds. A person might not want to give a gift after he has promised it; another person might not want the gift once he has asked for it. You should not mistakenly commit either of these forms of untruth.

THE KING said:

The duty of a kshatriya, O brahmin, is to fight and protect. It is said that kshatriyas are givers, so how could I accept anything from you?

THE BRAHMIN said:

I do not implore you, Your Majesty, nor have I entered 199.75
your home. But since you have come here and requested it, how could you not accept the gift?

DHARMA said:

Let there be no dispute between you two: know that I am Dharma, who has come here. A brahmin is bound to the rewards of giving, whereas a king is bound to the reward of truth.

HEAVEN said:

Know that it is I, Heaven, O Lord of kings, who has come here in an embodied form. Let there be no dispute between you: both of you are equal in terms of reward.

THE KING said:

I am not interested in heaven, so go, Heaven, just as you came! If the brahmin wishes to go to heaven, let him accept the reward I have acquired.

BRĀHMAṆA uvāca:

bālye yadi syād a|jñānān mayā hastaḥ prasāritaḥ,
nivṛtta|lakṣaṇaṃ dharmam upāse saṃhitāṃ japan.
199.80 nivṛttaṃ māṃ cirād, rājan, vipralobhayase katham?
svena kāryaṃ kariṣyāmi; tvatto n' êcche phalaṃ, nṛpa.
tapaḥ|svādhyāya|śīlo 'haṃ, nivṛttaś ca pratigrahāt.

RĀJ" ôvāca:

yadi, vipra, visṛṣṭaṃ te japyasya phalam uttamam,
āvayor yat phalaṃ kiṃ cit, sahitaṃ nau tad astv iha.
dvijāḥ pratigrahe yuktā; dātāro rāja|vaṃśa|jāḥ.
yadi dharmaḥ śruto, vipra, sah' âiva phalam astu nau.
mā vā bhūt saha|bhojyaṃ nau, madīyaṃ phalam āpnuhi!
pratīccha mat|kṛtaṃ dharmaṃ, yadi te mayy anugrahaḥ.

BHĪṢMA uvāca:

tato vikṛta|veṣau dvau puruṣau samupasthitau.
gṛhītv" ânyonyam āveṣṭya, ku|cailāv ūcatur vacaḥ.
199.85 «na me dhārayas'!» îty eko, «dhārayām'!» îti c' âparaḥ.
«ih' âsti nau vivādo 'yam, ayaṃ rāj" ânuśāsakaḥ.»

THE BRAHMIN said:

Although in my childhood I ignorantly stretched forth my hand to receive gifts, the religion I now venerate, as I quietly recite the Veda, is characterized by the cessation of action.

Why do you entice me, Your Majesty, even though I have 199.80
long since ceased to be involved in the world? I will carry out my duties alone; I do not wish to receive a reward from you, my king. I practice asceticism and Vedic recitation, and have ceased accepting gifts.

THE KING said:

O brahmin, if you have relinquished the supreme reward of your quiet recitation, let whatever the reward may be go to the two of us together.

Brahmins are bound to accept gifts, whereas men born in a royal lineage offer gifts. If I have learned the law of righteousness, O brahmin, let us both receive the reward together. Or let us not enjoy it together, and just accept my reward! Take away the merit I have created, if you would do me such a favor.

BHISHMA said:

All of a sudden, two badly clothed men came along. Grappling and wrestling with each other, the two badly dressed men spoke as follows.

One of them said: "You are not indebted to me!" The 199.85
other said: "I am indebted! We are in dispute about this, and here is the king, who governs."

«satyam bravīmy aham idaṃ: na me dhārayate bhavān.»
«an|ṛtaṃ vadas' îha tvam, ṛṇaṃ te dhārayāmy aham.»
tāv ubhau su|bhṛśaṃ taptau rājānam idam ūcatuḥ:
«parīkṣa† tvaṃ, yathā syāvo n' āvām iha vigarhitau.»

VIRŪPA uvāca:

dhārayāmi, nara|vyāghra, Vikṛtasy' êha goḥ phalam.
dadataś ca na gṛhṇāti Vikṛto me, mahī|pate.

VIKṚTA uvāca:

na me dhārayate kiṃ cid Virūpo 'yaṃ, nar'|âdhipa.
mithyā bravīty ayaṃ hi tvāṃ saty'|ābhāsaṃ, nar'|âdhipa.

RĀJ" ôvāca:

199.90 Virūpa, kiṃ dhārayate bhavān asya? bravītu me.
śrutvā tathā kariṣye 'ham, iti me dhīyate manaḥ.

VIRŪPA uvāca:

śṛṇuṣv' âvahito, rājan, yath" âitad dhārayāmy aham
Vikṛtasy' âsya, rāja'|rṣe, nikhilena, nar'|âdhipa.
anena dharma|prāpty|arthaṃ śubhā dattā pur", ân|agha,
dhenur viprāya, rāja'|rṣe, tapaḥ|svādhyāya|śīline.
tasyāś c' âyaṃ mayā, rājan, phalam abhyetya yācitaḥ.
Vikṛtena ca me dattaṃ viśuddhen' ântar|ātmanā.

One said: "I am telling the truth about this: this person is not indebted to me." The other said: "You are lying about this, for I owe you a debt."

Both the men spoke this to the king with much fervor and gusto, saying: "You should examine the matter, so that we will be free from blame."

VIRÚPA said:

I owe the reward of a cow to Víkrita here, tigerish man. But Víkrita will not accept it from me, Lord of the earth, even though I offer it to him.

VÍKRITA said:

This Virúpa owes me nothing, Lord of men. He is speaking falsely to you, ruler of men, but it appears to be true.

THE KING said:

Virúpa, please tell me, what do you owe this man? I have 199.90
made up my mind to act upon your words.

VIRÚPA said:

Listen attentively, Your Majesty, to how I owe a debt to Víkrita here, royal seer. Listen to it in full, ruler of men.

Earlier on, faultless one, in order to attain merit, Víkrita gave an auspicious gift of a milch cow to a brahmin practicing asceticism and Vedic recitation, royal seer. I then approached Víkrita, Your Majesty, and begged him for the reward gained in giving away the cow. Víkrita, acting with the purest of intentions, gave it to me.

tato me su|kṛtaṃ karma kṛtam ātma|viśuddhaye,
gāvau ca kapile krītvā vatsale, bahu|dohane:
199.95 te c' ôñcha|vṛttaye, rājan, mayā samapavarjite
yathā|vidhi, yathā|śraddhaṃ. tad asy' âhaṃ punaḥ prabho
ih' âdy' âiva gṛhītvā tu prayacche dvi|guṇaṃ phalam.
evaṃ syāt, puruṣa|vyāghra, kaḥ śuddhaḥ, ko 'tra doṣavān?
evaṃ vivadamānau svas tvām ih' âbhyāgatau nṛpa.
kuru dharmam a|dharmaṃ vā, vinaye nau samādadha!
yadi n' êcchati me dānaṃ yathā dattam anena vai,
bhavān atra sthiro bhūtvā mārge sthāpayit" âdya nau.

RĀJ" ôvāca:

dīyamānaṃ na gṛhṇāsi ṛṇaṃ kasmāt tvam adya vai?
yath" âiva te 'bhyanujñātaṃ, tathā gṛhṇīṣva mā ciram!

VIKṚTA uvāca:

199.100 dhārayām' îty anen' ôktaṃ, dadān' îti tathā mayā.
n' âyaṃ me dhārayaty adya, gacchatāṃ yatra vāñchati.

RĀJ" ôvāca:

dadato 'sya na gṛhṇāsi, viṣamaṃ pratibhāti me.
daṇḍyo hi tvaṃ mama mato, n' âsty atra khalu saṃśayaḥ.

Then, when I had bought two tawny looking cows, which were fond of their calves and yielded great amounts of milk, I performed a righteous deed in order to purify myself: I 199.95
handed the cows over to a brahmin who was living by gleaning grain, in the proper manner, and in complete faith, Your Majesty. So on this very day I received a reward from him, my Lord, but am offering one back that is twice as great. This is how it should be, tigerish man, so who is pure and who is at fault?

That is how we arrived here before you arguing with each other, Your Majesty. Please enforce right and wrong, and discipline us! If Víkrita does not wish to receive my gift of the merit I received from giving away two cows, just as he gave away his merit earlier on, you must stand firm in this matter and establish us on the true path.*

THE KING said:

Why do you now not accept this debt being repaid by Virúpa? As it has been promised to you, you must accept it without delay!

VÍKRITA said:

This man says that he is in debt but I say that I will give it 199.100
away. He owes me nothing today, and should go off wherever he pleases.

THE KING said:

As you will not accept what this man offers, it seems to me that there is an injustice. In this case, I have no doubt whatsoever that you should be punished.

VIKṚTA uvāca:

may" âsya dattaṃ, rāja'|rṣe, gṛhṇīyāṃ tat kathaṃ punaḥ?
kāmam atr' âparādho me, daṇḍam ājñāpaya, prabho!

VIRŪPA uvāca:

dīyamānaṃ yadi mayā n' êṣiṣyasi kathaṃ cana,
niyaṃsyati tvāṃ nṛ|patir ayaṃ dharm'|ânuśāsakaḥ.

VIKṚTA uvāca:

svaṃ mayā yāciten' êha dattaṃ. katham ih' âdya tat
gṛhṇīyāṃ? gacchatu bhavān, abhyanujñāṃ dadāni te.

BRĀHMAṆA uvāca:

199.105 śrutam etat tvayā, rājann, anayoḥ kathitaṃ dvayoḥ.
pratijñātaṃ mayā yat te, tad gṛhāṇ' â|vicāritam.

RĀJ" ôvāca:

prastutaṃ su|mahat kāryam; anayor gahvaraṃ yathā!
jāpakasya dṛḍhī|kāraḥ. katham etad bhaviṣyati?
yadi tāvan na gṛhṇāmi brāhmaṇen' âpavarjitam,
kathaṃ na lipyeyam ahaṃ pāpeṇa mahat" âdya vai?

BHĪṢMA uvāca:

tau c' ôvāca sa rāja'|rṣiḥ: «kṛta|kāryau gamiṣyathaḥ.
n' êdānīṃ mām ih' āsādya rāja|dharmo bhaven mṛṣā.
sva|dharmaḥ paripālyas tu rājñām, iti viniścayaḥ.
vipra|dharmaś ca gahano mām an|ātmānam āviśat.»

VÍKRITA said:

How can I again accept that which I gave away to him, royal seer? Granted that I am at fault in this case, you should order a beating, my lord!

VIRÚPA said:

If you will in no way accept that which I offer, the king should punish you, since he governs in accordance with righteousness.

VÍKRITA said:

Since it was requested of me, I gave away what I possessed. How, then, can I accept it back on the very same day? You should go, I give you my permission.

THE BRAHMIN said:

Your Majesty, you have heard what these two men have 199.105
had to say. So accept what I have promised you without hesitation.

THE KING said:

The matter that must be resolved is very complex; it is as if these two men find themselves in a deep cave! The Brahminic reciter stands firm. So how will it turn out? If I do not accept what the brahmin has given away, how will I not be tainted by great evil on this very day?

BHISHMA said:

The royal seer then told the two: "You have discharged your duty, so be off. This matter that has now burdened me should not be misconceived as the legal duty of a king. It is generally accepted that kings should uphold their individual duty. But I have encountered the thicket of a brahmin's

BRĀHMAṆA uvāca:

199.110 gṛhāṇa! dhāraye 'haṃ ca, yācitaṃ saṃśrutaṃ mayā.
na ced grahīṣyase, rājañ, śapiṣye tvāṃ, na saṃśayaḥ.

RĀJ" ôvāca:

dhig rāja|dharmaṃ, yasy' âyaṃ kāryasy' êha viniścayaḥ!
ity|arthaṃ me grahītavyaṃ. kathaṃ tulyaṃ bhaved iti?
eṣa pāṇir a|pūrvaṃ me nikṣep'|ârthaṃ prasāritaḥ:
yan me dhārayase, vipra, tad idānīṃ pradīyatām.

BRĀHMAṆA uvāca:

saṃhitāṃ japatā yāvān guṇaḥ kaś cid kṛto mayā,
tat sarvaṃ pratigṛhṇīṣva, yadi kiṃ cid ih' âsti me.

RĀJ" ôvāca:

jalam etan nipatitaṃ mama pāṇau, dvij'|ôttama.
samam astu: sah' âiv' âstu, pratigṛhṇātu vai bhavān.

VIRŪPA uvāca:

199.115 Kāma|Krodhau viddhi nau tvam,
āvābhyāṃ kārito bhavān!
«sah'» êti ca yad uktaṃ te,
samā lokās tav' âsya ca.
n' âyaṃ dhārayate kiṃ cij:
jijñāsā tvat|kṛte kṛtā.
Kālo, Dharmas, tathā Mṛtyuḥ,
Kāma|Krodhau tathā yuvām.

duty, and am drained of inspiration."

THE BRAHMIN said:

Accept it! I am indebted to you, for I promised what you begged from me. If you will not accept my gift, Your Majesty, I will definitely curse you. 199.110

THE KING said:

Woe is the duty of a king, the obligation that always requires a resolution in this world! I ought to accept the brahmin's gift for this sake. But how can there be equality? I have never before stretched out my hand to receive anything: now give me what you owe, brahmin.

THE BRAHMIN said:

While I quietly recited the Veda, I did something meritorious. Should I possess any such thing, accept it all.

THE KING said:

This is like water fallen into my hand, most excellent brahmin. But let there be equality between us: you should accept something from me—let the giving be joint.

VIRÚPA said:

Know us as Desire and Wrath, and it is we who have impelled you to act! Because you said the word "joint," the worlds allotted to both you and him will be equal. He owes you nothing: it has all been a test for your own sake. Time, Dharma and Death, as well as Desire and Anger, have appeared to you two for this reason. 199.115

sarvam anyonya|niṣkarṣe nighṛṣṭaṃ paśyatas tava.
gaccha lokāñ jitān svena karmaṇā, yatra vāñcchasi.

BHĪṢMA uvāca:

jāpakānāṃ phal'|âvāptir mayā te saṃpradarśitā,
gatiḥ, sthānaṃ ca, lokāś ca jāpakena yathā jitāḥ.
prayāti saṃhit'|âdhyāyī brahmāṇaṃ parame|ṣṭhinam,
atha v" âgniṃ samāyāti, sūryam āviśate 'pi vā.
199.120 sa taijasena bhāvena yadi tatra ramaty uta,
guṇāṃs teṣāṃ samādhatte rāgeṇa pratimohitaḥ.
evaṃ some tathā vāyau, bhūmy|ākāśa|śarīra|gaḥ:
sa|rāgas tatra vasati, guṇāṃs teṣāṃ samācaran.
atha tatra virāgī sa, gacchati tv atha saṃśayam.
param a|vyayam icchan sa tam ev' āviśate punaḥ.
amṛtāc c' âmṛtaṃ prāptaḥ,
śāntī|bhūto nir|ātmavān,
brahma|bhūtaḥ sa nir|dvaṃdvaḥ,
sukhī, śānto, nir|āmayaḥ.
brahma|sthānam an|āvartam, ekam a|kṣara|saṃjñakam,
a|duḥkham, a|jaraṃ, śāntaṃ sthānaṃ tat pratipadyate.

Everything you have witnessed has been an examination for the sake of ascertaining you mutually. So go, wherever you please, among the worlds conquered through your own deeds.

BHISHMA said:

I have declared to you the reward attained by quiet reciters, and how the quiet reciter secures a destiny, a station in which to abide and worlds.

The reciter of the Veda attains *brahman*, the supreme condition. Alternatively, he unites with fire or enters the
sun. If he finds pleasure through that lustrous state of be- 199.120
ing, being overcome by joy he develops their qualities.

It is exactly the same with the moon or the wind, or else he attains a body of earth or space—he abides impassioned by these objects, practicing their qualities.

But when he becomes tired of these things, he doubts their worth. Should he desire the supreme, immutable *brahman*, he enters into it once more.

Since he has become immortal, and has become tranquil and bodiless, he reaches the immortal. He becomes *brahman* and passes beyond duality and disease, experiencing bliss and peace.

He attains the condition of *brahman*, from which there is no return. This state is singular and called the "imperishable": it is a peaceful condition free from misery and decrepitude.

199.125 caturbhir lakṣaṇair hīnaṃ, tathā ṣaḍbhiḥ sa|ṣoḍaśaiḥ,
puruṣaṃ tam atikramya ākāśaṃ pratipadyate.
atha n' êcchati rāg'|ātmā, sarvaṃ tad adhitiṣṭhati.
yac ca prārthayate tac ca manasā pratipadyate.
atha vā c' êkṣate lokān sarvān niraya|saṃjñitān.
niḥ|spṛhaḥ† sarvato muktas: tatra vai ramate sukham.
evam eṣā, mahā|rāja, jāpakasya gatir yathā.
etat te sarvam ākhyātaṃ. kiṃ bhūyaḥ śrotum arhasi?

YUDHIṢṬHIRA uvāca:

200.1 KIM UTTARAṂ TADĀ tau sma cakratus tasya bhāṣite,
brāhmaṇo v" âtha vā rājā? tan me brūhi, pitā|maha.
atha vā tau gatau tatra yad etat kīrtitaṃ tvayā.
saṃvādo vā tayoḥ ko 'bhūt? kiṃ vā tau tatra cakratuḥ?

BHĪṢMA uvāca:

«tath"!» êty evaṃ pratiśrutya,
Dharmaṃ saṃpūjya ca, prabho,
Yamaṃ, Kālaṃ ca, Mmṛtyuṃ ca,
Svargaṃ saṃpūjya c' ârhataḥ.
pūrvaṃ ye c' âpare tatra sametā brāhmaṇa'|rṣabhāḥ,
sarvān saṃpūjya śirasā rājānaṃ so 'bravīd dvijaḥ:

Once he attains the cosmic person which is devoid of 199.125
the four characteristics, as well as the six and the sixteen, he enters into space. If he still feels some passion within himself, and does not desire to enter *brahman*, he presides over everything. Whatever he longs for can be attained through thought alone.

Alternatively, he observes the worlds and conceives the idea that they are all hells. Thus he becomes devoid of desire and is released from everything: he stops his pleasure right there.

This, great king, is how the quiet reciter attains his destiny. I have explained all this to you. What else do you wish to hear?

YUDHI·SHTHIRA said:

WHAT DID THE BRAHMIN and the king do after they had 200.1
been addressed by Virúpa? Please tell me that, grandfather.

Perhaps they went to those places just as you explained. But if not, what did they talk about? What did they do next?

BHISHMA said:

The brahmin assented to Virúpa's speech, Mighty King, saying "So be it!" After that he paid homage to Dharma, Yama, Time, Death and Heaven, those venerable beings. Once he had also payed homage to those bullish brahmins gathered in front and behind him by bowing his head, the brahmin spoke this to the king:

200.5 «phalen' ânena saṃyukto, rāja'|rṣe, gaccha mukhyatām!
bhavatā c' âbhyanujñāto japeyaṃ bhūya eva ha.
varaś ca mama pūrvaṃ hi datto devyā, mahā|bala:
‹śraddhā te japato nityaṃ bhavatv!› iti, viśāṃ pate.»

RĀJ" ôvāca:

yady evam a|phalā siddhiḥ śraddhā ca japituṃ tava,
gaccha, vipra, mayā sārdhaṃ: jāpakaṃ phalam āpnuhi!

BRĀHMAṆA uvāca:

kṛtaḥ prayatnaḥ su|mahān sarveṣāṃ saṃnidhāv iha.
saha tulya|phalāv āvāṃ gacchāvo yatra nau gatiḥ.

BHĪṢMA uvāca:

vyavasāyaṃ tayos tatra viditvā tridaś'|ēśvaraḥ,
saha devair upayayau, loka|pālais tath" âiva ca.
200.10 Sādhyāś ca, viśve Maruto, vādyāni su|mahānti ca,
nadyaḥ, śailāḥ, samudrāś ca, tīrthāni vividhāni ca,
tapāṃsi, saṃyoga|vidhir, vedāḥ, stobhāḥ, Sarasvatī,
Nāradaḥ Parvataś c' âiva; Viśvāvasur Hahā huhūḥ,
gandharvaś Citrasenaś ca parivāra|gaṇair yutaḥ,
nāgāḥ, siddhāś ca, munayo, deva|devaḥ Prajāpatiḥ,
Viṣṇuḥ sahasra|śīrṣaś ca devo '|cintyaḥ samāgamat.
avādyant' ântarikṣe ca bheryas tūryāṇi vā, vibho.

"Now that you are endowed with this reward, royal seer, 200.5
you shall become exalted! If you allow it, let me get on with my quiet recitation once again. O Mighty King, Lord of the earth, the goddess granted me a boon earlier on, saying: 'May your faith never fail you, as you practice quiet recitation!'."

THE KING said:

If you still have the faith to practice quiet recitation, despite the futility of the religious accomplishment you achieved thereby, then go with me, brahmin: attain the reward of quiet recitation!

THE BRAHMIN said:

I have made a monumental effort in front of everyone gathered here. So let us go together towards our destiny, partaking of the same reward.

BHISHMA said:

Once the Lord of the thirty gods understood that the two had made up their minds, he approached them accompanied by the gods and the protectors of the world.

There was tremendous music and they were joined by the 200.10
Sadhyas, all the *maruts*, the gods of the rivers, mountains and oceans, and by the gods of the various sacred bathing spots, ascetic practices, the rules of *yoga*, the Vedas and the chants that accompany the Sama Veda. Then there was the goddess Sarásvati, the royal seer Nárada, the seer Párvata, the *gandhárvas* including Vishva·vasu, Haha, Huhu and Chitra·sena with his retinue of servants; the serpent demons, the Siddhas, silent sages and Praja·pati, the god of gods. And finally Vishnu arrived, the thousand headed,

puṣpa|varṣāṇi divyāni tatra teṣāṃ mah"|ātmanām,
nanṛtuś c' âpsaraḥ|saṅghās tatra tatra samantataḥ.

200.15 atha Svargas tathā rūpī
brāhmaṇaṃ vākyam abravīt:
«saṃsiddhas tvaṃ, mahā|bhāgas.
tvaṃ ca siddhas tathā, nṛpa.»

atha tau sahitau, rājann, anyonya|vidhinā tataḥ,
viṣaya|pratisaṃhāram ubhāv eva pracakratuḥ.
prāṇ'|âpānau tath" ôdānaṃ samānaṃ vyānam eva ca,
evaṃ tau manasi sthāpya dadhatuḥ prāṇayor manaḥ.

upasthita|kṛtau tau ca nāsik'|âgram, adho bhruvoḥ,
bhru|kuṭyā c' âiva manasā, śanair dhārayatas tadā.
niśceṣṭābhyāṃ śarīrābhyāṃ, sthira|dṛṣṭī, samāhitau,
jit'|ātmānau tath" ādhāya mūrdhany ātmānam eva ca.

200.20 tālu|deśam ath' ôddālya brāhmaṇasya mah"|ātmanaḥ
jyotir jvālā su|mahatī, jagāma tri|divaṃ tadā.
hāhā|kāras tathā dikṣu sarveṣāṃ su|mahān abhūt;
taj jyotiḥ stūyamānaṃ sma Brahmāṇaṃ prāviśat tadā.

tataḥ «svāgatam» ity āha, tat tejaḥ prapitāmahaḥ
prādeśa|mātraṃ puruṣaṃ pratyudgamya, viśāṃ pate.

inconceivable god. All the while kettle drums and musical instruments resonated throughout the intermediate region, Mighty King.

Heavenly flowers rained down on those divine beings, and throngs of celestial nymphs danced here, there and all around. In the midst of this, Heaven, in his embod- 200.15
ied form, said this to the brahmin: "You are completely accomplished, and possess great fortune. You are also accomplished, Your Majesty."

And then, Your Majesty, in a mutual act the two of them together withdrew their senses from the sense objects, and held the five breaths—the *prana*, *apána*, *udána*, *samána* and *vyana*—in the mind, before fixing the mind on the two vital breaths.

They then focused these two breaths on the tip of the nose and gradually, concentrating with a frown, managed to hold the breaths just below the eyebrows. Being concentrated, with their bodies motionless and gazes fixed, these two men of self-mastery each focused the self in their heads.

And then a tremendous, burning flame split the palate 200.20
of the holy brahmin, and shot up to heaven. All the living beings in the different world regions made the magnificent sound of "Ha ha!" as that flame was praised and entered into the god Brahma.

Brahma—the great grandfather—advanced towards that flame, which was a person as big as the span between the thumb and forefinger, and said "Welcome!" my Lord.

bhūyaś c' âiv' âparaṃ prāha vacanaṃ madhuraṃ tadā:
«jāpakais tulya|phalatā yogānāṃ, n' âtra saṃśayaḥ.
yogasya tāvad etebhyaḥ pratyakṣaṃ phala|darśanam,
jāpakānāṃ viśiṣṭaṃ tu pratyutthānaṃ samāhitam.»
200.25 «uṣyatāṃ mayi!» c' êty uktv" âcetayat satataṃ punaḥ,
ath' āsyaṃ praviveś' âsya brāhmaṇo vigata|jvaraḥ.
rāj" âpy etena vidhinā bhagavantaṃ pitā|maham,
yath" âiva dvija|śārdūlas, tath" âiva prāviśat tadā.
svayaṃ|bhuvam atho devā abhivādya tato 'bruvan:
«jāpakānāṃ viśiṣṭaṃ tu pratyutthānaṃ samāhitam.
jāpak'|ârtham ayaṃ yatno, yad|arthaṃ vayam āgatāḥ.
kṛta|pūjāv imau tulyau tvayā, tulya|phalāv imau.
yoga|jāpakayor dṛṣṭaṃ phalaṃ su|mahad adya vai;
sarvāl̐ lokān atikramya, gacchetāṃ yatra vāñchitam.»

BRAHM" ÔVĀCA:

200.30 mahā|smṛtiṃ paṭhed yas tu,
tath" âiv' ânusmṛtiṃ śubhām,
tāv apy etena vidhinā
gacchetāṃ mat|salokatām.
yaś ca yoge bhaved bhaktaḥ, so 'pi, n' âsty atra saṃśayaḥ,
vidhin" ânena deh'|ânte mama lokān avāpnuyāt.
sādhaye, gamyatāṃ c' âiva yathā|sthānāni siddhaye.

Brahma uttered these sweet words as well: "The practitioners of quiet recitation undoubtedly attain the same reward as yogins. The latter also achieve the fruit of *yoga* that consists in seeing me face to face, but I rise in greeting specifically for the practitioners of quiet recitation."

As soon as Brahma said "Abide in me," he returned to 200.25
his perpetual contemplation, and then the brahmin, being free from all affliction, entered his mouth. The king too, by the same method, found himself in front of the blessed grandfather. And just like the tigerish brahmin, he entered the mouth of Brahma.

Then the gods saluted the self existent Brahma, and spoke this to him: "But you rise in greeting specifically for the practitioners of quiet recitation. The trouble you have gone to on behalf of a quiet reciter is the reason we have come here. You have payed these two equal homage, and they have attained the same reward. On this very day, we have witnessed a tremendous reward for both yogins and quiet reciters: having transcended all the worlds, let them go wherever they like."

BRAHMA said:

Both the person who recites the great tradition of the 200.30
Veda as well as the person who recites auspicious, minor traditions might, through this method, attain a place in my world. The person devoted to *yoga* can also obtain my worlds through this method, undoubtedly, when his body perishes. I command you to go back to your places and carry on with your duties.

BHĪṢMA uvāca:

ity uktvā sa tadā devas tatr' âiv' ântar|adhīyata.
āmantrya ca tato devā yayuḥ svaṃ svaṃ niveśanam.
te ca sarve mah"|ātmāno Dharmaṃ sat|kṛtya tatra vai
pṛṣṭhato 'nuyayū, rājan, sarve su|prīta|cetasaḥ.

etat phalaṃ jāpakānāṃ, gatiś c' âiṣā prakīrtitā
yathā|śrutaṃ, mahā|rāja. kiṃ bhūyaḥ śrotum icchasi?

BHISHMA said:

After that god had spoken, he disappeared on the spot. The gods also bid farewell and returned to their own abodes. Once those divine beings had honored Dharma they followed right behind him, Your Majesty, and were extraordinarily pleased.

I have proclaimed the reward and destiny attained by quiet reciters, as I have heard it, great king. What else would you like to hear?

201–206

THE DIALOGUE BETWEEN MANU AND BRIHAS·PATI

YUDHIṢṬHIRA uvāca:

201.1 KIṂ PHALAṂ JÑĀNA|yogasya,
vedānāṃ niyamasya ca?
bhūt'|ātmā vā kathaṃ jñeyas?
tan me brūhi, pitā|maha.

BHĪṢMA uvāca:

atr' âpy udāharant' îmam itihāsaṃ purātanam:
Manoḥ prajā|pater vādaṃ maha'|rṣeś ca Bṛhaspateḥ.
prajā|patiṃ śreṣṭhatamaṃ prajānāṃ
deva'|rṣi|saṃgha|pravaro maha"|rṣiḥ
Bṛhaspatiḥ praśnam imaṃ purāṇaṃ
papraccha, śiṣyo 'tha guruṃ praṇamya.

yat kāraṇaṃ, yatra vidhiḥ pravṛtto,
jñāne phalaṃ yat pravadanti viprāḥ,
yan mantra|śabdair a|kṛta|prakāśaṃ:
tad ucyatāṃ me, bhagavan, yathāvat.
201.5 sayac c' ârtha|śāstr'|āgama|mantra|vidbhir
yajñair an|ekair, atha go|pradānaiḥ,
phalaṃ mahadbhir yad upāsyate ca—
kiṃ tat? kathaṃ vā bhavitā, kva vā tat?
mahī, mahī|jāḥ, pavano, 'ntarikṣaṃ,
jal'|âukasaś c' âiva, jalaṃ, divaṃ ca,
div'|âukasaś c' âpi yataḥ prasūtās,
tad ucyatāṃ me, bhagavan, purāṇam.

YUDHI·SHTHIRA said:

WHAT REWARD IS yielded by the discipline of gnosis? 201.1
And what about the religious observances of the Vedas? How can the world self be perceived?* Please tell me this, grandfather.

BHISHMA said:

On this subject people relate the ancient tradition of a dialogue between Manu, progenitor of men, and the great seer Brihas·pati.* The great seer Brihas·pati—the most exalted among the congregation of celestial seers—put this ancient question to the most excellent progenitor of all creatures, after bowing to him as a pupil to a teacher.

BRIHAS·PATI said:

The cause of the world, in whom the religious order was set in motion; the reward that brahmins say is to be found in gnosis, and that upon which the sounds of the Vedic invocations shed no light: you should tell me this as it really is, Blessed One.

The reward that the great masters of the "Artha Shastra," 201.5
the Ágamas and Vedic mantras expect to gain through various sacrifices and giving away cows—what is that? How and where will it come about?

Tell me, Blessed One, about that ancient source from which everything is born: the earth and its creatures, the wind, the intermediate region, the water and its creatures, as well as heaven and the gods that dwell there.

jñānaṃ yataḥ prārthayate naro vai,
tatas tad|arthā bhavati pravṛttiḥ.
na c' âpy ahaṃ veda paraṃ purāṇaṃ,
mithyā|pravṛttiṃ ca kathaṃ nu kuryām?
ṛk|sāma|saṃghāṃś ca, yajūṃṣi c' âpi,
cchandāṃsi, nakṣatra|gatiṃ, niruktam
adhītya ca vyākaraṇaṃ sa|kalpaṃ,
śikṣāṃ ca, bhūta|prakṛtiṃ na vedmi.
sa me bhavāñ śaṃsatu sarvam etat,
sāmānya|śabdaiś ca viśeṣaṇaiś ca.
sa me bhavāñ śaṃsatu tāvad etaj:
jñāne phalaṃ karmaṇi vā yad asti,
201.10 yathā ca dehāc cyavate śarīrī,
punaḥ śarīraṃ ca yath" âbhyupaiti.

MANUR uvāca:

yad yat priyaṃ yasya, sukhaṃ tad āhus;
tad eva duḥkhaṃ pravadanty an|iṣṭam.
«iṣṭaṃ ca me syād, itarac ca na syād,»
etat|kṛte karma|vidhiḥ pravṛttaḥ.
«iṣṭaṃ tv an|iṣṭaṃ ca na māṃ bhajet'» êty
etat|kṛte jñāna|vidhiḥ pravṛttaḥ.
kām'|ātmakāś chandasi karma|yogā,
ebhir vimuktaḥ param aśnuvīta.
nānā|vidhe karma|pathe sukh'|ârthī
naraḥ pravṛtto na paraṃ† prayāti.

When a man longs for gnosis, his endeavors are motivated by that. But since I do not know that ancient, transcendent source, how can I ensure that my endeavors are not in vain? Although I have learned the collection of Rig and Sama hymns, the Yajus formulas, as well as the meters, astronomy, etymology, grammar, the sacrifice and the science of Vedic pronunciation, I do not know the origin of beings.

You should explain all this to me, in both general and specific terms. First of all, however, you should explain this: the reward gained through gnosis and that gained through action, and how the soul falls away from the body and reen- 201.10
ters another one.

MANU said:

They say that whatever pleases a person constitutes bliss, whereas that which is unwanted constitutes misery.

"May I have what I desire, but nothing other than this." Thinking in this way, a person follows the way of action. "May both the desirable and undesirable not come to me." Thinking in this way, however, a person follows the way of gnosis.

Those who are consumed by desire are bound to the rituals enjoined by the Veda, but when a person is released from these desires he attains the transcendent. The man who desires worldly bliss and follows the variegated path of action does not attain the transcendent.

BṚHASPATIR uvāca:

iṣṭaṃ tv an|iṣṭaṃ ca, sukh'|âsukhe ca
s'|āśīs tv avacchandati karmabhiś ca.

MANUR uvāca:

«ebhir vimuktaḥ param āviveśa,»
etat|kṛte '|karma|vidhiḥ pravṛttaḥ;
kām'|ātmakāṃś chandati karma|yoga,
ebhir vimuktaḥ param ādadīta.
ātm"|ādibhiḥ karmabhir idhyamāno,
dharme pravṛtto, dyutimān, sukh'|ârthī.
paraṃ hi tat karma|pathād apetaṃ
nir|āśiṣaṃ brahma|paraṃ hy avaiti.
201.15 prajāḥ sṛṣṭā manasā karmaṇā ca:
dvāv ev' âitau sat|pathau loka|juṣṭau.
dṛṣṭaṃ karma śāśvataṃ c' ântavac ca,
manas|tyāgaḥ kāraṇaṃ—n' ânyad asti.
sven' âtmanā cakṣur iva praṇetā,
niś"|âtyaye tamasā saṃvṛt'|ātmā.
jñānaṃ tu vijñāna|guṇena yuktaṃ,
karm' â|śubhaṃ paśyati varjanīyam.
sarpān, kuś'|âgrāṇi, tath" ôdapānaṃ
jñātvā manuṣyāḥ parivarjayanti;
a|jñānatas tatra patanti ke cij.
jñāne phalaṃ paśya yathā viśiṣṭam!

BRIHAS·PATI said:

A person full of desire fills himself with that which he desires and that which he does not, as well as pleasure and pain, through his acts.

MANU said:

"Freed from these, that person entered the transcendent." Thinking in this way, a person follows the way of inaction. The person attached to action finds pleasure in objects of desire, but once freed from these he perceives the transcendent.*

Illumined by practices concerning the self, in the course of following the religious life he becomes lustrous and pursues bliss. He attains the transcendent state of *brahman*, which is devoid of desire and beyond the path of action.

Offspring are created by means of the mind and ac- 201.15
tion: these are the two good paths that are practiced in the world. But when a person sees that *karma* is both continual and finite, mental renunciation must be his course of action—there is no other way.

When a person is shrouded in the darkness of dawn, it is as if his faculty of vision leads him by means of its own essence. In a similar way, when one's consciousness is endowed with the quality of perception it sees impure acts that ought to be avoided.

Upon becoming aware of snakes, wells and the sharp tips of *kusha* grass, men avoid them; it is only because of ignorance that some stumble upon them. Understand that this reward is specific to knowledge!

kṛtsnas tu mantro vidhivat prayukto,
yajñā yath"|ôktās tv iha dakṣiṇāś ca,
anna|pradānaṃ, manasaḥ samādhiḥ:
pañc'|ātmakaṃ karma|phalaṃ vadanti.
guṇ'|ātmakaṃ karma vadanti vedās,
tasmān mantro, mantra|pūrvaṃ hi karma.
«vidhir vidheyaṃ» manas" ôpapattiḥ,
phalasya bhoktā tu tathā śarīrī.
201.20 śabdāś ca, rūpāṇi, rasāś ca puṇyāḥ,
sparśāś ca, gandhāś ca śubhās tath" âiva,
naro na saṃsthāna|gataḥ prabhuḥ syād.
etat phalaṃ sidhyati karma|loke.
yad yac charīreṇa karoti karma,
śarīra|yuktaḥ samupāśnute tat,
śarīram ev' âyatanaṃ sukhasya,
duḥkhasya c' âpy āyatanaṃ śarīram.
vācā tu yat karma karoti kiṃ cid,
vāc" âiva sarvaṃ samupāśnute tat,
manas tu yat karma karoti kiṃ cin,
manaḥ|stha ev' âyam upāśnute tat.
yathā yathā karma|guṇaṃ phal'|ârthī
karoty ayaṃ karma|phale niviṣṭaḥ,
tathā tath" âyaṃ guṇa|saṃprayuktaḥ
śubh'|âśubhaṃ karma|phalaṃ bhunakti.
matsyo yathā srota iv' âbhipātī,
tathā kṛtaṃ pūrvam upaiti karma.
śubhe tv asau tuṣyati, duṣ|kṛte tu
na tuṣyate vai paramaḥ śarīrī.

They say the reward of action is fivefold: a person harnesses the entire Veda, according to the rule, as well as the sacrifices, as they are described, along with their fees, gifts of food, and concentration of the mind.

The Vedas state that ritual action is made up of subordinate parts—the Vedic incantations, for example, for ritual action is preceded by a Vedic incantation. Accomplishment comes through the thought "I, the religious agent, should perform the ritual," and so a person enjoys the rewards of his ritual deeds.

A man lacking in beauty might attain mastery over pleasurable sounds, visible forms and tastes, as well as pleasurable physical sensations and smells. This reward is accomplished in the realm of action. 201.20

A person experiences the results of his *karma* in the same body in which he commits it, for the body is the seat of both happiness and suffering.* In the same way, a person experiences in his speech and mind all the *karma* that he commits by means of his speech and mind respectively.

The person who desires rewards and is obsessed with the rewards of action acts on the sense objects. And so this person, by clinging on to sense objects, experiences the good and bad results of his action.

The *karma* committed in the past approaches its agent just like a fish rushes downstream. Hence the supreme soul experiences pleasure because of its good deeds, but experiences no pleasure because of its bad ones.

201.25 yato jagat sarvam idaṃ prasūtaṃ,
jñātv" ātmavanto vyatiyānti yat tat.
yan mantra|śabdair a|kṛta|prakāśaṃ,
tad ucyamānaṃ śṛṇu me, paraṃ yat.
rasair vimuktaṃ vividhaiś ca gandhair,
a|śabdam, a|sparśam, a|rūpavac ca,
a|grāhyam, a|vyaktam, a|varṇam, ekaṃ
pañca|prakārān sasṛje prajānām.
na strī, pumān, n' âpi na|puṃsakaṃ ca,
na san, na c' â|sat, sad|a|sac ca tan na,
paśyanti yad brahma|vido manuṣyās,
tad a|kṣaraṃ na kṣarat', îti viddhi.

MANUR uvāca:

202.1 A|KṢARĀT KHAṂ, tato vāyus, tato jyotis, tato jalam,
jalāt prasūtā jagatī. jagatyāṃ jāyate jagat.
etaiḥ śarīrair jalam eva gatvā;
jalāc ca tejaḥ, pavano, 'ntarikṣam.
khād vai nivartanti na bhāvinas te,
mokṣaṃ ca te vai param āpnuvanti.
n' ôṣṇaṃ, na śītaṃ, mṛdu, n' âpi tīkṣṇaṃ,
n' âmlaṃ, kaṣāyaṃ, madhuraṃ, na tiktam,
na śabdavan, n' âpi ca gandhavat tan,
na rūpavat tat parama|svabhāvam.
sparśaṃ tanur veda, rasaṃ ca jihvā,
ghrāṇaṃ ca gandhāñ, śravaṇau ca śabdān,
rūpāṇi cakṣur, na ca tat|paraṃ yad
gṛhṇanty an|adhyātma|vido manuṣyāḥ

Listen now as I describe that upon which the Vedic invocations shed no light—the supreme source from which the entire world was created. When self-controlled men know this, they transcend all things! 201.25

It is free from tastes and various sorts of smell, and devoid of sound, touch and visible form. Ungraspable, unmanifest, without any color and singular, it created the five classes of creatures.

The Vedic masters see that, which is not female, male, or neuter; it is neither existent nor non-existent, nor even existent and non-existent. Know it as the imperishable—that which does not fade away.

MANU said:

SPACE AROSE FROM the imperishable, from space came wind, from wind came fire, from fire came water, and from water the earth was created. Living creatures were born on the earth. 202.1

Men can go as far as water in their bodies; from water they go to fire, then wind, then space. The able do not return from space, but attain the transcendent state of liberation.

The ultimate, self-existent state is neither hot nor cold, neither soft nor sharp, neither sour nor astringent, neither sweet nor bitter. It has no sound, smell or visible form.

The body perceives touch, the tongue perceives taste, the nose perceives smell, the ears perceive sounds and the eye perceives visible forms, but those who do not know the supreme self cannot grasp that which is beyond these.

202.5 nivartayitvā rasanāṃ rasebhyo,
ghrāṇaṃ ca gandhāc, chravaṇau ca śabdāt,
sparśāt tvacaṃ, rūpa|guṇāt tu cakṣus,
tataḥ paraṃ paśyati svaṃ sva|bhāvam.
yato gṛhītvā hi karoti yac ca,
yasmiṃś ca tām ārabhate pravṛttim.
yasmiṃś ca, yad, yena ca, yaś ca kartā,
yat kāraṇaṃ: te samudāyam āhuḥ.
yad v" âpy abhūd† vyāpakaṃ sādhakaṃ ca,
yan mantravat sthāsyati c' âpi loke,
yaḥ sarva|hetuḥ param'|ârtha|kārī,†
tat kāraṇaṃ; kāryam ato yad anyat.
yathā hi kaś cit su|kṛtair manuṣyaḥ
śubh'|âśubhaṃ prāpnute 'th' â|virodhāt,
evaṃ śarīreṣu śubh'|âśubheṣu
sva|karma|jair jñānam idaṃ nibaddham.
yathā pradīptaḥ purataḥ pradīpaḥ
prakāśam anyasya karoti dīpyan,
tath" êha pañc'|êndriya|dīpa|vṛkṣā
jñāna|pradīptāḥ paravanta eva.
202.10 yathā ca rājñā bahavo hy amātyāḥ
pṛthak pramāṇaṃ pravadanti yuktāḥ,
tadvac charīreṣu bhavanti pañca.
jñān'|âika|deśaḥ paramaḥ sa tebhyaḥ.
yath" ârciṣo 'gneḥ, pavanasya vego,
marīcayo 'rkasya, nadīṣu c' āpaḥ
gacchanti c' âyānti ca saṃcarantyas,
tadvac charīrāṇi śarīriṇāṃ tu.
yathā ca kaś cit paraśuṃ gṛhītvā
dhūmaṃ na paśyej jvalanaṃ ca kāṣṭhe,

Turning the tongue back from tastes, the nose from 202.5
smells, the ears from sounds, the skin from physical contact and the eye from the various sorts of visible form, a person perceives the transcendent—his own inherent state.

When a man perceives something he performs an act and begins to exert himself for it. The object on which he acts, as well the act he performs, the means of action, the agent of action and his motive: these they call the totality.

According to the Vedas, that omnipresent and efficacious thing became manifest and will endure in the world. It is the ultimate cause—the cause of all things, and that which effects the highest goal. Everything else is just an effect.

A certain man will obtain good and bad results through his good deeds, without these obstructing each other. In the same way, consciousness is bound to handsome and ugly bodies because of the results of a person's *karma*.

Just as a lamp lit in front casts light on other things as it burns, so does a body when lit by consciousness become aware of other things through the light of the five senses.

Just as the many ministers a king employs give him ad- 202.10
vice separately, so too do the five forms of consciousness function within the body. But the self, the single source of consciousness, is beyond them.

The flames of a fire, the flight of the wind, the rays of the sun and the currents within rivers come and go, passing from one state to another. It is exactly the same for the bodies of embodied souls.

Just as a person would not be able to see smoke or a flame in a log by simply picking up an axe, so people do not see

tadvac charīr'|ôdara|pāṇi|pādaṃ
chittvā na paśyanti tato yad anyat.
tāny eva kāṣṭhāni yathā vimathya
dhūmaṃ ca paśyej jvalanaṃ ca yogāt.
tadvat sa|buddhiḥ samam indriy'|ātmā
budhaḥ† paraṃ paśyati taṃ sva|bhāvam.
yath" ātmano 'ṅgaṃ patitaṃ pṛthivyāṃ
svapn'|ântare paśyati c' ātmano 'nyat,
śrotr'|ādi|yuktaḥ sa|manāḥ† sa|buddhir†
liṅgāt tathā gacchati liṅgam anyat.
202.15 utpatti|vṛddhi|vyaya|saṃnipātair
na yujyate 'sau paramaḥ śarīrī.
anena liṅgena tu liṅgam anyad
gacchaty a|dṛṣṭaḥ phala|saṃniyogāt.
na cakṣuṣā paśyati rūpam ātmano;
na c' âpi saṃsparśam upaiti kiṃ cit.
na c' âpi taiḥ sādhayate tu kāryaṃ:
te taṃ na paśyanti, sa paśyate tān.
yathā samīpe jvalato 'nalasya
saṃtāpa|jaṃ rūpam upaiti kaś cit,
na c' âparaṃ rūpa|guṇaṃ bibharti.
tath" âiva tad dṛśyati rūpam asya.
tathā manuṣyaḥ parimucya kāyam
a|dṛśyam anyad viśate śarīram:
visṛjya bhūteṣu mahatsu dehaṃ,
tad|āśrayaṃ c' âiva bibharti rūpam.

what is beyond the body by cutting open its stomach, hands and feet.

When a person exerts himself and churns those logs he sees smoke and fire. In the same way a wise, an intelligent person of inner power perceives the unchanging, transcendent, self-existent state.

When dreaming a person can see his own body lying down on the ground, as something different from himself. In the same way, a person moves from one body to another in possession of all the sense faculties, such as hearing, as well as his mind and faculty of intelligence.

The supreme soul is dissociated from birth, growth, de- 202.15
cay and death. Because it is imbued with the rewards of its former deeds while in possession of "this" body, the invisible soul moves to another body.

One cannot see the visible form of the self with the eye: it cannot be sensed in any way. One does not accomplish one's religious goal through the sense faculties: they do not see the self, but it sees them.

Something might acquire a visible appearance on account of the heat of a flame burning nearby, but otherwise does not have any other appearance. The visible appearance of the self is apprehended in a similar manner.

Therefore a man abandons one body and enters a different, invisible one: he casts of his body into the great elements and bears a new form supported by them.

khaṃ, vāyum, agniṃ, salilaṃ, tath" ôrvīṃ
samantato 'bhyāviśate śarīrī.
nān"|āśrayāḥ karmasu vartamānāḥ
śrotr'|ādayaḥ pañca guṇāñ śrayante.
202.20 śrotraṃ khato, ghrāṇam atho pṛthivyās,
tejo|mayaṃ rūpam atho vipākaḥ.
jal'|āśrayaṃ teja uktaṃ, rasaṃ ca;
vāyv|ātmakaḥ sparśa|kṛto guṇaś ca.
mahatsu bhūteṣu vasanti pañca,
pañc'|êndriy'|ârthāś ca tath" êndriyeṣu.
sarvāṇi c' âitāni mano|'nugāni,
buddhiṃ mano 'nveti, matiḥ sva|bhāvam.
śubh'|âśubhaṃ karma kṛtaṃ, yad anyat,
tad eva pratyādadate sva|dehe.
mano 'nuvartanti par'|âvarāṇi,
jal'|âukasaḥ srota iv' ânukūlam.
calaṃ yathā dṛṣṭi|pathaṃ paraiti,
sūkṣmaṃ mahad rūpam iv' âbhibhāti,
sva|rūpam ālocayate ca rūpaṃ,
paraṃ tathā buddhi|pathaṃ paraiti.

MANUR uvāca:

203.1 YAD INDRIYAIS T' ûpahitaṃ, purastāt
prāptān guṇān saṃsmarate cirāya.
teṣv indriyeṣ' ûpahateṣu paścāt,
sa buddhi|rūpaḥ paramaḥ sva|bhāvaḥ.

The soul penetrates space, wind, fire, water and earth right through when it enters a body. When they are engaged in cognitive activities, the different senses have different physical loci and rest on the five sense objects.

The auditory faculty arises from space, the olfactory faculty arises from earth; visible form is a derivative that consists of fire. Fire is said to rest on water, as well as taste; the perceptible quality of touch is, essentially, wind. 202.20

The five sense faculties abide in the five great elements, and the five sense objects abide in the sense faculties. All of these are led by the mind, but the mind follows the faculty of intelligence, which in turn follows the self-existent one.

A person receives all the *karma* he commits in his own body, be it good, bad or neutral. A person's lofty and mean deeds follow the mind, just like aquatic creatures follow the water's current.

Just as a moving object comes into the field of one's vision, or a small object appears large, or one's own form is reflected in a mirror as a visible object, so too does the transcendent self come into the view of one's intelligence.

MANU said:

WHEN THE MIND is connected to the sense faculties, it 203.1
is able, for an extended period of time, to recall sense objects that it encountered earlier on. If, afterwards, the sense faculties are in any way hindered, the supreme, self-existent soul assumes the form of the faculty of intelligence.

yath" êndriy'|ârthān yugapat samantān
n' ôpekṣate kṛtsnam, a|tulya|kālam,
tathā calaṃ saṃcarate sa vidvāṃs.
tasmāt sa ekaḥ paramaḥ śarīrī.
rajas, tamaḥ, sattvam atho tṛtīyaṃ
gacchaty asau sthāna|guṇān virūpān.
tath" êndriyāṇy āviśate śarīrī,
hut'|âśanaṃ vāyur iv' êndhana|stham.
na cakṣuṣā paśyati rūpam ātmano,
na paśyati sparśanam indriy'|êndriyam.
na śrotra|liṅgaṃ, śravaṇe na darśanaṃ:
tathā kṛtaṃ paśyati, tad vinaśyati.

203.5 śrotr'|ādīni na paśyanti svaṃ svam ātmānam ātmanā.
sarva|jñaḥ sarva|darśī ca, sarva|jñas tāni paśyati.
yathā Himavataḥ pārśvaṃ, pṛṣṭhaṃ candramaso yathā,
na dṛṣṭa|pūrvaṃ manu|jair, na ca tan n' âsti tāvatā.
tadvad bhūteṣu bhūt'|ātmā sūkṣmo, jñān'|ātmavān asau
a|dṛṣṭa|pūrvaś cakṣurbhyāṃ, na c' âsau n' âsti tāvatā.
paśyann api yathā lakṣma, jagat some na vindati.
evam asti na c' ôtpannaṃ, na ca tan na parāyaṇam.

When different sense objects arise simultaneously all around him, a conscious person does not perceive them as a whole but only in succession: he encounters a changing world. Therefore a person's supreme soul must be singular.

The soul experiences passion, darkness and purity—the third—in the forms of the various objects of existence. Thus the soul enters into the sense faculties, just like wind enters into the fire that lies dormant in its kindling sticks.

One cannot perceive the visible form of the eye by means of the eye, one cannot perceive the faculty of touch or any other sense faculty.* The soul is not an object of hearing, and cannot be perceived through Vedic learning: it perceives acts of cognition, but they disappear.

The different sense faculties such as hearing cannot per- 203.5
ceive their own essence by themselves. But the soul is all-knowing and all-seeing; because it is all-knowing, it perceives the sense faculties.

Although men have never perceived the northern slopes of the Himalayas or the dark side of the moon, it does not mean that they do not exist. In the same way, although the subtle, individual self* that abides within living beings—the essence of which is consciousness—has never been perceived by the eyes, this does not mean that it does not exist.

A person can see the marks in the moon without perceiving the hare they resemble.* In the same way, the soul exists without appearing, and yet it is not as if it is not a person's ultimate purpose.

rūpavantam a|rūpatvād uday'|âstamane budhāḥ
dhiyā samanupaśyanti, tad|gatāḥ savitur gatim.

203.10 tathā buddhi|pradīpena dūra|sthaṃ su|vipaścitaḥ
pratyāsannaṃ ninīṣanti jñeyaṃ jñān'|âbhisaṃhitam.

na hi khalv an|upāyena kaś cid artho 'bhisidhyati:
sūtra|jālair yathā matsyān badhnanti jala|jīvinaḥ,
mṛgair mṛgāṇāṃ grahaṇaṃ, pakṣiṇāṃ pakṣibhir yathā,
gajānāṃ ca gajair. evaṃ† jñeyaṃ jñānena gṛhyate.

«ahir eva hy aheḥ pādān paśyat'» îti hi naḥ śrutam.
tadvan mūrtiṣu mūrti|sthaṃ jñeyaṃ jñānena paśyati.

n' ôtsahante yathā vettum indriyair indriyāṇy api,
tath" âiv' êha parā buddhiḥ paraṃ bodhyaṃ na paśyati.

203.15 yathā candro hy amāvāsyām a|liṅgatvān na dṛśyate,
na ca nāśo 'sya bhavati, tathā viddhi śarīriṇam.

kṣīṇa|kośo hy amāvāsyāṃ candramā na prakāśate.
tadvan mūrti|vimukto 'sau śarīrī n' ôpalabhyate.

When they reflect on the matter, wise men can perceive an embodied thing in terms of the formlessness inherent in that which rises and disappears. With that in mind, they understand the movement of the world-creator.

In the same way, with the light of their intelligence in- 203.10
spired men investigate objects of cognition upon which their consciousness focuses, both those in the distance and those nearby.

No purpose is accomplished without a method: fishermen catch fish with nets made of yarn, deer are trapped by means of decoy deer, birds are trapped by means of decoy birds and elephants are trapped by means of decoy elephants. In just the same way, objects of cognition are grasped by consciousness itself.

We have heard that only a snake can perceive its own tracks. In the same way, one perceives the embodied soul dwelling within embodied beings by means of consciousness.

People are incapable of apprehending the sense faculties by means of the sense faculties, just as the highest state of intelligence cannot perceive the highest object of understanding: the soul.

The new moon cannot be seen because it lacks a charac- 203.15
teristic sign, but it does not fail to exist. You should understand the embodied soul in just the same way.

When its cover has disappeared the new moon does not shine forth, just as the soul cannot be perceived when it is released from the body.

yathā kāś'|ântaraṃ prāpya candramā bhrājate punaḥ,
tadval liṅg'|ântaraṃ prāpya śarīrī bhrājate punaḥ.
janma, vṛddhiḥ, kṣayaś c' âsya pratyakṣeṇ' ôpalabhyate,
sā tu cāndramasī vṛttir, na tu tasya śarīriṇaḥ.
utpatti|vṛddhi|vyayato† yathā sa iti gṛhyate
candra eva tv amāvāsyāṃ, tathā bhavati mūrtimān.
203.20 n' ôpasarpad vimuñcad vā śaśinaṃ dṛśyate tamaḥ:
visṛjaṃś c' ôpasarpaṃś ca. tadvat paśya śarīriṇam.
yathā candr'|ârka|saṃyuktaṃ tamas tad upalabhyate,
tadvac charīra|saṃyuktaḥ śarīr" îty upalabhyate.
yathā candr'|ârka|nirmuktaḥ sa Rāhur n' ôpalabhyate,
tadvac charīra|nirmuktaḥ śarīrī n' ôpalabhyate.
yathā candro hy amāvāsyāṃ nakṣatrair yujyate gataḥ,
tadvac charīra|nirmuktaḥ phalair yujyati karmaṇaḥ.

MANUR uvāca:

204.1 YATHĀ VYAKTAM IDAṂ śete, svapne carati cetanam,
jñānam indriya|saṃyuktaṃ tadvat pretya bhav'|âbhavau.

The moon shines forth once more when it arrives at a different phase in its cycle of appearance, just as the soul become visible again when it enters a new body.

The moon's origin, waxing and waning are clearly perceived, but this is the cycle of the moon and not that of the soul.

The moon, when it begins a new cycle, is apprehended through its appearance, waxing and waning. The same is true of the embodied soul.

Darkness is not seen to creep up on the moon and then 203.20
release it: it is the moon itself that relinquishes the darkness and creeps forward. You should understand the manifestation of the embodied soul in just the same way.

Darkness can only be perceived in conjunction with the moon or sun. In the same way, the soul can only be perceived when connected to a body.

The soul is not perceived when it is released from the body, just as Rahu* is not perceived when released from contact with the moon or sun.

When there is a new moon it moves in conjunction with the constellations, just as the soul is governed by the rewards of its *karma* when released from the body.

MANU said:

A PERSON'S AWARENESS wanders about in a dream when 204.1
the body lies asleep, just as his consciousness—in conjunction with the sense faculties—wanders between the existent and non-existent when he dies.

yath" âmbhasi prasanne tu rūpaṃ paśyati cakṣuṣā,
tadvat prasann'|êndriyatvāj jñeyaṃ jñānena paśyati.
sa eva lulite tasmin yathā rūpaṃ na paśyati,
tath" êndriy'|ākulībhāve jñeyaṃ jñāne na paśyati.
a|buddhir a|jñāna|kṛtā, a|buddhyā kṛṣyate manaḥ.
duṣṭasya manasaḥ pañca saṃpraduṣyanti mānasāḥ.
204.5 a|jñāna|tṛpto viṣayeṣv avagāḍho na tṛpyate.
a|dṛṣṭavac ca bhūt'|ātmā viṣayebhyo nivartate.
tarṣa|cchedo na bhavati puruṣasy' êha kalmaṣāt:
nivartate tadā tarṣaḥ, pāpam anta|gataṃ yadā.
viṣayeṣu tu saṃsargāc, chāśvatasya tu saṃśrayāt,
manasā c' ânyath" ākāṅkṣan, paraṃ na pratipadyate.
jñānam utpadyate puṃsāṃ kṣayāt pāpasya karmaṇaḥ:
yath" ādarśa|tale prakhye paśyaty ātmānam ātmani.
prasṛtair indriyair duḥkhī, tair eva niyataiḥ sukhī.
tasmād indriya|rūpebhyo yacched ātmānam ātmanā.

When one's form is reflected in still water it can be seen through the faculty of vision. In the same way, one can perceive the soul by means of consciousness when the sense faculties are still.

But one cannot see one's form reflected in water when it is disturbed, just as one cannot perceive the soul in consciousness when the sense faculties are agitated.

A lack of intelligence is caused by a lack of consciousness, and the mind is dragged away by a lack of intelligence. In turn, the five forms of the mind—the five sense faculties—are defiled when the mind has become corrupt.

Not satisfied by consciousness itself, a person finds no 204.5
satisfaction by immersing himself in sense objects. It is because of its unseen *karma* that the individual self* returns to the sense objects.

In this world a person does not destroy his thirst through sin: only when he has done away with his evil *karma* does it cease.

Devoted to the eternal and yet attached to sense objects, a person does not attain the transcendent despite hoping to bring about this change.*

Men attain gnosis when their evil *karma* fades away: a person sees the self within as if in the clear surface of a mirror.

One experiences suffering when one's sense faculties are unleashed, but experiences bliss when they are controlled. Therefore one should restrain the self from the different sense objects by means of the self.

204.10 indriyebhyo manaḥ pūrvaṃ, buddhiḥ paratarā tataḥ.
buddheḥ parataraṃ jñānaṃ, jñānāt parataraṃ mahat.

a|vyaktāt prasṛtaṃ jñānaṃ, tato buddhis, tato manaḥ.
manaḥ śrotr'|ādibhir yuktaṃ śabd'|ādīn sādhu paśyati.

yas tāṃs tyajati śabd'|ādīn, sarvāś ca vyaktayas tathā,
vimuñcet prākṛtān grāmāṃs, tān muktv" â|mṛtam aśnute.

udyan hi savitā yadvat sṛjate raśmi|maṇḍalam,
sa ev' âstam apāgacchaṃs tad ev' ātmani yacchati.
antar'|ātmā tathā deham āviśy' êndriya|raśmibhiḥ,
prāpy' êndriya|guṇān pañca, so 'stam āvṛtya gacchati.

204.15 praṇītaṃ karmaṇā mārgaṃ
nīyamānaḥ punaḥ punaḥ
prāpnoty ayaṃ karma|phalaṃ,
pravṛttaṃ dharmam āptavān.

viṣayā vinivartante nir|āhārasya dehinaḥ,
rasa|varjaṃ; raso 'py asya paraṃ dṛṣṭvā nivartate.

buddhiḥ karma|guṇair hīnā yadā manasi vartate,
tadā saṃpadyate brahma tatr' âiva pralayaṃ gatam.
a|sparśanam, a|śṛṇvānam, an|āsvādam, a|darśanam,
a|ghrāṇam, a|vitarkaṃ ca sattvaṃ praviśate param.

manasy ākṛtayo magnā, manas tv abhigataṃ matim,
matis tv abhigatā jñānaṃ, jñānaṃ tv abhigataṃ param.

The mind comes before the sense faculties, intelligence is 204.10
beyond the mind, consciousness is beyond intelligence and the absolute is beyond consciousness.

Consciousness springs from the unmanifest and is followed by the faculty of intelligence and then the mind. The mind, in conjunction with the different sense faculties, is able to perceive sense objects.

Whoever abandons sense objects such as sound—and so all manifest forms—should let go of all the entire set of material objects, for once he does this he attains the immortal.

The sun shoots out its orb of rays when it rises, and then draws them back into itself when it sets. In the same way the inner self, once settled in the body, reaches out to the five sense objects through the rays of the sense faculties, before turning back and settling.

A person is repeatedly led along a path created by his own 204.15
karma. He reaps the retribution of his *karma*, and obtains the merit that he activated earlier.

Although objects disappear when the embodied soul is deprived of sustenance, desire does not disappear. But that also ceases when one sees the transcendent.*

When the faculty of intelligence abides in the mind and is deprived of the objects of sense activity, a person attains *brahman*, right there, in its devolved state. He enters the transcendent essence that is beyond touch, sound, taste, vision, smell and thought.

Sense objects are encompassed in the mind, the mind inclines towards intelligence, intelligence inclines towards consciousness and consciousness inclines towards the transcendent.

204.20 indriyair manasaḥ siddhir, na buddhiṃ budhyate mana
na buddhir budhyate '|vyaktaṃ, sūkṣmaṃ tv etāni paśyati

MANUR uvāca:

205.1 DUḤKH'|ÔPAGHĀTE śārīre mānase c' âpy upasthite,
yasmin na sakyate kartuṃ, yatnas taṃ n' ânucintayet.
bhaiṣajyam etad duḥkhasya yad etan n' ânucintayet,
cintyamānaṃ hi c' âbhyeti, bhūyaś c' âpi pravartate.
prajñayā mānasaṃ duḥkhaṃ
hanyāc, chārīram auṣadhaiḥ.
etad vijñāna|sāmarthyaṃ
na bālaiḥ samatām iyāt.
a|nityaṃ yauvanaṃ, rūpaṃ, jīvitaṃ, dravya|sañcayaḥ,
ārogyaṃ, priya|saṃvāso—gṛdhyet tatra na paṇḍitaḥ.
205.5 na jānapadikaṃ duḥkham ekaḥ śocitum arhati.
a|śocan pratikurvīta, yadi paśyed upakramam.
sukhād bahutaraṃ duḥkhaṃ jīvite, n' âsti saṃśayaḥ.
snigdhasya c' êndriy'|ârtheṣu mohān, maraṇam a|priyam.
parityajati yo duḥkhaṃ sukhaṃ c' âpy† ubhayaṃ naraḥ,
abhyeti brahma so 'tyantaṃ; na te śocanti paṇḍitāḥ.

The mind accomplishes its purposes through the sense faculties, but it cannot perceive the intelligence. The intelligence, in turn, cannot perceive the unmanifest, the subtle essence that perceives all these things. 204.20

MANU said:

WHEN THE AFFLICTION of physical or mental suffering 205.1
draws near, one should not dwell on the matter if one cannot do anything about it. The remedy for suffering is that one should not think about it, for suffering approaches the person who contemplates it and then prevails upon him to a greater degree.

One should dispel mental suffering through wisdom, and physical suffering through herbal remedies. This capacity to understand suffering should not be identified with the understanding of fools.

A wise man should not hanker after youth, physical appearance, lifespan, the accumulation of wealth, good health and companionship with his loved ones, for they are impermanent.

An individual should not grieve over the suffering of the 205.5
people. He should cure this suffering without grieving, if he sees a way of doing so.

There is no doubt that the suffering a person encounters throughout his life is greater than his happiness. Death is unwelcome to this person, who deludedly clings to the objects of the senses. But the man who lets go of both pleasure and pain attains the absolute state of *brahman*; those wise men do not grieve.

duḥkham arthā hi yujyante; pālane na ca te sukham.
duḥkhena c' âdhigamyante, nāśam eṣāṃ na cintayet.

jñānaṃ jñey'|âbhinirvṛttaṃ viddhi, jñāna|guṇaṃ manaḥ
prajñā|karaṇa|saṃyuktaṃ, tato buddhiḥ pravartate.

205.10 yad" â|karma|guṇ'|ôpetā buddhir manasi vartate,
tadā prajñāyate brahma dhyāna|yoga|samādhinā.

s" êyaṃ guṇavatī buddhir guṇeṣv ev' âbhivartate,
aparād abhiniḥsṛtya, gireḥ śṛṅgād iv' ôdakam.

yadā nir|guṇam āpnoti dhyānaṃ manasi pūrva|jam,
tadā prajñāyate brahma, nikaṣaṃ nikaṣe yathā.

manas tv apahṛtaṃ pūrvam indriy'|ârtha|nidarśakam,
na samakṣa|guṇ'|âpekṣi nir|guṇasya nidarśanam.

sarvāṇy etāni saṃvārya dvārāṇi manasi sthitaḥ,
manasy ek'|âgratāṃ kṛtvā tat paraṃ pratipadyate.

205.15 yathā mahānti bhūtāni nivartante guṇa|kṣaye,
tath" êndriyāṇy upādāya buddhir manasi vartate.

Material objects bestow suffering on a man—protecting hem will not bring you happiness. A person should not ontemplate the destruction of those things he pains himelf to attain.

Know that consciousness arises from the self, and that he mind is an evolvent of consciousness. When the mind is ngaged in the pursuit of wisdom, the faculty of intelligence ecomes active.

When the intelligence abides in the mind and is deprived 205.10
of the objects of sense activity, then *brahman* in realized, hrough a concentration engendered by the discipline of neditation.*

When the faculty of intelligence makes contact with the ense objects its activity is restricted to them, just like water treaming down from a particular mountain peak.

But when a person attains a mental state of meditation hat is devoid of objects, then *brahman* is realized, like a treak of gold on a touchstone.

When the mind is snatched away in an early stage of neditation, so that it perceives sense objects, since it oberves perceptible objects there is no perception of that vhich is beyond them.

When a person closes all his sense doors and rests in he mind, because he has made the mind one-pointed he eaches the transcendent.

The great elements vanish when material objects are dis- 205.15
olved, just as the faculty of intelligence takes hold of the ense faculties and abides within the mind.

yadā manasi sā buddhir vartate 'ntara|cāriṇī,
vyavasāya|guṇ'|ôpetā tadā saṃpadyate manaḥ.
guṇavadbhir guṇ'|ôpetaṃ yadā dhyāna|guṇaṃ manaḥ,
tadā sarvān guṇān hitvā nir|guṇaṃ pratipadyate.
a|vyaktasy' êha vijñāne n' âsti tulyaṃ nidarśanam.
yatra n' âsti pada|nyāsaḥ, kas taṃ viṣayam āpnuyāt?
tapasā c' ânumānena, guṇair, jātyā, śrutena ca
ninīṣet paramaṃ brahma, viśuddhen' ântar|ātmanā.
205.20 guṇa|hīno hi taṃ mārgaṃ bahiḥ samanuvartate.
guṇ'|âbhāvāt—prakṛtyā vā—nis|tarkyaṃ jñeya|saṃmitam.
nairguṇyād brahma c' āpnoti, sa|guṇatvān nivartate.
guṇa|pracāriṇī buddhir, hut'|âśana iv' êndhane.
yathā pañca vimuktāni indriyāṇi sva|karmabhiḥ,
tathā tat paramaṃ brahma vimuktaṃ prakṛteḥ param.
evaṃ prakṛtitaḥ sarve pravartante śarīriṇaḥ.
nivartante nivṛttau ca, sargaṃ n' âiv' ôpayānti ca.†

When the faculty of intelligence moves within and abides in the mind, since it is endowed with the quality of meditative resolve the mind becomes accomplished.

When the mind comes to be endowed with virtue—through the help of the virtuous—and possesses the quality of meditation, it abandons all sense objects and attains that which is beyond them

No perception in the world is equal to the realization of the unmanifest. Who could attain that sphere where there is no track?

One should investigate the supreme state of *brahman* with a pure heart, by means of asceticism, contemplation, moral virtues, one's true nature and sacred knowledge.

The person devoid of the prerequisite moral virtues moves 205.20
outside that path. Because it lacks all qualities—or else by its very nature—that which is reckoned as the self is beyond imagination.

One attains *brahman* when freed from sense objects, but returns to existence if attached to them. The faculty of intelligence clings to sense objects like a fire burning in its kindling sticks.

Like the five sense faculties when they are released from their own cognitive activity, the supreme *brahman* is released and transcends primordial matter.*

All embodied beings are therefore impelled into existence from primordial matter. But in a phase of cosmic dissolution they turn back and do not undergo creation.

puruṣaḥ, prakṛtir, buddhir, viśayāś c', êndriyāṇi ca,
ahaṃ|kāro, 'bhimānaś ca saṃbhūto bhūta|saṃjñakaḥ.

205.25 etasy' ādyā pravṛttis tu pradhānāt saṃpravartate;
dvitīyā mithuna|vyaktim a|viśeṣān niyacchati.

dharmād utkṛṣyate śreyas, tath" â|śreyo 'py a|dharmataḥ.
rāgavān prakṛtiṃ hy eti, virakto jñānavān bhavet.

MANUR uvāca:

206.1 YADĀ TAIḤ PAÑCABHIḤ pañca yuktāni manasā saha,
atha tad drakṣyase brahma, maṇau sūtram iv' ârpitam.

tad eva ca yathā sūtraṃ suvarṇe vartate punaḥ,
muktāsv, atha pravāleṣu, mṛn|maye, rājate tathā,
tadvad go|'śva manuṣyeṣu, tadvadd hasti|mṛg'|ādiṣu,
tadvat kīṭa|pataṃgeṣu prasakt' ātmā sva|karmabhiḥ.

yena yena śarīreṇa yad yat karma karoty ayam,
tena tena śarīreṇa tat tat phalam upāśnute.

206.5 yathā hy eka|rasā bhūmir oṣadhy|arth'|ânusāriṇī,
tathā karm'|ânugā buddhir antar|ātm'|ânudarśinī.

jñāna|pūrvā bhavel lipsā, lipsā|pūrv" âbhisaṃdhitā,
abhisaṃdhi|pūrvakaṃ karma; karma|mūlaṃ tataḥ phalam.*

The combination of spirit, primordial matter, the faculty of intelligence, sense objects, sense faculties, self-consciousness and conceit is called a human being.

The first phase of cosmic creation proceeds from unman- 205.25
ifest matter; the second phase controls the manifestation of complementary pairs from that homogeneous state.

Good fortune derives from righteousness, ill fortune is the result of evil. An impassioned person gets involved with primordial matter, but the dispassionate one attains gnosis.

MANU said:

WHEN THE FIVE sense faculties are united with the mind 206.1
and held back from the five sense objects, then you will perceive *brahman*, like a string threaded through a jewel.

Just as that same string may be threaded through gold, so it can also be threaded though pearls, pieces of coral, clay and silver. In the same way the self is bound to cows, horses, humans, elephants, deer, worms and birds, because of its *karma*.

A person experiences the retribution of his *karma* in the very same body in which he performs it.*

The earth has a single flavor which penetrates the sub- 206.5
stance of plants. The faculty of intelligence conforms to one's *karma* in the same way: its state of perception corresponds to one's inner state.

Consciousness precedes desire, desire precedes intention and intention precedes action; retribution is rooted in action.

phalaṃ karm'|ātmakaṃ vidyāt,
karma jñey'|ātmakaṃ tathā,
jñeyaṃ jñān'|ātmakaṃ vidyāj,
jñānaṃ sad|asad|ātmakam.

jñānānāṃ ca, phalānāṃ ca, jñeyānāṃ, karmaṇāṃ tathā
kṣay'|ânte yat phalaṃ vidyā, jñānaṃ jñeya|pratiṣṭhitam.

mahadd hi paramaṃ bhūtaṃ yat prapaśyanti yoginaḥ.
a|budhās taṃ na paśyanti hy ātma|sthaṃ guṇa|buddhayaḥ.

206.10 pṛthivī|rūpato rūpam apām iha mahattaram,
adbhyo mahattaraṃ tejas, tejasaḥ pavano mahān.
pavanāc ca mahad vyoma, tasmāt parataraṃ manaḥ,
manaso mahatī buddhir, buddheḥ kālo mahān smṛtaḥ.

kālāt sa bhagavān Viṣṇur, yasya sarvam idaṃ jagat,
n' ādir na madhyaṃ n' âiv' ântas tasya devasya vidyate.
an|āditvād, a|madhyatvād, an|antatvāc ca so '|vyayaḥ.
atyeti sarva|duḥkhāni, duḥkhaṃ hy antavad ucyate.

tad brahma paramaṃ proktaṃ,
tad dhāma paramaṃ padam.
tad gatvā kāla|viṣayād
vimuktā mokṣam āśritāḥ.

206.15 guṇeṣv ete prakāśante, nirguṇatvāt tataḥ param.
nivṛtti|lakṣaṇo dharmas tath" ānantyāya kalpate.

Know that action is the essence of retribution, a perceptible object is the essence of action, consciousness is the essence of a perceptible object, and that which is both existent and non-existent is the essence of consciousness.

Know that the reward gained when all states of consciousness, karmic retribution, perceptible objects and *karma* have faded away is a gnosis firmly established in the self.

The practitioners of *yoga* perceive that supreme, absolute being. Ignorant men do not perceive that which abides in the individual self, for their faculties of intelligence incline towards sense objects.

The form of water is greater than the form of earth, fire 206.10
is greater than water and wind is greater than fire. Space is greater than wind, the mind is beyond space, the faculty of intelligence is beyond the mind and time is held to be greater than that.

The blessed lord Vishnu is greater than time. The entire world abides in him, the god who has no beginning, middle or end. Because he lacks a beginning, middle and end he is immutable. He transcends all sufferings, for suffering is said to be finite.*

That is said to be the supreme *brahman*, the highest state or abode. Upon reaching it people are released from the sphere of time and abide in a state of deliverance.

These people become manifest in the world of objects, 206.15
although *brahman*, because he is devoid of objects, is therefore transcendent. The religion characterized by inaction thus leads to infinity.

Ṛco, Yajūṃṣi, Sāmāni śarīrāṇi vyapāśritāḥ,
jihv"|âgreṣu pravartante, yatna|sādhyā vināśinaḥ.
na c' âivam iṣyate brahma,
śarīr'|āśraya|saṃbhavam.
na yatna|sādhyaṃ tad brahma,
n' ādi|madhyaṃ na c' ântavat.
ṛcām ādis, tathā sāmnāṃ, yajuṣām ādir ucyate.
antaś c' ādimatāṃ dṛṣṭo, na tv ādir brahmaṇaḥ smṛtaḥ.
an|āditvād, an|antatvāt, tad an|antam ath' â|vyayam.
a|vyayatvāc ca nir|duḥkhaṃ; dvaṃdv'|âbhāvāt tataḥ param.
206.20 a|dṛṣṭato '|nupāyāc ca, pratisandheś ca karmaṇaḥ,
na tena martyāḥ paśyanti yena gacchanti tat param.
viṣayeṣu ca saṃsargāc, chāśvatasya ca darśanāt,
manasā c' ânyad ākāṅkṣan, paraṃ na pratipadyate.
guṇān yad iha paśyanti tad icchanty apare janāḥ.
paraṃ n' âiv' âbhikāṅkṣanti nirguṇatvād guṇ'|ârthinaḥ.
guṇair yas tv avarair yuktaḥ, kathaṃ vidyāt parān guṇān?
anumānādd hi gantavyaṃ guṇair avayavaiḥ param.
sūkṣmeṇa manasā vidmo, vācā vaktuṃ na śaknumaḥ.
mano hi manasā grāhyaṃ, darśanena ca darśanam.

The Rig, Yajur and Sama Vedas depend upon the bodies of people. They are produced at the tip of the tongue, and since they are formed by effort they are perishable.

But *brahman* cannot be sought that way, since he is the source and support of the body. That *brahman* cannot be won through effort, for it is without beginning, middle and end.

The Rig, Yajur and Sama Vedas are said to have a beginning. What has a beginning is seen to have an end, but *brahman* is not held to have a beginning.

Because it has no beginning or end, it is infinite and immutable. Because it is immutable it is devoid of suffering; because it is free from duality it is transcendent.

Since it is unseen, lacks an approach and resists action, 206.20
mortals do not see the way in which they attain that transcendent state.

Contemplating the eternal and yet attached to sense objects, a person does not attain the transcendent despite hoping for that otherness.*

Some people desire the sense objects that they see here. But those who covet sense objects do not desire the supreme state, because it is beyond all objects.

How can somebody who is attached to inferior objects know the higher ones? That which is beyond all individual objects can only be attained through contemplation.

We know that with a subtle mind, but cannot describe it in words. What is mental can only be grasped by the mind, and what is visual can only be grasped through vision.

206.25 jñānena nirmalī|kṛtya buddhiṃ, buddhyā manas tathā,
manasā c' êndriya|grāmam, a|kṣaraṃ pratipadyate.
buddhi|prahīṇo manasā samṛddho
nir|āśiṣaṃ nir|guṇam abhyupaiti.
paraṃ tyajant' îha vilobhyamānā
hut'|âśanaṃ vāyur iv' êndhana|stham.
guṇ'|ādāne viprayoge ca teṣāṃ,
manaḥ sadā buddhi|par'|âvarābhyām.
anen' âiva vidhinā saṃpravṛtto
guṇ'|âpāye brahma|śarīram eti.
a|vyakt'|ātmā puruṣo '|vyakta|karmā
so '|vyaktatvaṃ gacchati hy anta|kāle.
tair ev' âyaṃ c' êndriyair vardhamānair
glāyadbhir vā vartate karma|rūpaḥ.
sarvair ayaṃ c' êndriyaiḥ saṃprayukto
dehaḥ prāptaḥ, pañca|bhūt'|āśrayaḥ syāt.
n' â|sāmarthyād gacchati karmaṇ" êha,
hīnas tena paramеṇ' â|vyayena.
206.30 pṛthvyā naraḥ paśyati n' ântam asyā hy,
antaś c' âsyā bhavitā c', êti viddhi.
paraṃ nayant' îha vilobhyamānaṃ
yathā plavaṃ vāyur iv' ârṇava|stham.
divā|karo guṇam upalabhya nir|guṇo
yathā bhaved apagata|raśmi|maṇḍalaḥ,
tathā hy asau munir iha nirviśeṣavān
sa nir|guṇaṃ praviśati brahma c' â|vyayam.

By making the faculty of intelligence spotless through 206.25
consciousness, the mind spotless through the intelligence, and the senses spotless through the mind, a person attains the imperishable.

Abandoning the faculty of intelligence, the person of mental accomplishment approaches that which is beyond desire and devoid of sense objects. But those who are led astray by the world forsake the transcendent, like wind abandoning the fire that abides in its kindling sticks.

In grasping after objects or separation from them, the mind is always connected to high and low states of intelligence. With this rule in mind, the person who sets out to retreat from the sense objects enters the body of *brahman*.

The person whose self and deeds are unmanifest attains the unmanifest state at the time of death. But with his sense faculties increasing or decreasing in activity, a person exists in a state of action.

When the body is endowed with all the sense faculties it depends on the five elements. That person moves in accordance with his deeds in the world, not because he is incapable, but because he is bereft of the supreme, immutable *brahman*.

A man cannot foresee the end of this earth, but you 206.30
should know that it will indeed end. A man's deeds lead him to the transcendent, even though he is led astray by the world, just as the wind carries a boat in rough seas to shore.

The sun reaches out to objects but is deprived of them when its orb of rays disappear. In the same way a silent sage of this world enters the objectless, immutable *brahman* when he frees himself from all discrimination.

an|āgataṃ su|kṛtavatāṃ parāṃ gatiṃ
svayaṃ|bhuvaṃ prabhava|nidhānam a|vyayam
sanātanaṃ yad a|mṛtam a|vyayaṃ dhruvaṃ
nicāyya, tat param amṛtatvam aśnute.

When one reflects upon and then perceives the transcendent future destiny of the virtuous—that immutable, self-existent source and end of everything, which is everlasting, immortal, undecaying and intransient—then one attains the transcendent state of immortality.

207

A DISCOURSE ON THE ORIGIN OF GODS AND MEN

YUDHIṢṬHIRA uvāca:

207.1 PITĀ|MAHA MAHĀ|prājña,
puṇḍarīk'|âkṣam, a|cyutam,
kartāram a|kṛtaṃ, Viṣṇuṃ,
bhūtānāṃ prabhav'|âpyayam,
Nārāyaṇaṃ, Hṛṣīkeśaṃ, Govindam, a|parājitam,
tattvena, Bharata|śreṣṭha, śrotum icchāmi Keśavam.

BHĪṢMA uvāca:

śruto 'yam artho Rāmasya Jāmadagnyasya jalpataḥ,
Nāradasya ca deva'|rṣeḥ, Kṛṣṇadvaipāyanasya ca.
Asito Devalas, tāta, Vālmīkiś ca mahā|tapāḥ,
Mārkaṇḍeyaś ca Govinde kathayanty adbhutaṃ mahat.
207.5 Keśavo, Bharata|śreṣṭha, bhagavān īśvaraḥ prabhuḥ.
puruṣaḥ «sarvam» ity eva śrūyate, bahudhā vibhuḥ.
kiṃ tu yāni vidur loke brāhmaṇāḥ śārṅga|dhanvani
mahātmani, mahā|bāho, śṛṇu tāni, Yudhiṣṭhira.
yāni c' āhur, manuṣy'|êndra, ye purāṇa|vido janāḥ
karmāṇi tv iha Govinde, kīrtayiṣyāmi tāny aham.
mahā|bhūtāni bhūt'|ātmā mah"|ātmā puruṣ'|ôttamaḥ,
vāyur, jyotis, tathā c' āpaḥ, khaṃ ca, gāṃ c' ânvakalpayat.
sa sṛṣṭvā pṛthivīṃ c' âiva sarva|bhūt'|êśvaraḥ prabhuḥ,
apsv eva bhavanaṃ cakre mah"|ātmā puruṣ'|ôttamaḥ.
207.10 sarva|tejo|mayas tasmiñ śayānaḥ puruṣ'|ôttamaḥ,
so 'gra|jaṃ sarva|bhūtānāṃ Saṃkarṣaṇam akalpayat,
āśrayaṃ sarva|bhūtānāṃ manas", êti ha śuśruma.
sa dhārayati bhūtāni ubhe bhūta|bhaviṣyatī.

YUDHI·SHTHIRA said:

WISE GRANDFATHER, I would like to hear the truth about Vishnu, the lotus-eyed, unshakable one, the uncreated creator who is the origin and dissolution of all beings. That unconquered one is also known as Naráyana, Hrishi·kesha, Govínda, and Késhava, splendid Bhárata. 207.1

BHISHMA said:

I heard about this matter when Rama, the son of Jamad·agni, was talking about it; I also heard about it from the celestial seer Nárada, and Krishna Dvaipáyana. Ásita Dévala, the great ascetic Valmíki and Markandéya also narrate the great wonder of Govínda, my son.*

Késhava, splendid Bharata, is the blessed Lord and mas- 207.5
ter, the cosmic person known as "the whole." He is powerful in manifold ways.

Now learn about the exploits of great bow-wielding deity in this world, mighty-armed Yudhi·shthira, about which the brahmins are well-versed. I will proclaim the worldly acts of Govínda, Lord of men, that have been passed down by those who know the legends.

The world self*—the cosmic, supreme spirit—created the five elements of wind, fire, water, space and earth in succession. Once he had created the earth, the lord and master of all creatures—that cosmic, supreme spirit—fashioned an abode for himself in the waters.

The supreme spirit consists of nothing but radiance. As 207.10
he reclined there, in his abode, by means of his mind he emanated Bala·deva,* the first born of all livings beings and their refuge, so we have heard. Bala·deva supports all crea-

tatas tasmin mahā|bāho† prādur|bhūte mah"|ātmani,
bhāskara|pratimaṃ divyaṃ nābhyāṃ padmam ajāyata.
sa tatra bhagavān devaḥ puṣkare, bhrājayan diśaḥ,
Brahmā samabhavat, tāta, sarva|bhūta|pitā|mahaḥ.

tasminn api, mahā|bāho,† prādur|bhūte mah"|ātmani
tamasā pūrva|jo jajñe Madhur nāma mah"|âsuraḥ.
207.15 tam ugram ugra|karmāṇam ugraṃ karma samāsthitam,
brahmaṇ" ôpacitiṃ kurvañ jaghāna puruṣ'|ôttamaḥ.
tasya, tāta, vadhāt, sarve deva|dānava|mānavāḥ
Madhu|sūdanam ity āhur ṛṣabhaṃ sarva|Sātvatām.

Brahm" ânusasṛje putrān mānasān Dakṣa|saptamān:
Marīcim, Atry|Aṅgirasau,† Pulastyaṃ, Pulahaṃ, Kratum.
Marīciḥ Kaśyapaṃ, tāta, putram agra|jam agra|jaḥ
mānasaṃ janayām āsa taijasaṃ, brahmavittamam.

aṅguṣṭhāt sasṛje brahmā Marīcer api pūrva|jam,
so 'bhavad, Bharata|śreṣṭha, Dakṣo nāma prajā|patiḥ.
207.20 tasya pūrvam ajāyanta daśa tisraś ca, Bhārata,
prajā|pater duhitaras. tāsāṃ jyeṣṭh" âbhavad Ditiḥ.
sarva|dharma|viśeṣa|jñaḥ, puṇya|kīrtir, mahā|yaśāḥ
Mārīcaḥ Kaśyapas, tāta, sarvāsām abhavat patiḥ.

tures, both those in existence as well as those coming into existence.

After the manifestation of that cosmic being, mighty-armed one, a divine lotus as radiant as the sun emerged from within Vishnu's navel. And in that lotus the blessed god Brahma was born, lighting up space in all directions. He is the grandfather of all living beings, my son.*

After the manifestation of that cosmic being, mighty-armed one, a great demon called Madhu was the first creature to be born from the primeval darkness. But Vishnu, 207.15
the supreme being, strengthened himself with divine power and killed that terrifying demon, the one devoted to terrifying practices, whose deeds were terrifying. Because he had slain that demon, my son, all the gods, *dánava*s and men called him Madhu·súdana,* the bull of all the Satvats.

Then Brahma created seven sons, one after the other, from his mind. Daksha was one of these seven—the others were Maríchi, Atri, Ángiras, Pulástya, Púlaha and Kratu. Maríchi, who was born in the beginning, my son, first engendered his son Káshyapa, who was mind-born and lustrous, a supreme knower of *brahman*.

Brahma also created a son from his thumb even before Maríchi, splendid Bhárata. This was the patriarch called
Daksha. In the beginning thirteen daughters were born 207.20
to this patriarch, Bhárata, the eldest of whom was Diti. Káshyapa the son of Maríchi became their husband, my son. He was famous and renowned, a master of the specifics of all religious customs.

utpādya tu mahā|bhāgas tāsām avara|jā daśa,
dadau Dharmāya dharma|jño Dakṣa eva prajā|patiḥ.
Dharmasya Vasavaḥ putrā, Rudrāś c' â|mita|tejasaḥ,
Viśvedevāś ca, Sādhyāś ca, Marutvantaś ca, Bhārata.

aparāś ca yavīyasyas tābhyo 'nyāḥ sapta|viṃśatiḥ.
Somas tāsāṃ mahā|bhāgaḥ sarvāsām abhavat patiḥ.
207.25 itarās tu vyajāyanta gandharvāṃs, turagān, dvijān,
gāś ca, kiṃ|puruṣān, matsyān, udbhij|jāṃś ca vanas|patīn.

Ādityān Aditir jajñe deva|śreṣṭhān mahā|balān.
teṣāṃ Viṣṇur Vāmano 'bhūd, Govindaś c' âbhavat prabhuḥ
tasya vikramaṇāc c' âpi devānāṃ śrīr vyavardhata,
dānavāś ca parābhūtā, daiteyī c' āsurī prajā.

Vipracitti|pradhānāṃś ca dānavān asṛjad Danuḥ,
Ditis tu sarvān asurān mahā|sattvān ajījanat.

aho|rātraṃ ca kālaṃ ca yatha"|rtu Madhusūdanaḥ,
pūrv'|âhṇaṃ c' âpar'|âhṇaṃ ca sarvam ev' ânvakalpayat.†
207.30 pradhyāya so 'sṛjan meghāṃs, tathā sthāvara|jaṅgamān.
pṛthivīṃ so 'sṛjad viśvāṃ, sahitāṃ bhūri|tejasā.

The illustrious patriarch Daksha then begat ten more daughters. Being a master of religion, he handed them over to Dharma. The sons of Dharma were the Vasus, the *rudras* of immeasurable luster, the Vishve·devas, the Sadhyas and the *maruts*, O Bhárata.

The patriarch Daksha then begat twenty-seven younger daughters, and the illustrious Soma became their husband. It was these other daughters who gave birth to the *gan-* 207.25
dhárvas, horses, birds, cows, *kímpurushas*, fish, plants and trees.

Áditi gave birth to those most splendid of gods, the mighty Adítyas. Vishnu was born among them as the dwarf Vámana, and Govínda was their master. The effulgence of the gods grew after Vámana strode across the universe, and because of this the *dánavas* and the demonic offspring of Diti were defeated.*

It was Danu, one of the daughters of Daksha—the first son of Brahma—who gave birth to the *dánavas*, the foremost of whom was Vipra·chitti; and Diti—the eldest daughter of Daksha—who gave birth to all the *ásuras*, those mighty beings.

Madhu·súdana made the day and night, and time in its seasons, as well as the morning and evening, follow each other in order. After some contemplation, he created the 207.30
clouds and then all animate and inanimate things. He created the entire earth and sustained it with his vast energy.

tataḥ Kṛṣṇo mahā|bhāgaḥ punar eva, Yudhiṣṭhira,
brāhmaṇānāṃ śataṃ śreṣṭhaṃ mukhād ev' âsṛjat prabhuḥ.
bāhubhyāṃ kṣatriya|śataṃ, vaiśyānām ūrutaḥ śatam,
padbhyāṃ śūdra|śataṃ c' âiva Keśavo, Bharata'|ṛṣabha.

sa evaṃ caturo varṇān samutpādya mahā|tapāḥ,
adhyakṣaṃ sarva|bhūtānāṃ dhātāram akarot svayam.
veda|vidyā|vidhātāraṃ Brahmāṇam a|mita|dyutim,
bhūta|mātṛ|gaṇ'|âdhyakṣaṃ Virūpākṣaṃ ca so 'sṛjat.
207.35 śāsitāraṃ ca pāpānāṃ pitṝṇāṃ Sama|vartinam
asṛjat sarva|bhūt'|ātmā, nidhi|paṃ ca Dhan'|ēśvaraṃ.
yādasām asṛjan nāthaṃ Varuṇaṃ ca jal'|ēśvaram;
Vāsavaṃ sarva|devānām adhyakṣam akarot prabhuḥ.

yāvad yāvad abhūc chraddhā dehaṃ dhārayituṃ nṛṇām,
tāvat tāvad ajīvaṃs te: n' āsīd Yama|kṛtaṃ bhayam.
na c' âiṣāṃ maithuno dharmo babhūva, Bharata'|ṛṣabha:
saṃkalpād eva c' âiteṣām apatyam udapadyate.

tatas Tretā|yuge kāle saṃsparśāj jāyate prajā,
na hy abhūn maithuno dharmas teṣām api, jan'|âdhipa.
207.40 Dvāpare maithuno dharmaḥ prajānām abhavan, nṛpa.
tathā Kali|yuge, rājan, dvaṃdvam āpedire janāḥ.

And then, Yudhi·shthira, the illustrious lord Krishna emitted a hundred splendid brahmins out of his mouth. Késhava also issued a hundred kshatriyas from his arms, a hundred vaishyas from his thighs, and a hundred shudras from his feet, bullish Bhárata.

Possessing great ascetic power, he thus created the four classes and made himself the overseer and maintainer of all creatures. He created the immeasurably majestic Brahma to disseminate Vedic knowledge, as well as Shiva, the god with innumerable eyes, to oversee departed spirits and the group of divine mothers.*

Vishnu, the self of all creatures, created Yama—the im- 207.35
partial judge—to punish evil men and govern the ancestors. He also created Kubéra, the lord of wealth and guardian of treasure. The Lord created Váruna, the lord of water and sea monsters, and Indra, the overseer of all the gods.

So long as men believed they could hold on to their bodies, they lived: there was no fear of Yama back then. Nor was there any such thing as sexual intercourse among them, bullish Bhárata: their offspring arose through the mere wish for them.

But then, in the Treta age—the second world-age—creatures came to be born from physical contact, although there was still no sexual intercourse between people, my
lord. It was only in the Dvápara—the third world-age—that 207.40
sexual intercourse arose between creatures, Your Majesty. And it was only in the Kali age—the fourth and final world age—Your Majesty, that living beings separated into two genders.

eṣa bhūta|patis, tāta, sv|adhyakṣaś ca tath" ôcyate.
nir|apekṣāṃs ca, Kaunteya, kīrtayiṣyāmi; tān śṛṇu.

dakṣiṇā|patha|janmānaḥ sarve Naravar'|Āndhrakāḥ,
Guhāḥ, Pulindāḥ, Śabarāś, Cūcukā Madrakaiḥ saha.
uttarā|patha|janmānaḥ kīrtayiṣyāmi tān api:
Yauna|Kāmboja|Gāndhārāḥ, Kirātā barbaraiḥ saha.
ete pāpa|kṛtas, tāta, caranti pṛthivīm imām,
śvapāka|bala|gṛdhrāṇāṃ sa|dharmāṇo, nar'|âdhipa.

207.45 n' âite Kṛta|yuge, tāta, caranti pṛthivīm imām;
Tretā|prabhṛti vardhante te janā, Bharata'|rṣabha.
tatas tasmin mahā|ghore saṃdhyā|kāla upasthite
rājānaḥ samasajjanta samāsādy' êtar'|êtaram.

evam eṣa, Kuru|śreṣṭha, prādur bhūto mah"|ātmanā.
devaṃ deva'|rṣir ācaṣṭa Nāradaḥ sarva|loka|dṛk.
Nārado 'py atha Kṛṣṇasya paraṃ mene, nar'|âdhipa,
śāśvatatvaṃ, mahā|bāho, yathāvad, Bharata'|rṣabha.

evam eṣa mahā|bāhuḥ Keśavaḥ satya|vikramaḥ:
a|cintyaḥ puṇḍarīk'|âkṣo n' âiṣa kevala|mānuṣaḥ!

This Lord of creatures is said to be the benevolent overseer, my son. Listen now, son of Kunti, as I name those creatures who live without any care.

They include all those born in the South, such as the Nara·varas, Ándhrakas, Guhas, Pulíndas, Shábaras, Chúchukas and Mádrakas. I should mention all those born in the far North as well: the Yaunas, Kambójas, Gandháras, Kirátas and barbarians of the North. These evil men wander this earth, my son, following the ways of crows, vultures and those who cook dogs, Lord of men.

During the Krita age—the first world-age—my son, 207.45
these evil sorts did not wander the earth. It was only from the Treta age onwards that they began to thrive, bullish Bhárata. And then in that dreadful transition of time, from the Treta to the Dvápara age, kings attacked each other and fought battles.

Thus, splendid Kuru, the world was created by that cosmic being. According to the celestial seer Nárada, who beholds all worlds, he is the God. It was Nárada, my Lord, who correctly believed Krishna to be transcendent and eternal, O mighty-armed, bullish Bhárata.

The power of the mighty armed Késhava thus lies in truth—this inconceivable, lotus-eyed deity is by no means a man!

208

ON THE PATRIARCHS AND GODS

YUDHIṢṬHIRA uvāca:

208.1 KE PŪRVAM ĀSAN patayaḥ prajānāṃ, Bharata'|ṛṣabha?
ke ca' ṛṣayo mahā|bhāgā dikṣu pratyekaśaḥ smṛtāḥ?

BHĪṢMA uvāca:

śrūyatāṃ, Bharata|śreṣṭha, yan māṃ tvaṃ paripṛcchasi—
prajānāṃ patayo ye 'smin, dikṣu ye ca' ṛṣayaḥ smṛtāḥ.
ekaḥ svayaṃ|bhūr bhagavān ādyo Brahmā sanātanaḥ.
Brahmaṇaḥ sapta vai putrā mah"|ātmānaḥ svayaṃ|bhuvaḥ:
Marīcir, Atry|Aṅgirasau, Pulastyaḥ, Pulahaḥ, Kratuḥ,
Vasiṣṭhaś ca mahā|bhāgaḥ sadṛśo vai svayaṃ|bhuvā.
208.5 sapta Brahmāṇa ity ete purāṇe niścayaṃ gatāḥ.
ata ūrdhvaṃ pravakṣyāmi sarvān eva prajā|patīn.
Atri|vaṃśa|samutpanno Brahma|yoniḥ sanātanaḥ
Prācīnabarhir bhagavāṃs, tasmāt Prācetaso daśa.
daśānāṃ tanayas tv eko Dakṣo nāma prajā|patiḥ.
tasya dve nāmanī loke: Dakṣaḥ, Ka iti c' ôcyate.
Marīceḥ Kaśyapaḥ putras; tasya dve nāmanī smṛte:
Ariṣṭanemir ity ekaṃ, Kaśyap' êty apare viduḥ.
Atreś c' âiv' âurasaḥ śrīmān rājā Somaś ca vīryavān,
sahasraṃ yaś ca divyānāṃ yugānāṃ paryupāsitā.

YUDHI·SHTHIRA said:

IN THE BEGINNING, who were the progenitors of creatures, bullish Bhárata? And who were the illustrious seers, each one of whom is thought to inhabit a particular direction? 208.1

BHISHMA said:

You should listen, splendid Bhárata, to what you have quizzed me about—the progenitors of creatures and the seers that are believed to inhabit the different directions.

In the beginning there was only the blessed Lord Brahma, who is self-existent and eternal. Seven sons were born to that cosmic, self-existent one: Maríchi, Atri, Ángiras, Pulástya, Púlaha, Kratu and the illustrious Vasíshtha, who most
resembled the self-existent one.* According to ancient tra- 208.5
dition, these are known as the seven Bráhmanas. I will now give an account of all the patriarchs.

The primeval, blessed Prachína·barhis was born in the lineage of Atri, from the source of Brahma. From him were born the ten Prachétases. These ten had a single son, a patriarch called Daksha. He has two names in the world: Daksha and Ka, so it is said.

Káshyapa, the son of Maríchi, is said to have two names: Aríshta·nemi is one, although others know him simply as Káshyapa.

The son of Atri was the effulgent and valorous King Soma, who remained devout for a thousand celestial world-ages.

208.10 Aryamā c' âiva bhagavān, ye c' âsya tanayā, vibho,
ete pradeśāḥ kathitā bhuvanānāṃ prabhāvanāḥ.
Śaśabindoś ca bhāryāṇāṃ sahasrāṇi daś', â|cyuta,
ek'|âikasyāṃ sahasraṃ tu tanayānām abhūt tadā.
evaṃ śata|sahasrāṇi śataṃ† tasya mah"|ātmanaḥ
putrāṇāṃ ca, na te kaś cid icchanty anyaṃ prajā|patim.
prajām ācakṣate viprāḥ purāṇāḥ Śāśabindavīm,
sa Vṛṣṇi|vaṃśa|prabhavo mahā|vaṃśaḥ prajā|pateḥ.
ete prajānāṃ patayaḥ samuddiṣṭā yaśasvinaḥ;
ataḥ paraṃ pravakṣyāmi devāṃs tri|bhuvan'|ēśvarān.
208.15 Bhago, 'ṃśaś c', Âryamā c' âiva,
Mitro, 'tha Varuṇas tathā,
Savitā c' âiva, Dhātā ca,
Vivasvāṃś ca mahā|balaḥ,
Tvaṣṭā, Pūṣā, tath" âiv Êndro, dvādaśo Viṣṇur ucyate.
ity ete dvādaś' ādityāḥ Kaśyapasy' ātma|saṃbhavāḥ.
Nāsatyaś c' âiva Dasraś ca smṛtau dvāv Aśvināv api;
Mārtaṇḍasy' ātma|jāv etāv aṣṭamasya mah"|ātmanaḥ.
te ca pūrvaṃ surāś c' êti: dvi|vidhāḥ pitaraḥ smṛtāḥ.
Tvaṣṭuś c' âiv' ātma|jaḥ śrīmān Viśvarūpo mahā|yaśāḥ.
Ajaikapād, Ahirbudhnyo, Virūpākṣo 'tha Raivataḥ.
Haraś ca, Bahurūpaś ca, Tryambakaś ca Sureśvaraḥ,
208.20 Sāvitraś ca, Jayantaś ca, Pinākī c' Âparājitaḥ,
pūrvam eva mahā|bhāgā Vasavo 'ṣṭau prakīrtitāḥ.
eta evaṃ|vidhā devā Manor eva prajā|pateḥ.
te ca pūrvaṃ surāś c' êti: dvi|vidhāḥ pitaraḥ smṛtāḥ.

The blessed Áryaman* and his sons, Mighty King, have been described as the instructors and masters of creatures. 208.10

Shasha·bindu* had ten thousand wives, unshakable one, and then each one of them had a thousand sons. Thus the numinous Shasha·bindu had ten million sons, not one of whom wished there to be any other patriarch. The brahmins of old handed down their knowledge of the offspring of Shasha·bindu, for this patriarch's great lineage was the source of the Vrishni lineage.

I have listed the celebrated progenitors of all creatures; now I will outline the gods who rule over the triple world.

These are said to be Bhaga, Ansha, Áryaman, Mitra, 208.15
Váruna, Sávitri, Dhatri, the powerful Vivásvat, Tvashtri, Pushan, Indra and finally Vishnu, the twelfth. These are the twelve Adítyas, who are the offspring of Káshyapa. It is thought that Nasátya and Dasra—the two Ashvins—are the sons of the illustrious Martánda, the eighth in the above list.*

Thus the progenitors are believed to be twofold: these divinities and the gods mentioned earlier.

There is also Vishva·rupa—the effulgent, glorious one—who was the son of Tvashtri, as well as the following group:

Ajáikapad, Ahir·budhnya, Virupáksha, Ráivata, Hara,
Bahu·rupa, Tryámbaka, Suréshvara, Savítra, Jayánta, Piná- 208.20
kin and Aparájita. I have already proclaimed the illustrious eight Vasus.*

Such are the gods who descended from Manu the lord of creatures. Thus the progenitors are believed to be twofold: these divinities and the gods mentioned earlier.

śīla|yauvanatas tv anyas, tath" ânyaḥ Siddha|Sādhyayoḥ.
Ṛbhavo Marutaś c' âiva; devānāṃ c' ôdito gaṇaḥ.
evaṃ ete samāmnātā Viśvedevās tath" Âśvinau.
Ādityāḥ kṣatriyās teṣāṃ, viśaś ca Marutas tathā.
aśvinau tu smṛtau śūdrau tapasy ugre samāsthitau,
smṛtās tv aṅgiraso devā brāhmaṇā iti niścayaḥ.
208.25 ity etat sarva|devānāṃ cāturvarṇyaṃ prakīrtitam.
etān vai prātar utthāya devān yas tu prakīrtayet,
sva|jād anya|kṛtāc c' âiva sarva|pāpāt pramucyate.
Yavakrīto, 'tha Raibhyaś ca, Arvāvasu|Parāvasū,
Auśijaś c' âiva Kakṣīvān, Balaś c' Āṅgirasaḥ smṛtaḥ.
ṛṣir Medhātitheḥ putraḥ Kaṇvo, Barhiṣadas tathā,
trailokya|bhāvanās, tāta, prācyāṃ sapta' ṛṣayas tathā.
Unmuco Vimucaś c' âiva, Svastyātreyaś ca vīryavān,
Pramucaś c', Êdhmavāhaś ca, bhagavāṃś ca Dṛḍhavrataḥ,
Mitrā|Varuṇayoḥ putras tath" Âgastyaḥ pratāpavān:
208.30 ete brahma'|ṛṣayo nityam āśritā dakṣiṇāṃ diśam.
Uṣaṃguḥ, Kavaṣo, Dhaumyaḥ, Parivyādhaś ca vīryavān,
Ekataś ca, Dvitaś c' âiva, Tritaś c' âiva maha"|ṛṣayaḥ,
Atreḥ putraś ca bhagavāṃs, tathā Sārasvataḥ prabhuḥ:
ete c' âiva mah"|ātmānaḥ paścimām āśritā diśam.
Ātreyaś ca, Vasiṣṭhaś ca, Kāśyapaś ca mahān ṛṣiḥ,
Gautamo, 'tha Bharadvājo, Viśvāmitro 'tha Kauśikaḥ,
tath" âiva putro bhagavān Ṛcīkasya mah"|ātmanaḥ
Jamadagniś ca: sapt' âite udīcīm āśritā diśam.

It is said that there is another group of gods: the ribhus and maruts. They are distinguished by their virtue and youth, and are also distinct from the Siddhas and Sadhyas.

The Vishve·devas and Ashvins are also enumerated. The Adítyas are the kshatriyas among them, and the maruts are the vaishyas. It is held that the Ashvins, who practiced fierce asceticism, are shudras, and that the gods born from Ángiras are brahmins.

Thus I have explained the four classes of the gods. The 208.25
person who calls out the names of these gods when he rises at dawn is released from all evil, both that brought about by himself and that inflicted by others.

Yava·krita, the son of Rebha, Arva·vasu, Para·vasu, Kakshívat the son of Úshija, Bala the son of Ángiras, Kanva son of the seer Medhátithi and Barhi·shada promote welfare in the triple world, my son, and are the seven seers found in the East.

Únmucha, Vimucha, Svasty·atréya the valorous, Prámucha, Idhma·vaha, the blessed Dridha·vrata and Agástya, the
mighty son of Mitra and Váruna: these Brahminic seers are 208.30
always stationed in the Southern skies.

Ushángu, Kávasha, Dhaumya, Parivyádha the valorous, the great seers Ékata, Dvita and Trita, as well as the blessed son of Atri and Lord Sarásvata: these illustrious beings are found in the Western skies.*

Atréya, Vasíshtha, the great seer Káshyapa, Gáutama, Bharad·vaja, Vishva·mitra the son of Kúshika, and Jamad·agni, the blessed son of the illustrious Richíka: these seven are found in the northern skies.

ete pratidiśaṃ sarve kīrtitās tigma|tejasaḥ.
208.35 sākṣi|bhūtā mah"|ātmāno bhuvanānāṃ prabhāvanāḥ.
evam ete mah"|ātmānaḥ sthitāḥ pratyekaśo diśam.
eteṣāṃ kīrtanaṃ kṛtvā sarva|pāpāt pramucyate,
yasyāṃ yasyāṃ diśi hy ete, tāṃ diśaṃ śaraṇaṃ gataḥ;
mucyate sarva|pāpebhyaḥ, svastimāṃś ca gṛhān vrajet.

I have named all these intensely lustrous beings with reference to the directions. These illustrious beings, as wit- 208.35
nesses to everything and masters of the worlds, are each found in their own regions of the sky.

If a person repeats the names of these beings, he will be released from all evil and take refuge in that region in which those beings are found. Being released from all evil, he will attain good fortune and will be able to return to his home.

209

AN ACCOUNT OF THE CONFLICT BETWEEN DEMONS AND GODS

YUDHIṢṬHIRA uvāca:

209.1 PITĀ|MAHA MAHĀ|prājña, yudhi satya|parākrama,
śrotum icchāmi kārtsnyena Kṛṣṇam a|vyayam īśvaram.
yac c' âsya tejaḥ su|mahad, yac ca karma purātanam,
tan me sarvaṃ yathā|tattvaṃ brūhi tvaṃ, puruṣa'|rṣabha.
tiryag|yoni|gataṃ rūpaṃ kathaṃ dhāritavān prabhuḥ?
kena kārya|nisargeṇa? tam ākhyāhi, mahā|bala.

BHĪṢMA uvāca:

pur" âhaṃ mṛgayāṃ yāto, Mārkaṇḍey'|āśrame sthitaḥ.
tatr' âpaśyaṃ muni|gaṇān samāsīnān sahasraśaḥ.
209.5 tatas te madhu|parkeṇa pūjāṃ cakrur atho mayi,
pratigṛhya ca tāṃ pūjāṃ, pratyanandam ṛṣīn aham.
kath" âiṣā kathitā tatra Kaśyapena maha"|rṣiṇā.
manaḥ|prahlādinīṃ divyāṃ tām ih' âika|manāḥ śṛṇu.
purā dānava|mukhyā hi krodha|lobha|samanvitāḥ,
balena mattāḥ śataśo Narak'|ādyā mah"|âsurāḥ,
tath" âiva c' ânye bahavo dānavā yuddha|durmadāḥ,
na sahante sma devānāṃ samṛddhiṃ tām an|uttamām.
dānavair ardyamānās tu devā deva'|rṣayas tathā
na śarma lebhire, rājan, viśamānās tatas tataḥ.
209.10 pṛthivīm ārta|rūpāṃ te samapaśyan div'|âukasaḥ,
dānavair abhisaṃstīrṇāṃ ghora|rūpair mahā|balaiḥ,
bhār'|ārtām, a|prahṛṣṭāṃ ca, duḥkhitāṃ, saṃnimajjatīm.
ath' Āditeyāḥ saṃtrastā Brahmāṇam idam abruvan:

YUDHI·SHTHIRA said:

WISE GRANDFATHER, you whose valor in battle derives from truth, I would like to hear a full account of Krishna, the immutable Lord. 209.1

Please tell me everything as it really is, bullish man, about his tremendous energy and primeval deeds.

And explain to me, mighty one, how and why the Lord assumed the form of an animal.

BHISHMA said:

Long ago, when I was out hunting, I found myself at Markandéya's hermitage. There I saw a troop of silent sages
seated in their thousands. After accepting the offering of 209.5
milk and honey with which they paid me homage, I saluted them. Now listen attentively to the delightful story of heavenly events that the great seer Káshyapa narrated on that occasion.

Once upon a time there was an angry, greedy bunch of leading *dánava*s and hundreds of great *ásura*s under the leadership of Náraka. Intoxicated by their own strength, and joined by many other *dánava*s eager for battle, they could not tolerate the incomparable prosperity of the gods.

These *dánava*s harassed the gods and celestial seers, who could not find a safe haven no matter where they searched,
Your Majesty. The gods saw that the earth was in a per- 209.10
ilous state because it was plagued by these terrible, mighty *dánava*s—oppressed by this heavy burden the earth was gloomy and miserable and began to sink. And so the Adítyas, trembling with fear, petitioned Brahma as follows:

«katham̩ śakṣyāmahe, Brahman,
dānavair abhimardanam?»
svayam̩|bhūs tān uvāc' êdam̩:
«nisr̩ṣṭo 'tra vidhir mayā.
te vareṇ' âbhisam̩pannā, balena ca madena ca,
n' âvabudhyanti sam̩mūḍhā Viṣṇum a|vyakta|darśanam,
varāha|rūpiṇam̩ devam a|dhr̩ṣyam a|marair api.
eṣa vegena gatvā hi yatra te dānav'|âdhamāḥ,
209.15 antar|bhūmi|gatā ghorā nivasanti sahasraśaḥ,
śamayiṣyati!» tac chrutvā jahr̩ṣuḥ sura|sattamāḥ.
tato Viṣṇur mahā|tejā vārāham̩ rūpam āsthitaḥ,
antar|bhūmim̩ sam̩praviśya jagāma Diti|jān prati.
dr̩ṣṭvā ca sahitāḥ sarve daityāḥ sattvam a|mānuṣam,
prasahya tarasā sarve sam̩tasthuḥ kāla|mohitāḥ.
tatas te samabhidrutya varāham̩ jagr̩huḥ samam,
sam̩kruddhāś ca varāham̩ tam̩ vyakarṣanta samantataḥ.
dānav'|êndrā mahā|kāyā, mahā|vīryā, bal'|ôcchritāḥ
n' âśaknuvam̩ś ca kim̩ cit te tasya kartum̩ tadā, vibho.
209.20 tato 'gacchan vismayam̩ te Dānav'|êndrā bhayam̩ tadā,
sam̩śayam̩ gatam ātmānam̩ menire ca sahasraśaḥ.
tato dev'|âdhidevaḥ sa yog'|ātmā yoga|sārathiḥ
yogam āsthāya bhagavām̩s tadā, Bharata|sattama,
vinanāda mahā|nādam̩ kṣobhayan daitya|dānavān,
sam̩nāditā yena lokāḥ sarvāś c' âiva diśo daśa.

"O Brahma, how might we withstand the onslaught of these *dánavas*?"

The self-existent one replied: "In this matter I have already ordained what is to be done. The *dánavas* have been fortified by a boon, and by their strength and rapturous excitement. But in their state of infatuation they have not noticed Vishnu, the invisible one. Bearing the form of a boar, this god is invincible even among the immortals. He has
hastened to the lair of those vile *dánavas*, those terrible crea- 209.15
tures living below the ground in their thousands. He will subdue them!"

Upon hearing this the exalted gods were overjoyed. And then, assuming the form of a boar, and endowed with great energy, Vishnu entered the earth and sought out the sons of Diti.

All the *daityas* saw that inhuman creature at once and, dumbfounded by their imminent death, endured its advance with all their might. They rushed toward the boar and grabbed hold of it together, and in their rage proceeded to drag it hither and thither. But the *dánava* lords, although massive, valorous and powerful, were not able to do anything to it, Mighty King. Because of this they became as- 209.20
tonished and afraid, and thousands of them began to doubt themselves.

And so the supreme, blessed god began to wield the magical power with which he was imbued and of which he was a master, exalted Bhárata. He roared a mighty roar that resounded throughout the ten directions and all the worlds, and shook the *daityas* and *dánavas* to their core.

tena saṃnāda|śabdena lokānāṃ kṣobha āgamat,
saṃtrastāś ca bhṛśaṃ loke devāḥ Śakra|puro|gamāḥ.
nir|viceṣṭaṃ jagac c' âpi babhūv' âtibhṛśaṃ tadā,
sthāvaraṃ jaṅgamaṃ c' âiva tena nādena mohitam.
209.25 tatas te dānavāḥ sarve tena nādena bhīṣitāḥ,
petur gat'|āsavaś c' âiva, Viṣṇu|tejaḥ|pramohitāḥ.
Rasātala|gataś c' âpi varāhas tri|daśa|dviṣām
khurair vidārayām āsa māṃsa|medo|'sthi|saṃcayān.
nādena tena mahatā «sanātana» iti smṛtaḥ.
padma|nābho mahā|yogī, bhūt'|ācāryaḥ sa bhūta|rāṭ.
tato deva|gaṇāḥ sarve pitā|maham upābruvan
tatra gatvā mah"|ātmānam, ūcuś c' âiva jagat|patim:
«nādo 'yaṃ kīdṛśo, deva? n' âitaṃ vidma vayaṃ, vibho.
ko 'sau hi, kasya vā nādo yena vihvalitaṃ jagat?
209.30 devāś ca dānavāś c' âiva mohitās tasya tejasā,
etasminn antare Viṣṇur vārāhaṃ rūpam āsthitaḥ
udatiṣṭhan, mahā|bāho, stūyamāno maha"|ṛṣibhiḥ.»

PITĀ|MAHA uvāca:

nihatya dānava|patīn mahā|varṣmā, mahā|balaḥ
eṣa devo mahā|yogī bhūt'|ātmā, bhūta|bhāvanaḥ,
sarva|bhūt'|êśvaro, yogī, munir, ātmā tath" ātmanaḥ.
sthirībhavata, Kṛṣṇo 'yaṃ, sarva|vighna|viṇāśanaḥ.

The sound of that roar made the worlds shake and the gods, led by Indra, trembled violently in fear: the world was without any sign of movement at that moment when all animate and inanimate things were stupefied by the roar of Vishnu.

That roar terrified the entire mass of *dánava*s, and they 209.25
fell down, drained of spirit, stupefied by the power of Vishnu. Still bearing the form of a boar in the Rasátala hell, Vishnu lacerated the flesh, fat and bones of those enemies of the gods with his hoofs.

Because of that great roar Vishnu is regarded as "the primeval one." This lotus-naveled god who possesses great magical power is the teacher and king of creatures. After these events all the troops of gods approached Brahma, the cosmic grandfather and Lord of the world, and addressed him as follows, saying:

"What sort of roar was that, O god? We do not know this, mighty one. What was that roar which shook the earth,
and who roared it? At the moment when Vishnu assumed 209.30
the form of a boar and rose up to the praise of the great seers, the gods and *dánava*s were stupefied by his power, mighty-armed one."

THE GRANDFATHER said:

This god of such massive proportions, strength and magic power—the one who slew the *dánava* leaders—is the world-self,* the creator of all creatures. He is the Lord of all creatures, the wielder of magic power, the silent sage and inner self within the body. Fortify yourselves, for this is Krishna, the destroyer of all obstacles!

kṛtvā karm' âtisādhv etad a|śakyam, a|mita|prabhaḥ
samāyātaḥ svam ātmānaṃ mahā|bhāgo mahā|dyutiḥ.
padma|nābho mahā|yogī, mah"|ātmā bhūta|bhāvanaḥ.
na saṃtāpo, na bhīḥ kāryā, śoko vā, sura|sattamāḥ.
209.35 vidhir eṣa, prabhāvaś ca, Kālaḥ saṃkṣaya|kārakaḥ.
lokān dhārayatā tena nādo mukto mah"|ātmanā.
sa eṣa hi mahā|bāhuḥ, sarva|loka|namas|kṛtaḥ,
a|cyutaḥ, puṇḍarīk'|âkṣaḥ, sarva|bhūt'|ādir īśvaraḥ.

Once he had carried out this impossible, awesome deed, this illustrious god of immeasurable luminosity and great glory returned to his true state.

The lotus-naveled one is the wielder of magic power, the cosmic self that creates all creatures, so there is no need for anguish, dread or sorrow, exalted gods.

He is the divine order itself, as well as creation, Time, and 209.35
the agent of cosmic destruction. The worlds are sustained by him, the cosmic being who released that roar.

He is the mighty-armed deity that all worlds worship, the unshakable, lotus-eyed Lord who is the source of all living beings.

210–217
THE DIALOGUE BETWEEN A MASTER AND PUPIL

YUDHIṢṬHIRA uvāca:

210.1 YOGAṂ ME PARAMAṂ, tāta, mokṣasya vada, Bhārata.
tam ahaṃ tattvato jñātum icchāmi, vadatāṃ vara.

BHĪṢMA uvāca:

atr' âpy udāharant' îmam itihāsaṃ purātanam:
saṃvādaṃ mokṣa|saṃyuktaṃ śiṣyasya guruṇā saha.
kaś cid brāhmaṇam āsīnam ācāryam ṛṣi|sattamam,
tejo|rāśiṃ, mah"|ātmānaṃ, satya|sandhaṃ, jit'|êndriyam
śiṣyaḥ parama|medhāvī, śreyo|'rthī, su|samāhitaḥ
caraṇāv upasaṃgṛhya sthitaḥ prāñjalir abravīt.
210.5 «upāsanāt prasanno 'si yadi vai, bhagavan, mama,
saṃśayo me mahān kaś cit, tan me vyākhyātum arhasi.
kutaś c' âhaṃ, kutaś ca tvaṃ? tat samyag brūhi yat param.
kathaṃ ca sarva|bhūteṣu sameṣu, dvija|sattama,
samyag|vṛttā nivartante, viparītāḥ kṣay'|ôdayāḥ?
vedeṣu c' âpi yad vākyaṃ, laukikaṃ vyāpakaṃ ca yat,
etad vidvan, yathā|tattvaṃ sarvaṃ vyākhyātum arhasi.»

GURUR uvāca:

śṛṇu, śiṣya mahā|prājña, brahma|guhyam idaṃ param,
adhyātmaṃ sarva|vidyānām āgamānāṃ ca yad vasu.

YUDHI·SHTHIRA said:

SPEAK TO ME, Bhárata, about the highest yogic discipline 210.1
that leads to liberation. I wish to know about that as it really is, most eloquent speaker.

BHISHMA said:

On this subject people relate the ancient tradition of a dialogue on liberation between a master and his pupil.

There was once a great Brahminic teacher, an exalted seer of immense luster who had mastered his senses and was devoted to the truth. He had a pupil who was highly intelligent and very focused, a seeker of divine felicity. Once, when the teacher was sitting down, the pupil embraced his feet and then stood up cupping his hands in reverence, saying:

"If you are satisfied with my devotion, venerable one, you 210.5
should clear up this great doubt of mine. What is the source from which you and I originated? Give me a thorough explanation of the transcendent.

If all living beings are equal, exalted brahmin, how is it that those who conduct themselves impeccably are born again whereas deviants attain the destruction of rebirth?

Since you understand the injunctions of the Vedas and worldly convention, please explain everything as it really is."

THE MASTER said:

You must learn, wise pupil, about the transcendent mystery that is *brahman*, the supreme self which is the treasure of all sacred knowledge and scripture.

Vāsudevaḥ param idaṃ, viśvasya brahmaṇo mukham,
satyaṃ, jñānam, atho yajñas, titikṣā, dama, ārjavam.
210.10 puruṣaṃ sanātanaṃ Viṣṇuṃ yaṃ taṃ veda|vido viduḥ
sarga†|pralaya|kartāram, a|vyaktaṃ brahma śāśvatam.

tad idaṃ, brahma, Vārṣṇeyam itihāsaṃ śṛṇuṣva me:
brāhmaṇo brāhmaṇaiḥ śrāvyo, rājanyaḥ kṣatriyais tathā,
vaiśyo vaiśyais tathā śrāvyaḥ, śūdraḥ śūdrair mahā|manāḥ,
māhātmyaṃ deva|devasya Viṣṇor a|mita|tejasaḥ.
arhas tvam asi, kalyāṇaṃ Vārṣṇeyaṃ śṛṇu, yat param.

kāla|cakram an|ādy|antaṃ bhāv'|âbhāva|sva|lakṣaṇam
trailokyaṃ sarva|bhūt'|ēśe cakravat parivartate.
yat tad a|kṣaram, a|vyaktam, a|mṛtaṃ brahma śāśvatam
vadanti, puruṣa|vyāghra, Keśavaṃ puruṣa'|rṣabham.
210.15 pitṝn, devān, ṛṣīṃś c' âiva, tathā vai yakṣa|rākṣasān,
nāg'|âsura|manuṣyāṃś ca sṛjate paramo '|vyayaḥ;
tath" âiva veda|śāstrāṇi, loka|dharmāṃś ca śāśvatān
pralaye† prakṛtiṃ prāpya, yug'|ādau sṛjate prabhuḥ.

The transcendent is Vasudéva, the source of the whole world. He is truth, knowledge, the sacrifice, forbearance, restraint and honesty. Vedic masters know him as Vishnu, 210.10
the primeval person and agent of cosmic creation and destruction—he is the eternal, unmanifest *brahman*.

O brahmin, you must learn from me the legend of the descendent of the Vrishni tribe—the ode to Vishnu, that immeasurably radiant god of gods. A brahmin should learn about it from brahmins, a kshatriya should learn about it from kshatriyas, a vaishya should learn about it from vaishyas and distinguished shudras should learn about it from other shudras. You are worthy, so listen to this auspicious legend of the descendent of the Vrishni tribe. It is supreme!

The wheel of time has neither beginning nor end, it is characterized by both existence and non-existence. It encompasses the three worlds and revolves, like a wheel, within the lord of all creatures. People say, tigerish man, that the imperishable, unmanifest, immortal and eternal *brahman* is Késhava, that bull of a man.

This supreme, immutable being created the ancestors, 210.15
gods, seers, *yakshas*, *rákshasas*, *nagas*, demons and men.

He also created the Vedas, the treatises and the world's religious laws that last for ever. In a period of cosmic destruction the Lord assumes his natural state, but at the beginning of a world age he resumes his creative activity.

yatha" rtāv ṛtu|liṅgāni nānā|rūpāṇi paryaye
dṛśyante tāni tāny eva, tathā bhāvā yug'|ādiṣu.
atha yad yad yadā bhāti Kāla|yogād yug'|ādiṣu,
tat tad utpadyate jñānaṃ loka|yātrā|vidhāna|jam.
yug'|ânte 'ntar|hitān vedān s'|êtihāsān maha"|rṣayaḥ
lebhire tapasā, pūrvam anujñātāḥ svayaṃ|bhuvā.
210.20 veda|vid veda bhagavān ved'|âṅgāni Bṛhaspatiḥ,
Bhārgavo nīti|śāstraṃ tu jagāda jagato hitam.
gāndharvaṃ Nārado veda, Bharadvājo dhanur|graham,
deva'|rṣi|caritaṃ Gārgyaḥ, Kṛṣṇātreyaś cikitsitam.
nyāya|tantrāṇy an|ekāni tais tair uktāni vādibhiḥ.
hetv|āgama|sad|ācārair yad uktaṃ, tad upāsyatām.
an|ādyaṃ tat paraṃ brahma na devā na' rṣayo viduḥ.
ekas tad veda bhagavān dhātā Nārāyaṇaḥ prabhuḥ.
Nārāyaṇād ṛṣi|gaṇās, tathā mukhyāḥ sur'|âsurāḥ,
rāja'|rṣayaḥ purāṇāś ca paramaṃ duḥkha|bheṣajam.
210.25 puruṣ'|âdhiṣṭhitān bhāvān prakṛtiḥ sūyate yadā,
hetu|yuktam ataḥ pūrvaṃ jagat saṃparivartate.
dīpād anye yathā dīpāḥ pravartante sahasraśaḥ,
prakṛtiḥ sūyate tadvad ānantyān, n' âpacīyate.

Just as the various characteristics of the seasons appear in a regular order in the course of time, so too do living beings appear whenever a world age begins. At the beginning of a world age Time impels consciousness to appear; it becomes manifests in order to regulate worldly existence.

At the end of a world age, when the Vedas and legends have vanished from the world, the great seers discover them once again through their asceticism, with the prior assent
of the self-existent one. The venerable Brihas·pati, a Vedic 210.20
master, discovered the supplementary works of the Veda, whereas the son of Bhrigu transmitted the treatise on political science, for the benefit of the world. Nárada discovered the science of music, Bharad·vaja the art of archery, Gargya the adventures of the celestial seers and Krishnatréya the science of medicine.

Various teachers transmitted the numerous works on logic. Since their conduct was impeccable and their doctrines rational, the works they transmitted ought to be venerated.

Neither the gods nor the seers know that transcendent *brahman* which has no beginning. Only the lord Naráyana, the blessed creator, knows it. The hosts of seers, the foremost gods and *ásuras*, as well as the royal seers of old acquired the ultimate remedy for suffering from Naráyana.

If primordial matter creates living beings presided over 210.25
by the spirit, in the beginning the world exists in connection with a cause. Just as thousands of lamps are lit from a single lamp, so primordial matter creates infinite things without diminution.*

a|vyaktāt karma|jā buddhir ahaṃ|kāraṃ prasūyate.
ākāśaṃ c' âpy ahaṃ|kārād, vāyur ākāśa|saṃbhavaḥ.
vāyos tejas, tataś c' āpa, adbhyo 'tha vasudh" ôdgatā.
mūla|prakṛtayo hy aṣṭau, jagad etāsv avasthitam.
jñān'|êndriyāṇy ataḥ pañca, pañca karm'|êndriyāṇy api,
viṣayāḥ pañca c' âikaṃ ca: vikāre ṣo|ḍaśaṃ manaḥ.

210.30 śrotraṃ, tvak, cakṣuṣī, jihvā,
ghrāṇaṃ jñān'|êndriyāṇy atha.
pādau, pāyur, upasthaś ca,
hastau, vāk karmaṇām† api.
śabdaḥ, sparśaś ca, rūpaṃ ca, raso, gandhas tath" âiva ca.
vijñeyaṃ vyāpakaṃ cittaṃ: teṣu sarva|gataṃ manaḥ.

rasa|jñāne tu jihv" êyaṃ, vyāhṛte vāk tath" ôcyate.
indriyair vividhair yuktaṃ sarvaṃ vyaktaṃ manas tathā.
vidyāt tu ṣo|ḍaś' âitāni daivatāni vibhāgaśaḥ,
deheṣu jñāna|kartāram upāsīnam upāsate.

tadvat soma|guṇā jihvā, gandhas tu pṛthivī|guṇaḥ,
śrotraṃ nabho|guṇaṃ c' âiva, cakṣur agner guṇas tathā,
sparśaṃ vāyu|guṇaṃ vidyāt sarva|bhūteṣu sarvadā.

210.35 manaḥ sattva|guṇaṃ prāhuḥ,
sattvam a|vyakta|jaṃ tathā.
sarva|bhūt'|ātma|bhūta|sthaṃ
tasmād budhyeta buddhimān.

Intelligence is born from unmanifest matter through its *karma*, and this in turn gives rise to self-consciousness. Space arises from self-consciousness, and wind from space.* Fire comes from wind, and is followed by water and then earth. These are the eight original forms of primordial matter, on which the world is founded. After that came the five faculties of cognition, the five faculties of action, the five objects of cognition and the one further item—the mind, or sixteenth modification.

The cognitive faculties are the ear, the skin, eyes, tongue and nose. The faculties of action are the feet, anus, penis, hands and speech. The objects of cognition are sound, touch, visible form, taste and smell. One should understand that thought is omnipresent: the mind pervades all objects of cognition.

The tongue is said to be involved in the cognition of taste, speech is involved in saying something. All manifest objects are connected to their respective sense faculties and the mind. One should know these sixteen "deities" separately, which venerate the agent of consciousness who abides in all bodies.

In a similar manner one should understand the tongue as an evolvent of water, smell as a perceptible quality of earth, the ear as an evolvent of space, vision as an evolvent of fire, and touch as a perceptible quality of wind. These are always found among all living beings. They say that the mind is an evolvent of substance, and that substance arises from the unmanifest. Therefore an intelligent man should understand that the unmanifest abides as the self in all creatures.*

ete bhāvā jagat sarvaṃ vahanti sa|car'|âcaram,
śritā vi|rajasaṃ devaṃ yam āhuḥ prakṛteḥ param.
nava|dvāraṃ puraṃ puṇyam etair bhāvaiḥ samanvitam
vyāpya śete mahān ātmā, tasmāt «puruṣa» ucyate.
a|jaraḥ so, '|maraś c' âiva, vyakt'|âvyakt'|ôpadeśavān,
vyāpakaḥ, sa|guṇaḥ, sūkṣmaḥ, sarva|bhūta|guṇ'|āśrayaḥ.

yathā dīpaḥ prakāś'|ātmā, hrasvo vā yadi vā mahān,
jñān'|ātmānaṃ tathā vidyāt puruṣaṃ sarva|jantuṣu.
210.40 śrotraṃ vedayate vedyaṃ, sa śṛṇoti, sa paśyati:
kāraṇaṃ tasya deho 'yaṃ, sa kartā sarva|karmaṇām.

agnir dāru|gato yadvad bhinne dārau na dṛśyate,
tath" âiv' ātmā śarīra|stho yogen' âiv' ânudṛśyate.
agnir yathā hy upāyena, mathitvā dāru, dṛśyate,
tath" âiv' ātmā śarīra|stho yogen' âiv' âtra dṛśyate.

nadīṣv āpo yathā yuktā, yathā sūrye marīcayaḥ
saṃtatatvād yathā yānti, tathā dehāḥ śarīriṇām.

svapna|yoge yath" âiv' ātmā pañc'|êndriya|samāyutaḥ
deham utsṛjya vai yāti, tath" âiv' ātm" ôpalabhyate.

These "states" bear this entire world of mobile and immobile things, but they depend on the spotless god that is said to transcend primeval matter. The nine-doored, auspicious city (*pura*) of the body is endowed with these states. The cosmic self pervades and abides (*shi*) within the body, and so is called "spirit" (*púrusha*). That is beyond decrepitude and death, and comprises the terms "manifest" and "unmanifest;" it is all-pervasive and endowed with evolvents, but also subtle and the refuge of all evolvents and creatures.

Just as the essence of a lamp, be it small or large, is illumination, so one should know that the essence of the spirit
who abides within all creatures is consciousness. The ear 210.40
senses its object of cognition, but it is the self that hears and sees: with the body as its foundation, it is the agent of all acts.

The fire latent within a piece of lumber cannot be seen when the lumber is split. In the same way the self abides in the body but can only be seen through the practice of *yoga*. Fire can be seen once the piece of lumber has been churned in the proper manner. In the same way, the self that abides in the body can only be seen through the practice of *yoga*.

Water is connected to the rivers, just as the sun's rays are connected to the sun. They move in a seamless flow, just like the bodies of embodied souls.

When the self is overcome by sleep, it remains connected to the five sense faculties. One should understand that the self relinquishes the body and moves on at the time of death in just the same way.

210.45 karmaṇā bādhyate rūpaṃ, karmaṇā c' ôpalabhyate.
karmaṇā nīyate 'nyatra sva|kṛtena balīyasā.
sa tu dehād yathā dehaṃ
tyaktv" ânyaṃ pratipadyate,
tath" ânyaṃ saṃpravakṣyāmi
bhūta|grāmaṃ sva|karma|jam.

GURUR uvāca:†

211.1 CATUR|VIDHĀNI bhūtāni sthāvarāṇi carāṇi ca,
a|vyakta|prabhavāny āhur, avyakta|nidhanāni ca.
a|vyakta|lakṣaṇaṃ vidyād a|vyakt'|ātm'|ātmakaṃ manaḥ.
yath" âśvattha|kaṇīkāyām antar|bhūto mahā|drumaḥ
niṣpanno dṛśyate vyaktam, a|vyaktāt saṃbhavas tathā.
abhidravaty ayas|kāntam ayo niś|cetanaṃ yathā,
sva|bhāva|hetu|jā bhāvā yadvad anyad ap' īdṛśam,
tadvad a|vyakta|jā bhāvāḥ kartuḥ kāraṇa|lakṣaṇāḥ;
a|cetanāś cetayituḥ kāraṇād abhisaṃhatāḥ.
211.5 na bhūr, na khaṃ, dyaur, bhūtāni,
na' rṣayo, na sur'|âsurāḥ,
n' ânyad āsīd ṛte jīvam,
āsedur na tu saṃhatam,
pūrvaṃ nityaṃ sarva|gataṃ mano|hetum a|lakṣaṇam.
a|jñāna|karma nirdiṣṭam, etat kāraṇa|lakṣaṇam.
tat kāraṇair hi saṃyuktaṃ kārya|saṃgraha|kārakam:
yen' âitad vartate cakram an|ādi|nidhanaṃ mahat.

A person's body is destroyed by his own *karma*, but is also taken up because of his *karma*: he is led elsewhere by the efficacy of his own deeds. Just as he abandons one body and moves from it to the next, so will I explain how the other classes of beings are reborn due to their own *karma*. 210.45

THE MASTER said:

LIVING BEINGS, both the mobile and immobile, are of four kinds. They say that their origin lies in the unmanifest, as does their end. One should also know that the mind is characterized by the unmanifest—that is its essence. 211.1

A great tree lies hidden within a pipal seed and is only seen clearly when it has sprung up. Existence emerges from the unmanifest in just the same way.

Just as an insentient piece of iron rushes towards a lodestone, and just as creatures are caused by their inherent nature and are reborn in a body of a similar nature, thus an agent's states arise from unmanifest matter and are characterized by this cause. Although this agent is sentient, his states are insentient and assailed by their cause.

There was no earth, space, heaven or material elements, and no seers, gods or *ásuras*. There was nothing apart from the soul—the elements had not yet overwhelmed that primeval, homogenous state which was unchanging, all-pervading, the root cause of mind and without characteristic. 211.5

Unmanifest matter is characterized as the cause—its creative activity is said to lead to ignorance. Through its connection to the material elements it brings about a multitude

a|vyakta|nābhaṃ, vyakt'|āraṃ,
vikāra|parimaṇḍalam,
kṣetra|jñ'|âdhiṣṭhitaṃ cakraṃ
snigdh'|âkṣaṃ vartate dhruvam.
snigdhatvāt tilavat sarvaṃ cakre 'smin pīḍyate jagat,
tila|pīḍair iv' ākramya, bhogair a|jñāna|saṃbhavaiḥ.
211.10 karma tat kurute tarṣād, ahaṃ|kāra|parigrahāt.
kārya|kāraṇa|saṃyoge sa hetur upapāditaḥ.
n' âbhyeti kāraṇaṃ kāryaṃ, na kāryaṃ kāraṇaṃ tathā.
kārya|vyaktena karaṇe Kālo bhavati hetumān.
hetu|yuktāḥ prakṛtayo, vikārāś ca parasparam
anyonyam abhivartante puruṣ'|âdhiṣṭhitāḥ sadā.
rājasais tāmasair bhāvaiś cyuto, hetu|bal'|ânvitaḥ
kṣetra|jñam ev' ânuyāti, pāṃsur vāt'|ērito yathā.
na ca taiḥ spṛśyate bhāvair, na te tena mah"|ātmanā.
sa|rajasko '|rajaskaś ca n' âiva vāyur bhaved yathā:
211.15 tath" âitad antaraṃ vidyāt sattva|kṣetrajñayor budhaḥ.
abhyāsāt sa tathā yukto na gacchet prakṛtiṃ punaḥ.

of effects: thus it turns the great wheel of existence, which is without beginning or end.

The hub of the wheel is unmanifest matter, its spokes are the manifest, and its felly is the modifications of the manifest. The axis of the wheel is oiled, and it revolves incessantly, presided over by the field-knower.

The entire world is crushed in this wheel, by the pleasures that arise from ignorance, just as sesame seeds are crushed because of their oiliness. It is as if the whole world is attacked by sesamum grinders.*

A person performs a deed because of thirst, when he is 211.10
possessed by self-consciousness. And in the connection between cause and effect a karmic condition is brought into being.

A cause does not draw near to its effect and an effect does not meet its cause. When something is accomplished through the manifestation of an effect, it is Time that is causally potent.

The eight forms of primeval matter are linked to a cause; their modifications are mutually causative. These continue in existence symbiotically, ever presided over by the spirit.

When shaken by states of passion and darkness, the soul is possessed by the power of causality. It follows the field-knower, just like dust blown by the wind.

The cosmic self is not touched by those states, nor are they touched by it. The wind never contains dust and then
loses it: the wise man should understand this difference 211.15
between substance and the field-knower. Disciplined by this contemplation, he will not return to primordial matter again.

samdeham etam utpannam acchinad bhagavān ṛṣiḥ.
tathā vārtāṃ samīkṣeta kṛta|lakṣaṇa|saṃmitām.
bījāny agny|upadagdhāni na rohanti yathā punaḥ,
jñāna|dagdhais tathā kleśair n' ātmā saṃpadyate punaḥ.

GURUR uvāca:

212.1 PRAVṚTTI|LAKṢAṆO dharmo yathā samupalabhyate.
teṣāṃ vijñāna|niṣṭhānām anyat tattvaṃ na rocate.
dur|labhā veda|vidvāṃso ved'|ôkteṣu vyavasthitāḥ,
prayojana|mahatvāt† tu mārgam icchanti saṃstutam.
sadbhir ācaritatvāt tu vṛttam etad a|garhitam.
iyaṃ sā buddhir abhyetya yayā yāti parāṃ gatim.
śarīravān upādatte mohāt sarvān parigrahān,
krodha|lobh'|ādibhir bhāvair yukto rājasa|tāmasaiḥ.
212.5 n' â|śuddham ācaret tasmād abhīpsan deha|yāpanam:
karmaṇā vivaraṃ kurvan na lokān āpnuyāc chubhān.
loha|yuktaṃ yathā hema, vipakvaṃ na virājate.
tath" â|pakva|kaṣāy'|ākhyaṃ vijñānaṃ na prakāśate.
yaś c' â|dharmaṃ carel lobhāt kāma|krodhāv anuplavan,
dharmyaṃ panthānam ākramya s'|ânubandho vinaśyati.
śabd'|ādīn viṣayāṃs tasmān na saṃrāgād ayaṃ vrajet;
krodho, harṣo, viṣādaś ca jāyante ha parasparāt.

The venerable seer cut away this doubt when it arose. Therefore one should consider that existence is regulated by attributes that are caused.

Just as seeds burned by fire will not sprout again, so too will the self not be reborn when its defilements are burned by gnosis.

THE MASTER said:

PEOPLE TAKE UP the religion characterized by action in 212.1
various ways. But for those devoted to perception, no other reality appeals.

It is hard to find Vedic masters who are established in Vedic lore—those who, with the loftiest of motives, seek out the path that is praised. Since it is practiced by the virtuous, this conduct is not censured. This is the understanding with which they approach and attain the transcendent condition.

Possessed by states of passion and darkness such as anger and greed, a person deludedly grasps after all objects.
Because of this one should not perform impure acts in the 212.5
hope of maintaining the body: making oneself vulnerable in this way, one will not attain resplendent worlds.

When gold is mixed with iron the end product will not gleam. In the same way a person's consciousness will not shine forth if its defilements have not been burned away.

The person who acts unrighteously, out of greed or because of desire and anger, he transgresses the path of righteousness and is destroyed along with his attachments. Therefore one should not pursue sensual objects—such as

pañca|bhūt'|ātmake dehe sattve rājasa|tāmase
kam abhiṣṭuvate c' âyaṃ? kaṃ vā krośati, kiṃ vadan?
212.10 sparśa|rūpa|ras'|ādyeṣu saṅgaṃ gacchanti bāliśāḥ.
n' âvagacchanti vijñānād ātmānaṃ pārthivaṃ guṇam.

mṛn|mayaṃ śaraṇaṃ yadvan mṛd" âiva parilipyate,
pārthivo 'yaṃ† tathā deho mṛd|vikārān na naśyati.
madhu, tailaṃ, payaḥ, sarpir, māṃsāni, lavaṇaṃ, guḍaḥ,
dhānyāni, phala|mūlāni mṛd|vikārāḥ sah" âmbhasā.

yadvat kāntāram ātiṣṭhan n' āutsukyaṃ samanuvrajet,
grāmyam āhāram ādadyād a|svādv api hi yāpanam;
tadvat saṃsāra|kāntāram ātiṣṭhañ śrama|tat|paraḥ,
yātr"|ârtham adyād āhāraṃ, vyādhito bheṣajaṃ yathā.
212.15 satya|śauc'|ārjava|tyāgair, varcasā, vikrameṇa ca,
kṣāntyā, dhṛtyā ca, buddhyā ca, manasā, tapas" âiva ca
bhāvān sarvān upāvṛttān samīkṣya viṣay'|ātmakān,
śāntim icchann a|dīn'|ātmā saṃyacched indriyāṇi ca.

sattvena, rajasā c' âiva, tamasā c' âiva mohitāḥ
cakravat parivartante hy a|jñānāj jantavo bhṛśam.
tasmāt samyak parīkṣeta doṣān a|jñāna|saṃbhavān,
a|jñāna|prabhavaṃ duḥkham ahaṃ|kāraṃ parityajet.

sound—with an inflamed heart, or else anger, excitement and depression will arise one after the other.

Who is there to praise in this body of five elements, with its states of purity, passion and darkness? Who would one yell at, and what would one say? Simpletons become at- 212.10
tached to such things as touch, visible form and taste, and with this understanding do not understand that the body is only a derivative of earth.

Just as a refuge made of earth can only be soiled by earth, so this body made of earth will not perish through that which is derived from the earth. Honey, sesame oil, milk, ghee, meat, salt, treacle, grain, fruits and roots are all modifications of the earth and water.

When he enters the wilderness a man should not cross it impatiently—he should take food from the villages, even if it is tasteless, in order to sustain himself. In the same way, the person intent on striving across the wilderness of transmigration should take medical sustenance in order to sustain himself when ill.

Contemplating that all the states that afflict him are 212.15
caused by the sense objects, the noble person who seeks peace should control his sense faculties by means of truth, pure conduct, honesty, renunciation, vigor and courage, forbearance, resolve, intelligence, contemplation and asceticism.

Deluded by purity, passion and darkness, creatures revolve in transmigration due to their ignorance, just like a wheel with unstoppable momentum. Therefore one should make a thorough examination of the faults caused by ig-

mahā|bhūtān', îndriyāṇi, guṇāḥ, sattvaṃ, rajas, tamaḥ,
trailokyaṃ s'|ēśvaraṃ sarvam ahaṃ|kāre pratiṣṭhitam.

212.20 yath" êha niyataḥ kālo darśayaty ārtavān guṇān,
tadvad bhūteṣv ahaṃ|kāraṃ vidyād karma|pravartakam.

sammohakaṃ tamo vidyāt kṛṣṇam a|jñāna|saṃbhavam,
prīti|duḥkha|nibaddhāṃś ca samastāṃs trīn atho guṇān.
sattvasya, rajasaś c' âiva, tamasaś ca nibodha tān.

prasādo, harṣa|jā prītir, a|saṃdeho, dhṛtiḥ, smṛtiḥ—
etān sattva|guṇān vidyād. imān rājasa|tāmasān:
kāma|krodhau, pramādaś ca,
lobha|mohau, bhayaṃ, klamaḥ,
viṣāda|śokāv, a|ratir,
māna|darpāv, an|āryatā.

doṣāṇām evam|ādīnāṃ parīkṣya guru|lāghavam,
vimṛśed ātma|saṃsthānam ek'|âikam anusaṃtatam.

YUDHIṢṬHIRA uvāca:

212.25 ke doṣā manasā tyaktāḥ? ke buddhyā śithilī|kṛtāḥ?
ke punaḥ punar āyānti, ke mohād a|phalā iva?

norance, and then abandon the suffering it brings about—which is self-consciousness.

Everything—the triple world along with its ruler, the great elements, the sense faculties, their objects and the states of purity, passion and darkness—is rooted in self-
consciousness. Just as time, in its regular cycles, manifests 212.20
the material evolvents of the world in a regular order, so one should understand that the self-consciousness found within all living beings sets in motion their *karma*.

One should understand that the deluding state of darkness is a sort of blackness caused by ignorance, and that when the three psychosomatic states are united, they are accompanied by joy and suffering. Listen now to the different states of purity, passion and darkness.

One should understand that tranquility, the joy born from excitement, clarity of mind, resolve and recollection are the different sorts of purity, and that the following are those born from passion and darkness: desire, anger, negligence, greed, delusion, fear, languor, depression, sorrow, discontent, conceit, pride and ignobility.

Examining the strength or weakness of faults such as these, one should contemplate each one of them, successively, as they occur in oneself.

YUDHI·SHTHIRA said:

What faults are abandoned by means of the mind? Which 212.25
ones are unloosed by the intelligence? Which ones return to a person again and again, and which ones, out of ignorance, appear to be ineffective?

keṣāṃ bal'|âbalaṃ buddhyā hetubhir vimṛśed budhaḥ?
eṣa me saṃśayas, tāta, tan me brūhi, pitā|maha.

BHĪṢMA uvāca:

doṣair mūlād avacchinnair viśuddh'|ātmā vimucyate.
vināśayati saṃbhūtam ayas|mayam ayo yathā,
tath" â|kṛt'|ātmā saha|jair doṣair naśyati tāmasaiḥ.
rājasaṃ tāmasaṃ c' âiva, śuddh'|ātmakam a|kalmaṣam:
tat sarvaṃ dehināṃ bījaṃ; sattvam ātmavataḥ samam.
tasmād ātmavatā varjyaṃ rajaś ca tama eva ca.
rajas|tamobhyāṃ nirmuktaṃ sattvaṃ nirmalatām iyāt.
212.30 atha vā mantravad brūyur ātm'|ādānāya duṣ|kṛtam.
sa vai hetur: an|ādāne śuddha|dharm'|ânupālane.
rajas" â|dharma|yuktāni kāryāṇy api samāpnute,
artha|yuktāni c âtyarthaṃ kāmān sarvāṃś ca sevate.
tamasā lobha|yuktāni krodha|jāni ca sevate
hiṃsā|vihār'|âbhiratas, tandrī|nidrā|samanvitaḥ.

Upon the strengths and weaknesses of which faults should a wise man reflect through his intelligence and reasoned arguments? This is my doubt, dear grandfather, please explain it to me.

BHISHMA said:

A pure person is liberated when his faults are cut off at their root. Just as rust annihilates iron when it arises, so too does an incomplete man perish because of his innate faults, those inner states of darkness.

States of passion and darkness, and those spotless states of purity: all that is the seed for the origination of embodied creatures. But the purity of those who are self-controlled is always constant.

Therefore a self-controlled man ought to avoid passion and darkness. Released from their grip, he will arrive at an untainted state of purity.

Alternatively, some might say that a deed requiring a 212.30
Vedic invocation is incorrect when it comes to grasping the self. That is indeed a cause: not of grasping the self, but of preserving the religion of ritual purity.

A person motivated by passion accomplishes tasks of an unrighteous nature, and pursues all sensual pleasures and matters of material gain to an excessive degree.

Out of darkness he resorts to matters associated with greed, as well as those which arise from anger. Such a person delights in violent pursuits, and is dominated by lethargy and sleep.

sattva|sthaḥ sāttvikān bhāvāñ śuddhān paśyati saṃśritaḥ.
sa dehī vimalaḥ śrīmāñ śraddhā|vidyā|samanvitaḥ.

GURUR uvāca:

213.1 RAJASĀ SĀDHYATE mohas tamasā, Bharata'|rṣabha,
krodha|lobhau, bhayaṃ, darpa; eteṣāṃ sādhanāc chuciḥ.
paramaṃ param'|ātmānaṃ, devam a|kṣayam a|vyayam,
Viṣṇum a|vyakta|saṃsthānaṃ vidus taṃ deva|sattamam.
tasya māyā|pinaddh'|âṅgā, naṣṭa|jñānā, vicetasaḥ.
mānavā jñāna|saṃmohāt tataḥ krodhaṃ prayānti vai.
krodhāt kāmam avāpy', âtha lobha|mohau ca mānavāḥ,
māna|darpāv, ahaṃ|kāram; ahaṃ|kārāt tataḥ kriyāḥ.
213.5 kriyābhiḥ sneha|saṃbandhaḥ,†
snehāc chokam anantaram.
sukha|duḥkha|kriy"|ārambhāj
janm'|âjanma|kṛta|kṣaṇāḥ.†
janmato garbha|vāsaṃ tu śukra|śoṇita|saṃbhavam,
purīṣa|mūtra|vikleda†|śoṇita|prabhav'|āvilam.
tṛṣṇ"|âbhibhūtas tair baddhas tān ev' âbhipariplavan

The person grounded in purity, however, perceives wholesome states of purity in himself and embraces them. Endowed with faith and knowledge, that person becomes spotless and effulgent.

THE MASTER said:

PASSION AND DARKNESS lead to delusion, bullish Bhárata, 213.1
as well as anger, greed, fear and pride. By mastering these one attains purification.

The ultimate, supreme self, the unfailing, immutable deity that is Vishnu, the one whose condition is unmanifest—they believe he is the most exalted of gods.

With their bodies shrouded in the magical power of that god and their consciousness corrupt, men become confounded, and in that confused state of mind they become angry.

Because of anger men are subjected to desire, greed, delusion, conceit, pride and self-consciousness; it is self-consciousness that leads to action.

Actions lead to the bond of attachment, and attachment 213.5
leads to endless sorrow. Undertaking acts that lead to pleasure and pain, people are subjected to repeated rebirth.

In order to be reborn an embryo must arise from the combination of semen and blood. It is then polluted by the production of feces, urine moisture and blood. The person overcome with thirst is bound by these, and hastens towards them.

saṃsāra|tantra|vāhinyas tatra budhyeta yoṣitaḥ.
prakṛtyā kṣetra|bhūtās tā, narāḥ kṣetra|jña|lakṣaṇāḥ.
tasmād et" â|viśeṣeṇa†na c' âbhīyur vipaścitaḥ,†
kṛtyā hy etā ghora|rūpā, mohayanty a|vicakṣaṇān.
rajasy antarhitā mūrtir indriyāṇāṃ sanātanī.

213.10 tasmāt tad|ātmakād rāgād bījāj jāyanti jantavaḥ.
sva|deha|jān a|sva|saṃjñān yadvad aṅgāt kṛmīṃs tyajet,
sva|saṃjñān a|svakāṃs tadvat suta|saṃjñān kṛmīṃs tyajet.

śukrato rasataś c' âiva dehāj jāyanti jantavaḥ.
sva|bhāvāt karma|yogād vā tān upekṣeta buddhimān.

rajas tamasi paryastaṃ, sattvaṃ ca rajasi sthitam.
jñān'|âdhiṣṭhānam a|vyaktaṃ, buddhy|ahaṃ|kāra|lakṣaṇam.

tad bījaṃ dehinām āhus, tad bījaṃ jīva|saṃjñitam.
karmaṇā kāla|yuktena saṃsāra|parivartanam.

ramaty ayaṃ yathā svapne manasā, dehavān iva.
karma|garbhair guṇair dehī garbhe tad upalabhyate.

In this matter one should understand that it is women who bring about the continuity of transmigration. Women are, essentially, the field, whereas men have the characteristic of being the field-knower. Therefore perceptive men should not approach women without a particular reason to do so, for women are evil sorceresses who delude the witless with their terrifying forms. Their physical form is always shrouded in the passion of their sense faculties.

Therefore people are born from the seed of passion, the 213.10
essence of which is woman. Just as a person would cast off worms born on one's own body, which are not called one's own property, so should one abandon those worms called "sons," since they are not one's own even though called just that.

People are born from the semen and juice found in the body. But a wise man should think that they are born because of their inherent nature, or else the yoke of *karma*.

Passion is shrouded in darkness, and purity abides within passion. Unmanifest matter is presided over by consciousness, and is characterized by the faculty of intelligence and self-consciousness.

They say that the seed termed "soul" is the source of all embodied creatures. It revolves in transmigration because of its *karma*, which is impelled by time.

During sleep the soul finds pleasure through the mind, as if it were embodied. In just the same way, the embodied soul in the womb is grasped by the qualities contained within its *karma*.

213.15 karmaṇā bīja|bhūtena codyate yad yad indriyam,
jāyate tad ahaṃ|kārād, rāga|yuktena cetasā.

śabda|rāgāc chrotram asya jāyate ’|bhāvit’|ātmanaḥ,
rūpa|rāgāt tathā cakṣur, ghrāṇaṃ gandha|cikīrṣayā.

sparśane tvak, tathā vāyuḥ prāṇ’|āpāna|vyapāśrayaḥ.
vyān’|ôdānau samānaś ca pañcadhā deha|yāpanam.

saṃjātair jāyate gātraiḥ karma|jair varṣmaṇā vṛtaḥ,
duḥkh’|ādy|antair duḥkha|madhyair naraḥ śārīra|mānasaiḥ.

duḥkhaṃ vidyād upādānād, abhimānāc ca vardhate.
tyāgāt tebhyo nirodhaḥ syān, nirodha|jño vimucyate.

213.20 indriyāṇāṃ rajasy eva pralaya|prabhavāv ubhau
parīkṣya saṃcared vidvān yathāvac chāstra|cakṣuṣā.

jñān’|êndriyāṇ’ îndriy’|ârthān n’ ôpasarpanty a|tarṣulam.
hīnaiś ca karaṇair dehī na dehaṃ punar arhati.

Whatever sense faculty is prompted into action by a karmic seed, that arises from self-consciousness, when one's mind is bound by passion. 213.15

Hearing arises in an undeveloped person because of his passion for sound, vision arises because of his passion for visible form, whereas smell arises from the desire for scent.

Touch requires skin and the internal wind which is not supported by the *prana*, the in-breath, and the *apána*, the breath that moves down. But along with the *vyana*—the diffused breath—the *udána*—the breath that moves upward—and the *samána*—the link breath—they sustain the body in five ways.

A man endowed with a body is born with physical and mental faculties. They arise at the same time because of his past *karma*, but their beginning, middle and end is mired in suffering.

Understand that suffering arises from grasping and increases through arrogance. The cessation of these is attained through letting go, and the person who realizes this cessation is released.

The sense faculties are activated and deactivated in a state of passion. When a learned man has contemplated this he should conduct himself properly, in accordance with his understanding of the treatises. 213.20

The cognitive faculties do not obtrude on the sense objects when a person lacks desire. And when a person abandons cognitive action, he will not be reborn.

GURUR uvāca:

214.1 ATR' ÔPĀYAṂ pravakṣyāmi, yathāvac chāstra|cakṣuṣā.
tad|vijñānāc† caran, rājan, prāpnuyāt paramāṃ gatim.
sarveṣām eva bhūtānāṃ puruṣaḥ śreṣṭha ucyate.
puruṣebhyo dvij|ān āhur, dvijebhyo mantra|darśinaḥ.
sarva|bhūt'|ātma|bhūtās te sarva|jñāḥ, sarva|darśinaḥ
brāhmaṇā veda|śāstra|jñās, tattv'|ârtha|gata|niścayāḥ.
netra|hīno yathā hy ekaḥ kṛcchrāṇi labhate 'dhvani,
jñāna|hīnas tathā loke. tasmāj jñāna|vido 'dhikāḥ.
214.5 tāṃs tān upāsate dharmān dharma|kāmā yath"|āgamam.
na tv eṣām artha|sāmānyam antareṇa guṇān imān.
vāg|deha|manasāṃ śaucaṃ,
kṣamā, satyaṃ, dhṛtiḥ, smṛtiḥ:
sarva|dharmeṣu dharma|jñā
jñāpayanti guṇāñ chubhān.
yad idaṃ brahmaṇo rūpaṃ brahma|caryam iti smṛtam,
paraṃ tat sarva|dharmebhyas, tena yānti parāṃ gatim.
liṅga|saṃyoga|hīnaṃ yac, chabda|sparśa|vivarjitam,
śrotreṇa śravaṇaṃ c 'âiva, cakṣuṣā c' âiva darśanam,
vāk|saṃbhāṣā|pravṛttaṃ yat, tan manaḥ|parivarjitam;
buddhyā c' âdhyavasīyīta brahma|caryam a|kalmaṣam.

THE MASTER said:

I WILL NOW deliver a discourse on method, according to my understanding of the treatises. When a man conducts himself in accordance with his perception of it, Your Majesty, he will attain the supreme destiny. 214.1

Among all living beings a man is said to be the best. Brahmins are the best among men, so they say, and those who comprehend the Vedas are superior to brahmins. But those brahmins who become the self of all living beings, who are all-knowing, all-seeing and know the Vedas as well as the treatises—they are in no doubts as to the true nature of things.

In this world a man who does not attain gnosis is like a lonely blind man who encounters difficulties along a path. Therefore men who attain gnosis are superior.

Men dedicated to righteousness follow the religious practices prescribed by tradition. But apart from the qualities they acquire, these men do not attain the same goal. 214.5

Masters of religion prescribe these pure qualities in all religious practices: purity of speech, body and mind, along with forbearance, truth, resolve and recollection.

The celibate life is held to be the visible form of *brahman*. This method, by which people attain the transcendent state, is beyond all mundane religious practices.

Aided by his intelligence a person should undertake a spotless life of celibacy, which is devoid of bodily contact, sound and touch. It consists of learning with the ears and perceiving with vision, but avoids the thought brought about by speech and conversation.

214.10 samyag|vṛttir Brahma|lokaṃ
prāpnuyān; madhyamaḥ surān;
dvij'|āgryo jāyate vidvān
kanyasīṃ vṛttim āsthitaḥ.
su|duṣ|karaṃ brahma|caryam upāyaṃ tatra me śṛṇu!
saṃpradīptam udīrṇaṃ ca nigṛhṇīyād dvijo rajaḥ.
yoṣitāṃ na kathā śrāvyā, na nirīkṣyā nir|ambarāḥ,
kathaṃ cid darśanād āsāṃ dur|balān āviśed† rajaḥ.
rāg'|ôtpannaś caret kṛcchram, mah"|ārtiḥ praviśed apaḥ.
magnaḥ svapne ca manasā, trir japed Aghamarṣaṇam.
pāpmānaṃ nirdahed evam antarbhūta|rajo|mayam
jñāna|yuktena manasā saṃtatena vicakṣaṇaḥ.
214.15 kuṇap'|â|medhya|saṃyuktaṃ
yadvad a|cchidra|bandhanam,
tadvad deha|gataṃ vidyād
ātmānaṃ deha|bandhanam.
vāta|pitta|kaphān,† raktaṃ,
tvaṅ|māṃsaṃ, snāyum, asthi ca,
majjāṃ—dehaṃ sirā|jālais
tarpayanti rasā nṛṇām.
daśa vidyād dhamanyo 'tra pañc'|êndriya|guṇ'|āvahāḥ,
yābhiḥ sūkṣmāḥ pratāyante dhamanyo 'nyāḥ sahasraśaḥ.
evam etāḥ śirā|nadyo raso|dā deha|sāgaram
tarpayanti yathā|kālam, āpagā iva sāgaram.

Impeccable conduct leads to the world of Brahma. A person of mediocre conduct might reach the gods, whereas the person who follows this practice to a tiny degree is reborn as a learned, respectable brahmin. 214.10

Listen now as I divulge the method involved in this arduous life of celibacy!

The brahmin should suppress passion when it is excited and blazes forth. He should not listen to the chatter of young women, and should not look at them when they are naked, since passion enters the weak with a mere glance at a naked women.

If passion does arise in him his life becomes difficult. He will feel great pain, and so should immerse himself in water. If there is a nocturnal emission of semen while he sleeps, because of his dreams, he should recite the 'Agha·márshana' three times.*

With a mind continually disciplined by knowledge, the discerning student thus burns away the evil that consists of his inner passion.

He should realize that the self within is bound to the body just like an unbroken tether is connected to a ritually impure corpse. 214.15

Various juices nourish the human body—the inner winds, phlegm, bile, blood, skin, flesh, sinew, bones and bone marrow—through a network of veins. Ten channels convey the nutrients of the juices to the sense faculties, so one should understand. Thousands of other, subtler veins spread out from the ten principle veins. Therefore these veins and channels, bearing juice, nourish the ocean that is the body, just as rivers reach the ocean in due course.

madhye ca hṛdayasy' âikā śirā tatra mano|vahā
śukraṃ saṃkalpa|jaṃ nṝṇāṃ sarva|gātrair vimuñcati.

214.20 sarva|gātra|pratāyinyas tasyā hy anugatāḥ śirāḥ
netrayoḥ pratipadyante, vahantyas taijasaṃ guṇam.

payasy antar|hitaṃ sarpir yadvan nirmathyate khajaiḥ,
śukraṃ nirmathyate tadvad deha|saṃkalpa|jaiḥ khajaiḥ.

svapne 'py evaṃ yath" âbhyeti manaḥ|saṃkalpa|jaṃ rajaḥ,
śukraṃ saṃkalpa|jaṃ dehāt sṛjaty asya mano|vahā.

maha"|rṣir bhagavān Atrir veda tac chukra|saṃbhavam.
tri|bījam, Indra|daivatyaṃ, tasmād indriyam ucyate.

ye vai śukra|gatiṃ vidyur bhūta|saṃkara|kārikām,
vi|rāgā dagdha|doṣās te n' āpnuyur deha|saṃbhavam.

214.25 guṇānāṃ sāmyam āgamya, manas" âiva mano|vaham
deha|karmā nudan prāṇān, anta|kāle vimucyate.

bhavitā manaso jñānaṃ, mana eva prajāyate:
jyotiṣmad, vi|rajo nityaṃ, mantra|siddhaṃ mah"|ātmanām.

tasmāt tad|abhighātāya, karma kuryād a|kalmaṣam,
rajas tamaś ca hitv" êha, yath"|êṣṭāṃ gatim āpnuyāt.

One vein runs through the middle of the heart—the *mano·vaha*. It distributes the essential juice produced by a person's intentions throughout the body. The subsidiary 214.20
veins of the *mano·vaha* spread out through all parts of the body. Bearing the quality of fire, they reach the eyes.

Just as the ghee hidden within milk can be produced by churning it with churning sticks, so too can the essential juice be produced by churning with the ladle of a person's bodily intentions. In this way the passion born from the mind's intentions arises even in sleep, and because of this intention the *mano·vaha* emits the semen from the body.

The venerable Atri, a great seer, knew the origin of this essential juice. It has three seeds and is presided over by the deity Indra. It is because of this that the sense faculties are called *índriyas*.*

Understanding that the movements of a person's essential juices cause the intermixing of beings, men become dispassionate and burn away their sins so that they are not reborn in another body. Achieving an equilibrium of the dif- 214.25
ferent juices and subduing the *mano·vaha*, the acts of the body and breaths by means of the mind, a person attains liberation at the time of death.

Although consciousness arises in the mind, it is the mind alone that is reborn—within holy men it becomes luminous, permanently free from passion and accomplished in Vedic invocation.

Therefore, in order to ward off rebirth a person should perform deeds that are spotless. By abandoning passion and darkness, he will attain the destiny he so desires.

taruṇ'|âdhigataṃ jñānaṃ jarā|durbalatāṃ gatam.
vipakva|buddhiḥ kālena ādatte mānasaṃ balam.
su|durgam iva panthānam atītya guṇa|bandhanam,
yathā paśyet tathā doṣān atīty' â|mṛtam aśnute.

GURUR uvāca:

215.1 DUR|ANTEṢV INDRIY'|ârtheṣu saktāḥ sīdanti jantavaḥ.
ye tv a|saktā mah"|ātmānas, te yānti paramāṃ gatim.
janma|mṛtyu|jarā|duḥkhair, vyādhibhir, mānasa|klamaiḥ
dṛṣṭv" âiva saṃtataṃ lokaṃ, ghaṭen mokṣāya buddhimān.
vāṅ|manobhyāṃ śarīreṇa śuciḥ syād an|ahaṃ|kṛtaḥ.
praśānto jñānavān bhikṣur nir|apekṣaś caret sukham.
atha vā manasaḥ saṅgaṃ paśyed bhūt'|ânukampayā;
tatr' âpy upekṣāṃ kurvīta, jñātvā karma|phalaṃ jagat.
215.5 yat kṛtaṃ syāc chubhaṃ karma, pāpaṃ vā yadi v" âśnute.
tasmāc chubhāni karmāṇi kuryād vāg|buddhi|karmabhiḥ.†
a|hiṃsā, satya|vacanaṃ, sarva|bhūteṣu c' ārjavam,
kṣamā c' âiv', â|pramādaś ca: yasy' âite sa sukhī bhavet.
tasmāt samāhitaṃ buddhyā mano bhūteṣu dhārayet.*
yaś c' âinaṃ paramaṃ dharmaṃ sarva|bhūta|sukh'|āvaham
duḥkhān niḥ|saraṇaṃ veda, sarva|jñaḥ sa sukhī bhavet.
tasmāt samāhitaṃ buddhyā mano bhūteṣu dhārayet.

The knowledge a person acquires in youth is weakened by decrepitude. But if a person cultivates his intelligence for a long time, he acquires mental power.

When a person passes beyond the virtually impassable path bound by three psychosomatic states, since he gains vision he transcends all sin and attains the immortal.

THE MASTER said:

SENSE OBJECTS LEAD to misery, and those attached to 215.1
them perish. But holy men who are free from attachment attain the highest destiny.

As soon as a wise man sees that the world is enveloped in the sufferings of birth, death, decrepitude, illness and mental tribulation, he ought to strive for liberation.

He should be pure in speech, thought and body, and free from self-consciousness. Serene, wise and devoid of desire, the mendicant should wander blissfully.

If he sees an attachment in his mind, out of compassion for living beings he should make himself indifferent to it, for he understands that the world is the result of *karma*.

He experiences the results of the acts he commits, be they 215.5
pure or evil. Therefore he should perform pure acts of word, thought and deed.

Whoever is patient, diligent, non-violent, honest and sincere toward all living beings will attain bliss.

Therefore he should concentrate the mind through the faculty of intelligence, and focus it on all living beings. The one who understands the highest truth, which brings bliss to all living beings and is the way out of suffering—that all-knowing person attains bliss. Thus he should concentrate

n' âpadhyāyen, na spṛhayen, n' â|baddhaṃ cintayed a|sat.
ath' â|mogha|prayatnena mano jñāne niveśayet.
vāc"|âmogha|prayāsena mano|jñaṃ tat pravartate,
215.10 vivakṣatā ca sad|vākyaṃ dharmaṃ sūkṣmam avekṣatā.

satyāṃ vācam a|hiṃsrāṃ ca vaded an|apavādinīm;
kalk'|âpetām, a|paruṣām, a|nṛśaṃsām, a|paiśunām.
īdṛg alpaṃ ca vaktavyam a|vikṣiptena cetasā,
vāk|prabaddho hi saṃsāro; vi|rāgād vyāhared yadi.

buddhy" âpy anugṛhītena manasā karma tāmasam,
rajo|bhūtair hi karaṇaiḥ karmaṇi pratipadyate.
sa duḥkhaṃ prāpya loke 'smin narakāy' ôpapadyate.
tasmān mano|vāk|śarīrair ācared dhairyam ātmanaḥ.

prakīrṇa|meṣa|bhāro† hi yadvad dhāryeta dasyubhiḥ
pratilomāṃ diśaṃ buddhvā, saṃsāram a|budhās tathā.
215.15 tam eva ca yathā dasyuḥ kṣiptvā gacchec chivāṃ diśam,
tathā rajas|tamaḥ|karmāṇy utsṛjya prāpnuyāc chubham.

niḥ|saṃdigdham an|īho vai, muktaḥ sarva|parigrahaiḥ,
vivikta|cārī, laghv|āśī, tapasvī, niyat'|êndriyaḥ.

the mind with the faculty of intelligence, and focus it on all living beings.

He should not think ill of anyone, long for anything, or 215.10
contemplate what he does not own—which does not really exist. With an unfailing effort he should turn his mind towards gnosis. By means of an unfailing effort of speech, the person who observes the subtle religion and wishes to speak good words attains an agreeable state.

He should speak words that are true, harmless and not abusive; they should not be mean, harsh, cruel or calumnious. A person with collected thoughts should only speak such words, for transmigration is bound by speech. If a person should speak let it be without any passion.

Even when the mind is imbued with intelligence, action can be mired in darkness. When a person's sense faculties are impassioned he proceeds to act, and will experience misery in this world and then be reborn in hell. Therefore he should practice inner calming, through acts of mind, speech and body.

Just as robbers would corral their scattered flock of sheep upon realizing they are in hostile territory, thus is the lot of ignorant people in samsara.

Just as a robber who lets go of this burden might find safe 215.15
territory, so too does a person find felicity by relinquishing acts of passion and darkness.

Devoid of all possessions, living in isolation, eating little, practicing asceticism and controlling his senses, a man certainly becomes indifferent.

jñāna|dagdha|parikleśaḥ, prayoga|ratir, ātmavān,
niṣ|pracāreṇa manasā paraṃ tad adhigacchati.

dhṛtimān ātmavān buddhiṃ nigṛhṇīyād a|saṃśayam.
mano buddhyā nigṛhṇīyād, viṣayān manas" ātmanaḥ.

nigṛhīt'|êndriyasy' âsya kurvāṇasya mano vaśe
devatās saṃprakāśante† hṛṣṭā yānti tam īśvaram.

215.20 tābhiḥ saṃyukta|manaso brahma tat saṃprakāśate:
etaiś c' âpagataiḥ† sattve brahma|bhūyāya kalpate.

atha vā na pravarteta, yoga|tantrair upakramet.
yena tantrayatas tantraṃ vṛttiḥ syāt, tat tad ācaret.

kaṇa|kulmāṣa|piṇyāka|śāka|yāvaka|saktavaḥ
tathā mūla|phalaṃ bhaikṣyaṃ paryāyeṇ' ôpayojayet.

āhāra|niyamaṃ c' âiva deśe kāle ca sāttvikam
tat parīkṣy' ânuvarteta tat pravṛtty|anupūrvakam.

pravṛttaṃ n' ôparundheta, śanair agnim iv' êndhayet,
jñān'|ânvitaṃ tathā jñānam arkavat saṃprakāśate.

215.25 jñān'|âdhiṣṭhānam a|jñānaṃ trīl lokān adhitiṣṭhati.
vijñān'|ânugataṃ jñānam a|jñānen' âpakṛṣyate.

His defilements burned away by gnosis, the self-controlled man finds pleasure in his religious practices and attains the transcendent by means of a still mind.

Resolute and self-controlled, he should certainly restrain his faculty of intelligence. He should restrain the mind through his faculty of intelligence, and keep sense objects away from himself by means of his mind.

The "deities"—or sense faculties—of a man who restrains them and controls his mind become radiant. Bristling with rapture, they enter that man of power.

When his mind and sense faculties are integrated *brah-* 215.20
man shines forth: when his senses settle into a state of purity, he is fit for the state of *brahman*.

Should he not wish to remain active in the world, he should proceed according to the practices of *yoga*. He should practice a method that is comparable to the conduct of a person threading a loom.

He may eat corn, gruel, oil-cakes, potherbs, barley-gruel, groats, roots and fruits as almsfood, in a fixed routine.

He should experiment with restricting his food to that which is pure and to be eaten only at specific times and places, and then stick to a regular routine.

Just as one would kindle a fire gradually, and not obstruct it when it has been produced, so does one's consciousness shine forth like the sun when it has been intensified by gnosis.

The ignorance that rules the three worlds is presided over 215.25
by consciousness, but when consciousness is disturbed by sense cognition it is dragged down by ignorance.

pṛthaktvāt saṃprayogāc ca n' âsūyur veda śāśvatam.
sa tayor apavarga|jño vīta|rāgo vimucyate.
vayo|'tīto jarā|mṛtyū jitvā, brahma sanātanam
a|mṛtaṃ tad avāpnoti, yat tad a|kṣaram a|vyayam.

GURUR uvāca:

216.1 NIṢ|KALMAṢAṂ BRAHMA|caryam icchatā carituṃ sadā
nidrā sarv'|ātmanā tyājyā, svapna|doṣān avekṣatā.
svapne hi rajasā dehī, tamasā c' âbhibhūyate.
deh'|ântaram iv' āpannaś caraty apagata|spṛhaḥ.
jñān'|âbhyāsāj jāgaraṇaṃ jijñās"|ârtham an|antaram;
vijñān'|âbhiniveśāt tu sa jāgarty a|niśaṃ sadā.
atr' āha ko nv ayaṃ bhāvaḥ svapne viṣayavān iva?
pralīnair indriyair dehī vartate dehavān iva.
216.5 atr' ôcyate yathā hy etad veda yog'|ēśvaro Hariḥ,
tath" âitad upapann'|ârthaṃ† varṇayanti maha"|rṣayaḥ.
indriyāṇāṃ śramāt svapnam āhuḥ sarva|gataṃ budhāḥ.
manasas tv a|pralīnatvāt tat tad āhur nidarśanam.

Affected by states of separation and conjunction, the spiteful man does not realize the eternal. But when he realizes his emancipation from these two states, he becomes devoid of passion and is liberated.

Transcending old-age, he conquers decrepitude and death and realizes *brahman*, which is primeval, immortal, imperishable and immutable.

THE MASTER said:

THE PERSON WHO wishes to follow the pure life of celibacy 216.1
for the rest of his life should make every effort to abandon sleep, once he has become aware of its faults. For it is during sleep that the soul is overcome with passion and darkness. It seems to enter another body and wander about without any purpose.

Disciplining himself in consciousness, he should always remain awake in order to attain gnosis. Because of his devotion to perception he is ever awake and takes no sleep.

But what is this state of sleep said to be, in which a person seems to be aware of sense objects? The soul acts as if it possesses a body, although at the time its sense faculties rest within.

Herein, it is said that the great seers describe the matter 216.5
just as Hari, the lord of *yoga*, understands it, once they have realized its meaning.*

Wise men say that sleep is a universal phenomenon that arises when the sense faculties become weary. They say that when the mind is not withdrawn, it perceives different objects.

kārye vyāsakta|manasaḥ saṃkalpo jāgrato hy api
yadvan mano|rath'|āiśvaryaṃ, svapne tadvan mano|gatam.†

saṃsārāṇām a|saṃkhyānāṃ kām'|ātmā tad avāpnuyāt.
manasy antar|hitaṃ sarvaṃ sa ved' ôttama|pūruṣaḥ†
guṇānām api yad yat tat,† karmaṇā c' âpy upasthitam,
tat tac chaṃsanti bhūtāni, mano yad bhāvitaṃ yathā.

216.10 tatas tam upasarpante guṇā rājasa|tāmasāḥ,
sāttvikā vā yathā|yogam, ānantarya|phal'|ôdayam.
tataḥ paśyanty a|saṃbuddhyā vāta|pitta|kaph'|ôttarān
rajas|tamo|gatair bhāvais. tad apy āhur dur|atyayam.

prasannair indriyair yad yat saṃkalpayati mānasam,
tat tat svapne 'py upagate mano hṛṣyan nirīkṣate.
vyāpakaṃ sarva|bhūteṣu vartate '|pratighaṃ manaḥ.
ātma|prabhāvāt taṃ vidyāt, sarvā hy ātmani devatāḥ.

manasy antar|hitaṃ dvāraṃ, deham āsthāya mānasam,†
yad yat sad a|sad a|vyaktaṃ, svapity asmin nidarśanam.
sarva|bhūt'|ātma|bhūta|sthaṃ tam adhyātma|guṇaṃ viduḥ.

216.15 lipseta manasā yaś ca saṃkalpād aiśvaraṃ guṇam,
ātma|prasādāt† taṃ vidyāt, sarvā hy ātmani devatāḥ.

When he is awake, a person whose mind is occupied with his work has intentions, and his thoughts in sleep conform to the power of these fancies.

The person obsessed by sensual pleasure might realize these fancies, after being reborn countless times; the supreme spirit knows all this that is hidden within the mind. People commend whatever sort of object is brought about through one's *karma*, no matter how this fancy is brought about.

Therefore a person is subjected to states of passion, dark- 216.10
ness or purity, according to circumstances, and he receives their effects immediately. Thus people experience excesses of wind, bile and phlegm caused by states of passion and darkness, but fail to understand them. That is hard to overcome, so they say.

When sleep overcomes a person he sees the delightful fancies conjured up when his sense faculties were inactive. The mind dominates all living beings, and operates without any obstruction. One should know the self through one's own endeavors, for all the senses reside in the self.*

Once a person enters his "mental" body—the door hidden within the mind—a person perceives, during his sleep, that which is unmanifest and comprises both the existent and non-existent. That abides within as the self of every being; they know it as a derivative of the supreme self.

The person who desires to gain the quality of meditative 216.15
power, by means of thought and intention, should realize that through inner tranquility, when all the senses abide within.

evaṃ hi tapasā yuktam arkavat tamasaḥ param.
trailokya|prakṛtir dehī, tamaso 'nte mah''|ēśvaraḥ.
tapo hy adhiṣṭhitaṃ devais, tapo|ghnam asurais tamaḥ.
etad dev'|âsurair guptaṃ tad āhur jñāna|lakṣaṇam.
sattvaṃ, rajas tamaś c' êti dev'|âsura|guṇān viduḥ.
sattvaṃ deva|guṇaṃ vidyād, itarāv āsurau guṇau.
brahma tat paramaṃ jñānam, a|mṛtaṃ jyotir a|kṣaram,
ye vidur bhāvit'|ātmānas, te yānti paramāṃ gatim.
216.20 hetumac chakyam ākhyātum etāvaj jñāna|cakṣuṣā.
pratyāhāreṇa vā śakyam a|kṣaraṃ brahma veditum.

GURUR uvāca:

217.1 NA SA VEDA PARAṂ brahma, yo na veda catuṣṭayam,
vyakt'|âvyaktaṃ ca yat tattvaṃ samproktaṃ parama'|rṣiṇā.
vyaktaṃ mṛtyu|mukhaṃ vidyād,
a|vyaktam a|mṛtaṃ padam.
pravṛtti|lakṣaṇaṃ dharmam
ṛṣir Nārāyaṇo 'bravīt,
tatr' âiv' âvasthitaṃ sarvaṃ trailokyaṃ sa|car'|âcaram.
nivṛtti|lakṣaṇaṃ dharmam a|vyaktaṃ brahma śāśvatam.

That which is beyond darkness is connected to the practice of asceticism, and is like fire. The soul has the nature of the triple world, but once it has gone beyond darkness it attains great power. The gods preside over asceticism, the *ásuras* preside over the darkness that destroys it. They say that the gods protect this asceticism characterized by gnosis from the demons.

It is believed that the states of purity, passion and darkness are found among the gods and demons. But one should understand that purity is the state found among the gods, whereas the other two are found among the demons.

Once they know *brahman*, the supreme state of consciousness that is immortal, radiant and imperishable, men of inner cultivation attain the highest destiny.

It is possible to pronounce this much rationally, provided 216.20
one possesses the eye of knowledge. But by withdrawing the senses from their objects, it is possible to realize the imperishable *brahman*.

THE MASTER said:

UNLESS ONE KNOWS the set of four,* one cannot real- 217.1
ize the transcendent *brahman*—the reality that has been explained by the supreme seer to comprise both the manifest and unmanifest. One should know that the manifest is the door to death, whereas the unmanifest is the immortal state.

The seer Naráyana expounded the religious order characterized by worldly endeavor, and the entire triple world of mobile and immobile beings is founded on just that. But

pravṛtti|lakṣaṇaṃ dharmaṃ Prajāpatir ath' âbravīt.
pravṛttiḥ punar|āvṛttir, nivṛttiḥ paramā gatiḥ.
217.5 tāṃ gatiṃ paramām eti nivṛtti|paramo muniḥ.
jñāna|tattva|paro nityaṃ śubh'|âśubha|nidarśakaḥ.

tad evam etau vijñeyāv avyakta|puruṣāv ubhau.
avyakta|puruṣābhyāṃ tu yat syād anyan mahattaram?
taṃ viśeṣam avekṣeta viśeṣeṇa vicakṣaṇaḥ.
an|ādy|antāv ubhāv etāv, a|liṅgau c' âpy ubhāv api.
ubhau nityāv, a|vicalau, mahadbhyaś ca mahattarau.

sāmānyam etad ubhayor; evaṃ hy anyad viśeṣaṇam.
prakṛtyā sarga|dharmiṇyā tathā tri|guṇa|dharmayā,
viparītam ato vidyāt kṣetra|jñasya sva|lakṣaṇam,
217.10 prakṛteś ca vikārāṇāṃ draṣṭāram a|guṇ'|ânvitam.

a|grāhyau puruṣāv etāv, a|liṅgatvād a|saṃhatau.
saṃyoga|lakṣaṇ'|ôtpattiḥ karmaṇā gṛhyate yathā;
karaṇaiḥ karma|nirvṛttiḥ kartā yad yad viceṣṭate.
kīrtyate śabda|saṃjñābhiḥ «ko 'ham? eṣo 'py? asāv?» iti.

the religious order characterized by otherworldly inaction is identical with the unmanifest, eternal *brahman*.

Praja·pati, the lord of creatures, also expounded the religious order characterized by worldly endeavor. Worldly endeavor leads to reincarnation, whereas otherworldly inaction leads to the highest destiny. The silent sage who is de- 217.5
voted to inaction attains the highest destiny. Through his continual devotion to states of consciousness, he sees what is pure and impure.

Therefore one should understand this pair: unmanifest matter and spirit. What other thing could be greater than them?* A discerning man should particularly perceive the distinction between the two. Both are without beginning and end, both have no characteristic mark. Both are permanent, immovable and beyond the macrocosmic faculty of intelligence.

This is the similarity between the two—the distinction between them lies elsewhere. Since primordial matter is characterized by creation and the three psychosomatic states of purity, passion and darkness, understand that the characteristic of the field-knower is quite different from this, and 217.10
that the one who observes the modifications of primordial matter is not connected to the three psychosomatic states.

These two entities—the observer and primordial matter—are ungraspable; because they lack characteristics they are uncompounded. The characteristics of connection come into being and are acquired through *karma*; *karma* is produced through the acts that the person, as an agent, commits himself to. The agent is explained through the clear

uṣṇīṣavān yathā vastrais tribhir bhavati saṃvṛtaḥ,
saṃvṛto 'yaṃ tathā dehī sattva|rājasa|tāmasaiḥ.
tasmāc catuṣṭayaṃ vedyam etair hetubhir āvṛtam.
yathā|saṃjño hy ayaṃ samyag anta|kāle na muhyati.

śriyaṃ divyām abhiprepsur, varṣmavān, manasā śuciḥ,
śārīrair niyamair ugraiś caren niṣ|kalmaṣaṃ tapaḥ.
217.15 trailokyaṃ tapasā vyāptam antar|bhūtena bhāsvatā;
sūryaś ca candramāś c' âiva bhāsatas tapasā divi.

prakāśas tapaso jñānaṃ: loke saṃśabditaṃ tapaḥ;
rajas|tamo|ghnaṃ yat karma tapasas, tat sva|lakṣaṇam.
brahma|caryam a|hiṃsā ca śārīraṃ tapa ucyate,
vāṅ|mano|niyamaḥ samyaṅ mānasaṃ tapa ucyate.

vidhi|jñebhyo dvi|jātibhyo grāhyam annaṃ viśiṣyate;
āhāra|niyamen' âsya pāpmā śāmyati rājasaḥ.
vaimanasyaṃ ca viṣaye yānty asya karaṇāni ca,
tasmāt tan|mātram ādadyād, yāvad atra prayojanam.
217.20 anta|kāle bal'|ôtkarṣāc chanaiḥ kuryād an|āturaḥ,
evaṃ yuktena manasā jñānaṃ yad upapadyate.

understanding of the questions "Who am I? Who is this? Who is that?"

Just as a man wearing a turban swathes himself in three cloths, so too is this soul enveloped by states of purity, passion and darkness. One should know, therefore, that the set of four* is concealed by these causes. The person who has a perfect understanding of this will not be perplexed at the time of death.

The pure hearted person who longs to achieve divine felicity should observe pure ascetic practices by performing fierce physical restraints. The triple world is permeated by 217.15
this hidden, resplendent asceticism; it is because of this ascetic power that the sun and moon shine in the heavens above.

Asceticism is praised in this world: the light it produces is gnosis; the action that destroys passion and darkness is a particular characteristic of it. It is said that physical asceticism consists of celibacy and non-violence; mental asceticism is said to be the complete control of speech and mind.

The best food should be taken from brahmins learned in the ritual method; the evil that arises from passion is pacified by restraint in food. Acting on a sense object leads to dejection, and so one should take only as much food as one's purpose demands.

At the time of death one should make a supreme effort 217.20
to gradually free oneself from affliction; gnosis is attained by disciplining the mind in this manner.

rajo|varjyo 'py ayaṃ dehī dehavāñ śabdavac caret,
kāryair a|vyāhata|matir, vairāgyāt prakṛtau sthitaḥ.
ā dehād a|pramādāc ca deh'|ântād vipramucyate.

hetu|yuktaḥ sadā sargo bhūtānāṃ, pralayas tathā.
para|pratyaya|sarge tu niyatir n' ânuvartate,
bhāv'|ânta|prabhav'|â|prajñā† āsate ye viparyayam.

dhṛtyā dehān dhārayanto, buddhi|saṃkṣipta|cetasaḥ,
sthānebhyo dhvaṃsamānāś ca: sūkṣmatvāt tān upāsate.

217.25 yath"|āgamaṃ ca gatvā vai buddhyā tatr' âiva budhyate,
deh'|ântaṃ kaś cid anvāste bhāvit'|ātmā nir|āśrayam.

yukto dhāraṇayā kaś cit,† sataḥ ke cid upāsate,
abhyasyanti paraṃ devaṃ vidyā†|saṃśabdit'|â|kṣaram.
anta|kāle hy upāsante, tapasā dagdha|kilbiṣāḥ,
sarva ete mah"|ātmāno gacchanti paramāṃ gatim.

sūkṣmaṃ viśeṣaṇaṃ teṣām avekṣec chāstra|cakṣuṣā.
deh'|ântaṃ paramaṃ vidyād vimuktam a|parigraham,
antarikṣād anyataraṃ dhāraṇ"|āsakta|mānasam.

A person should avoid passion and wander like sound, even in his embodied state. His thoughts unencumbered by duties, through dispassion he abides in his true nature. If he remains diligent for as long as he has a body, he is released at the time of death.

The creation and dissolution of living beings is brought about by a cause. Fate has no part to play in the arising of a thing from a cause, but those who do not understand the origin and end of living beings think differently.

Those who sustain their bodies through resolve, gather their thoughts in the faculty of intelligence and withdraw from their positions in the world are revered because of their subtlety.

Another person practices in accordance with the scrip- 217.25
tures, and understands their teachings through his faculty of intelligence. This person of inner cultivation waits for death, which is without any physical locus.

One person is disciplined in meditative absorption, others venerate virtuous men and yet others focus on the transcendent deity, the imperishable that is eulogized as "knowledge." Engaged in these various practices at the time of death, their sins burned away by asceticism, all of these holy men attain the ultimate destiny.

Through understanding this teaching one should note the subtle distinction between these three types. And one should understand their death as the ultimate release free from grasping —a state of mind immersed in meditative absorption that lies beyond the sky.

martya|lokād vimucyante vidyā|saṃsakta|cetasaḥ.
217.30 brahma|bhūtā, vi|rajasas tato yānti parāṃ gatim.

evam ek'|âyanaṃ dharmam āhur veda|vido janāḥ,
yathā|jñānam upāsantaḥ sarve yānti parāṃ gatim.

kaṣāya|varjitaṃ jñānaṃ yeṣām utpadyate '|calam,
yānti te 'pi parāl̐ lokān, vimucyante yathā|balam.

bhagavantam a|jaṃ divyaṃ Viṣṇum a|vyakta|saṃjñitam
bhāvena yānti śuddhā ye jñāna|tṛptā nir|āśiṣaḥ.

jñātv" ātma|sthaṃ Hariṃ c' âiva na nivartanti te '|vyayāḥ.
prāpya tat paramaṃ sthānaṃ modante '|kṣaram a|vyayam.

etāvad etad vijñānam: etad asti ca n' âsti ca.
tṛṣṇā|baddhaṃ jagat sarvaṃ cakravat parivartate.

217.35 bisa|tantur yath" âiv' âyam antaḥ|sthaḥ sarvato bise,
tṛṣṇā|tantur an|ādy|antas tathā deha|gataḥ sadā.

sūcyā sūtraṃ yathā vastre saṃsārayati vāyakaḥ,
tadvat saṃsāra|sūtraṃ hi tṛṣṇā|sūcyā nibadhyate.

vikāraṃ, prakṛtiṃ c' âiva, puruṣaṃ ca sanātanam
yo yathāvad vijānāti, sa vi|tṛṣṇo vimucyate.

Their thoughts immersed in knowledge, these men are
released from the world of mortals. Having attained iden- 217.30
tification with *brahman*, and being devoid of passion, they attain the supreme destiny. Therefore the Vedic masters say that religion has one end, since all those who practice in accordance with their understanding attain the transcendent destiny. Attaining an unshakeable knowledge devoid of defilement, they attain transcendent worlds and are liberated in accordance with their religious ability.

Some, purified by meditative cultivation, satiated by gnosis and freed from desire, attain the blessed Vishnu, who is unborn, divine, and known as the "unmanifest." Once they have perceived Hari abiding within they become immutable and do not return; they attain the ultimate condition, imperishable and undecaying, and rejoice.

This is the extent of perception: this exists, this does not exist. The entire world is bound by thirst, and revolves like a wheel.

Just as lotus fiber is found throughout a lotus plant, so 217.35
does the soul always exist in the body; its "fiber" is thirst and yet it lacks a beginning and end.

Just as a weaver strings a thread through a garment with a shuttle, so is the thread of transmigration bound in place by the shuttle of thirst.

The person who perceives primordial matter, its modification and the primeval spirit as it really is becomes devoid of thirst and is released.

prakāśaṃ bhagavān etad ṛṣir Nārāyaṇo ’|mṛtam
bhūtānām anukamp’|ârthaṃ jagāda jagato gatiḥ.

The blessed seer Naráyana, destiny of the whole world, uttered this illuminating teaching on the immortal out of compassion for all living beings.

218–219

THE TEACHINGS OF PANCHA·SHIKHA

YUDHIṢṬHIRA uvāca:

218.1 KENA VṚTTENA, VṚTTA|jña,
Janako Mithil'|âdhipaḥ
jagāma mokṣaṃ mokṣa|jño,
bhogān utsṛjya mānuṣān?

BHĪṢMA uvāca:

atr' âpy udāharant' îmam itihāsaṃ purātanam:
yena vṛttena dharma|jñaḥ sa jagāma mahat sukham.
Janako jana|devas tu Mithilāyāṃ jan'|âdhipaḥ
aurdhvadehika|dharmāṇām āsīd yukto vicintane.
tasya sma śatam ācāryā vasanti satataṃ gṛhe,
darśayantaḥ pṛthag dharmān nānā|pāṣaṇḍa|vādinaḥ.†
218.5 sa teṣāṃ pretya|bhāve ca pretya|jātau viniścaye,
āgama|sthaḥ sa bhūyiṣṭham, ātma|tattve na tuṣyati.
tatra Pañcaśikho nāma Kāpileyo mahā|muniḥ
paridhāvan mahīṃ kṛtsnāṃ jagāma Mithilām atha,
sarva|saṃnyāsa|dharmāṇāṃ tattva|jñāna|viniścaye
su|paryavasit'|ârthaś ca, nir|dvaṃdvo, naṣṭa|saṃśayaḥ.
ṛṣīṇām āhur ekaṃ taṃ, yaṃ kām'|ân|āvṛtaṃ nṛṣu,
śāśvataṃ sukham atyantam anvicchantaṃ su|dur|labham:
yam āhuḥ Kapilaṃ sāṃkhyāḥ, parama'|rṣiṃ Prajāpatim,
sa manye tena rūpeṇa vismāpayati hi svayam!

YUDHI·SHTHIRA said:

ONCE HE HAD abandoned human pleasures, master of conduct, what practice did King Jánaka of Míthila follow in order to realize and perceive liberation? 218.1

BHISHMA said:

On this subject people relate the ancient tradition of the conduct through which that master of religion attained great bliss.

King Jánaka of Míthila was dedicated to the contemplation of different systems of metaphysics, and a hundred teachers proclaiming various heresies were permanent residents in his home, each teaching him their individual doctrines. He was greatly learned in scriptural knowledge, but 218.5
was not satisfied with their opinions on the state after death, reincarnation or the true nature of the self.

At that time there was a great sage called Pancha·shikha, a follower of Kápila, who arrived at Míthila in the course of wandering the entire earth. He had fully accomplished his purpose by working out a true understanding of all renunciant doctrines, and so had annihilated his doubts and passed beyond duality.

There was one individual among the seers who, they say, avoided the sensual pleasures of men while searching for that final, eternal bliss so hard to attain: the Samkhya followers call him Kápila, as well as Praja·pati, the supreme seer. Methinks that he astonished people with his own appearance!

218.10 Āsureḥ prathamaṃ śiṣyaṃ, yam āhuś cira|jīvinam,
pañca|srotasi yaḥ satram āste varṣa|sahasrikam.
yatra c' āsīnam āgamya Kāpilaṃ maṇḍalaṃ mahat,
«pañca|srotasi niṣṇātaḥ, pañca|rātra|viśāradaḥ,
pañca|jñaḥ, pañca|kṛt, pañca|
guṇaḥ Pañcaśikhaḥ smṛtaḥ.»*
puruṣ'|âvastham a|vyaktaṃ
param'|ârthaṃ nibodhayat.†
iṣṭa|satreṇa saṃpṛṣṭo bhūyaś ca tapas" Āsuriḥ,
kṣetra|kṣetra|jñayor vyaktiṃ bubudhe deva|darśanaḥ.
yat tad ek'|â|kṣaraṃ brahma nānā|rūpaṃ pradṛśyate,
Āsurir maṇḍale tasmin pratipede tad a|vyayam.
218.15 tasya Pañcaśikhaḥ śiṣyo mānuṣyā payasā bhṛtaḥ.
brāhmaṇī Kapilā nāma kā cid āsīt kuṭumbinī.
tasyāḥ putratvam āgamya striyāḥ sa pibati stanau.
tataḥ sa Kāpileyatvaṃ lebhe, buddhiṃ ca naiṣṭhikīm.
etan me bhagavān āha Kāpileyasya saṃbhavam:
tasya tat Kāpileyatvaṃ, sarva|vittvam an|uttamam.

Pancha·shikha was the principle disciple of Ásuri. They 218.10
say he was long-lived, and had sat at the confluence of five streams for a "sacrificial" session that lasted a thousand years.

After he had arrived at a sitting of the great brotherhood of Kápila, he realized the supreme goal, the unmanifest condition of spirit.

"He was deeply versed in the stream of five, and skilled in the practice of five nights. He knew the five things, carried out the five acts, possessed the five qualities and was known as Pancha·shikha."

Ásuri had the appearance of a god and was ardent in his ascetic practices. After being quizzed by Kápila, who had completed a long "sacrificial" session, he realized the distinction between the "field" and the "field-knower." In that brotherhood of Kápila, Ásuri attained *brahman*, which is single, imperishable and immutable—the one whose manifold forms are witnessed in the world.

His disciple Pancha·shikha was raised on the milk of a 218.15
certain brahmin woman called Kapilá. Pancha·shikha became her son, and used to drink from her breast. Hence he became a son of Kapilá and eventually attained the highest understanding.

The blessed one informed me of all this on the origin of Pancha·shikha Kapiléya—how he became the son of Kapilá and attained the incomparable state of omniscience.

sāmānyaṃ Janakaṃ jñātvā dharma|jño jñānam uttamam
upetya śatam ācāryān mohayām āsa hetubhiḥ.
Janakas tv abhisaṃraktaḥ Kāpiley'|ânudarśanāt,
utsṛjya śatam ācāryān pṛṣṭhato 'nujagāma tam.

218.20 tasmai parama|kalyāya praṇatāya ca dharmataḥ,
abravīt paramaṃ mokṣaṃ yat tat Sāṃkhye 'bhidhīyate.
jāti|nirvedam uktvā sa karma|nirvedam abravīt.
karma|nirvedam uktvā ca sarva|nirvedam abravīt.

yad|arthaṃ dharma|saṃsargaḥ,
karmaṇāṃ ca phal'|ôdayaḥ,
tad† an|āśvāsikaṃ: mohaṃ,
vināśi, calam, a|dhruvam.

dṛśyamāne vināśe ca pratyakṣe loka|sākṣike,
āgamāt «param ast'» îti bruvann api parājitaḥ.
an|ātmā hy, ātmano mṛtyuḥ: kleśo, mṛtyur, jar", āmayaḥ.
ātmānaṃ manyate mohāt: tad a|samyak paraṃ matam.

218.25 atha ced evam apy asti yal loke n' ôpapadyate,
«a|jaro 'yam a|mṛtyuś ca,» rāj" âsau manyate yathā.

Knowing that Jánaka was a fair man, Pancha·shikha, a master of religion who had attained the supreme understanding, bewildered those one hundred teachers with his reasoning. Pleased by the appearance of Kapiléya, Jánaka dismissed his teachers and pursued him.

Kapiléya taught the highest liberation, as it is described 218.20
in the Samkhya teaching, to that supremely able king who bowed in homage according to religious custom. He told him about disillusionment with birth, religious deeds and finally everything.

PANCHA·SHIKHA said:

The purpose for which a person adheres to religious custom and then receives the retribution of its rites lacks any consolation: it is deluding, destructible, unsteady and transient.

When destruction is perceived and actually observed in the world, a person will be defeated if he depends upon the testimony of scriptures in stating that the transcendent exists.

The transcendent is certainly not the individual self, since the individual self is subject to death: affliction, death, decrepitude and illness affect it. A person thinks it is the individual self because of his delusion, but that is the wrong way to consider the transcendent.

If one holds that what does not appear in the world exists, 218.25
it is just like thinking of the king "He is beyond decrepitude and death!"

«asti n' âst'» îti c' âpy etat, tasminn a|sati lakṣaṇe,
kim adhiṣṭhāya tad brūyāl loka|yātrā|viniścayam?

pratyakṣaṃ hy etayor mūlaṃ kṛt'|ânt'|āitihyayor api:
pratyakṣeṇ' āgamo bhinnaḥ, kṛt'|ânto vā na kiṃ cana,
yatra yatr' ânumāne 'smin kṛtaṃ bhāvayato 'pi ca.

n' ânyo jīvaḥ śarīrasya nāstikānāṃ mate sthitaḥ,
reto vaṭa|kaṇīkāyāṃ ghṛta|pāk'|âdhivāsanam.
jātiḥ smṛtir ayas|kāntaḥ sūrya|kānto; 'mbu|bhakṣaṇam.

218.30 pretī|bhūte 'tyayaś c' âiva, devat"|ādy|upayācanam.
mṛte karma|nivṛttiś ca: pramāṇam iti niścayaḥ.

nanv ete hetavaḥ santi ye ke cin mūrti|saṃsthitāḥ,
a|mūrtasya hi mūrtena sāmānyaṃ n' ôpapadyate.

a|vidyā|karma|tṛṣṇānāṃ† ke cid āhuḥ punar|bhave,
kāraṇaṃ lobha|mohau tu doṣāṇāṃ tu niṣevaṇam.

"It both exists and does not exist;" this is one way of thinking about the transcendent. But since such a characteristic is not found, with reference to what could one say that it has been understood according to worldly events?

Direct perception is the root of both empirical proof and traditional teaching. Scripture is refuted by direct perception, otherwise an empirical proof would count for nothing at all, even for the person who promotes a practice based on a deduction about a particular perception.*

In the opinion of heretic materialists, the soul does not abide in the body as a separate entity—its existential state is just like the germ in the seed of a banyan tree, or the ghee that permeates cooked food. They say that birth and recollection occur automatically, just like the action of a lodestone or sun-stone. The soul's existence ought to be understood through the analogy of tasting salty water, since salt is tasted throughout the water.

They say that when a person dies he is destroyed, even 218.30
though people solicit the gods and so on in prayer. When a man dies his action ceases, and this, they say, is the proof for the materialist position.

But surely all these arguments are concerned with physical form, and yet there can be no identity between that which has form and that which does not.

Some say that greed, delusion, and the habitual tendency towards other vices are the cause of the rebirth of ignorance, *karma* and thirst.

a|vidyāṃ kṣetram āhur hi, karma bījaṃ tathā kṛtam.
tṛṣṇā|saṃjananaṃ sneha: eṣa teṣāṃ punar|bhavaḥ.
tasmin vyūḍhe† ca dagdhe ca, citte† maraṇa|dharmiṇi,
anyo 'nyāj jāyate dehas: tam āhuḥ sattva|saṃkṣayam.

218.35 yadā sva|rūpataś c' ânyo jātitaḥ śubhato 'rthataḥ,
katham asmin sa ity eva† saṃbandhaḥ?† syād a|saṃhitam.
evaṃ sati ca kā prītir dāna|vidyā|tapo|balaiḥ?
yad asy' ācaritaṃ karma sarvam anyat prapadyate.
api hy ayam ih' âiv' ânyaiḥ prākṛtair duḥkhito bhavet;
sukhito duḥkhito v" âpi. dṛśy'|âdṛśya|vinirṇayaḥ.
tathā hi musalair hanyuḥ śarīraṃ, tat punar bhavet
pṛthag|jñānaṃ yad anyac ca; yen' âitan n' ôpapadyate.
ṛtu|saṃvatsarau tithyaḥ† śīt'|ôṣṇau 'tha priy'|âpriye:
yath" âtītāni paśyanti, tādṛśaḥ sattva|saṃkṣayaḥ.

These—the Buddhists—say that ignorance is the field, the act committed is the seed and the arising of thirst is the moisture necessary for its germination: this, for them, accounts for rebirth.

When the seed that causes an existence develops and is burned away, and since the mind is characterized by death, another body is born from another seed: that, they say, constitutes the dissolution of a living thing.

If, however, the new body is different in terms of its na- 218.35
ture, origin, virtue and cause, how could it be connected to the previous one? It must be unconnected

If individual existence is indeed thus, how could anyone experience joy through the power of one's former charity, knowledge or asceticism? Every deed a person performs would turn into something different.

Moreover, a person would be made to experience suffering in this world because of the wicked acts of others; he would feel happiness and suffering in just this way. This settles the matter of that which is visible—a person—and that which is invisible—his *karma*.

According to the Buddhists, although people might slay a body with maces, the individual consciousness reborn would be different; the consciousness of the person dying would not be reborn through that new individual consciousness.

According to fatalists, the dissolution of a living thing is analogous to the natural way in which they understand that the seasons, years, lunar days, cold, heat, pleasure and pain disappear.

218.40 jarayā 'bhiparītasya mṛtyunā ca vināśinā
dur|balaṃ dur|balaṃ pūrvaṃ gṛhasy' êva vinaśyati.
indriyāṇi, mano, vāyuḥ, śoṇitaṃ, māṃsam, asthi ca
ānupūrvyā vinaśyanti, svaṃ dhātum upayānti ca.
loka|yātrā vighātaś ca dāna|dharma|phal'|āgame,
tad|arthaṃ veda|śabdāś ca vyavahārāś ca laukikāḥ.
iti samyaṅ manasy ete bahavaḥ santi hetavaḥ.
«etad ast', îdam ast'» îti, na kiṃ cit pratidṛśyate!
teṣāṃ vimṛśatām eva tat tat samabhidhāvatām,
kva cin niviśate buddhis, tatra jīryati vṛkṣavat.
218.45 evam arthair an|arthaiś ca duḥkhitāḥ sarva|jantavaḥ,
āgamair apakṛṣyante hasti|pair hastino yathā.
arthāṃs tath" âtyanta†|sukh'|āvahāṃś ca
lipsanta ete bahavo viśuṣkāḥ!
mahattaraṃ duḥkham anuprapannā,
hitv" āmiṣaṃ mṛtyu|vaśaṃ prayānti.
vināśino hy a|dhruva|jīvitasya
kiṃ bandhubhir bhinna|parigrahaiś ca?
vihāya yo gacchati sarvam eva,
kṣaṇena gatvā na nivartate ca.

The person seized by decrepitude and the destructive 218.40
power of death becomes weaker, gradually, just like a house, and eventually perishes.

The sense faculties, mind, internal wind, blood, flesh and bones are destroyed one after the other and enter their own essence.

But continued existence in the world and its destruction depend on receiving the retribution of acts of charity and religion, and for this there are Vedic invocations and worldly practices.

These, therefore, are the many arguments that one might believe to be true. People think "This exists, that exists," but nothing is witnessed!

While people consider these arguments and jump to this or that conclusion, their faculties of intelligence incline towards a particular idea and wither away in that state, just like a tree.

All creatures suffer because of their achievements and 218.45
calamities, and are drawn away by events that assail them, just like elephants led away by their mahouts.

Innumerable are the thirsty souls who lust after the objects that bring excessive bliss! But they experience terrible suffering, and once they abandon the pleasures of the flesh they enter the dominion of death.

A person will eventually die since life is transient, so what is the point of kinsmen or destructible possessions? A person abandons everything and departs—he disappears in an instant and does not return.

bhū|vyoma|toy'|ânala|vāyavo 'pi
sadā śarīraṃ pratipālayanti.
it' îdam ālakṣya ratiḥ kuto bhaved?
vināśino 'py asya na śarma vidyate.

idam an|upadhi vākyam a|cchalaṃ,
parama|nirāmayam ātma|sākṣikam
nara|patir abhivīkṣya vismitaḥ,
punar anuyoktum idaṃ pracakrame.

BHĪṢMA uvāca:

219.1 JANAKO JANA|DEVAS tu jñāpitaḥ parama'|rṣiṇā
punar ev' ânupapraccha sāṃparāye bhav'|âbhavau:
«bhagavan, yadi na pretya saṃjñā bhavati kasya cit,
evaṃ sati kim a|jñānaṃ, jñānaṃ vā kiṃ kariṣyati?
sarvam uccheda|niṣṭhaṃ syāt:
paśya c' âitad, dvij'|ôttama.
a|pramattaḥ pramatto vā
kiṃ viśeṣaṃ kariṣyati?
a|saṃsargo hi bhūteṣu saṃsargo vā vināśiṣu
kasmai kriyeta kalpyeta? niścayaḥ ko 'tra tattvataḥ?»

BHĪṢMA uvāca:

219.5 tamasā hi praticchannaṃ, vibhrāntam iva c' āturam
punaḥ praśamayan vākyaiḥ kaviḥ Pañcaśikho 'bravīt.

Earth, space, water, fire and wind maintain the body without fail. In consideration of this, how could anyone indulge in pleasure? There is no refuge for that which is destructible.

BHISHMA said:

This teaching is free from deception and deceit, it is supremely beneficial and bears witness unto the self. Upon contemplating it King Jánaka was astonished, and decided to question Pancha·shikha further.

BHISHMA said:

AFTER BEING INSTRUCTED by that supreme seer, King Já- 219.1
naka once again quizzed him on existence and non-existence in the state after death:

"Perhaps, venerable sir, a person is insentient after death. If so, what difference does it make if a person is ignorant or knowledgeable?*

Consider, eminent brahmin, that everything ends in destruction. If so, what difference does it make if a person lives diligently or negligently?

Association or dissociation with perishable living beings affects or happens to whom? How should this matter be resolved, in accordance with the way things truly are?"

BHISHMA said:

The king was shrouded in darkness, seemingly confused 219.5
and tormented, but the sage Pancha·shikha soothed him with further teachings.

uccheda|niṣṭhā n' êh' âsti, bhāva|niṣṭhā na vidyate.
ayaṃ hy api samāhāraḥ śarīr'|êndriya|cetasām:
vartate pṛthag anyonyam apy, apāśritya karmasu.

dhātavaḥ pañcadhā: toyaṃ,† khaṃ, vāyur, jyotiṣo, dharā
te sva|bhāvena tiṣṭhanti, viyujyante sva|bhāvataḥ.

ākāśo, vāyur, ūṣmā ca, sneho, yac c' âpi pārthivaḥ:
eṣa pañca|samāhāraḥ, śarīram iti n' âikadhā.
jñānam, ūṣmā ca, vāyuś ca: tri|vidhaḥ karma|saṃgrahaḥ.

indriyāṇ', îndriy'|ârthāś ca, sva|bhāvaś, cetanā, manaḥ,
prāṇ'|âpānau, vikāraś ca: dhātavaś c' âtra niḥsṛtāḥ.

219.10 śravaṇaṃ, sparśanaṃ, jihvā, dṛṣṭir, nāsā tath" âiva ca:
indriyāṇ' îti pañc' âite, citta|pūrvaṃ|gatā guṇāḥ.

tatra vijñāna|saṃyuktā tri|vidhā vedanā† dhruvā:
sukha|duḥkh" êti yām āhur, a|duḥkhām, a|sukh" êti ca.

śabdaḥ, sparśaṃ ca, rūpaṃ ca, raso, gandhaś ca, mūrtaya
ete hy ā maraṇāt pañca. ṣaḍ guṇā jñāna|siddhaye.

teṣu karma|visargaś ca, sarva|tattv'|ârtha|niścayaḥ.
tam āhuḥ «paramaṃ śukraṃ buddhir» ity a|vyayaṃ mahat.

PANCHA·SHIKHA said:

Things do not end in destruction in this world; there is no termination of a living being. A person is an aggregate of body, senses and consciousness: each functions separately, and yet symbiotically, resting upon a person's *karma*.

There are five elements: space, wind, fire, water and earth. They persist in a person because of his inherent nature, but they are essentially distinct.

The body is a collection of five things—space, wind, heat, liquid and earth—and so is not a unitary substance. Its acts are threefold: those of cognition, heat and wind.

The elements are found in the sense faculties, the sense objects, inherent nature, intelligence, mind, the in-breath, the out-breath and digestion.

The five sense faculties are hearing, touching, tasting, 219.10
seeing and smelling. These evolvents are dominated by the mind.

Only three sorts of feeling accompany the consciousness found in the body: pleasurable, painful or neither pleasurable nor painful, so they say.

The body has five sensations which persist until death: sound, touch, visible form, taste and smell. Six evolvents—the five senses plus the mind—are required to effect cognition.

Sense activity is directed towards the sense objects and determines the meaning of every object. The thing they call the "supreme seed or intelligence" is immutable and macrocosmic.

imaṃ guṇa|samāhāram ātma|bhāvena paśyataḥ,
a|samyag|darśanair duḥkham an|antaṃ n' ôpaśāmyati.

219.15 «an|ātm"» êti ca yad dṛṣṭaṃ,
«te n' âhaṃ, na mam'» êty api,
vartate kim|adhiṣṭhānāt
prasaktā duḥkha|saṃtatiḥ?

atra «samyag|vadho» nāma tyāga|śāstram an|uttamam
śṛṇu, yat tava mokṣāya bhāṣyamāṇaṃ bhaviṣyati.
tyāga eva hi sarveṣāṃ yuktānām api karmaṇām,
nityaṃ mithyā|vinītānāṃ kleśo duḥkha|vaho mataḥ.
dravya|tyāge tu karmāṇi, bhoga|tyāge vratāny api.
sukha|tyāge tapo|yogaṃ, sarva|tyāge samāpanā.
tasya mārgo 'yam a|dvaidhaḥ sarva|tyāgasya darśitaḥ,
viprahāṇāya duḥkhasya: dur|gatis tv anyathā bhavet.

219.20 pañca jñān'|êndriyāṇy uktvā manaḥ|ṣaṣṭhāni cetasi,
bala|ṣaṣṭhāni vakṣyāmi pañca karm'|êndriyāṇi tu.
hastau karm'|êndriyaṃ jñeyam, atha pādau gat'|îndriyam
prajan'|ānandayoḥ śepho, nisarge pāyur indriyam.

Should a person perceive this collection of evolvents in terms of his own existence, because of such incorrect states of understanding his endless suffering is not pacified.

When an object of perception is considered as "That is 219.15
not the self, they are not I, nor mine," on what basis would the stream of misery that adheres to a person continue?

In this matter listen to the highest instruction in abandoning; it is called "the true vanquisher," and will lead to your liberation even as I speak unto you.

The abandoning of all one's prescribed acts is the only way, for sin is thought to inflict continual misery on those who have been incorrectly disciplined.

Ritual acts are prescribed in order to abandon possessions, religious vows are prescribed in order to abandon enjoyment. The discipline of asceticism is for abandoning bliss, whereas completion comes when a person abandons everything.

This nondual path is taught for the abandonment of everything. It leads to the cessation of a person's misery—without it, a person would be reborn in a miserable existence.

I have mentioned the five cognitive faculties, the mind 219.20
being the "sixth," that abide in the faculty of intelligence. Now I will outline the five faculties of action; strength is their "sixth."

One should know that the hands are the organs of action, the feet are the organs of motion, the penis is for begetting offspring and experiencing bliss, and that the anus is for defecation.

vāk ca śabda|viśeṣ'|ârtham. iti pañc'|ânvitaṃ viduḥ.
evam ekādaś' âitāni buddhy" āśu visṛjen manaḥ.

karṇau, śabdaś ca, cittaṃ ca, trayaḥ śravaṇa|saṃgrahe.
tathā sparśe, tathā rūpe, tath" âiva rasa|gandhayoḥ.

evaṃ pañca|trikā hy ete guṇās tad|upalabdhaye,
yen' âyaṃ tri|vidho bhāvaḥ paryāyāt samupasthitaḥ.

219.25 sāttviko, rājasaś c' âpi, tāmasaś c' âpi, te trayaḥ,
tri|vidhā vedanā yeṣu prasūtā sarva|sādhanā.

praharṣaḥ, prītir, ānandaḥ, sukhaṃ, saṃśānta|cittatā
a|kutaś|cit kutaś cid vā, cintitaḥ sāttviko guṇaḥ.

a|tuṣṭiḥ, paritāpaś ca, śoko, lobhas, tath" â|kṣamā,
liṅgāni rajasas tāni; dṛśyante hetv|a|hetutaḥ.

a|vivekas, tathā mohaḥ, pramādaḥ, svapna|tandritā,
kathaṃ cid api vartante, vividhās tāmasā guṇāḥ.

atra yat prīti|saṃyuktaṃ kāye manasi vā bhavet,
«vartate sāttviko bhāva» ity apekṣeta tat tathā.

219.30 yat tv a|saṃtoṣa|saṃyuktam a|prīti|karam ātmanaḥ;
«pravṛttaṃ raja» ity evaṃ tatas tad api cintayet.

Speech is the faculty for articulating sound. Thus it is known that a person is endowed with these five faculties. It is the mind that activates these eleven faculties; it does this through the quick movements of the faculty of intelligence.

The three things necessary for the cognition of sound are the ears, the sound itself and the mind. Three things are also needed in order to perceive touch, visible form, taste and smell.

Thus these five sets of three evolvents are required in order to perceive an object, and it is because of this object that the three psychosomatic states overwhelm a person in turn.

These three states are purity, passion and darkness. Three 219.25
sorts of feeling are generated in these states, and these complete every act of cognition.

Excitement, joy, ecstasy, bliss and peaceful states of mind may or may not have a clear cause. They are thought to be different sorts of purity.

Displeasure, torment, sorrow, greed and impatience are the characteristics of passion. Their cause may or may not be clear.

A lack of discrimination, bewilderment, carelessness, sleep and lethargy come about in various ways. They are the different sorts of darkness.

When an experience of joy arises in one's body or mind, one should consider that a state of purity has come about.

When an unpleasant experience arises it leads to displea- 219.30
sure in a person, and one should contemplate the fact that passion has been activated.

atha yan moha|saṃyuktaṃ kāye manasi vā bhavet,
a|pratarkyam, a|vijñeyaṃ, tamas tad upadhārayet.
śrotram vyom'|āśritaṃ bhūtaṃ;
śabdaḥ śrotraṃ samāśritaḥ.
n' ôbhayaṃ śabda|vijñāne,
vijñānasy' êtarasya vā.
evaṃ tvak, cakṣuṣī, jihvā, nāsikā c' êti pañcamī,
sparśe, rūpe, rase, gandhe. tāni ceto manaś ca tat.
sva|karma|yugapad|bhāvo daśasv eteṣu tiṣṭhati.
cittam ekādaśaṃ viddhi, buddhir dvādaśamī bhavet.
219.35 teṣām a|yugapad|bhāva ucchedo n' âsti tāmase.
āsthito yugapad|bhāvo, vyavahāraḥ sa laukikaḥ.
indriyāṇy api sūkṣmāṇi dṛṣṭvā pūrva|śrut'|āgamāt,
cintayan n' ânuparyeti tribhir ev' ânvito guṇaiḥ.
yat tamo|'pahataṃ cittam āśu saṃhāram a|dhruvam
karoty uparamaṃ kāye, tad āhus tāmasaṃ budhāḥ.
yad yad āgama|saṃyuktaṃ na kṛcchram anupaśyati.
atha tatr' âpy upādatte, tamo vyaktam iv' ân|ṛtam.

When an experience of bewilderment arises in one's body or mind, indistinguishable and incognizable, one should regard it as darkness.*

The substratum of the faculty of hearing is space; sound rests upon the faculty of hearing. Two things are not enough for the cognition of sound, or indeed any another cognition.

The same is true of the skin, eyes, tongue and nose—the fifth—and their objects: touch, visible forms, taste and smell. These require consciousness and the mind for an act of cognition.

The simultaneity between this group of ten—the five senses and their objects—in an act of cognition is due to a person's *karma*. Know that the mind is the eleventh, and that the faculty of intelligence is the twelfth.

When there is no such simultaneity it is because a state 219.35
of darkness persists. But a simultaneity between senses and objects brings about worldly intercourse.

If a person contemplates the understanding of the subtle senses already gained through scriptural learning, he will not continue to be possessed by the three psychosomatic states.

The mind weakened by darkness quickly contracts, and is unstable. It leads to inactivity in the body, a state that wise men call "darkness."

A person considers whatever is contained in scripture without much difficulty. But even if he clings on to this, darkness manifest itself as a form of untruth.

evam eṣa prasaṃkhyātaḥ sva|karma|pratyayo guṇaḥ
kathaṃ cid vartate samyak, keṣāṃ cid vā nivartate.
219.40 etad āhuḥ samāhāraṃ «kṣetram» adhyātma|cintakāḥ.
sthito manasi yo bhāvaḥ, sa vai «kṣetra|jña» ucyate.
evaṃ sati ka ucchedaḥ, śāśvato vā kathaṃ bhavet?
sva|bhāvād vartamāneṣu sarva|bhūteṣu hetutaḥ.
yath" ârṇava|gatā nadyo vyaktīr jahati nāma ca,
na ca svatāṃ† niyacchanti. tādṛśaḥ sattva|saṃkṣayaḥ.
evaṃ sati kutaḥ saṃjñā pretya|bhāve punar bhavet,
pratisaṃmiśrite jīve† gṛhyamāṇe ca sarvataḥ?
imāṃ ca yo veda vimokṣa|buddhim,
ātmānam anvicchati c' â|pramattaḥ,
na lipyate karma|phalair an|iṣṭaiḥ,
patraṃ bisasy' êva jalena siktam.
219.45 dṛḍhair hi pāśair bahubhir vimuktaḥ,
prajā|nimittair api daivataiś ca.
yadā hy asau sukha|duḥkhe jahāti,
muktas, tad" āgryāṃ gatim ety a|liṅgaḥ.
śruti|pramāṇ'|āgama|maṅgalaiś ca
śete jarā|mṛtyu|bhayād a|bhītaḥ.
kṣīṇe ca puṇye, vigate ca pāpe,
tato|nimitte ca phale vinaṣṭe,
a|lepam ākāśam a|liṅgam evam
āsthāya paśyanti mahadd hy† a|saktāḥ.

But even this state is reckoned to be caused by a person's own *karma*. Somehow or other it is effectively set in motion, but for some it ceases to be.

Those who contemplate the supreme self call this collection of things the "field." The "field-knower" is said to be an essence that abides within the mind. 219.40

This being so, given that all existing beings have a causal dependence on their inherent nature—how could they be annihilated or eternal?

When rivers flow into the sea they abandon their visible forms and name, and do not hold on to their own individuality. The dissolution of living beings is just the same.

This being so, when the soul is assimilated and completely integrated into the absolute, how could there be any further consciousness after death?

The vigilant person who masters this understanding of liberation and seeks the self is not tainted by the unpleasant results of his *karma*, just like a lotus leaf is not made wet by water.

He is released from the innumerable bonds that shackle 219.45
him firmly, including those caused by his offspring and those that come about by chance. When he abandons pleasure and pain, he attains liberation—he leaves his body and attains the highest destiny.

Through the auspicious sayings of those scriptures whose authority is the Vedas, a person becomes tranquil and has no fear of decrepitude and death. When their stock of merit and evil has disappeared, and the retribution it causes destroyed, detached people go to space, which is free from taint and characteristic, and perceive the absolute.

yath" ōrṇa|nābhiḥ parivartamānas
tantu|kṣaye tiṣṭhati pātyamānaḥ,
tathā vimuktaḥ prajahāti duḥkhaṃ,
vidhvaṃsate loṣṭha iv' âdrim ṛcchan.
yathā ruruḥ śṛṅgam atho purāṇaṃ
hitvā, tvacaṃ v" âpy urago yathā ca
vihāya gacchaty an|avekṣamāṇas,
tathā vimukto vijahāti duḥkham.
drumaṃ yathā v" âpy udake patantam
utsṛjya pakṣī nipataty a|saktaḥ,
tathā hy asau sukha|duḥkhe vihāya
muktaḥ: par'|ârdhyāṃ gatim ety a|liṅgaḥ
219.50 api ca bhavati Maithilena gītaṃ
nagaram upāhitam agnin" âbhivīkṣya:
«na khalu mama hi dahyate 'tra kiṃ cit!»
svayam idam āha kila sma bhūmi|pālaḥ.

idam amṛta|padaṃ niśamya rājā
svayam iha Pañcaśikhena bhāṣyamāṇam,
nikhilam abhisamīkṣya niścit'|ârthaḥ,
parama|sukhī vijahāra vīta|śokaḥ.
imaṃ hi yaḥ paṭhati mokṣa|niścayaṃ,
mahī|pate, satatam avekṣate tathā,
upadravān n' ânubhavaty a|duḥkhitaḥ,
pramucyate Kapilam iv' âitya Maithilaḥ.

A spider circumambulating its web is made to fall—but still survives—when the threads are destroyed. In just the same way a liberated person abandons misery like a clod of earth crushed by a pounding stone.

Just like an antelope abandons its old horns, or a snake goes off without a care in the world once it has shed its slough, so too does the liberated person abandon misery.

A bird relinquishes a tree falling into the water and flies off, since it is free of burdens. The person who abandons pleasure and pain is liberated in the same way: when he abandons the body he attains the highest destiny.

When the king of Míthila saw that his city had been 219.50
burned down he said: "Nothing whatsoever of mine has been burned here!"

BHISHMA said:

Once King Jánaka had listened to the path to the immortal as described by Pancha·shikha, and investigated it thoroughly so that he had resolved his purpose, he experienced supreme bliss and was freed from sorrow.

The person who recites this inquiry into liberation and always reflects on it, Lord of the earth, will be freed from misery and never experience misfortune. He will be liberated just like the king of Míthila was after his meeting with Kápila.

220

IN PRAISE OF RESTRAINT

YUDHIṢṬHIRA uvāca:*

220.1 KIṂ KURVAN SUKHAM āpnoti,
kiṃ kurvan duḥkham āpnuyāt?
kiṃ kurvan nirbhayo loke
siddhaś carati, Bhārata?

BHĪṢMA uvāca:

damam eva praśaṃsanti vṛddhāḥ śruti|samādhayaḥ
sarveṣām eva varṇānāṃ, brāhmaṇasya viśeṣataḥ.
n' â|dāntasya kriyā|siddhir yathāvad upapadyate:
kriyā tapaś ca satyaṃ ca dame sarvaṃ pratiṣṭhitam.
damas tejo vardhayati, pavitraṃ dama ucyate.
vi|pāpmā, nir|bhayo, dāntaḥ puruṣo vindate mahat.
220.5 sukhaṃ dāntaḥ prasvapiti, sukhaṃ ca pratibudhyate.
sukhaṃ loke viparyeti, manaś c' âsya prasīdati.
tejo damena dhriyate. tatra tīkṣṇo 'dhigacchati
a|mitrāṃś ca bahūn nityaṃ, pṛthag ātmani paśyati.
kravyādbhya iva bhūtānām a|dāntebhyaḥ sadā bhayam.
teṣāṃ vipratiṣedh'|ârthaṃ rājā sṛṣṭaḥ svayaṃ|bhuvā.
āśrameṣu ca sarveṣu dama eva viśiṣyate.
yac ca teṣu phalaṃ dharme, bhūyo dānte tad ucyate.
teṣāṃ liṅgāni vakṣyāmi, yeṣāṃ samudayo damaḥ:
a|kārpaṇyam, a|saṃrambhaḥ, saṃtoṣaḥ, śraddadhānatā,
220.10 a|krodha, ārjavaṃ nityaṃ, n' âtivādo, na mānitā,†
guru|pūj" ân|asūyā ca, dayā bhūteṣv, a|paiśunam,

YUDHI·SHTHIRA said:

By what means does a person experience pleasure or 220.1
pain? How can a person free himself from fear and
wander the world in this accomplished state, Bhárata?

BHISHMA said:

The elders who meditate on the Vedas recommend restraint for all classes of men, and especially for a brahmin. A man does not accomplish his actions in the correct manner if he is not restrained: action, asceticism and truth are all rooted in restraint.

Restraint increases a person's luster and is said to be a means of purification. The restrained man frees himself from evil and fear, and finds the absolute.

The restrained man sleeps blissfully and wakes up in a 220.5
state of bliss. He lives happily in this world, and has a tranquil mind.

A man's luster is preserved through restraint. Because of restraint, a perceptive man will find the many enemies that always lurk within, and perceive them individually.

People are always afraid of those without restraint, just as they fear predators. In order to restrain them, the self-existent *brahman* created the king.

Restraint is specified for all religious paths. The reward attained through righteousness is said to become bountiful through restraint.

I will outline the characteristics of those in whom restraint arises. They are: munificence, repose, contentment,
faith; perpetual honesty and the absence of anger, abu- 220.10
sive language and conceit; homage towards one's teacher,

jana|vāda|mṛṣā|vāda|stuti|nindā|vivarjanam.
sādhu|kāmaś ca spṛhayen n' āyatiṃ, pratyayo nṛṣu.†
a|vaira|kṛt, s'|ûpacāraḥ,
samo nindā|praśaṃsayoḥ.
su|vṛttaḥ, śīla|saṃpannaḥ,
prasann'|ātm", ātmavān prabhuḥ.
prāpya loke ca sat|kāraṃ, svargaṃ vai pretya gacchati.
dur|gamaṃ sarva|bhūtānāṃ prāpayan modate sukhī.
sarva|bhūta|hite yukto na sma yo dviṣate janam;
mahā|hrada iv' â|kṣobhya prajñā|tṛptaḥ prasīdati.
220.15 a|bhayaṃ yasya bhūtebhyaḥ, sarveṣām a|bhayaṃ yataḥ.
namasyaḥ sarva|bhūtānāṃ dānto bhavati buddhimān.
na hṛṣyati mahaty arthe, vyasane ca na śocati.
sa vai parimita|prajñaḥ sa dānto dvija ucyate.
karmabhiḥ śruta|saṃpannaḥ, sadbhir ācaritaḥ, śuciḥ.
sad" âiva dama|saṃyuktas, tasya bhuṅkte mahā|phalam.
an|asūyā, kṣamā, śāntiḥ, saṃtoṣaḥ, priyavāditā,
satyaṃ, dānam, an|āyāso—n' âiṣa mārgo dur|ātmanām.
kāma|krodhau ca, lobhaś ca, parasy' ērṣyā, vikatthanā,
kāma|krodhau vaśe kṛtvā brahma|cārī jit'|êndriyaḥ
220.20 vikramya ghore tamasi brāhmaṇaḥ saṃśita|vrataḥ
kāl'|ākāṅkṣī carel lokān, nirapāya iv' ātmavān.

goodwill, sympathy towards living beings, the absence of calumny; the avoidance of gossip, false talk, praise and blame. Wishing to do good, he should not look to the future; such a person has confidence in his fellow men.

He causes no enmity, is easy to approach and is indifferent to both blame and praise. He is well-behaved and steeped in virtue, a controlled man of inner tranquility and self-mastery. He attains respect in this world, and when he dies he goes to heaven. Attaining that which all living beings find difficult to attain, he rejoices in his bliss.

Devoted to the welfare of all beings, he does not hate anyone; satiated by wisdom he is tranquil, just like a great,
imperturbable lake. Other creatures pose no danger to him, 220.15
and he incites no fear in them. All livings should pay homage to this man who is restrained and wise.

He is not excited when he attains great wealth and feels no sorrow in a disaster; the restrained man of determined wisdom is said to be a brahmin. Through his endeavors he masters the Vedas; being pure, he is visited by virtuous men. He is always devoted to restraint and so enjoys its great reward.

Goodwill, forbearance, peace, contentment, kind words, truth, restraint and ease: this path is not for the wicked, whose path involves lust, anger, greed, bragging and envy of others. But the celibate student who controls his lust and anger will master his senses.

Striving on through the terrible darkness, the brahmin 220.20
should stick to his vows and wander the worlds, waiting for his end, being just like an immortal in his self-control.

221

IN PRAISE OF FASTING

YUDHIṢṬHIRA uvāca:

221.1 DVI|JĀTAYO VRAT'|ôpetā yad idaṃ bhuñjate haviḥ,
annaṃ brāhmaṇa|kāmāya katham etat, pitā|maha?

BHĪṢMA uvāca:

a|ved'|ôkta|vrat'|ôpetā bhuñjānāḥ kārya|kāriṇaḥ.
ved'|ôkteṣu ca bhuñjānā vrata|luptā,† Yudhiṣṭhira.

YUDHIṢṬHIRA uvāca:

yad idaṃ tapa ity āhur upavāsaṃ pṛthag|janāḥ,
etat tapo, mahā|rāja? ut' āho kiṃ tapo bhavet?

BHĪṢMA uvāca:

māsa|pakṣ'|ôpavāsena manyante yat tapo janāḥ,
ātma|tantr'|ôpaghātas tu, na tapas tat satāṃ matam.
221.5 tyāgaś ca saṃnatiś c' âiva śiṣyate tapa uttamam.
sad" ôpavāsī sa bhaved, brahma|cārī sadā bhavet
muniś ca syāt sadā vipro, daivataṃ ca sadā bhajet.
kuṭumbiko dharma|kāmaḥ sad" â|svapnaś ca, Bhārata.
a|māṃs'|ādī sadā ca syāt, pavitraś ca sadā japet.
amṛt'|āśī sadā ca syād, devat"|âtithi|pūjakaḥ.

YUDHI·SHTHIRA said:

WHEN BRAHMINS undertake religious vows, they eat the burned offerings of the ritual. But how can such food be agreeable to them, grandfather? 221.1

BHISHMA said:

Only those who undertake religious vows not prescribed by the Veda eat when carrying out their ritual obligations. Those who eat while performing rites prescribed by the Veda break their vow, Yudhi·shthira.

YUDHI·SHTHIRA said:

Ordinary people say that fasting is asceticism. But is it really asceticism, great king? If not, what else could asceticism be?

BHISHMA said:

People believe that asceticism is accrued through fasting every lunar month or fortnight. But since that hinders the means of realizing the self, virtuous men do not consider it to be asceticism.

Renunciation and humility are distinguished as the highest form of asceticism. A man should always fast and observe a celibate life. 221.5

A brahmin should always be sagacious and worship the gods. As a householder, he should dedicate himself to religion and always avoid sleep, Bhárata.

He must never eat meat, and should silently recite the Vedas in a state of purity. He should always eat ambrosia and pay homage to gods and guests.

vighas'|āśī sadā ca syāt, sadā c' aiv' âtithi|vrataḥ.
śraddadhānaḥ sadā ca syād, devatā|dvija|pūjakaḥ.

YUDHIṢṬHIRA uvāca:

katham sad" ôpavāsī syād? brahma|cārī katham bhavet?
vighas'|āśī katham ca syāt, sadā c' aiv' âtithi|vrataḥ?

BHĪṢMA uvāca:

221.10 antarā prātar|āśaṃ ca sāyam|āśaṃ tath" âiva ca,
sad" ôpavāsī sa bhaved, yo na bhuṅkte 'ntarā punaḥ.
bhāryāṃ gacchan brahma|cārī ṛtau bhavati vai dvijaḥ.
ṛta|vādī bhaven nityaṃ jñāna|nityaś ca yo naraḥ.
na bhakṣayed vṛthā|māṃsam, a|māṃs'|āśī bhavaty api.
dāna|nityaḥ, pavitraś ca, a|svapnaś ca div" â|svapan.
bhṛty"|âtithiṣu yo bhuṅkte bhuktavatsu sadā sadā,
a|mṛtaṃ kevalaṃ bhuṅkte, iti viddhi, Yudhiṣṭhira.
a|bhuktavatsu n' âśnānaḥ satataṃ yas tu vai dvijaḥ,
a|bhojanena ten' âsya jitaḥ svargo bhavaty uta.
221.15 devatābhyaḥ, pitṛbhyaś ca, bhṛtyebhyo, 'tithibhiḥ saha
avaśiṣṭaṃ tu yo 'śnāti, tam āhur vighas'|āśinam.
teṣāṃ lokā hy a|paryantāḥ sadane Brahmaṇā saha.
upasthitāś c' âpsarobhiḥ pariyānti div'|âukasaḥ.

He should always eat the remains of an oblation, and constantly observe the vow of hospitality to guests. Ever faithful, he should pay homage to the gods and brahmins.

YUDHI·SHTHIRA said:

How can a person continually observe a fast? How should he observe the vow of celibacy? How should he eat the remains of an oblation, and always observe the vow of hospitality to guests?

BHISHMA said:

The person who does not eat between the morning and 221.10
evening meal is the one who observes a continual fast.

By only approaching his wife when she is in season, the brahmin observes the vow of celibacy. This man should always speak the truth and be committed to knowledge.

He is a non-meat eater if he does not eat meat prepared for his own use. He becomes pure through constant charity, and does not sleep so long as he does not nap during the day.

You should know, Yudhi·shthira, that a man eats nothing but ambrosia if he always takes his food after his servants and guests have eaten. The brahmin never eats before they
have eaten and in that way conquers heaven. The person 221.15
who eats what is left over from the offerings to the gods, ancestors, servants and guests is said to be the one who eats the remains of an oblation.

They attain worlds without limit in an abode with Brahma. Celestial nymphs approach them, and the gods flock to them.

devatābhiś ca ye sārdhaṃ, pitṛbhyaś c' ôpabhuñjate,
ramante putra|pautraiś ca, teṣāṃ gatir an|uttamā.

Eating with the gods and ancestors, and finding pleasure in their sons and grandsons, people obtain an incomparable destiny.

222

THE DIALOGUE BETWEEN INDRA AND PRAHRÁDA

YUDHIṢṬHIRA uvāca:

222.1 YAD IDAM KARMA loke 'smiñ
śubhaṃ vā yadi v" â|śubham,
puruṣaṃ yojayaty eva
phala|yogena, Bhārata.
kart" âsti tasya puruṣa, ut' āho n', êti saṃśayaḥ.
etad icchāmi tattvena tvattaḥ śrotuṃ, pitā|maha.

BHĪṢMA uvāca:

atr" âpy udāharant' îmam itihāsaṃ purātanam:
Prahrādasya ca saṃvādam Indrasya ca, Yudhiṣṭhira.
a|saktaṃ, dhūta|pāpmānaṃ, kule jātaṃ, bahu|śrutam,
a|stabdham, an|ahaṃ|kāraṃ, sattva|sthaṃ, samaye ratam,
222.5 tulya|nindā|stutiṃ, dāntaṃ, śūny'|āgāra|nivāsinam,
car'|âcarāṇāṃ bhūtānāṃ vidita|prabhav'|âpyayam,†
a|krudhyantam a|hṛṣyantam a|priyeṣu priyeṣu ca,
kāñcane v" âtha loṣṭhe vā ubhayoḥ sama|darśanam,
ātma|niḥśreyasi† jñāne dhīraṃ, niścita|niścayam,†
par'|âvara|jñaṃ bhūtānāṃ, sarva|jñaṃ, sama|darśanam,
Śakraḥ Prahrādam āsīnam ek'|ānte saṃyat'|êndriyam,
bubhutsamānas tat|prajñām abhigamy' êdam abravīt:
«yaiḥ kaś cit saṃmato loke guṇaiḥ syāt puruṣo nṛṣu,
bhavaty an|apagān sarvāṃs tān guṇāl lakṣayāmahe.
222.10 atha te lakṣyate buddhiḥ samā bāla|janair iha.
ātmānaṃ manyamānaḥ sañ, śreyaḥ kim iha manyase?

YUDHI·SHTHIRA said:

WHATEVER ACT A man commits in this world, be it good or bad, it binds him because of the connection to its retribution, Bhárata. But I doubt whether or not a man is really the agent of his action. I would like to hear the truth of this matter from you, grandfather. 222.1

BHISHMA said:

On this subject people relate the ancient tradition of a dialogue between Prahráda and Indra, Yudhi·shthira.*

Detached and expunged of evil, Prahráda had been born into a respectable family and was very learned. He was free from obstinacy and self-consciousness, steadfast in his purity and devoted to the law. Indifferent to blame and praise, 222.5
he was restrained and frequented empty houses; he knew the origin and end of all mobile and immobile beings.

He could not be angered or excited by pleasant or unpleasant things, and regarded gold and a clod of earth as the same. Acquainted with a knowledge of the self's felicity, he was possessed of a resolute conviction. He could recognize who was superior and inferior among living beings, for he was all-knowing and impartial in his understanding.

One time, when Prahráda was seated in a secluded place with his sense faculties under control, he was approached by Shakra who, wanting to know about his wisdom, said this:

"We note that you are not lacking in all those qualities because of which any man will be esteemed by others in this world. Your intelligence seems just like that of a child. 222.10

baddhaḥ pāśaiś, cyutaḥ sthānād, dviṣatāṃ vaśam āgataḥ,
śriyā vihīnaḥ, Prahrāda, śocitavye na śocasi.
prajñā|lābhāt tu, Daiteya, ut' āho dhṛtimattayā?
Prahrāda, sukha|rūpo 'si paśyan vyasanam ātmanaḥ.»
iti saṃcoditas tena dhīro niścita|niścayaḥ
uvāca ślakṣṇayā vācā svāṃ prajñām anuvarṇayan.

PRAHRĀDA uvāca:

pravṛttiṃ ca nivṛttiṃ ca bhūtānāṃ yo na budhyate,
tasya stambho bhaved bālyān. n' âsti stambho 'nupaśyataḥ.
222.15 sva|bhāvāt saṃpravartante, nivartante tath" âiva ca
sarve bhāvās tath" â|bhāvāḥ; puruṣ'|ârtho na vidyate.
puruṣ'|ârthasya c' â|bhāve n' âsti kaś cic ca kārakaḥ.
svayaṃ na kurvatas tasya jātu māno bhaved iha?
yas tu kartāram ātmānaṃ manyate, sādhv a|sādhu vā,
tasya doṣavatī prajñā a|tattva|jñ", êti me matiḥ.

Since you contemplate the self, what do you think is the most felicitous thing in the world?

Being under the control of your enemies, you are bound in chains and have lost your eminent position. You have lost your effulgence, Prahráda, but you do not lament your lamentable state. Is it because you have attained wisdom, son of Diti, or because you are endowed with resolve? Your appearance is agreeable, Prahráda, although you are fully aware of this disaster that has befallen you."

Upon being challenged by Shakra, Prahráda, who was wise and resolute in his conviction, spoke in eloquent words and described his own wisdom as follows.

PRAHRÁDA said:

A person will become obstinate if he does not understand the appearance and disappearance of living beings; this is because of his foolishness. But the person who sees this is not obstinate.

All things that come into being are impelled by their in- 222.15
herent nature, and it is this that causes things to cease and become non-existent. There is no such thing as human effort. Because there is no such thing as human effort, there can be no such thing as an agent. And if a person cannot act by his own means, why would he ever become conceited in this world? The person who thinks of himself as an agent, whether of good or bad deeds, suffers from a defiled understanding. It is my opinion that he does not understand the way things really are.

yadi syāt puruṣaḥ kartā, Śakr', ātma|śreyase dhruvam,
ārambhās tasya sidhyeyur, na tu jātu parābhavet.
an|iṣṭasya hi nirvṛttir, a|nivṛttiḥ priyasya ca
lakṣyate '|yatamānānām. puruṣ'|ârthas tataḥ kutaḥ?
222.20 an|iṣṭasy' âbhinirvṛttim iṣṭa|saṃvṛttim eva ca
a|prayatnena paśyāmaḥ. keṣāṃ cit tat sva|bhāvataḥ.
pratirūpatarāḥ ke cid dṛśyante buddhimattarāḥ,
virūpebhyo 'lpa|buddhibhyo lipsamānā dhan'|āgamam.

sva|bhāva|preritāḥ sarve niviśante guṇā yadā
śubh'|âśubhās, tadā tatra kasya kiṃ māna|kāraṇam?
sva|bhāvād eva tat sarvam, iti me niścitā matiḥ.
ātma|pratiṣṭhā, prajñā vā—mama n' âsti tato 'nyathā.

karma|jaṃ tv iha manyante phala|yogaṃ śubh'|âśubham.
karmaṇāṃ viṣayaṃ kṛtsnam ahaṃ vakṣyāmi. tac chṛṇu!
222.25 yathā vedayate kaś cid odanaṃ vāyaso hy adan,
evaṃ sarvāṇi karmāṇi sva|bhāvasy' âiva lakṣaṇam.

vikārān eva yo veda, na veda prakṛtiṃ parām,
tasya stambho bhaved bālyān. n' âsti stambho 'nupaśyataḥ.

If it is true that a man can be the agent of his own felicity, Shakra, he would accomplish his endeavors and never be defeated. Undesirable things arise and pleasant things do not stop even if people do not exert themselves. So how can there be human effort?

We see that undesirable things arise and that desirable 222.20
things pass away without making any effort—this is due to the inherent nature of particular people. Even excessively beautiful and intelligent people are seen to scrounge wealth from those who are deformed and of little intelligence.

All the experiential qualities that enter a person, which are both good and bad, are determined by one's inherent nature. In this matter what reason is there for conceit, and who would entertain it? I am of the resolute opinion that everything is caused by a person's inherent nature. The same applies to one's stability or wisdom—I do not see how it could be otherwise.

Since some people think that a person's connection with good and bad rewards arises from worldly action, I will explain the entire sphere of actions. Listen to this!

All acts are characteristic of one's inherent nature alone, 222.25
in the same way that a crow eating rice pudding can't help but make the fact known.

The person who perceives changes in his state, but not his true nature beyond them, will become obstinate because of his foolishness. But it is not so for the person who sees this.

sva|bhāva|bhāvino bhāvān sarvān ev' êha niścayāt
budhyamānasya darpo vā māno vā kiṃ kariṣyati?
veda dharma|vidhiṃ kṛtsnaṃ, bhūtānāṃ c' âpy a|nityatām!
tasmāc, Chakra, na śocāmi, sarvaṃ hy ev' êdam antavat.
nir|mamo, nir|ahaṃ|kāro, nir|āśīr, mukta|bandhanaḥ,
sva|stho, vyapetaḥ paśyāmi bhūtānāṃ prabhav'|âpyayau.
222.30 kṛta|prajñasya, dāntasya, vi|tṛṣṇasya, nir|āśiṣaḥ
n' āyāso vidyate, Śakra, paśyato lokam a|vyayam.
prakṛtau ca vikāre ca na me prītir, na ca dviṣe.
dveṣṭāraṃ ca na paśyāmi yo mām adya mamāyate.
n' ōrdhvaṃ, n' âvāṅ, na tiryak ca,
na kva cic, Chakra, kāmaye,
na hi jñeye, na vijñāne,
na jñāne karma vidyate.

ŚAKRA uvāca:

yen' âiṣā labhyate prajñā, yena śāntir avāpyate,
prabrūhi tam upāyaṃ me samyak, Prahrāda, pṛcchataḥ.

PRAHRĀDA uvāca:

ārjaven', â|pramādena, prasāden', âtmavattayā,
vṛddha|śuśrūṣayā, Śakra, puruṣo labhate mahat.
222.35 sva|bhāvāl labhate prajñāṃ, śāntim eti sva|bhāvataḥ.
sva|bhāvād eva tat sarvaṃ, yat kiṃ cid anupaśyasi.

There is no doubt that all the world's living beings come into existence because of their inherent nature. For the person who is aware of this, what will pride or conceit achieve? I know the religious order in its totality, and the impermanence of all beings! Therefore I feel no sorrow, Shakra, for the entire world is finite.

Devoid of possessiveness, self-consciousness, desire and bondage, I have found contentment and detachment and can see the origin and end of all beings.

The person who attains this wisdom is restrained and free 222.30
from thirst and desire. There is no trouble for that person who sees the immutable world, Shakra.

I feel neither joy in my true nature nor aversion to my changing states. I see no enemy who envies me now.

My desire goes nowhere, Shakra, neither above, below or across, and I do not act on any perceptible object, or on the cognition and full awareness of it.

SHAKRA said:

Tell me that method by which you have attained this wisdom and peace, Prahráda, since I have asked about it in the correct manner.

PRAHRÁDA said:

A man obtains esteem through honesty, diligence, tranquility, self-control and obedience to his elders, Shakra. But 222.35
he attains wisdom and peace through his inherent nature. Everything—whatever you can see—arises from its inherent nature.

ity ukto Daitya|patinā Śakro vismayam āgamat.
prītimāṃś ca tadā, rājaṃs, tad vākyaṃ pratyapūjayat
sa tad" âbhyarcya Daity'|êndraṃ trailokya|patir īśvaraḥ,
asur'|êndram upāmantrya jagāma svaṃ niveśanam.

BHISHMA said:

Addressed in this manner by the lord of the *daityas*, Shakra was astonished. Feeling great joy, Your Majesty, he paid homage to that teaching. The Lord and ruler of the triple world then praised the leader of the *daityas* and demons, saluted him and returned to his own abode.

223–225

THE DIALOGUE BETWEEN INDRA AND BALI

YUDHIṢṬHIRA uvāca:

223.1 YAYĀ BUDDHYĀ mahī|pālo bhraṣṭa|śrīr vicaren mahīm
Kāla|daṇḍa|viniṣpiṣṭas, tan me brūhi, pitā|maha.

BHĪṢMA uvāca:

atr' âpy udāharant' îmam itihāsaṃ purātanam:
Vāsavasya ca saṃvādaṃ, Baler Vairocanasya ca.
pitā|maham upāgamya, praṇipatya kṛt'|âñjaliḥ,
sarvān ev' âsurāñ jitvā, Baliṃ papraccha Vāsavaḥ:
yasya sma dadato vittaṃ na kadā cana hīyate,
taṃ Baliṃ n' âdhigacchāmi. Brahmann, ācakṣva me Balim.
223.5 sa vāyur, varuṇaś c' âiva, sa raviḥ, sa ca candramāḥ.
so 'gnis tapati bhūtāni, jalaṃ ca sa bhavaty uta.
taṃ Baliṃ n' âdhigacchāmi.
Brahmann, ācakṣva me Balim.
sa eva hy astam ayate,
sa sma vidyotate diśaḥ;
sa varṣati sma varṣāṇi yathā|kālam a|tandritaḥ.
taṃ Baliṃ n' âdhigacchāmi. Brahmann, ācakṣva me Balim.

BRAHM" ôvāca:

n' âitat te sādhu, Maghavan, yad enam anupṛcchasi.
pṛṣṭas tu n' ân|ṛtaṃ brūyāt. tasmād vakṣyāmi te Balim.
uṣṭreṣu, yadi vā goṣu, khareṣv, aśveṣu vā punaḥ
variṣṭho bhavitā jantuḥ śūny'|āgāre, Śacī|pate.

YUDHI·SHTHIRA said:

WHEN A KING has been crushed by the staff of Time and has lost his effulgence, what would his state of mind be as he wanders the earth? Please tell me this, grandfather. 223.1

BHISHMA said:

On this subject people relate the ancient tradition of a dialogue between Indra, chief of the Vasus, and Bali, the son of the demon Viróchana.

Indra approached Brahma, the grandfather, and bowed down holding his hands together in reverence. Since he had just conquered all the demons, he asked him about Bali:

"I have not found Bali, the one whose wealth never dwindles even when he gives it away. Please tell me where he is,
Brahma. He is the wind, ocean, sun and moon. He is the 223.5
fire that heats living beings, and he is also the water.

I cannot find that Bali, Brahma, so please tell me where he is. It is he who lights up the directions of the sky and then sets; he sends down the rains at the appropriate time, and yet remains unwearied. I cannot find that Bali, Brahma: please tell me where he is."

BRAHMA said:

It is not right, Mághavat, that you inquire after him. But when a person is asked, he should not say anything that is untrue. Therefore, I will tell you where Bali is.

That supreme being will be found living in an empty house among camels, cows, donkeys or horses, O husband of Shachi.

ŚAKRA uvāca:

223.10 yadi sma Balinā, Brahmañ,
śūny'|āgāre sameyivān,
hanyām enaṃ na vā hanyāṃ?
tad, Brahmann, anuśādhi mām.

BRAHM" ôvāca:

mā sma, Śakra, baliṃ hiṃsīr, na Balir vadham arhati.
nyāyas tu, Śakra, praṣṭavyas tvayā, Vāsava, kāmyayā.

BHĪṢMA uvāca:

evam ukto bhagavatā mah"|Êndraḥ pṛthivīṃ tadā
cacār' Âirāvata|skandham adhiruhya, śriyā vṛtaḥ.
tato dadarśa sa Baliṃ khara|veṣeṇa saṃvṛtam,
yath"|ākhyātaṃ bhagavatā śūny'|āgāra|kṛt'|ālayam.

ŚAKRA uvāca:

khara|yonim anuprāptas tuṣa|bhakṣo 'si, Dānava.
iyaṃ te yonir adhamā śocasy, āho na śocasi?
223.15 a|dṛṣṭaṃ bata paśyāmi dviṣatāṃ vaśam āgatam,
śriyā vihīnaṃ mitraiś ca, bhraṣṭa|vīrya|parākramam.
yat tad yāna|sahasrais tvaṃ jñātibhiḥ parivāritaḥ,
lokān pratāpayan sarvān yāsy asmān a|vitarkayan.
tvan|mukhāś c' âiva Daiteyā vyatiṣṭhaṃs tava śāsane;
a|kṛṣṭa|pacyā ca mahī tav' āiśvarye babhūva ha.
idaṃ ca te 'dya vyasanaṃ. śocasy, āho na śocasi?

SHAKRA said:

If I meet Bali in an empty house, Brahma, please tell me whether or not I should kill him. 223.10

BRAHMA said:

You should not harm Bali, Shakra, and you should not slay him. If you wish ask him about method, O Shakra, leader of the Vasus.

BHISHMA said:

After he had been addressed by the blessed Brahma, the great Indra climbed on to the shoulders of his elephant Airávata and wandered the earth, shrouded in effulgence. After some time he saw Bali in the form of a donkey. And just as the blessed Brahma had said, he had made his abode in empty house.

SHAKRA said:

You have been reborn as a donkey eating the husks of grain, *dánava*. Do you lament this inferior birth of yours, or not?

Alas! I see you in an unprecedented condition—under 223.15
the control of your enemies, deprived of your effulgence and friends, devoid of your valor and power. You used to travel with a thousand carriages, surrounded by your kinsmen, all the while scorching the worlds without any consideration for us.

You were the leader of the *daitéyas*, who were dispersed far and wide under your rule; under your sovereignty, the earth used to yield its crop without being plowed. Do you lament this disaster that has now befallen you, or not?

yad" âtiṣṭhaḥ samudrasya pūrva|kūle vilelihan,
jñātīn vibhajato vittaṃ, tad" āsīt te manaḥ katham?
yat te sahasra|samitā nanṛtur deva|yoṣitaḥ,
223.20 bahūni varṣa|pūgāni vihāre dīpyataḥ śriyā,
sarvāḥ puṣkara|mālinyaḥ, sarvāḥ kāñcana|sa|prabhāḥ—
katham adya tadā c' âiva manas te, Dānav'|ēśvara?
chatraṃ tav' āsīt sumahat sauvarṇaṃ, ratna|bhūṣitam;
nanṛtus tatra gandharvāḥ ṣaṭ|sahasrāṇi saptadhā.
yūpas tav' āsīt su|mahān yajataḥ sarva|kāñcanaḥ,
yatr' âdadaḥ sahasrāṇi ayutānāṃ gavāṃ daśa,
an|antaraṃ sahasreṇa—tad" āsīd, Daitya, kā matiḥ?
yadā ca pṛthivīṃ sarvāṃ yajamāno 'nuparyagāḥ
śamyā|kṣepeṇa vidhinā, tad" āsīt kiṃ tu te hṛdi?
223.25 na te paśyāmi bhṛṅgāraṃ, na cchatraṃ, vyajane na ca,
Brahma|dattāṃ ca te mālāṃ na paśyāmy, asur'|âdhipa.

BALIR uvāca:

na tvaṃ paśyasi bhṛṅgāraṃ, na cchatraṃ, vyajane na ca,
Brahma|dattāṃ ca me mālāṃ na tvaṃ drakṣyasi, Vāsava.
guhāyāṃ nihitāni tvaṃ mama ratnāni pṛcchasi:
yadā me bhavitā kālas, tadā tvaṃ tāni drakṣyasi.
na tv etad anurūpaṃ te
yaśaso vā kulasya ca,
samṛddh'|ârtho 'samṛddh'|ârthaṃ
yan māṃ katthitum icchasi.

When you stood on the eastern shore of the ocean, lapping up your success, what did you think, as you divided up your wealth among your kinsmen? Celestial maidens danced in their thousands for you, all of them lustrous as 223.20
gold and adorned with lotus garlands, as you passed many years glowing with effulgence in this pleasurable state.

What did you think then, and what do you think now, *dánava* lord? You used to have an enormous, golden umbrella adorned with jewels, where forty-two thousand *gandhárva*s danced for you.

When you offered a sacrifice, you had a tremendous sacrificial pillar made entirely of gold where you used to offer cows in their billions and then immediately a thousand more. What was your state of mind, at that time, O *daitya*?

When you offered a sacrifice, you used to circumambulate the entire earth as you followed the custom of hurling your staff. At that time what did you feel?

I do not see your golden vase, umbrella or fans, never 223.25
mind the garland given to you by Brahma, *ásura* lord.

BALI said:

You do not see my golden vase, umbrella or fans, and you will not see the garland given to me by Brahma, O Indra. The jewels of mine that you ask about are hidden in a cave: when my time comes, you will see them. But it does not befit your reputation or race that you, who abounds in wealth, would wish to abuse me, who does not.

na hi duḥkheṣu śocante, na prahṛṣyanti ca' rddhiṣu†
kṛta|prajñā, jñāna|tṛptāḥ, kṣāntāḥ santo manīṣiṇaḥ.
223.30 tvaṃ tu prākṛtayā buddhyā, Puraṃdara, vikatthase.
yad" âham iva bhāvī syās,† tadā n' âivaṃ vadiṣyasi.

BHĪṢMA uvāca:

224.1 PUNAR EVA TU taṃ Śakraḥ prahasann idam abravīt
niḥśvasantaṃ yathā nāgaṃ, pravyāhārāya, Bhārata.

ŚAKRA uvāca:

yat tad yāna|sahasreṇa jñātibhiḥ parivāritaḥ,
lokān pratāpayan sarvān yāsy asmān a|vitarkayan.
dṛṣṭvā su|kṛpaṇāṃ c' êmām avasthām ātmano, Bale,
jñāti|mitra|parityaktaḥ, śocasy, āho na śocasi?
prītiṃ prāpy' â|tulāṃ pūrvaṃ, lokāṃś c' ātma|vaśe sthitān,
vinipātam imaṃ bāhyaṃ śocasy, āho na śocasi?

BALIR uvāca:

224.5 a|nityam upalakṣy' êha kāla|paryāya|dharmataḥ,
tasmāc, Chakra, na śocāmi, sarvaṃ hy ev' êdam antavat.
antavanta ime dehā bhūtānām ca, sur'|âdhipa.
tena, Śakra, na śocāmi, n' âparādhād idaṃ mama.
jīvitaṃ ca śarīraṃ ca jāty" âiva saha jāyate.
ubhe saha vivardhete, ubhe saha vinaśyataḥ.

Wise men satiated by gnosis do not lament their sufferings or delight in their successes. They are patient, virtuous and sagacious. But you brag, Puran·dara, because of your 223.30
vulgar mind. When I am able you will not speak thus.

BHISHMA said:

ANYWAY, BHÁRATA, Shakra simply smiled and for the sake 224.1
of further discussion said this to Bali, who was hissing like a snake.

SHAKRA said:

You used to travel with a thousand carriages, surrounded by your kinsmen, all the while scorching the worlds without any consideration for us.

Seeing this extremely wretched state of yours, Bali, in which your kinsmen and friends have abandoned you, do you feel any lamentation or not? In the past, when the worlds were under your control, you experienced incomparable joy. So do you lament this unprecedented loss of status or not?

BALI said:

I have come, in this world, to understand the imper- 224.5
manence of that characterized by the procession of time. Therefore I do not grieve, Shakra, for everything in this world is finite. The bodies of living creatures are finite, ruler of the gods. Therefore I do not grieve, Shakra, for this is no fault of mine.

The soul and the body are born together at the time of birth. Both become manifest together, and both perish together.*

na h' īdṛśam ahaṃ bhāvam a|vaśaḥ prāpya kevalam,
yad evam abhijānāmi, kā vyathā me vijānataḥ?
bhūtānāṃ nidhanaṃ niṣṭhā, srotasām iva sāgaraḥ.
n' âitat samyag vijānanto narā muhyanti, vajra|dhṛk.
224.10 ye tv evaṃ n' âbhijānanti rajo|moha|parāyaṇāḥ,
te kṛcchraṃ prāpya sīdanti, buddhir yeṣāṃ praṇaśyati.
buddhi|lābhāt tu puruṣaḥ sarvaṃ tudati kilbiṣam.
vi|pāpmā labhate sattvaṃ, sattva|sthaḥ saṃprasīdati.
tatas tu ye nivartante, jāyante vā punaḥ punaḥ,
kṛpaṇāḥ paritapyante, tair arthair abhicoditāḥ.
artha|siddhim, an|arthaṃ, ca jīvitaṃ, maraṇaṃ tathā,
sukha|duḥkha|phale c' âiva na dveṣmi na ca kāmaye.
hataṃ hanti hato hy eva, yo naro hanti kaṃ cana.
ubhau tau na vijānīto yaś ca hanti, hataś ca yaḥ.
224.15 hatvā jitvā ca, Maghavan, yaḥ kaś cit puruṣāyate,
a|kartā hy eva bhavati, kartā hy eva karoti tat.
ko hi lokasya kurute vināśa|prabhavāv ubhau?
kṛtaṃ hi tat kṛten' âiva; kartā tasy' âpi c' âparaḥ.
pṛthivī, jyotir, ākāśam, āpo, vāyuś ca pañcamaḥ—
etad|yonīni bhūtāni. tatra kā paridevanā?

But I am not completely without power having attained such a state as this. Since I understand it thus, how could I be perturbed?

The end of all living beings is death, just like the end of all rivers is the ocean. Men who do not perceive this correctly are deluded, thunderbolt-wielder.

Those possessed by passion and delusion do not under- 224.10
stand it thus. Upon encountering hardship they become depressed, and their intelligence disappears.

When a man acquires intelligence he wards off all sin. Freed from evil he obtains goodness, steadfast in which he becomes serene. But those who turn away from goodness are reborn over and over again. Driven by material objects, these wretches are tormented.

The attainment of wealth, disappointment, life and death: I neither desire nor feel aversion towards the pleasure or pain of karmic retribution.

One man kills another, but it is really just one dead person killing another; neither of them perceives who kills and
who is killed. Whoever kills or conquers for personal gain, 224.15
Mághavat, is not really an agent but thinks of himself as such when he does something.

Who brings about the creation and destruction of the world? Only what has been done in the past acts in the present; the agent of the deed is different from what one thinks.

Earth, fire, space, water and wind—the five elements are the source of living beings. What is there to lament in this?

mahā|vidyo 'lpa|vidyaś ca, balavān dur|balaś ca yaḥ,
darśanīyo virūpaś ca, su|bhago dur|bhagaś ca yaḥ—
sarvaṃ Tālaḥ samādatte gambhīraḥ svena tejasā.
tasmin Tāla|vaśaṃ prāpte kā vyathā me vijānataḥ?
224.20 dagdham ev' ânudahati, hatam ev' ânuhanyate,
naśyate naṣṭam ev' âgre: labdhavyaṃ labhate naraḥ.
n' âsya dvīpaḥ, kutaḥ pāro, n' âvāraḥ saṃpradṛśyate?
n' ântam asya prapaśyāmi vidher divyasya cintayan.
yadi me paśyataḥ Kālo bhūtāni na vināśayet,
syān me harṣaś ca, darpaś ca, krodhaś c' âiva, Śacī|pate.
tuṣa|bhakṣaṃ tu māṃ jñātvā pravivikta|jane gṛhe,
bibhrataṃ gārdabhaṃ rūpam, āgatya parigarhase.
icchann ahaṃ vikuryāṃ hi rūpāṇi bahudh" ātmanaḥ
vibhīṣaṇāni, yān' īkṣya palāyethās tvam eva me.
224.25 Kālaḥ sarvaṃ samādatte, Kālaḥ sarvaṃ prayacchati.
Kālena vihitaṃ sarvaṃ: mā kṛthāḥ, Śakra, pauruṣam!
purā sarvaṃ pravyathitaṃ mayi kruddhe, Puraṃdara.
avaimi tv asya lokasya dharmaṃ, Śakra, sanātanam.
tvam apy evam avekṣasva. m" ātmanā vismayaṃ gamaḥ!
prabhavaś ca prabhāvaś ca n' ātma|saṃsthaḥ kadā cana.

Whether a person is very learned or not, strong or weak, handsome or ugly, fortunate or unfortunate, Time, mysterious in its own power, takes everything away. Since I perceive that everything is under the control of Time, how could I be perturbed?

A man gets burned after burning something, killed af- 224.20
ter killing something and destroyed after destroying something: he gets what he deserves.

Time is like an ocean without an island. How could it have a far shore when a near shore cannot be perceived? I cannot see an end to the divine order despite my contemplations.

If I were to see that Time does not destroy living beings, then I might be subject to excitement, pride and anger, O husband of Shachi.

You have realized that I eat husks of grain in a house without people, bearing the form of an ass, and so abuse me. I could, if I wished, mutate into many different, terrifying forms so that you would flee if you were to see them.

Time takes everything away and brings everything into 224.25
being. Everything is ordered by Time: do not believe in human effort, Shakra!

In the past, Indra, everything would tremble in fear when I became angry. But now I understand the eternal religious order of the world, Shakra. You too should consider this. Do not be astonished! Creation and efficacy are never in one's control.

kaumāram eva te cittaṃ, tath" âiv' âdya yathā purā.
samavekṣasva, Maghavan, buddhiṃ vindasva naiṣṭhikīm.
devā, manuṣyāḥ, pitaro, gandharv'|ôraga|rākṣasāḥ
āsan sarve mama vaśe. tat sarvaṃ vettha, Vāsava.
224.30 «namas tasyai diśe 'py astu, yasyāṃ Vairocano Baliḥ!»
iti mām abhyapadyanta buddhi|mātsarya|mohitāḥ.
n' âhaṃ tad anuśocāmi, n' âtma|bhraṃśaṃ, Śacī|pate.
evaṃ me niścitā buddhiḥ: śāstus tiṣṭhāmy ahaṃ vaśe.
dṛśyate hi kule jāto, darśanīyaḥ, pratāpavān,
duḥkhaṃ jīvan sah"|āmātyo: bhavitavyaṃ hi tat tathā.
dauṣkuleyas tathā mūḍho, dur|jātaḥ, Śakra dṛśyate
sukhaṃ jīvan sah"|āmātyo: bhavitavyaṃ hi tat tathā.
kalyāṇī, rūpa|saṃpannā dur|bhagā, Śakra, dṛśyate,
a|lakṣaṇā vi|rūpā ca su|bhagā dṛśyate parā.
224.35 n' âitad asmat|kṛtaṃ, Śakra, n' âitac, Chakra, tvayā kṛtam
yat tvam evaṃ|gato, Vajrin, yac c' âpy evaṃ|gatā vayam.
na karma bhavitā 'py etat kṛtaṃ mama, Śata|krato!
ṛddhir v" âpy atha vā na' rddhiḥ—paryāya|kṛtam eva tat.
paśyāmi tvāṃ virājantaṃ deva|rājam avasthitam,
śrīmantaṃ dyutimantaṃ ca, garjamānaṃ mam' ôpari.
evaṃ n' âiva, na cet Kālo mām ākramya sthito bhavet.
pātayeyam ahaṃ tv" âdya sa|vajram api muṣṭinā!

Your mind is still juvenile, just like it was in the past. Think about this, Mághavat, and you might find the highest understanding.

All the gods, humans, ancestors, *gandhárvas*, *nagas* and *rákshasas* used to be under my control. You know all this, Indra.

All of them were deluded by envy and so honored me, 224.30
saying "Homage to that region of the sky in which Bali the son of Viróchana abides!" But I do not lament my loss of status, husband of Shachi, for I am of the resolute understanding that I will remain under the control of the ruler—Time.

One can see that a handsome, formidable person from a good family may live an unhappy life, along with his companions: things may be thus. But one can also see that a fool from a low family and an inferior class might live a happy life with his companions, Shakra: things may be thus. One can see that a beautiful, good-looking woman might be unfortunate, Shakra, whereas another unremarkable, ugly woman might be blessed by good fortunate.

I have not caused your present state, Shakra, nor have 224.35
you caused this present state of mine, thunderbolt-wielder! And I will commit no such act in the future, Indra of the hundred sacrifices! Whether or not I achieve success or failure depends on the procession of Time.

I behold you, shining forth in your position as the king of gods, effulgent and glorious, roaring away above me. But things would not be thus if Time did not continue to affect me after its attack. I would smite down you and your thunderbolt with my fist right now! But this is not a time for

na tu vikrama|kālo 'yaṃ: śānti|kālo 'yam āgataḥ.
Kālaḥ sthāpayate sarvaṃ, Kālaḥ pacati vai tathā.

224.40 māṃ ced abhyāgataḥ Kālo dānav'|ēśvaram ūrjitam,†
garjantaṃ, pratapantaṃ ca: kam anyaṃ n' āgamiṣyati?
dvādaśānāṃ tu bhavatām Ādityānāṃ mah"|ātmanām
tejāṃsy ekena sarveṣāṃ, deva|rāja, dhṛtāni me.
aham ev' ôdvahāmy āpo, visṛjāmi ca, Vāsava;
tapāmi c' âiva trailokyaṃ, vidyotāmy aham eva ca.
saṃrakṣāmi, vilumpāmi, dadāmy aham ath' ādade,
saṃyacchāmi, niyacchāmi, lokeṣu prabhur īśvaraḥ.

tad adya vinivṛttaṃ me prabhutvam, amar'|âdhipa.
Kāla|sainy'|âvagāḍhasya sarvaṃ na pratibhāti me.

224.45 n' âhaṃ kartā, na c' âiva tvaṃ, n' ânyaḥ kartā, Śacī|pate.
paryāyeṇa hi bhujyante lokāḥ, Śakra, yadṛcchayā.

māsa|mās'|ârdha|veśmānam, aho|rātr'|âbhisaṃvṛtam,
ṛtu|dvāraṃ, vāyu|mukham āhur† veda|vido janāḥ.

āhuḥ sarvam idaṃ cintyaṃ janāḥ ke cin manīṣayā.
asyāḥ pañc' âiva cintāyāḥ paryeṣyāmi ca pañcadhā.

gambhīraṃ, gahanaṃ brahma,
mahat toy'|ârṇavaṃ yathā,
an|ādi|nidhanaṃ c' āhur,
a|kṣaraṃ kṣaram eva ca.
sattveṣu liṅgam āviśya nir|liṅgam api tat svayam,
manyante dhruvam ev' âinaṃ ye janās tattva|darśinaḥ.

valor: the time for peace has arrived. Time sets everything up and then cooks it.

Thundering and harassing others, I was the mighty lord 224.40
of the *dánavas*. If Time has attacked me, who else might it not approach? I alone upheld the power of the twelve Adítyas, those venerable and illustrious beings, O king of the gods. I used to draw the waters upwards and then release them as rain, Vásava; I used to heat and illuminate the triple world. I was the powerful master of the worlds who would protect and destroy, give and take, reward and suppress.

Today my supremacy has disappeared, O ruler of the immortals. Since I was overcome by the army of Time nothing appeals to me. Neither I, nor you, nor anyone else is an 224.45
agent, husband of Shachi. The worlds are consumed by the procession of Time, Shakra, and quite by chance.

The Vedic masters say that Time has its abode in the months and half-months, and is concealed by the days and nights. It is the door to the seasons and the opening of the wind.

Some men say that the entire world can be conceived through inspired thinking. I will investigate each five of these contemplations in five ways.

Just like a great flood of water, *brahman* is deep and mysterious. It is without beginning and end and comprises both the imperishable and perishable, so they say. In itself it is incorporeal, but it enters the bodies of creatures. Those who see the truth think that it is intransient.

224.50 bhūtānāṃ tu viparyāsaṃ kurute bhagavān iti.
na hy etāvad bhaved gamyaṃ, na yasmāt prabhavet punaḥ.
gatiṃ hi sarva|bhūtānām a|gatvā kva gamiṣyati?
yo dhāvatā na hātavyas, tiṣṭhann api na hīyate.
tam indriyāṇi sarvāṇi n' ânupaśyanti pañcadhā.
āhuś c' âinaṃ ke cid agniṃ, ke cid āhuḥ Prajāpatim.
ṛtūn, mās'|ârdha|māsāṃś ca, divasāṃś ca, kṣaṇāṃs tathā,
pūrv'|âhṇam apar'|âhṇaṃ ca, madhy'|âhnam api c' âpare,
muhūrtam api c' âiv' āhur ekaṃ santam an|ekadhā.
taṃ Kālam iti jānīhi, yasya sarvam idaṃ vaśe.
224.55 bahūn' Îndra|sahasrāṇi samatītāni, Vāsava,
bala|vīry'|ôpapannāni, yath" âiva tvaṃ, Śacī|pate.
tvām apy ati|balaṃ, Śakra, deva|rājaṃ bal'|ôtkaṭam,
prāpte kāle mahā|vīryaḥ Kālaḥ saṃśamayiṣyati.
ya idaṃ sarvam ādatte, tasmāc, Chakra, sthiro bhava!
mayā tvayā ca pūrvaiś ca na sa śakyo 'tivartitum.
yām etāṃ prāpya jānīṣe rājya|śriyam an|uttamām,
«sthitā may'» îti, tan mithyā: n' âiṣā hy ekatra tiṣṭhati.
sthitā h' Îndra|sahasreṣu tvad|viśiṣṭatameṣv iyam.
māṃ ca lolā parityajya, tvām agād, vibudh'|âdhipa.
224.60 m" âivaṃ, Śakra, punaḥ kārṣīḥ. śānto bhavitum arhasi!
tvām apy evaṃ|vidhaṃ jñātvā, kṣipram anyaṃ gamiṣyati.

Therefore the Blessed One brings about the disintegra- 224.50
tion of living beings. But that much cannot be perceived, since a person cannot master him.

Where can one go when one has reached the destiny of all living beings? He cannot be abandoned by running away, and he does not relinquish the person who stands still.

The five sense faculties cannot see him. Some say he is fire, others call him Praja·pati. Others say he is the seasons, the months, the fortnight, the days, the hours, the morning, the evening, midday or the moment. He is one but has innumerable forms. Know him as Time, by whom the entire world is controlled.

Many thousands of Indras have passed away, Vásava, de- 224.55
spite being endowed with strength and valor—the same will happen to you, husband of Shachi.

Although you are excessively strong, Shakra, as the king of the gods abounding in power, Time is awesomely powerful. When your time comes it will destroy you. It takes everything away, so stand firm, Shakra! It is impossible that you, or I, or anybody before us could escape it.

You think "It abides in me alone!" but that is the wrong way to consider this incomparable, imperial effulgence that you have attained. It does not rest in one place for it is found among thousands of Indras, most notably in you. But being fickle it abandoned me and came to you instead, O ruler of the gods.

Do not act in this way, Shakra. Be peaceful! For when 224.60
it realizes what you are like, it will quickly find its way to someone else.

BHĪṢMA uvāca:

225.1 ŚATA|KRATUR ath' âpaśyad Baler dīptāṃ mah"|ātmanaḥ
sva|rūpiṇīṃ śarīrādd hi niṣkrāmantīṃ tadā śriyam.
tāṃ dṛṣṭvā prabhayā dīptāṃ bhagavān Pāka|śāsanaḥ
vismay'|ôtphulla|nayano Baliṃ papraccha Vāsavaḥ.

ŚAKRA uvāca:

Bale, k' êyam apakrāntā rocamānā śikhaṇḍinī
tvattaḥ? sthitā sa|keyūrā, dīpyamānā sva|tejasā.

BALIR uvāca:

na h' îmām āsurīṃ vedmi, na daivīṃ ca, na mānuṣīm.
tvam enāṃ pṛccha vā mā vā. yath"|êṣṭaṃ kuru, Vāsava!

ŚAKRA uvāca:

225.5 kā tvaṃ Baler apakrāntā rocamānā śikhaṇḍinī?
ajānato mam' ācakṣva nāma|dheyaṃ, śuci|smite.
kā tvaṃ tiṣṭhasi māṃ evaṃ dīpyamānā sva|tejasā?
hitvā daitya|varaṃ, subhru? tan mam' ācakṣva pṛcchataḥ.

ŚRĪR uvāca:

na māṃ Virocano veda,
n' âyaṃ Vairocano Baliḥ.
āhur māṃ «Duḥsah"» êty evaṃ,
«Vidhits"» êti ca māṃ viduḥ.

BHISHMA said:

AND THEN INDRA of the hundred sacrifices saw Shri, the goddess of fortune, in her own blazing form leaving the body of Bali the great.* Upon seeing her blazing with brilliant light, the blessed Vásava, punisher of Paka the *daitya*, once again questioned Bali, his eyes wide open in astonishment. 225.1

SHAKRA said:

Who is this resplendent, crested being that leaves you, Bali? She has bracelets on her upper arms, and blazes with her own luster.

BALI said:

I do not know whether she is a demon, a goddess or a human being. Ask her, or maybe not. Do what you want, Vásava!

SHAKRA said:

Who are you, resplendent and crested, who has just left Bali? Tell me your name for I do not know it, sweetly smiling one. Who are you, standing next to me, blazing with your own luster? Now that you have abandoned the chief of the *daitya*s, beautiful browed lady, please tell me since I ask. 225.5

SHRI said:

Viróchana does not know me, nor does his son Bali. They call me the "Dúhsaha"—the irresistible one—or simply "Vidhítsa"—intention.

«Bhūtir, Lakṣm"» īti mām āhuḥ,
«Śrīr» ity evaṃ ca, Vāsava.
tvaṃ māṃ, Śakra na jānīṣe,
sarve devā na māṃ viduḥ.

ŚAKRA uvāca:

kim idaṃ tvaṃ mama kṛte, ut' āho Balinaḥ kṛte
Duḥsahe, vijahāsy enaṃ cira|saṃvāsinī satī?

ŚRĪR uvāca:

225.10 no dhātā na vidhātā māṃ vidadhāti kathaṃ cana.
kālas tu, Śakra, paryāgān; m" âinaṃ, Śakr', âvamanyathāḥ!

ŚAKRA uvāca:

kathaṃ tvayā Balis tyaktaḥ? kim|arthaṃ vā, śikhaṇḍini?
kathaṃ ca māṃ na jahyās tvaṃ? tan me brūhi, śuci|smite.

ŚRĪR uvāca:

satye sthit" âsmi, dāne ca, vrate, tapasi c' âiva hi,
parākrame ca, dharme ca; parācīnas tato Baliḥ.
brahmaṇyo 'yaṃ purā bhūtvā, satya|vādī, jit'|êndriyaḥ,
abhyasūyad brāhmaṇānām, ucchiṣṭaś c' âspṛśad ghṛtam.
yajña|śīlaḥ sadā bhūtvā, mām eva yajate svayam.
provāca lokān mūḍh'|ātmā, Kālen' ôpanipīḍitaḥ.
225.15 apākṛtā tataḥ, Śakra, tvayi vatsyāmi, Vāsava.
a|pramattena dhāry" âsmi tapasā vikrameṇa ca.

They also call me Bhuti, Lakshmi and Shri as well, O Vásava. You do not know me, Shakra, and nor do any of the gods.

SHAKRA said:

O Dúhsaha, is it because of me or because of Bali that you abandon him? You have abided in Bali for a long time.

SHRI said:

Neither the creator nor the ordainer controls me in any 225.10
way. Time has simply elapsed, Shakra—do not despise him!

SHAKRA said:

How come you have abandoned Bali? What is the purpose of this, crested one? And how might you not leave me? Tell me this, sweetly smiling one.

SHRI said:

I abide in truth, charity, religious vows, asceticism, courage and righteousness, but Bali has turned away from these. In the past he was pious, honest and and a master of his senses. But then he started to resent brahmins, and handled ghee in a state of impurity.

He always performed his sacrificial duties zealously, and offered his sacrifices to me alone. But then he foolishly
praised the worlds and so was oppressed by Time. I have 225.15
left him, Shakra, and will abide in you, Vásava. You must support me with diligence, asceticism and vigor.

ŚAKRA uvāca:

n' âsti deva|manuṣyeṣu sarva|bhūteṣu vā pumān,
yas tvām eko viṣahituṃ śaknuyāt, kamal'|ālaye?

ŚRĪR uvāca:

n' âiva devo, na gandharvo, n' âsuro, na ca rākṣasaḥ,
yo mām eko viṣahituṃ śaktaḥ kaś cit, Puraṃdara.

ŚAKRA uvāca:

tiṣṭhethā mayi nityaṃ tvaṃ yathā, tad brūhi me, śubhe!
tat kariṣyāmi te vākyam, ṛtaṃ tad vaktum arhasi.

ŚRĪR uvāca:

sthāsyāmi nityaṃ, dev'|êndra, yathā tvayi, nibodha tat.
vidhinā veda|dṛṣṭena caturdhā vibhajasva mām.

ŚAKRA uvāca:

225.20 ahaṃ vai tvāṃ nidhāsyāmi yathā|śakti, yathā|balam.
na tu me 'tikramaḥ syād vai sadā, Lakṣmi, tav' ântike.
bhūmir eva manuṣyeṣu dhāriṇī bhūta|bhāvinī.
sā te pādaṃ titikṣeta, samarthā h', îti me matiḥ.

ŚRĪR uvāca:

eṣa me nihitaḥ pādo, yo 'yaṃ bhūmau pratiṣṭhitaḥ.
dvitīyaṃ, Śakra, pādaṃ me tasmāt su|nihitaṃ kuru!

SHAKRA said:

Is there no man among the gods, humans and other living beings who is able to overpower you all by himself, lotus dweller?

SHRI said:

There is no god, *gandhárva*, demon or *rákshasa* who can overpower me by himself, Puran·dara.

SHAKRA said:

Tell me how you will always reside within me, auspicious one. I will do whatever you say, so answer me truly.

SHRI said:

Listen to how I will always abide in you, lord of the gods. You must divide me into four parts, according to the Vedic prescription.

SHAKRA said:

I will consign you as you say, with all my power and 225.20
might. I will never commit a transgression in your presence, Lakshmi. The earth alone blesses all living beings and supports men. May it bear a quarter of you, for I think that it is capable of doing so.

SHRI said:

I lay down this quarter of mine, so that it is established in the earth. Now consign my second quarter, Shakra. Do it well!

ŚAKRA uvāca:

āpa eva manuṣyeṣu dravantyaḥ paricāriṇīḥ.
tās te pādaṃ titikṣantām, alam āpas titikṣitum.

ŚRĪR uvāca:

eṣa me nihitaḥ pādo, yo 'yam apsu pratiṣṭhitaḥ.
tṛtīyaṃ, Śakra, pādaṃ me tasmāt su|nihitaṃ kuru!

ŚAKRA uvāca:

225.25 yasmin vedāś ca yajñāś ca, yasmin devāḥ pratiṣṭhitāḥ,
tṛtīyaṃ pādam agnis te su|dhṛtaṃ dhārayiṣyati.

ŚRĪR uvāca:

eṣa me nihitaḥ pādo yo 'yam agnau pratiṣṭhitaḥ.
caturthaṃ, Śakra, pādaṃ me tasmāt su|nihitaṃ kuru!

ŚAKRA uvāca:

ye vai santo manuṣyeṣu brahmaṇyāḥ satya|vādinaḥ,
te te pādaṃ titikṣantām; alaṃ santas titikṣitum.

ŚRĪR uvāca:

eṣa me nihitaḥ pādo, yo 'yaṃ satsu pratiṣṭhitaḥ.
evaṃ hi nihitāṃ, Śakra, bhūteṣu paridhatsva mām!

ŚAKRA uvāca:

bhūtānām iha yo vai tvāṃ mayā vinihitāṃ satīm
upahanyāt, sa me dhṛṣyas. tathā śṛṇvantu me vacaḥ!

SHAKRA said:

The waters flow and circulate among human beings. Let them bear a quarter of you, for they are able to do so.

SHRI said:

I lay down this quarter of mine, so that it is established in the waters. Now consign my third quarter, Shakra. Do it well!

SHAKRA said:

Fire will be able to give excellent support to your third quarter, for the Vedas, the sacrifices and the gods are established in it. 225.25

SHRI said:

I lay down this quarter of mine, so that it is established in fire. Now consign my fourth quarter, Shakra. Do it well!

SHAKRA said:

Let those men who are virtuous, pious and honest bear a quarter of you, as they are able to do so.

SHRI said:

I lay down this quarter of mine, so that it is established in the virtuous. You must protect me, Shakra, thus consigned to different entities!

SHAKRA said:

I will attack any creature here that tries to harm you, for it is I who has deposited your four quarters. Take heed of my words!

tatas tyaktaḥ Śriyā rājā Daityānāṃ Balir abravīt.

BALIR uvāca:

225.30 yāvat purastāt pratapet, tāvad vai dakṣiṇāṃ diśam,
paścimāṃ tāvad ev' âpi, tath" ôdīcīṃ divā|karaḥ.
tathā madhyaṃ|dine sūryo n' âstam eti yadā, tadā
punar dev'|âsuraṃ yuddhaṃ bhāvi; jet" âsmi vas tadā.
sarva|lokān yad" āditya eka|sthas tāpayiṣyati,
tadā dev'|âsure yuddhe jet" âhaṃ tvāṃ, Śata|krato.

ŚAKRA uvāca:

brahmaṇ" âsmi samādiṣṭo, «na hantavyo bhavān,» iti
tena te 'haṃ, Bale, vajraṃ na vimuñcāmi mūrdhani.
yath"|êṣṭaṃ gaccha, daity'|êndra, svasti te 'stu, mah"|âsura.
ādityo n' âiva tapitā kadā cin madhyataḥ sthitaḥ.
225.35 sthāpito hy asya samayaḥ pūrvam eva svayaṃ|bhuvā:
ajasraṃ pariyāty eṣa, satyen' âvatapan prajāḥ.
ayanaṃ tasya ṣaṇ|māsān uttaraṃ, dakṣiṇaṃ tathā,
yena saṃyāti lokeṣu śīt'|ôṣṇe visṛjan raviḥ.

BHĪṢMA uvāca:

evam uktas tu daity'|êndro balir Indreṇa, Bhārata,
jagāma dakṣiṇām āśām, udīcīṃ tu Puraṃdaraḥ.
ity etad Balinā gītam an|ahaṃ|kāra|saṃjñitam
vākyaṃ śrutvā Sahasr'|âkṣaḥ kham ev' āruruhe tadā.

BHISHMA said:

But then Bali, the king of the *daityas* who had been abandoned by Shri, spoke.

BALI said:

As long as the sun shines in the East, so will it shine in the South, the West and the North. But when the sun does not start to set after midday, there will be a war between the *ásuras* and gods once again, and I will conquer you. 225.30

When the sun remains in the same place scorching all the worlds, I will conquer you in the war between the *ásuras* and gods, O Indra of the hundred sacrifices.

SHAKRA said:

As Brahma has forbidden me from killing you, I will not fire my thunderbolt at your head, Bali! Go where you want, *daitya* lord, and may you have good fortune, great demon. The sun will never halt at its meridian and scorch the worlds.

The self-existent Brahma has already established the rule 225.35
for this: the sun revolves without stopping, heating creatures by means of the truth. For six months its course lies in the North and for six months it lies in the South. Following this path through the worlds, the sun diffuses cold and heat.

BHISHMA said:

Once Bali the leader of the *daityas* had been addressed by Indra, he went off to the South, and Puran·dara headed north, Bhárata. Thus Bali sung a song that lacked any sense of self-consciousness, and once the thousand-eyed Indra heard it, he ascended into the sky.

226

THE DIALOGUE BETWEEN INDRA AND NÁMUCHI

BHĪṢMA uvāca:

226.1 ATR’ ÂIV’ ÔDĀHARANT’ îmam itihāsaṃ purātanam:
Śata|kratoś ca saṃvādaṃ Namuceś ca, Yudhiṣṭhira.
śriyā vihīnam āsīnam, a|kṣobhyam iva sāgaram,
bhav’|âbhava|jñaṃ bhūtānām ity uvāca Puraṃ|daraḥ:
«baddhaḥ pāśaiś, cyutaḥ sthānād, dviṣatāṃ vaśam āgataḥ,
śriyā vihīno, Namuce, śocasy, āho na śocasi?»

NAMUCIR uvāca:

a|nivāryeṇa śokena śarīraṃ c’ ôpatapyate.
amitrāś ca prahṛṣyanti, śoke n’ âsti sahāyatā.
226.5 tasmāc, Chakra, na śocāmi; sarvaṃ hy ev’ êdam antavat.
saṃtāpād bhraśyate rūpaṃ, saṃtāpād bhraśyate śriyaḥ,
saṃtāpād bhraśyate c’ āyur, dharmaś c’ âiva, sur’|ēśvara.
vinīya khalu tad duḥkham āgataṃ vaimanasya|jam,
dhyātavyaṃ manasā hṛdyaṃ kalyāṇaṃ saṃvijānatā.
yadā yadā hi puruṣaḥ kalyāṇe kurute manaḥ,
tadā tasya prasidhyanti sarv’|ârthā, n’ âtra saṃśayaḥ.
ekaḥ śāstā na dvitīyo ’sti śāstā,
garbhe śayānaṃ puruṣaṃ śāsti śāstā.
ten’ ânuyuktaḥ, pravaṇād iv’ ôdakaṃ:
yathā niyukto ’smi tathā vahāmi.
bhav’|âbhavau tv abhijānan, garīyo

BHISHMA said:

ON THE VERY SAME subject, people relate the ancient tradition of a dialogue between Indra of the hundred sacrifices and Námuchi, O Yudhi·shthira. 226.1

Devoid of his effulgence, the seated Námuchi was as unshakeable as the ocean. He understood the existence and non-existence of living beings, and Puran·dara spoke thus to him:

"Under the control of your enemies and bound in chains, you have lost your eminent position. Devoid of effulgence, Námuchi, do you feel any lamentation or not?"

NÁMUCHI said:

The sorrow that afflicts the body cannot be warded off. One's enemies rejoice then, for there is no companionship
in sorrow. But I do not grieve because of this, Shakra, for 226.5
everything in this world is finite. One's beauty, good fortune, longevity and righteousness vanish because of affliction, O Lord of the gods.

The person who understands this should dispel the misery that arises from depression, and meditate on the good that abides within the heart. Whenever a man keeps his mind to the good, all his aims will undoubtedly be accomplished.

There is only one ruler, and no second, who rules over the embryo lying in the womb. I follow his order like water running down a slope: I conduct myself just as I am directed to. I understand existence and non-existence, and know what is most important and felicitous, but still do not

jānāmi śreyo na tu tat karomi!†
āśāsu dharmyāsu parāsu kurvan,
yathā niyukto 'smi, tathā vahāmi.

226.10 yathā yath" âsya prāptavyaṃ, prāpnoty eva tathā tathā:
bhavitavyaṃ yathā yac ca, bhavaty eva tathā tathā.
yatra yatr' âiva saṃyukto dhātrā garbhe punaḥ punaḥ,
tatra tatr' âiva vasati, na yatra svayam icchati.
bhāvo yo 'yam anuprāpto, bhavitavyam idaṃ mama:
iti yasya sadā bhāvo, na sa muhyet kadā cana.
paryāyair hanyamānānām abhiyoktā na vidyate.
duḥkham etat tu, yad dveṣṭā «kart" âham» iti manyate.
ṛṣīṃś ca, devāṃś ca, mah"|âsurāṃś ca,
traividya|vṛddhāṃś ca, vane munīṃś ca
kān āpado† n' ôpanamanti loke?
par'|âvara|jñās tu na saṃbhramanti.

226.15 na paṇḍitaḥ krudhyati, n' âbhipadyate,
na c' âpi saṃsīdati, na prahṛṣyati.
na c' ârtha|kṛcchra|vyasaneṣu śocate,
sthitaḥ prakṛtyā Himavān iv' â|calaḥ.
yam artha|siddhiḥ paramā na mohayet,
tath" âiva kāle vyasanaṃ na mohayet,
sukhaṃ ca duḥkhaṃ ca tath" âiva madhyamaṃ
niṣevate yaḥ, sa dhuraṃ|dharo naraḥ.
yāṃ yām avasthāṃ puruṣo 'dhigacchet,
tasyāṃ ramet' â|paritapyamānaḥ.
evaṃ pravṛddhaṃ praṇuden† mano|jaṃ,
saṃtāpam āyāsa|karaṃ† śarīrāt.

do that! Acting according to other, righteous aspirations, I conduct myself just as I am directed to.

One receives what one ought to receive: only that which 226.10
ought to come into being comes into being. A person abides in whatever womb the creator places him over and over again, and not in one that he himself chooses. The state I have attained is only that which I should attain: a person should never delude himself, for his existence is always thus.

There is no enemy of those killed by the procession of Time. This is suffering, to which the person who considers himself an agent is averse.

Who are the seers, gods, great *ásura*s, elders steeped in the triple knowledge and silent sages in the forest that calamities do not approach in this world? But those who understand both the inferior and the superior are not perplexed.

Wise men are not angry or aggressive and do not become 226.15
depressed or excited. They do not grieve over difficult matters or disasters but abide in their true nature, just like the unshakeable Himalaya.

The man who is not deluded by accomplishing the ultimate goal, or stupefied when a disaster eventually comes his way, who endures pleasurable, painful and neutral experiences—he is preeminent.

A person should find pleasure in whatever condition he falls into, without being tormented. And so one must expel desire from the body when it arises, for it is an affliction that causes suffering.

tat sadaḥ† sat|pariṣat|sabhā|sadaḥ,†
prāpya yo† na kurute sadā bhayam,
dharma|tattvam avagāhya buddhimān
yo 'bhyupaiti, sa dhuram|dharaḥ pumān.
prājñasya karmāṇi dur|anvayāni:
na vai prājño muhyati moha|kāle.
sthānāc cyutaś cen na mumoha c' ôttamas
tāvat kṛcchrām āpadaṃ prāpya vṛddhaḥ.

226.20 na mantra|bala|vīryeṇa, prajñayā, pauruṣeṇa ca,
na śīlena, na vṛttena, tathā n' âiv ârtha|saṃpadā
a|labhyaṃ labhate martyas. tatra kā paridevanā?
yad evam anujātasya dhātāro vidadhuḥ purā,
tad ev' ânucariṣyāmi. kiṃ me mṛtyuḥ kariṣyati?
labdhavyāny eva labhate, gantavyāny eva gacchati.
prāptavyāny eva prāpnoti duḥkhāni ca sukhāni ca.
etad viditvā kārtsnyena yo na muhyati mānavaḥ,
kuśalī sarva|duḥkheṣu, sa vai sarva|dhano naraḥ.

The wise man who never feels fear when he arrives at an assembly—a gathering or congregation of worthy people, in other words—since he only approaches once he has steeped himself in religious truth, he is preeminent.

The acts of a wise man are hard to fathom: he is not deluded in a time of delusion. Even if that supreme, venerable, person loses his status upon encountering a miserable misfortune, he is not deluded.

Not through the efficacy and power of the Vedic mantras, 226.20
nor through wisdom, human effort, virtue, good behavior, or the accomplishment of his aims does a mortal attain that which is impossible to attain. What is there to lament in this?

I will therefore follow what the divinities ordained in the past for one reborn in a state like mine. What will death do with me?

A person gets only what he should get, and achieves only what he should achieve. He experiences only the sufferings and pleasures that he deserves.

The man who understands this in its entirety, who is not deluded but skilled in all sufferings, he alone possesses all riches.

227

ANOTHER DIALOGUE BETWEEN INDRA AND BALI

YUDHIṢṬHIRA uvāca:

227.1 MAGNASYA VYASANE kṛcchre kiṃ śreyaḥ puruṣasya hi
bandhu|nāśe, mahī|pāla, rājya|nāśe 'tha vā punaḥ?
tvaṃ hi naḥ paramo vaktā loke 'smin, Bharata'|rṣabha.
etad bhavantaṃ pṛcchāmi, tan me tvaṃ vaktum arhasi.

BHĪṢMA uvāca:

putra|dāraiḥ sukhaiś c' âiva viyuktasya, dhanena vā,
magnasya vyasane kṛcchre, dhṛtiḥ śreyas|karī, nṛpa.
dhairyeṇa yuktaṃ satataṃ śarīraṃ na viśīryate.
vi|śokatā sukhaṃ dhatte, dhatte c' ārogyam uttamam.
227.5 ārogyāc ca śarīrasya sa punar vindate śriyam.
yaś† ca prājño naras, tāta, sāttvikīṃ vṛttim āsthitaḥ,
tasy' âiśvaryaṃ ca, dhairyaṃ ca, vyavasāyaś ca karmasu.
atr' âiv' ôdāharant' îmam itihāsaṃ purātanam:
Bali|Vāsava|saṃvādaṃ punar eva, Yudhiṣṭhira.
vṛtte dev'|âsure yuddhe daitya|dānava|saṃkṣaye,
Viṣṇu|krānteṣu lokeṣu, deva|rāje Śata|kratau,
ijyamāneṣu deveṣu, cāturvarṇye vyavasthite,
samṛddha|mātre trailokye, prīti|yukte svayaṃ|bhuvi,
Rudrair, Vasubhir, Ādityair, Aśvibhyām, api ca' ṛṣibhiḥ,
227.10 gandharvair, bhujag'|êndraiś ca,
siddhaiś c' ânyair vṛtaḥ prabhuḥ
catur|dantaṃ su|dāntaṃ ca

YUDHI·SHTHIRA said:

WHAT IS BEST for a man beset by a terrible disaster 227.1
such as the loss of his kinsmen or kingdom, Lord of the earth? We think that you are the supreme teacher of this world, bullish Bhárata. Since I have inquired about this, please explain it to me.

BHISHMA said:

When a man is beset by a terrible disaster, and is separated from his sons, wives, pleasures or wealth, it is resolve that secures his felicity, Your Majesty.

If one's body is perpetually endowed with determination, it does not disintegrate. Freedom from sorrow brings bliss
and excellent health. Endowed with good health, a man 227.5
finds felicity. The wise man who adheres to pure conduct, my son, will find sovereignty, determination, and resolve in his deeds.

On this very subject people relate an ancient tradition, Yudhi·shthira: another dialogue between Bali and Vásava. When the war between the gods and demons was over and the *daitya*s and *dánava*s had been destroyed, Vishnu stepped over the worlds and Indra of the hundred sacrifices was established as king of the gods. At that time the gods were worshipped with sacrifices, and the system of four classes was established.

The triple world was completely prosperous, and Brahma was filled with joy. And then, surrounded by the *rudra*s, Vasus, Adítyas, Ashvin twins, seers, *gandhárva*s, serpent lords, 227.10
Siddhas and others, Lord Shakra mounted Airávata—the well tamed leader of the elephants who, with his four tusks,

vāraṇ'|êndraṃ śriyā vṛtam
āruhy' Āirāvataṃ Śakras
trailokyam anusaṃyayau.

sa kadā cit samudr'|ânte kasmiṃś cid giri|gahvare
Baliṃ Vairocaniṃ vajrī dadarś', ôpasasarpa ca.
tam Airāvata|mūrdha|sthaṃ prekṣya deva|gaṇair vṛtam
sur'|êndram Indraṃ daity'|êndro na śuśoca, na vivyathe.
dṛṣṭvā tam a|vikāra|sthaṃ tiṣṭhantaṃ nir|bhayaṃ Balim,
adhirūḍho dvipa|śreṣṭham ity uvāca Śata|kratuḥ:

«daitya, na vyathase. śauryād, atha vā vṛddha|sevayā,
tapasā, bhāvitatvād vā, sarvath" âitat su|duṣkaram.
227.15 śatrubhir vaśam ānīto, hīnaḥ† sthānād an|uttamāt,
Vairocane, kim āśritya śocitavye na śocasi?

śraiṣṭhyaṃ prāpya sva|jātīnāṃ,
mahā|bhogān an|uttamān,
hṛta|sva|ratna|rājyas tvaṃ
brūhi, kasmān na śocasi?
īśvaro hi purā bhūtvā pitṛ|paitāmahe pade,
tat tvam adya hṛtaṃ dṛṣṭvā sapatnaiḥ kiṃ na śocasi?

baddhaś ca Vāruṇaiḥ pāśair, vajreṇa ca samāhataḥ
hṛta|dāro, hṛta|dhano, brūhi kasmān na śocasi?
naṣṭa|śrīr, vibhava|bhraṣṭo yan na śocasi duṣ|karam,
trailokya|rājya|nāśe hi ko 'nyo jīvitum utsahet?»

was enveloped in effulgence—and traversed the triple world.

Eventually this thunderbolt-wielding god reached the end of the oceans and came upon a mountain cave in which he saw Bali, son of Viróchana. That leader of *daitya*s saw Indra, lord of the gods, mounted on the head of Airávata and surrounded by the hosts of gods. But he did not lament and was not perturbed. Still mounted on Airávata, and seeing that Bali did not move and stood still without any fear, Indra of the hundred sacrifices said:

"You are not perturbed, *daitya*. Whether this is because of your valor, reverence for the elders, asceticism or inner development, it is a virtually impossible feat. You have 227.15
fallen into the hands of your enemies, and have lost your incomparable position. What is the reason, Vairóchani, that do you not lament that which you ought to lament?

You had attained superiority among your own kind and incomparable good fortune. But your jewels and kingdom have been taken away, so tell me—why do you not lament? You were previously the lord, in the position held by your father and grandfather, but have seen it taken away by your enemies. So why do you not lament?

You have been struck down by my thunderbolt, and are bound by the snares of Váruna, god of the sea. Your wives and wealth have been taken away, so tell me—why do you not lament? Deprived of your effulgence and stripped of your power, you do not lament this disaster. Who else could bear to live when his dominion over the triple world has been destroyed?"

227.20 etac c' ânyac ca paruṣaṃ bruvantaṃ paribhūya tam
śrutvā sukham a|saṃbhrānto Balir Vairocano 'bravīt.

BALIR uvāca:

nigṛhīte mayi bhṛśaṃ, Śakra, kiṃ katthitena te?
vajram udyamya tiṣṭhantaṃ paśyāmi tvāṃ, Puraṃdara.
a|śaktaḥ pūrvam āsīs tvaṃ, kathaṃ cic chaktatāṃ gataḥ.
kas tvad|anya imāṃ vācaṃ su|krūrāṃ vaktum arhati?
yas tu śatror vaśa|sthasya śakto 'pi kurute dayām
hasta|prāptasya vīrasya, taṃ c' âiva puruṣaṃ viduḥ.
a|niścayo hi yuddheṣu dvayor vivadamānayoḥ
ekaḥ prāpnoti vijayam, ekaś c' âiva parājayam.
227.25 mā ca te bhūt sva|bhāvo 'yam iti te, deva|puṃgava!
īśvaraḥ sarva|bhūtānāṃ vikrameṇa jito balāt.
n' âitad asmat|kṛtaṃ, Śakra,
n' âitac, Chakra, kṛtam tvayā,
yat tvam evaṃ|gato, vajrin,
yad v" âpy evaṃ|gatā vayam.
aham āsaṃ yath" âdya tvaṃ, bhavitā tvaṃ yathā vayam.
m" âvamaṃsthā «mayā karma duṣ|kṛtaṃ kṛtam» ity uta.
sukha|duḥkhe hi puruṣaḥ paryāyeṇ' âdhigacchati.
paryāyeṇ' âsi Śakratvaṃ prāptaḥ, Śakra, na karmaṇā.
Kālaḥ kāle nayati māṃ, tvāṃ ca Kālo nayaty ayam.
ten' âhaṃ tvaṃ yathā n' âdya, tvaṃ c' âpi na yathā vayam.

Bali, son of Viróchana, listened to Indra insulting him 227.20
with this and other cutting statements. But he did not becoming agitated and spoke this willingly.

BALI said:

While I am restrained so excessively, Shakra, what is the point of boasting? I see you standing there, Puran·dara, with your thunderbolt raised. In the past you lacked power, but have gained it now by chance. Who else but you could speak these excessively cruel words? They call him a man who although able shows mercy to the enemy he controls, the hero whom he has in the palm of his hand.

In battles between two disputants, it is uncertain who
will achieve victory and who will be conquered. Do not let 227.25
your true nature be thus, bullish god! Even the Lord of all living beings can be forcibly conquered by valor.

The state you find yourself in now is due to no act of mine, Shakra, thunderbolt wielder, just as the state I find myself in now is not due to any act of yours. I used to be exactly like you are now, and you will eventually end up like me. Do not despise me, thinking that you have done a very difficult deed.

A person experiences pleasure and pain in the course of Time. You attained your current status through the procession of Time, and not through any act of yours, Shakra. Time will eventually subdue me, just as it will subdue you. That is why I am not in your state now, and you are not in mine.

227.30 na mātṛ|pitṛ|śuśrūṣā, na ca daivata|pūjanam,
n' ânyo guṇa|samācāraḥ puruṣasya sukh'|āvahaḥ.
na vidyā, na tapo, dānaṃ, na mitrāṇi, na bāndhavāḥ
śaknuvanti paritrātuṃ naraṃ Kālena pīḍitam.
n' āgāminam an|arthaṃ hi pratighāta|śatair api
śaknuvanti prativyoḍhum ṛte buddhi|balān narāḥ.
paryāyair hanyamānānāṃ paritrātā na vidyate,
idaṃ tu duḥkhaṃ yac, Chakra, «kart" âham» iti manyase.
yadi kartā bhavet, kartā na kriyeta kadā cana.
yasmāt tu kriyate kartā, tasmāt kart" âpy an|īśvaraḥ.
227.35 Kālen' âham tvām ajayaṃ, Kālen' âhaṃ jitas tvayā.
gantā gatimatāṃ Kālaḥ: Kālaḥ kalayati prajāḥ.
Indra, prākṛtayā buddhyā
pralayaṃ n' âvabudhyase.
ke cit tvāṃ bahu manyante
śraiṣṭhyaṃ prāptaṃ sva|karmaṇā.
katham asmad|vidho nāma, jānan loka|pravṛttayaḥ,
Kālen' âbhyāhataḥ śocen, muhyed v" âpy atha vibhramet?
nityaṃ Kāla|parītasya, mama vā mad|vidhasya vā,
buddhir vyasanam āsādya bhinnā naur iva sīdati.
ahaṃ ca, tvaṃ ca, ye c' ânye bhaviṣyanti sur'|âdhipāḥ,
te sarve, Śakra, yāsyanti mārgam Indra|śatair gatam.
227.40 tvām apy evaṃ su|dur|dharṣaṃ jvalantaṃ parayā śriyā,
Kāle pariṇate Kālaḥ kālayiṣyati mām iva.
bahūn' Îndra|sahasrāṇi daivatānāṃ yuge yuge
abhyatītāni Kālena, Kālo hi dur|atikramaḥ.

Obedience to one's parents, reverence to the gods and 227.30
the practice of any virtue will not bring a man happiness. Knowledge, asceticism, charity, friends and kinsmen are unable to save a man who is oppressed by Time. Men are not able to repel misfortune when it comes, even with a hundred attempts, without the power of their intelligence.

There is no savior for those struck down by the procession of Time, Shakra, but you think that you are the agent of this suffering of mine. If there truly was such a thing as an agent he would never be acted upon. But since the so-called
agent is in fact acted upon, it means that he lacks power. I 227.35
once conquered you by means of Time, and you have now conquered me by means of Time. Time is the real mover within things that have motion, and that which carries off all creatures.

Because of your inferior intelligence, Indra, you do not understand dissolution, and some really to think that you have attained superiority through your own deeds. How could someone like me lament? I been struck down by Time and understand worldly endeavors, so how could I become bewildered or confused? It is certain that the intelligence of anyone overcome by Time—such as myself or someone like me—would sink like a boat scuppered by a disaster.

You, I, and all the other future commanders of the gods will follow the path traversed by hundreds of Indras in the
past, O Shakra. When Time ripens within you it will carry 227.40
you off, just like it carried me off, despite the fact that you are virtually invincible and blazing with great effulgence. Many thousands of Indras have passed away among the

idaṃ tu labdhvā saṃsthānam ātmānaṃ bahu manyase,
sarva|bhūta|bhavaṃ devaṃ brahmāṇam iva śāśvatam.
na c' êdam a|calaṃ sthānam anantaṃ v" âpi kasya cit,
tvaṃ tu bāliśayā buddhyā «mam' êdam» iti manyase.

a|viśvaste viśvasiṣi, manyase v" ā|dhruve dhruvam.
nityaṃ Kāla|parīt'|ātmā bhavaty evaṃ, sur'|ēśvara.

227.45 «mam' êyam» iti mohāt tvaṃ rāja|śriyam abhīpsasi.
n' êyaṃ tava, na c' âsmākaṃ, na c' ânyeṣāṃ sthirā sadā.
atikramya bahūn anyāṃs tvayi tāvad iyaṃ gatā,
kaṃ cit kālam iyaṃ sthitvā tvayi, Vāsava, cañcalā.

gaur nivāsam iv' ôtsṛjya punar anyaṃ gamiṣyati,
rāja|lokā hy atikrāntā, yān na saṃkhyātum utsahe.
tvatto bahutarāś c' ânye bhaviṣyanti, Puraṃdara.

sa|vṛkṣ'|âuṣadhi|ratn" êyaṃ, saha|sattva|van'|ākarā,
tān idānīṃ na paśyāmi, yair bhukt" êyaṃ purā mahī:
Pṛthur, Ailo, Mayo, Bhīmo, Narakaḥ, Śambaras tathā,
227.50 Aśvagrīvaḥ, Pulomā ca, Svarbhānur, Amitadhvajaḥ,
Prahrādo, Namucir, Dakṣo, Vipracittir, Virocanaḥ,
Hrīniṣevaḥ, Suhotraś ca, Bhūrihā, Puṣpavān, Vṛṣaḥ,
Satyeṣur, Ṛṣabho, Bāhuḥ, Kapilāśvo, Virūpakaḥ,
Bāṇaḥ, Kārtasvaro, Vahnir, Viśvadaṃṣṭro, 'tha Nairṛtiḥ,
Saṃkoco, 'tha Varitākṣo, Varāhāśvo, Ruciprabhuḥ,
Viśvajit, Pratirūpaś ca, Vṛṣāṇḍo, Viṣkaro, Madhuḥ,
Hiraṇyakaśipuś c' âiva, Kaiṭabhaś c' âiva Dānavaḥ.

gods of each world age because of Time, the insurmountable one.

Having gained this condition you take pride in yourself, as if you were Brahma, the eternal god who is the source of all beings. This condition is not unshakeable or unlimited, whoever attains it, but because of your infantile understanding you think that it is yours.

You trust that in which no trust can be found, and think that the intransient is found in the transient. But the person affected by Time always behaves in this manner, Lord of the gods.

You deludedly think that you possess the royal effulgence 227.45
that you have sought. But it never stands firm in you, me, or anyone else. It has left many others before residing in you, and after some time you will feel it start to waver.

Like a cow leaving its home and going to another one, this effulgence has left so many royal worlds that I am unable to count them. There will be many more after you, Puran·dara.

I do not see them now, those who used to enjoy the earth, with her trees, plants, jewels, and all its living beings and forests: Prithu, Aila, Maya, Bhima, Náraka, Shámbara,
Ashva·griva, Pulóman, Svar·bhanu, Ámita·dhvaja, Prahrá- 227.50
da, Námuchi, Daksha, Vipra·chitti, Viróchana, Hri·nishéva, Suhótra, Bhúrihan, Púshpavat, Vrisha, Satyéshu, Ríshabha, Bahu, Kapiláshva, Virúpaka, Bana, Karta·svara, Vahni, Vishva·danshtra, Náirriti, Sankócha, Varitáksha, Varaháshva, Ruchi·prabhu, Víshvajit, Pratirúpa, Vrishánda, Víshkara, Madhu, Hiránya·káshipu, and Káitabha the *dánava*.

daiteyā dānavāś c' âiva sarve te Nairṛtaiḥ saha,
ete c' ânye ca bahavaḥ pūrve pūrvatarāś ca ye,
227.55 daity'|êndrā dānav'|êndrāś ca yāṃś c' ânyān anuśuśruma:
bahavaḥ pūrva|daity'|êndrāḥ saṃtyajya pṛthivīṃ gatāḥ,
Kālen' âbhyāhatāḥ sarve, Kālo hi balavattaraḥ.
sarvaiḥ kratu|śatair iṣṭaṃ, na tvam ekaḥ «Śata|kratuḥ.»
sarve dharma|parāś c' āsan, sarve satata|satriṇaḥ.
antarikṣa|carāḥ sarve, sarve 'bhimukha|yodhinaḥ.
sarve saṃhanan'|ôpetāḥ, sarve parigha|bāhavaḥ.
sarve māyā|śata|dharāḥ, sarve te kāma|rūpiṇaḥ.
sarve samaram āsādya na śrūyante parājitāḥ.
sarve satya|vrata|parāḥ, sarve kāma|vihāriṇaḥ.
227.60 sarve veda|vrata|parāḥ, sarve c' âiva bahu|śrutāḥ;
sarve saṃmatam aiśvaryam īśvarāḥ pratipedire.
na c' āiśvarya|madas teṣāṃ bhūta|pūrvo mah"|ātmanām:
sarve yath"|ârha|dātāraḥ, sarve vigata|matsarāḥ.
sarve sarveṣu bhūteṣu yathāvat pratipedire,
sarve Dākṣāyaṇī|putrāḥ Prājāpatyā mahā|balāḥ.
jvalantaḥ pratapantaś ca Kālena pratisaṃhṛtāḥ.
tvaṃ c' âiv' êmāṃ yadā bhuktvā pṛthivīṃ tyakṣase punaḥ,
na śakṣyasi tadā, Śakra,
niyantuṃ śokam ātmanaḥ.
muñc' êcchāṃ kāma|bhogeṣu!
muñc' êmaṃ śrī|bhavaṃ madam!
227.65 evaṃ sva|rājya|nāśe tvaṃ śokaṃ saṃprasahiṣyasi.

All these *daitéyas* and *dánavas*, along with the sons of Nírriti and the generations that came before them, plus 227.55 all the other *daitéya* and *dánava* lords that we have heard about—these numerous *daitéya* lords of the past disappeared and ended up on the earth. All were struck down by Time, for that is more powerful than them. All of them performed hundreds of sacrifices—it is not only you who goes by the name of "one hundred sacrifices."

All of them were committed to religion, all offered *soma* sacrifices perpetually. All of them flew about in the sky, all fought battles from the front. All of them were robust, their arms resembling iron bars. All of them were adept in hundreds of magical tricks, and all were able to assume different forms at will.

All were not known to be defeated once they entered into battle. All of them were committed to the vow of truth, and were very fond of sexual pleasure. All of them were 227.60 committed to the Vedic vows, and highly learned. All these lords attained what is believed to be sovereignty. But these illustrious beings were not intoxicated by their sovereignty in the past: all made donations depending on the worth of the recipient, and all were devoid of jealousy.

They all behaved properly towards other living beings, these mighty sons of Diti, descendants of Praja·pati. But 227.65 Time destroyed those radiant, illuminous beings, and you too, when you abandon this earth after enjoying its pleasures, will not be able to control your own sorrow, Shakra. Let go of this desire to enjoy sensual pleasures! Let go of this intoxicating state of effulgence! For when your dominion is destroyed, you will have to endure sorrow.

śoka|kāle śuco mā tvaṃ, harṣa|kāle ca mā hṛṣaḥ.
atīt'|ânāgataṃ† hitvā pratyutpannena vartaya!
māṃ ced abhyāgataḥ Kālaḥ sad|āyuktam a|tandritaḥ—
kṣamasva, na cirād, Indra, tvām apy upagamiṣyati.
trāsayann iva, dev'|êndra, vāgbhis takṣasi mām iha.
saṃyate mayi nūnaṃ tvam ātmānaṃ bahu manyase.
Kālaḥ prathamam āyān māṃ, paścāt tvām anudhāvati.
tena garjasi, dev'|êndra, pūrvaṃ Kāla|hate mayi.
ko hi sthātum alaṃ loke mama kruddhasya saṃyuge?
227.70 Kālas tu balavān prāptas, tena tiṣṭhasi, Vāsava.
yat tad varṣa|sahasr'|ântaṃ pūrṇaṃ bhavitum arhati,
yathā me sarva|gātrāṇi na su|sthāni mah'|âujasaḥ.
aham Aindrāc cyutaḥ sthānāt, tvam Indraḥ prakṛto divi,
su|citre jīva|loke 'sminn upāsyaḥ Kāla|paryayāt.
kiṃ hi kṛtvā tvam Indro 'dya, kiṃ vā kṛtvā vayam cyutāḥ?
kālaḥ kartā vikartā ca—
sarvam anyad a|kāraṇam.
nāśaṃ, vināśam, aiśvaryaṃ,
sukhaṃ, duḥkhaṃ, bhav'|âbhavau
vidvān prāpy' âivam aty|arthaṃ
na prahṛṣyen na ca vyathet.
tvam eva h', Îndra, vetth' āsmān,
ved' âhaṃ tvāṃ ca, Vāsava.
227.75 vikatthase† māṃ kiṃ ca tvaṃ Kālena, nir|apatrapa?

In a time of sorrow you should not lament, in a time of excitement you should not become excited. Relinquish the past and future and live in the present! If Time, ever vigilant, has approached me, who adheres to virtue—just you wait, Indra, it will soon come after you.

You cut me with your words, Lord of the gods, but only appear to frighten me. Now that I am imprisoned you take pride in yourself. Time came to me first—and is going after you next. Therefore you roar, O Lord of the gods, but I had already been struck down by Time.

When I was angered, who in this world was capable of 227.70
standing against me in battle? But Time, the mighty one, confronted me and so you stand before me now, Vásava. At the end of a thousand years all your limbs will feel uncomfortable, just like mine do, in spite of my great energy.

I have fallen away from my position as Indra, whereas you have been appointed Indra in heaven. Because of the procession of Time, you will be venerated in this diverse world of living creatures. But what have you done to become Indra now, and what have I done for this loss of status? Time is the creator and destroyer—everything else lacks efficacy.

When a wise man encounters excessive destruction, annihilation, supremacy, pleasure, pain, existence and nonexistence, he does not feel excitement or get perturbed.

You know me, Indra, and I know you, Vásava. So why 227.75
do you abuse me, shameless one, when Time has brought this about?

tvam eva hi purā vettha yat tadā pauruṣaṃ mama;
samareṣu ca vikrāntaṃ paryāptaṃ tan|nidarśanam.
Ādityāś c' âiva, Rudrāś ca, Sādhyāś ca Vasubhiḥ saha
mayā vinirjitāḥ pūrvaṃ, Marutaś ca, Śacī|pate!
tvam eva, Śakra, jānāsi, dev'|âsura|samāgame
sametā vibudhā bhagnās tarasā samare mayā.
parvatāś c' â|sakṛt kṣiptāḥ sa|vanāḥ sa|van'|âukasaḥ,
sa|ṭaṅka|śikharā bhagnāḥ samare mūrdhni te mayā!
kiṃ nu śakyaṃ mayā kartuṃ? Kālo hi dur|atikramaḥ.
227.80 na hi tvāṃ n' ôtsahe hantuṃ sa|vajram api muṣṭinā!
na tu vikrama|kālo 'yaṃ, kṣamā|kālo 'yam āgataḥ.
tena tvāṃ marṣaye, Śakra, dur|marṣaṇataras tvayā.
taṃ māṃ pariṇate kāle parītaṃ Kāla|vahninā,
niyataṃ kāla|pāśena baddhaṃ, Śakra, vikatthase.
ayaṃ sa puruṣaḥ śyāmo, lokasya dur|atikramaḥ,
baddhvā tiṣṭhati māṃ raudraḥ,
paśuṃ raśanayā yathā.
lābh'|âlābhau, sukhaṃ, duḥkhaṃ,
kāma|krodhau, bhav'|âbhavau,
vadha|bandha|pramokṣaṃ ca: sarvaṃ Kālena labhyate.
n' âhaṃ kartā, na kartā tvaṃ, kartā yas tu sadā prabhuḥ.
227.85 so 'yaṃ pacati Kālo māṃ, vṛkṣe phalam iv' āgatam.
yāny eva puruṣaḥ kurvan sukhaiḥ Kālena yujyate,
punas tāny eva kurvāṇo duḥkhaiḥ Kālena yujyate.
na ca Kālena kāla|jñaḥ spṛṣṭaḥ śocitum arhati.
tena, Śakra, na śocāmi, n' âsti śoke sahāyatā.

You know how heroic I was in the past; that I was valorous and able in battles proves this. In the past I conquered the Adítyas, the *rudras*, the Sadhyas, the Vasus and the *maruts*, O husband of Shachi! And you know that in the conflict between *ásuras* and gods I decimated the company of gods with my martial force.

I felled mountains, repeatedly, along with the forests and 227.80
their inhabitants. In battle I shattered mountain peaks and crags on your head! But what can I do? Time is insurmountable. It is not that I am unable to strike down you and your thunderbolt with my fist!

This is not the time for valor, however—the time for patience has arrived. Therefore I will tolerate you, Shakra, although it is impossible for you to tolerate me.

When my time came I was overcome by the fire of Time —you humiliate someone who has been suppressed and bound by the chain of Time, Shakra. Time is the black person whom the world cannot cannot escape. This fierce one has bound me and lingers, as if binding an animal with a rope.

Gain, loss, pleasure, pain, lust, anger, existence, nonexistence and the release from torture and imprisonment: all these are caused by Time. I am not an agent, and neither
are you; the real agent is ever the master of all. It is Time 227.85
that has cooked me, like a fruit ripened on a tree.

By doing various things a person will receive pleasures in the course of time. But in doing such things that person will, in the course of time, come into contact with sufferings. The person who understands Time ought not to grieve

yadā hi śocataḥ śoko vyasanaṃ n' âpakarṣati,
sāmarthyaṃ śocato n' âst' îty, ato 'haṃ n' âdya śocimi.

evam uktaḥ sahasr'|âkṣo bhagavān Pāka|śāsanaḥ
pratisaṃhṛtya saṃrambham ity uvāca śata|kratuḥ.

sa|vajram udyataṃ bāhuṃ dṛṣṭvā, pāśāṃś ca Vāruṇān,
227.90 kasy' êha na vyathed buddhir? Mṛtyor api jighāṃsataḥ.
sā te na vyathate buddhir, a|calā tattva|darśinī.
dhruvaṃ na vyathase 'dya tvaṃ dhairyāt, satya|parākrama.
ko hi viśvāsam artheṣu śarīre vā śarīra|bhṛt
kartum utsahate loke dṛṣṭvā saṃprasthitaṃ jagat?
aham apy evam ev' âinaṃ lokaṃ jānāmy a|śāśvatam,
Kāl'|âgnāv āhitaṃ ghore, guhye, satata|ge, '|kṣare.
na c' âtra parihāro 'sti Kāla|spṛṣṭasya kasya cit;
sūkṣmāṇāṃ mahatāṃ c' âiva bhūtānāṃ paripacyatām.
an|īśasy' â|pramattasya, bhūtāni pacataḥ sadā,
227.95 a|nivṛttasya Kālasya kṣayaṃ prāpto na mucyate.
a|pramattaḥ pramatteṣu Kālo jāgarti dehiṣu.

when touched by it. Therefore I do not lament, Shakra, for there is no companionship in lamentation.

If lamentation cannot rid a grieving person of a calamity, that grieving person will have no strength, and so I no longer lament.

BHISHMA said:

When Indra of the hundred sacrifices had been addressed thus, that blessed, thousand-eyed destroyer of Paka suppressed his anger and spoke as follows.

INDRA said:

Whose state of mind would not be perplexed upon see- 227.90
ing my arm held aloft bearing a thunderbolt, as well as the chains of Váruna? It would be so even for Death, the one who wishes to kill. But your state of mind is not perplexed; it is steady, and sees the truth. It is certainly because of your determination that you are not perplexed today, you who possess the power of truth.

When he sees how the world works, which person in this world is able to have any trust in material objects or the body? For what it is worth, I know that this world is not eternal, but rests upon the terrible fire of Time, whose movements are always concealed and unfailing.

When someone is touched by Time there is no avoiding it; living beings are cooked by Time, whether they are
small or massive. Time has no master and vigilantly cooks 227.95
living beings without stopping. It never ceases, and when a person encounters its destructive effects there is no escape.

prayatnen' âpy apakrānto dṛṣṭa|pūrvo na kena cit;
purāṇaḥ śāśvato dharmaḥ, sarva|prāṇa|bhṛtāṃ samaḥ.
Kālo na parihāryaś ca, na c' âsy' âsti vyatikramaḥ;
aho|rātrāṃś ca, māsāṃś ca, kṣaṇān, kāṣṭhā, lavān, kalāḥ
saṃpīḍayati yaḥ Kālo, vṛddhiṃ vārdhuṣiko yathā.
«idam adya kariṣyāmi, śvaḥ kart" âsm'» îti vādinam
Kālo harati saṃprāpto, nadī|vega iva drumam.
«idānīṃ tāvad ev' âsau mayā dṛṣṭaḥ! kathaṃ mṛtaḥ?»
227.100 iti Kālena hriyatāṃ
pralāpaḥ śrūyate nṛṇām.
naśyanty arthās, tathā bhogāḥ,
sthānam, aiśvaryam eva ca:
jīvitaṃ jīva|lokasya Kālen' āgamya nīyate.
ucchrāyā vinipāt'|ântā, bhāvo '|bhāvaḥ sa eva ca.
a|nityam a|dhruvaṃ sarvaṃ, vyavasāyo hi duṣ|karaḥ.
sā te na vyathate buddhir: a|calā tattva|darśinī.
aham āsaṃ purā c' êti, manas" âpi na budhyase.†
Kālen' ākramya loke 'smin pacyamāne balīyasā,
a|jyeṣṭham a|kaniṣṭhaṃ ca kṣipyamāṇo na budhyate.
īrṣy"|âbhimāna|lobheṣu, kāma|krodha|bhayeṣu ca,
227.105 spṛhā|moh'|âbhimāneṣu lokaḥ sakto vimuhyati.
bhavāṃs tu bhāva|tattva|jño, vidvāñ, jñāna|tapo|'nvitaḥ,
Kālaṃ paśyati su|vyaktaṃ, pāṇāv āmalakaṃ yathā.

Time is vigilant and keeps watch over living beings who are negligent.

Nobody has ever seen Time overcome by any sort of effort; it is the ancient and eternal law of righteousness, and treats all creatures equally. Time cannot be avoided or bypassed; it counts the days, nights, months, hours, minutes, seconds and moments like a moneylender counts his profit.

"Today I will do this, tomorrow I will do that." To the person who speaks thus, Time appears and takes him away, just like the current of a river takes away a tree. "I have seen this person just now! How can he have died?" Such chatter 227.100
is heard of men being taken away by Time.

A person's wealth, pleasures, position and power perish: Time approaches a living thing in the world of the living and leads it away. Growth ends in ruin, existence ends in non-existence. Everything is impermanent and transient, a conviction that is hard to stick to.

Your state of mind is not perplexed: it is steady and sees the truth. In the past I was exactly thus, but you cannot understand this even by thinking it through.

In this world assailed by Time and cooked by its exceptional power, a person is not aware of being neither the eldest nor the youngest even as he is cast away.

Stuck in jealousy, arrogance, greed, lust, anger, fear, desire, delusion and conceit, the world is utterly bewildered. 227.105
But you understand the truth of existence—you are wise, steeped in knowledge and asceticism, and see Time clearly, like a plum in your hand.

Kāla|cāritra|tattva|jñaḥ, sarva|śāstra|viśāradaḥ:
Vairocane, kṛt'|ātm" âsi, spṛhaṇīyo vijānatām.
sarva|loko hy ayaṃ, manye, buddhyā parigatas tvayā,
viharan sarvato|mukto, na kva cit pariṣajjase.
rajaś ca hi tamaś ca tvāṃ spṛśate na jit'|êndriyam.
niṣ|prītiṃ naṣṭa|saṃtāpam, ātmānaṃ tvam upāsase.
su|hṛdaṃ sarva|bhūtānāṃ, nir|vairaṃ, śānta|mānasam,
227.110 dṛṣṭvā tvāṃ mama saṃjātā tvayy anukrośinī matiḥ.
n' âham etādṛśaṃ buddhaṃ hantum icchāmi bandhane,
ānṛśaṃsyaṃ paro dharmo hy, anukrośaś ca me tvayi.
mokṣyante Vāruṇāḥ pāśās tav' ême kāla|paryayāt,
prajānām upacāreṇa. svasti te 'stu, mah"|âsura!
yadā śvaśrūṃ snuṣā† vṛddhāṃ paricāreṇa yokṣyate,
putraś ca pitaraṃ mohāt preṣayiṣyati karmasu;
brāhmaṇaiḥ kārayiṣyanti vṛṣalāḥ pāda|dhāvanam;
śūdrāś ca brāhmaṇīṃ bhāryām upayāsyanti nir|bhayāḥ,
vi|yoniṣu vimokṣyanti bījāni puruṣā yadā;
227.115 saṃkaraṃ kāṃsya|bhāṇḍaiś ca, baliṃ c' âiva ku|pātrakaiḥ,
cāturvarṇyaṃ yadā kṛtsnam a|maryādaṃ bhaviṣyati,
ek'|êikas te tadā pāśaḥ kramaśaḥ pratimokṣyate.
asmattas te bhayaṃ n' âsti, samayaṃ pratipālaya,
sukhī bhava, nir|ābādhaḥ, sva|stha|cetā, nir|āmayaḥ.

You have a true understanding of the movement of Time, and are skilled in all the treatises: you are complete, Vairóchani, and the envy of perceptive men. I think that your understanding encompasses this whole world, since you abide in a state of complete release, and are not attached to anything.

Passion and darkness do not touch you, since you have mastered your senses. Being beyond joy and affliction, you meditate on the self.

Sympathy towards you is stirred within me, since I see 227.110
you as the friend of all living beings, free from enmity and with a peaceful mind. I do not wish to punish such a wise man by imprisoning him, for I am full of benevolence—the highest religion—and compassion.

Because of your civility towards creatures, the chains of Váruna which shackle you will be loosed with the passage of Time. Good luck to you, great *ásura*!

When a daughter-in-law shackles her aged mother-in-law with the tasks of a servant, and the son, out of ignorance, presses his father into work; when wicked men make brahmins wash their feet; when shudras fearlessly take
brahmin women as wives, and men impregnate low caste 227.115
women; when rubbish is kept in brass vessels and ritual oblations are contained in impure bowls, and when the entire civilization of four classes transgresses its limits, then each one of your chains will gradually be released.

You have nothing to fear from us so keep your word and be happy, secure and free from disease, your mind content.

tam evam uktvā bhagavāñ Śata|kratuḥ
pratiprayāto gaja|rāja|vāhanaḥ.
vijitya sarvān asurān sur'|âdhipo
nananda harṣeṇa, babhūva c' âika|rāṭ.
maha"|rṣayas tuṣṭuvur añjasā ca taṃ
Vṛṣākapiṃ sarva|car'|âcar'|ēśvaram.
Himāpaho havyam uvāha c' âdhvare,
tath" â|mṛtaṃ c' ârpitam īśvaro 'pi hi.
dvij'|ôttamaiḥ sarva|gatair abhiṣṭuto,
vidīpta|tejā, gata|manyur īśvaraḥ
praśānta|cetā, muditaḥ svam ālayaṃ
tri|viṣṭapaṃ prāpya mumoda Vāsavaḥ.

BHISHMA said:

When the blessed Indra of the hundred sacrifices had addressed Bali he went off, carried by the king of the elephants. The commander of the gods then conquered all the *ásuras*, and being the single ruler, he rejoiced in his happiness.

The great seers immediately praised Indra, the lord of all mobile and immobile creatures. Agni carried the sacrificial oblations to him, and the lord drank the ambrosia on offer.

Worshipped by the most eminent brahmins from all regions, the lord was devoid of anger and his luster blazed forth. Tranquil minded and overjoyed, Vásava returned to his own abode in heaven and rejoiced there.

228

THE DIALOGUE BETWEEN INDRA AND SHRI

YUDHIṢṬHIRA uvāca:

228.1 PŪRVA|RŪPĀṆI ME, rājan, puruṣasya bhaviṣyataḥ,
parābhaviṣyataś c' âiva, tan me brūhi, pitā|maha.

BHĪṢMA uvāca:

mana eva manuṣyasya pūrva|rūpāṇi śaṃsati
bhaviṣyataś ca, bhadraṃ te, tath" âiva na bhaviṣyataḥ.
atr' âpy udāharant' îmam itihāsaṃ purātanam:
Śriyā Śakrasya saṃvādaṃ. taṃ nibodha, Yudhiṣṭhira.
mahatas tapaso vyuṣṭyā paśyal̃ lokau par'|âvarau,
sāmānyam ṛṣibhir gatvā Brahma|loka|nivāsibhiḥ,
228.5 Brahm' êv' â|mita|dīpt'|âujāḥ, śānta|pāpmā mahā|tapāḥ,
vicacāra yathā|kāmaṃ triṣu lokeṣu Nāradaḥ.
kadā cit prātar utthāya, pispṛkṣuḥ salilaṃ śuci,
dhruva|dvāra|bhavāṃ Gaṅgāṃ jagām', âvatatāra ca.
sahasra|nayanaś c' âpi Vajrī Śambara|Pāka|hā
tasyā deva'|rṣi|juṣṭāyās tīram abhyājagāma ha.
tāv āplutya yat'|ātmānau kṛta|japyau samāsatuḥ
nadyāḥ pulinam āsādya sūkṣma|kāñcana|vālukam.
puṇya|karmabhir ākhyātā deva'|rṣi|kathitāḥ kathāḥ,
cakratus tau tath" āsīnau maha"|rṣi|kathitās tathā.

YUDHI·SHTHIRA said:

WHAT ARE THE portents of my future success as a person, Your Majesty, and what are the portents of my failure? Please tell me that, grandfather. 228.1

BHISHMA said:

Only the mind can disclose the portents of a person's future success or failure. May you be fortunate! On this subject people relate the ancient tradition of a dialogue between Shri and Shakra. Listen to it, Yudhi·shthira.

As a reward of his great asceticism, Nárada could see this world and the world beyond, and had attained the status
of the seers living in the Brahma worlds. Blazing with im- 228.5
measurable luster, he was just like Brahma himself. He had pacified his evil and attained great ascetic power, and so wandered among the three worlds as he pleased.

Upon arising one morning and wishing to bathe in pure water, he descended to the Ganges, whose waters gush from a steady source. At the same time the thousand-eyed, thunderbolt-wielding Indra who destroyed Shámbara and Paka visited the bank of that river, the one that the celestial seer Nárada found so agreeable.

Once these two beings of inner control had bathed and completed their Vedic recitation, they found a sandbank of fine, golden sand and sat down together. Once seated, the two talked about the legends handed down by the celestial seers who had performed auspicious deeds, as well as the tales handed down by great seers.

228.10 pūrva|vṛtta|vyapetāni kathayantau samāhitau
atha bhāskaram udyantaṃ, raśmi|jāla|puras|kṛtam,
pūrṇa|maṇḍalam ālokya tāv utthāy' ôpatasthatuḥ.
abhitas t' ûdayantaṃ tam arkam, arkam iv' âparam,
ākāśe dadṛśe jyotir udyat'|ârciḥ, sama|prabham.
tayoḥ samīpaṃ taṃ prāptaṃ pratyadṛśyata, Bhārata,
tat suparṇ'|ârka|racitam āsthitaṃ Vaiṣṇavaṃ padam.
bhābhir a|pratimaṃ bhāti, trailokyam avabhāsayat.
tatr' âbhirūpa|śobhābhir apsarobhiḥ puras|kṛtām,
bṛhatīm, aṃśumat|prakhyāṃ, bṛhad|bhānor iv' ârciṣam,
228.15 nakṣatra|kalp'|ābharaṇāṃ tāṃ mauktika|sama|srajam
Śriyaṃ dadṛśatuḥ Padmāṃ sākṣāt padma|dala|sthitām.
s" âvaruhya vimān'|âgrād, aṅganānām an|uttamā
abhyāgacchat tri|lok'|ēśaṃ deva'|rṣiṃ c' âpi Nāradam.
Nārad'|ânugataḥ sākṣān Maghavāṃs tām upāgamat
kṛt'|âñjali|puṭo devīṃ, nivedy' ātmānam ātmanā.
cakre c' ân|upamāṃ pūjāṃ tasyāś c' âpi sa sarva|vit
deva|rājaḥ Śriyaṃ, rājan, vākyaṃ c' êdam uvāca ha.

ŚAKRA uvāca:

kā tvaṃ, kena ca kāryeṇa saṃprāptā, cāru|hāsini?
kutaś c' âgamyate, subhru? gantavyaṃ kva ca te, śubhe?

Whilst they were absorbed in their discussion about the 228.10
details of past events, they saw that the rising sun, preceded by its net of rays, had become full in the sky and so they stood up and worshipped it.

While the sun was rising, however, in its vicinity a light of equal radiance appeared in the sky. It was streaming with rays, and looked just like another sun. They noticed it as it moved towards them, Bhárata, that light following the heavenly course of the beautiful-rayed sun. It shone with unparalleled radiance, illuminating the triple world.

It was Shri that the two of them saw with their own eyes, preceded by celestial nymphs of beautiful splendor. That great lady had the appearance of the sun, and indeed was
just like a ray of light emitted by it. Also called Padma, she 228.15
was standing on the petal of a lotus with garlands as bright as pearls, wearing jewelry that looked like the stars.

Descending from the edge of her flying chariot, that incomparable lady approached the Lord of the triple world and the celestial seer Nárada. Clasping his hands together in reverence, and promptly followed by Nárada, Mághavat approached the goddess and introduced himself to her. The all-knowing king of the gods payed incomparable homage to Shri and uttered these words, Your Majesty.

SHAKRA said:

Who are you, and what is your business here, sweetly-smiling one? Where have you come from, beautiful browed lady? And where will you go, auspicious one?

ŚRĪR uvāca:

228.20 puṇyeṣu triṣu lokeṣu sarve sthāvara|jaṅgamāḥ
mam' ātma|bhāvam icchanto yatante param'|ātmanā.
s' âhaṃ vai paṅka|je jātā sūrya|raśmi|vibodhite
bhūty|arthaṃ sarva|bhūtānāṃ: Padmā Śrīḥ padma|mālinī.
aham Lakṣmīr, ahaṃ Bhūtiḥ, Śrīś c' âhaṃ, Bala|sūdana.
ahaṃ śraddhā ca, medhā ca, saṃnatir, vijitiḥ, sthitiḥ.
ahaṃ dhṛtir, ahaṃ siddhir; ahaṃ tvad|bhūtir eva ca.
ahaṃ svāhā svadhā c' âiva, saṃnatir, niyatiḥ, smṛtiḥ.
rājñāṃ vijayamānānāṃ sen'|âgreṣu dhvajeṣu ca
nivāse dharma|śīlānāṃ viṣayeṣu pureṣu ca.
228.25 jita|kāśini śūre ca saṃgrāmeṣv a|nivartini
nivasāmi manuṣy'|êndre sad" âiva, Bala|sūdana.
dharma|nitye, mahā|buddhau, brahmaṇye, satya|vādini,
praśrite, dāna|śīle ca sad" âiva nivasāmy aham.
asureṣv avasaṃ pūrvaṃ, satya|dharma|nibandhanā.
viparītāṃs tu tān budhvā, tvayi vāsam arocayam.

ŚAKRA uvāca:

kathaṃ|vṛtteṣu daityeṣu tvam avātsīr, var'|ānane?
dṛṣṭvā ca kim ih' āgās tvaṃ hitvā daiteya|dānavān?

SHRI said:

Desiring my state, all the animate and inanimate beings 228.20
of this auspicious, triple world exert themselves with all their heart. I am the one who was born in a lotus awakened by the rays of the sun, for the prosperity of all living beings: I am Padma, or Shri, the one who wears a garland of lotuses.

I am Lakshmi, I am Bhuti, and I am Shri, O destroyer of Bala. I am faith, intelligence, humility, triumph and stability. I am determination and accomplishment; I alone constitute your prosperity. I am the ritual utterances "svaha" and "svadha:" I am humility, control and recollection.

I abide at the front of victorious kings' armies, and on their banners; I live in the dominions and cities of those
who are steeped in righteousness. I always abide in the lord 228.25
of men, the hero who has the appearance of a conqueror and does not turn away from battle, O destroyer of Bala.

I always abide in the person who is committed to religion, highly intelligent, pious, honest, courteous and steeped in charity. In the past I dwelled among the *ásuras*, for I was bound to the religion of truth. But when I became aware of their deviance from truth, I thought it suitable to abide in you.

SHAKRA said:

When you abided in the *daityas*, pretty faced goddess, how did they conduct themselves? And what did you witness that compelled you to abandon the *daityas* and *dánavas* and come here?

ŚRĪR uvāca:

sva|dharmam anutiṣṭhatsu, dhairyād a|caliteṣu ca,
svarga|mārg'|âbhirāmeṣu sattveṣu niratā hy aham.
228.30 dān'|âdhyayana|yajñ'|êjyā, pitṛ|daivata|pūjanam,
gurūṇām atithīnāṃ ca teṣāṃ satyam avartata.

su|saṃmṛṣṭa|gṛhāś c' āsañ, jita|strīkā, hut'|âgnayaḥ,
guru|śuśrūṣakā, dāntā, brahmaṇyāḥ satya|vādinaḥ,
śraddadhānā, jita|krodhā, dāna|śīl", ân|asūyavaḥ,
bhṛta|putrā, bhṛt'|âmātyā, bhṛta|dārā hy an|īrṣavaḥ.

a|marṣeṇa na c' ânyonyaṃ spṛhayante kadā cana,
na ca jāt' ûpatapyanti dhīrāḥ para|samṛddhibhiḥ.
dātāraḥ, saṃgṛhītāra, āryāḥ, karuṇa|vedinaḥ,
mahā|prasādā, ṛjavo, dṛḍha|bhaktā, jit'|êndriyāḥ,
228.35 saṃtuṣṭa|bhṛtya|sacivāḥ, kṛta|jñāḥ, priya|vādinaḥ,
yath"|ârha|mān'|ârtha|karā, hrī|niṣevā, yata|vratāḥ,
nityaṃ parvasu su|snātāḥ, sv|anuliptāḥ, sv|alaṃ|kṛtāḥ,
upavāsa|tapaḥ|śīlāḥ, pratītā, brahma|vādinaḥ.

n' âinān abhyudiyāt sūryo, na c' âpy āsan prage|śayāḥ.
rātrau dadhi ca saktūṃś ca nityam eva vyavarjayan.
kālyaṃ ghṛtaṃ c' ânvavekṣan, prayatā, brahma|vādinaḥ.
maṅgalyāny api c' âpaśyan, brāhmaṇāṃś c' âpy apūjayan.

SHRI said:

I am devoted to people who follow their duties resolutely and do not waver, those who find pleasure in following the path to heaven. They are charitable, recite the Vedas and 228.30
offer sacrifices. They revere the ancestors and deities, and are honest to their teachers and guests.

The *daitya*s lived in houses that were well swept, their women were controlled and they offered oblations into the ritual fire. They were obedient to their teachers, restrained, pious and honest. They were faithful, in control of their anger, of a charitable disposition and lacking in spite. They looked after their offspring, companions and wives without feeling envy.

Those wise beings never envied each other indignantly, and did not torment themselves over the successes of others. Those noble ones were charitable and restrained, and spoke with sympathy. Their tranquility was profound; they were honest, steadfastly pious and had mastered their senses.

Their servants and companions were content, for they 228.35
were appreciative and kindly spoken. They bestowed honor and wealth on everyone according to their worth, maintained their modesty and stuck to their vows. On sacred days they were always well bathed, anointed and adorned. Observing fasts and asceticism, they were trusting and uttered Vedic prayers.

The sun could not rise above them, for they never slept in the morning. They always avoided eating curds and groats in the night. They would look at the dawn and ghee, and were religious, uttering the Vedic prayers. They approved of auspicious prayers and revered brahmins. When they spoke

sadā hi vadatāṃ dharmaṃ, sadā c' â|pratigṛhṇatām,
ardhaṃ ca rātryāḥ svapatāṃ, divā c' â|svapatāṃ tathā,
228.40 kṛpaṇ'|ânātha|vṛddhānāṃ, dur|bal'|ātura|yoṣitām
dāyaṃ ca saṃvibhāgaṃ ca nityam ev' ânvamodatām.
trastaṃ, viṣaṇṇam, udvignaṃ,
bhay'|ārtaṃ, vyādhitaṃ, kṛśam,
hṛta|svaṃ, vyasan'|ārtaṃ ca
nityam āśvāsayanti te.
dharmam ev' ânvavartanta, na hiṃsanti paras|param.
anukūlāś ca kāryeṣu, guru|vṛddh'|ôpasevinaḥ.
pitṝn dev'|âtithīṃś c' âiva yathāvat te 'bhyapūjayan.
avaśeṣāṇi c' âśnanti, nityaṃ satya|tapo|dhṛtāḥ.
n' âike 'śnanti su|saṃpannaṃ, na gacchanti para|striyam.
sarva|bhūteṣv avartanta yath" ātmani dayāṃ prati.
228.45 n' âiv' ākāśe, na paśuṣu, vi|yonau ca, na parvasu
indriyasya visargaṃ te rocayanti kadā cana.
nityaṃ dānaṃ, tathā dākṣyam, ārjavaṃ c' âiva nityadā,
utsāho, 'th' ân|ahaṃ|kāraḥ, paramaṃ sauhṛdaṃ, kṣamā,
satyaṃ, dānaṃ, tapaḥ, śaucaṃ,
kāruṇyaṃ, vāg a|niṣṭhurā,
mitreṣu c' ân|abhidrohaḥ:
sarvaṃ teṣv abhavat, prabho.
nidrā, tandrīr, a|saṃprītir, asūy", âth' ân|avekṣitā,
a|ratiś ca, viṣādaś ca, spṛhā c' âpy aviśan na tān.
s" âham evaṃ|guṇeṣv eva Dānaveṣv avasaṃ purā,
prajā|sargam upādāya n' âikaṃ yuga|viparyayam.
228.50 tataḥ kāla|viparyāse teṣāṃ guṇa|viparyayāt
apaśyaṃ nirgataṃ dharmaṃ kāma|krodha|vaś'|ātmanām.

it was always about religion, and they never accepted gifts.
They slept for only half the night, and never during the day.
They always took pleasure in giving and distributing gifts 228.40
among the pitiable, helpless and aged, as well as women,
the weak and sick.* They always relieved those who were
fearful, depressed, anxious, distressed by fear, ill, emaciated,
robbed or struck by a calamity. They followed religion and
did not harm each other. They conformed to their duties,
and served their teachers and elders.

They duly revered the ancestors, gods and their guests.
They ate only what remained after the rituals, and were unfailing in their observance of truth and asceticism. Some
did not eat delicacies, none of them committed adultery.
They acted towards living beings with the same sympathy
as they did towards themselves.

They did not think it fitting to discharge semen into 228.45
empty space, cattle or a member of a low caste, and not at
all on holy days. They were always charitable, industrious,
honest, persevering, devoid of egotism, patient and most
friendly.

They never lacked any of the following qualities, my
Lord: truth, charity, asceticism, purity, compassion, gentle
speech and benevolence towards their friends. Sleep, laziness, displeasure, envy, thoughtlessness, discontent, depression and covetousness did not possess them.

In the past I abided in the *dánava*s when they were in
possession of such qualities, and not just for the duration
of one generation and their offspring. However, over the 228.50
course of time their qualities changed; they fell under the

sabhā|sadām ca vṛddhānām satām kathayatām kathāḥ,
prāhasann abhyasūyaṃś ca sarva|vṛddhān guṇ'|âvarāḥ.
yuvānaś ca samāsīnā vṛddhān api gatān sataḥ,
n' âbhyutthān'|âbhivādābhyām yathā|pūrvam apūjayan.

vartayaty eva pitari putraḥ prabhavate tathā,
a|bhṛtyā bhṛtyatām prāpya khyāpayanty an|apatrapāḥ.
tathā dharmād apetena karmaṇā garhitena ye
mahataḥ prāpnuvanty arthāṃs, teṣām tatr' âbhavat spṛhā.
228.55 uccaiś c' âbhyavadan rātrau, nīcais tatr' âgnir ajvalat.
putrāḥ pitṝn atyacaran, nāryaś c' âtyacaran patīn.

mātaram, pitaram, vṛddham, ācāryam, atithim, gurum
gurutvān n' âbhyanandanta, kumārān n' ânvapālayan.
bhikṣām, balim a|dattvā ca svayam annāni bhuñjate,
an|iṣṭvā, '|saṃvibhajy' âtha pitṛ|dev'|âtithīn, gurūn.

na śaucam anurudhyanta teṣām sūda|janās tathā
manasā, karmaṇā, vācā; bhakṣyam āsīd an|āvṛtam.
viprakīrṇāni dhānyāni, kāka|mūṣika|bhojanam.
apāvṛtam payo 'tiṣṭhad, ucchiṣṭāś c' âspṛśan ghṛtam.
228.60 kuddālam, dātra|piṭakam prakīrṇam kāṃsya|bhājanam,
dravy'|ôpakaraṇam sarvam n' ânvavaikṣat kuṭumbinī.
prākār'|āgāra|vidhvaṃsān na sma te pratikurvate,
n' ādriyante paśūn baddhvā yavasen' ôdakena ca.

sway of lust and anger, and I saw that righteousness had abandoned them.

When the virtuous elders were sat in discussion at an assembly, the morally inferior among them indignantly ridiculed them. When the elders departed these youths remained seated, and so did not revere them by rising respectfully and saluting them, as in the past.

A son would control his father even if he still worked, and those who had been independent became servants and disclosed the matter without any shame. Some achieved great profit through despicable deeds beyond the pale of righteousness, and took pleasure in doing so. They talked 228.55
in loud voices during the night, and their fire burned ever lower. Sons disobeyed fathers, wives disobeyed husbands.

They did not acknowledge the respectability of their mothers, fathers, elders, preceptors, guests or teachers, and they did not cherish their children. They did not offer alms or oblations, and ate food by themselves without offering sacrifices to the ancestors or deities, and without distributing food to guests or teachers.

Their cooks did not observe the code of purity, in thought, deed or word, and their food was left uncovered. Their grain was scattered about, so that it was left as food for crows and mice. Their milk was left open, and their ghee was handled by the impure.

Their spades, sickles, baskets and copper vessels were dis- 228.60
ordered, and the woman of the house did not look after any of their goods or paraphernalia. They did not mend the ruins of walls or homes, and did not tend to their tethered cattle with fodder or water.

bālānāṃ prekṣamāṇānāṃ svayaṃ bhakṣyam abhakṣayan,
tathā bhṛtya|janaṃ sarvam asaṃtarpya ca dānavāḥ.
pāyasaṃ, kṛsaraṃ, māṃsam, apūpān, atha śaṣkulīḥ
apācayann ātmano 'rthe, vṛthā|māṃsāny abhakṣayan.

utsūrya|śāyinaś c' āsan, sarve c' āsan prage|niśāḥ,
avartan kalahāś c' âtra divā|rātraṃ gṛhe gṛhe.
228.65 an|āryāś c' âryam āsīnaṃ paryupāsan na tatra ha,
āśrama|sthān vidharma|sthāḥ prādviṣanta paras|param.
saṃkarāś c' âbhyavartanta: na ca śaucam avartata.

ye ca veda|vido viprā, vispaṣṭam an|ṛcaś ca ye,
nir|antara|viśeṣās te bahumān'|âvamānayoḥ.
hāram, ābharaṇaṃ, veṣaṃ, gataṃ, sthitam, avekṣitam:
asevanta bhujiṣyā vai dur|jan'|ācaritaṃ vidhim.
striyaḥ puruṣa|veṣeṇa, puṃsaḥ strī|veṣa|dhāriṇaḥ
krīḍā|rati|vihāreṣu parāṃ mudam avāpnuvan.

prabhavadbhiḥ purā dāyān arhebhyaḥ pratipāditān
228.70 n' âbhyavartanta nāstikyād, vartantaḥ saṃbhaveṣv api.
mitreṇ' âbhyarthitaṃ mitram artha|saṃśayite kva cit
vāla|koṭy|agra|mātreṇa sv'|ârthen' âghnata tad|vasu.

para|sv'|ādāna|rucayo, vipaṇa|vyavahāriṇaḥ
adṛśyant' ārya|varṇeṣu śūdrāś c' âpi tapo|dhanāḥ!
adhīyante '|vratāḥ ke cid, vṛthā|vratam ath' âpare.
a|śuśrūṣur guroḥ śiṣyaḥ, kaś cic chiṣya|sakho guruḥ.

The *dánavas* ate all their food themselves while their children looked on, without even feeding their servants. They had rice-dessert, *pilau*, meat, flour-cakes and rice-cakes cooked for themselves, and ate meat prepared specifically for them.

All of them stayed in bed as the sun rose, sleeping well into the morning, about which disputes raged day and night in house after house. The ignoble did not venerate a 228.65
seated nobleman; being committed to irreligious practices they despised hermits, and were despised by them in turn. There was an intermingling of castes: purity was not upheld.

There was no clear difference of respect and contempt between brahmins who had mastered the Vedas and those had not. Slaves adopted the conduct of scoundrels—stealing, wearing jewelry and clothes; going off, standing still and staring at people. Women wore the clothes of men, and men wore the clothes of women. They experienced the highest joy when occupied with play or pleasure.

Because of a lack of faith, they did not procure the gifts 228.70
that powerful men of the past offered to those who were worthy, being only concerned with present occurrences. A friend would query a friend about some doubtful matter, and destroy his property for his own advantage—for nothing more than the tip of a horse's hair.

They approved of stealing and made their living through trade. Shudras steeped in asceticism were even seen among the noble classes! Some recited the Vedas without following the requisite vows, others followed useless vows. Pupils disobeyed their teachers, and some teachers even befriended their pupils.

pitā c' âiva, janitrī ca śrāntau vṛtt'|ôtsavāv iva.
a|prabhutve sthitau vṛddhāv, annaṃ prārthayataḥ sutān.
tatra veda|vidaḥ prājñā, gāmbhīrye sāgar'|ôpamāḥ,
228.75 kṛṣy|ādiṣv abhavan saktā, mūrkhāḥ śrāddhāny abhuñjata.
prātaḥ prātaś ca su|praśnaṃ kalpanaṃ preṣaṇa|kriyāḥ
śiṣy'|ânuprahitās† teṣām akurvan guravaḥ svayam.
śvaśrū|śvaśurayor agre vadhūḥ preṣyān aśāsata,
anvaśāsac ca bhartāraṃ samāhvāy' âbhijalpatī.†
prayatnen' âpi c' ârakṣac cittaṃ putrasya vai pitā,
vyabhajac c' âpi saṃrambhād duḥkha|vāsaṃ tath" âvasat.
agni|dāhena, corair vā, rājabhir vā hṛtaṃ dhanam
dṛṣṭvā dveṣāt prāhasanta suhṛt|saṃbhāvitā hy api.
kṛta|ghnā, nāstikāḥ, pāpā, guru|dār'|âbhimarṣinaḥ,
228.80 a|bhakṣya|bhakṣaṇa|ratā, nir|maryādā, hata|tviṣaḥ.
teṣv evam|ādīn ācārān ācaratsu viparyaye,
n' âhaṃ, dev'|êndra, vatsyāmi dānaveṣv, iti me matiḥ.
tan māṃ svayam anuprāptām abhinanda, Śacī|pate!
tvay" ârcitāṃ māṃ, dev'|ēśa, puro|dhāsyanti devatāḥ.
yatr' âhaṃ, tatra mat|kāntā, mad|viśiṣṭā, mad|arpaṇāḥ:
sapta devyo Jay"|âṣṭamyo vāsam eṣyanti te 'ṣṭadhā.
āśā, śraddhā, dhṛtiḥ, kśāntir, vijitiḥ, saṃnatiḥ, kṣamā,
aṣṭamī vṛttir etāsāṃ puro|gā, Pāka|śāsana.

Fathers and mothers were wearied, as if having just cele- 228.75
brated a festival. Aged parents lacked any power, and asked their sons for food. Even the wise Vedic masters, who were as deep as the ocean, practiced trades such as agriculture and foolishly ate at *shraddha* ceremonies.*

Every morning, urged on by their pupils, teachers took care of menial tasks and ceremoniously inquired about their students' welfare.

A wife, in the presence of her in-laws, would chastise the servants and call her husband to chastise him, all the while chattering away. A father would make great efforts to protect the mind of his son, but then the son would angrily cut him off and live a miserable life.

Even people respected by their friends burst into laughter, out of malice, when they saw another person's wealth being burned by fire, or taken by robbers or kings. They were ungrateful, heretical and evil, and touched the wives
of their teachers. Unrestrained and bereft of beauty, they 228.80
delighted in eating forbidden foods.

Since they follow practices such as these, and have deviated from the old ways, I will no longer abide among the *dánava*s, O Lord of the gods—this is my decision. So rejoice in the fact that I have come in person, husband of Shachi! Since I am revered by you, the gods will honor me, Lord of the gods.

Those who I love, distinguish and entrust are found where I abide: the seven goddesses along with Jaya, the eighth, all eight of whom will find my abode. Hope, faith, resolve, forbearance, success, humility, patience and good conduct,

tāś c' âhaṃ c' âsurāṃs tyaktvā, yuṣmad|viṣayam āgatā.
228.85 tri|daśeṣu nivatsyāmo dharma|niṣṭh"|ântar|ātmasu.

ity ukta|vacanāṃ devīm prīty|arthaṃ ca nanandatuḥ
Nāradaś c' âtra deva'|rṣir, Vṛtra|hantā ca Vāsavaḥ.
tato 'nala|sakho vāyuḥ pravavau deva|vartmasu†
iṣṭa|gandhaḥ, sukha|sparśaḥ, sarv'|êndriya|sukh'|āvahaḥ.
śucau v" âbhyarthite deśe tri|daśāḥ prāyaśaḥ sthitāḥ,
Lakṣmī|sahitam āsīnaṃ Maghavantaṃ didṛkṣavaḥ.
tato divaṃ prāpya sahasra|locanaḥ
śriy" ôpapannaḥ,† su|hṛdā maha"|rṣiṇā,
rathena hary|aśva|yujā sura'|rṣabhaḥ
sadaḥ surāṇām abhisatkṛto yayau.
228.90 ath' êṅgitaṃ vajra|dharasya Nāradaḥ,
Śriyaś ca devyā manasā vicārayan,
Śriyai śaśaṃs' âmara|dṛṣṭa|pauruṣaḥ
Śivena tatr' āgamanaṃ maha"|rṣibhiḥ.
tato 'mṛtaṃ dyauḥ pravavarṣa bhāsvatī
pitā|mahasy' āyatane svayaṃ|bhuvaḥ.
an|āhatā dundubhayo 'tha nedire,
tathā prasannāś ca diśaś cakāśire.

the eighth, are prominent in these goddesses, destroyer of Paka.

We have abandoned the demons and come to your dominion. We will live among the thirty gods in heaven, for 228.85
their commitment to religion comes from within.

BHISHMA said:

Once the goddess had uttered this speech, the celestial seer Nárada and Indra, the slayer of Vritra,* were delighted and overjoyed. Then the wind, a friend of fire, started to blow along the paths of the gods. Bearing desirable smells and a pleasant feeling, this wind brings bliss to all the sense faculties.

Virtually all the gods assembled in the requested place of purity, and saw Mághavat sitting with Lakshmi. Then the bullish god with one thousand eyes, accompanied by Shri and his friend the great seer, ascended to heaven on a chariot drawn by Indra's bay horse; they were honored as they approached the abode of the gods.

Understanding the intentions of the thunderbolt-wielder 228.90
and the goddess Shri, Nárada, whose power the immortals had recognized, announced their arrival, as did Shri, Shiva and other great seers. Heaven was radiant and showered down nectar on the dominion of Brahma, the self-existent grandfather. The drums of heaven began to roar although nobody struck them, and the cardinal points shone forth in their pellucidity.

yatha"|rtu sasyeṣu vavarṣa Vāsavo,
na dharma|mārgād vicacāla kaś cana.
an|eka|ratn'|ākara|bhūṣaṇā ca bhūḥ,
su|ghoṣa|ghoṣā bhuvan'|âukasāṃ jaye.
kriy"|âbhirāmā manu|jā manasvino
babhuḥ śubhe puṇya|kṛtāṃ pathi sthitāḥ.
nar'|âmarāḥ, kiṃnara|yakṣa|rākṣasāḥ
samṛddhimantaḥ su|manasvino 'bhavan.
na jātv a|kāle kusumaṃ, kutaḥ phalaṃ
papāta vṛkṣāt pavan'|ēritād api.
rasa|pradāḥ kāma|dughāś ca dhenavo,
na dāruṇā vāg vicacāra kasya cit.
228.95 imāṃ saparyāṃ saha sarva|kāma|daiḥ
Śriyāś ca Śakra|pramukhaiś ca daivataiḥ,
paṭhanti ye vipra|sadaḥ|samāgatāḥ,
samṛddha|kāmāḥ śriyam āpnuvanti te.
tvayā, Kurūṇāṃ vara, yat pracoditaṃ
bhav'|âbhavasy' êha paraṃ nidarśanam,
tad adya sarvaṃ parikīrtitaṃ mayā;
parīkṣya tattvaṃ parigantum arhasi.

Vásava showered rain upon the crops, as it was the season to do so, and no one deviated from the path of righteousness. The earth was adorned with mines abounding in gems, and all sorts of lovely sounds could be heard at the triumph of the gods. Men delighted in religious rites and were wise, steadfastly following the pure path of those who perform auspicious acts. Men, immortals, *kínnaras*, *yakshas* and *rákshasas* were successful and wise.

Flowers never fell from the trees, not to mention fruit, even when they were shaken by the wind. Milch cows yielded nectar and objects of desires, and nobody uttered any cruel words.

Those who gather in an assembly of brahmins to recite 228.95
this ode to Shri and the gods fronted by Shakra who grant all desires, they will achieve their desires and attain good fortune.

These are the indications of worldly success and failure that you asked about, supreme Kuru. You should examine everything I have just explained and understand its truth.

229
THE DIALOGUE BETWEEN JAIGISHÁVYA AND ÁSITA

YUDHIṢṬHIRA uvāca:

229.1 KIṂ|ŚĪLAḤ, KIṂ|samācāraḥ,
kiṃ|vidyaḥ, kiṃ|parākramaḥ
prāpnoti brahmaṇaḥ sthānaṃ,
yat paraṃ prakṛter dhruvam?

BHĪṢMA uvāca:

mokṣa|dharmeṣu niyato, laghv|āhāro, jit'|êndriyaḥ,
prāpnoti brahmaṇaḥ sthānaṃ, tat paraṃ prakṛter dhruvam.
atr' âpy udāharant' îmam itihāsaṃ purātanam:
Jaigīṣavyasya saṃvādam Asitasya ca, Bhārata.
Jaigīṣavyaṃ mahā|prajñaṃ, dharmāṇām āgat'|āgamam,
a|krudhyantam, a|hṛṣyantam, Asito Devalo 'bravīt.

DEVALA uvāca:

229.5 na prīyase vandyamāno, nindyamāno na kupyase.
kā te prajñā? kutaś c' âiṣā, kiṃ te tasyāḥ parāyaṇam?

BHĪṢMA uvāca:

iti ten' ânuyuktaḥ sa tam uvāca mahā|tapāḥ
mahad vākyam a|saṃdigdhaṃ, puṣkal'|ârtha|padaṃ, śuci.

JAIGĪṢAVYA uvāca:

yā gatir, yā parā kāṣṭhā, yā śāntiḥ puṇya|karmaṇām,
tāṃ te 'haṃ saṃpravakṣyāmi mahatīm, ṛṣi|sattama.

YUDHI·SHTHIRA said:

WITH WHAT VIRTUES, practices, knowledge and exertions can one attain the condition of *brahman*, that intransient state beyond primordial matter? 229.1

BHISHMA said:

A man can attain the condition of *brahman*, the intransient state beyond primordial matter, if he is committed to practices that lead to liberation, takes little food and masters his senses.

On this subject, people relate the ancient tradition of a dialogue between Jaigishávya and Ásita, O Bhárata. Jaigishávya was a man of great wisdom, a master of the treatises on religious practices, and devoid of anger and excitement. He was addressed by Ásita Dévala as follows.

DÉVALA said:

You feel no joy when you are praised, and do not get angry when you are despised. What wisdom have you attained? What is its source—what is its essence? 229.5

BHISHMA said:

Thus questioned by Dévala, the great ascetic delivered a remarkable teaching to him, one that was clear, pure and full of meaningful words.

JAIGISHÁVYA said:

I will outline the deportment of those who have performed auspicious deeds, exalted seer, as well as the transcendent goal and peace they attain.

nindatsu ca samā nityaṃ, praśaṃsatsu ca, Devala,
nihnavanti ca ye, teṣāṃ samayaṃ su|kṛtaṃ ca yat.
uktāś ca na vadiṣyanti vaktāram a|hite hitam,
pratihantuṃ na c' êcchanti hantāraṃ vai manīṣiṇaḥ.

229.10 n' â|prāptam anuśocanti, prāpta|kālāni kurvate.
na c' âtītāni śocanti, na c' âiva pratijānate.
saṃprāptāyāṃ ca pūjāyāṃ kāmād artheṣu, Devala,
yath"|ôpapattiṃ kurvanti śaktimantaḥ kṛta|vratāḥ.

pakva|vidyā, mahā|prājñā, jita|krodhā, jit'|êndriyāḥ,
manasā karmaṇā vācā n' âparādhyanti karhi cit.
an|īrṣavo, na c' ânyonyaṃ vihiṃsanti kadā cana,
na ca jāt' ûpatapyante dhīrāḥ para|samṛddhibhiḥ.
nindā|praśaṃse c' âty|arthaṃ na vadanti parasya ye,
na ca nindā|praśaṃsābhyāṃ vikriyante kadā cana.

229.15 sarvataś ca praśāntā ye, sarva|bhūta|hite ratāḥ,
na krudhyanti, na hṛṣyanti, n' âparādhyanti karhi cit.
vimucya hṛdaya|granthiṃ caṅkramanti yathā|sukham.
na yeṣāṃ bāndhavāḥ santi, ye c' ânyeṣāṃ na bāndhavāḥ.
a|mitrāś ca na santy eṣāṃ, ye c' â|mitrā na kasya cit.
ya evaṃ kurvate martyāḥ, sukhaṃ jīvanti sarvadā.

ye dharmaṃ c' ânurudhyante dharma|jñā, dvija|sattama,
ye hy ato vicyutā mārgāt, te hṛṣyanty udvijanti ca.
āsthitas tam ahaṃ mārgam asūyiṣyāmi kaṃ katham?
nindyamānaḥ praśasto vā, hṛṣye 'haṃ kena hetunā?

They always remain equanimous when people abuse or praise them, Dévala, and conceal their observances along with their good deeds. These wise men will not reply when someone intent on giving them trouble addresses them, they have no wish to strike back at someone who strikes them.

They do no lament what they do not possess, and only 229.10
act on what is present. They do not grieve what has passed away or acquiesce to anything. If they are revered, Dévala, these able practitioners of religious vows act on things as they happen, of their own free will.

Possessing immense wisdom and perfect knowledge, along with mastery of their anger and sense faculties, they do not wrong anyone in thought, deed or word. Since they are free from envy, wise men never harm each other and are never tormented by the successes of somebody else. Because they do not abuse or praise another person excessively, they are never affected by abuse or praise.

Those who are completely serene and delight in the wel- 229.15
fare of all living beings cannot be incited to anger or excitement; they do not wrong anyone. Releasing the knot in the heart, they wander about as they like. They have no companions, and are not the companions of others. They have no enemies, and are enemies to nobody. Mortals who act thus pass their lives in constant bliss.

These masters of religion live in accordance the religious law, exalted brahmin. But those who fall away from this path feel excitement and agitation. I have practiced that path, so who could I envy, and how? Whether I am abused or praised, what could cause me to become excited?

229.20 yad yad icchanti, tat tasmād apigacchantu mānavāḥ:
na me nindā|praśaṃsābhyāṃ hrāsa|vṛddhī bhaviṣyataḥ.
amṛtasy' êva saṃtṛpyed avamānasya tattva|vit;
viṣasy' êv' ôdvijen nityaṃ saṃmānasya vicakṣaṇaḥ.
avajñātaḥ sukhaṃ śete, iha c' âmutra c' â|bhayam.
vimuktaḥ sarva|doṣebhyo, yo 'vamantā sa vadhyate.†
parāṃ gatiṃ ca ye ke cit prārthayanti manīṣiṇaḥ
etad vrataṃ samāhṛtya, sukham edhanti te janāḥ.
sarvataś ca samāhṛtya
kratūn sarvāñ jit'|êndriyaḥ
prāpnoti brahmaṇaḥ sthānaṃ,
yat paraṃ prakṛter dhruvam.
229.25 n' âsya devā, na gandharvā, na piśācā, na rākṣasāḥ
padam anvavarohanti prāptasya paramāṃ gatim.

Therefore let men get whatever they want—I will not be 229.20
slighted through abuse or elevated through praise.

The person who understands the way things really are should delight in contempt, as if it were a nectar: the discerning man is always wary of honor, as if it were a poison. The man who is despised sleeps blissfully, and has nothing to fear in in this world and the world beyond. He is released from all sin, whereas the person who despises another is struck down. When wise men who long for the transcendent goal undertake this vow, they find bliss.

By completely withdrawing all one's desires, the one who masters the senses attains the condition of *brahman*, the
intransient state beyond primordial matter. The gods, *gan-* 229.25
*dhárva*s, *pisháchas* and *rákshasas* do not reach the state of that person who has attained the highest destiny.

230
THE DIALOGUE BETWEEN VASUDÉVA AND UGRA·SENA

YUDHIṢṬHIRA uvāca:

230.1 PRIYAḤ SARVASYA lokasya, sarva|sattv'|âbhinanditā
guṇaiḥ sarvair upetaś ca, ko nv asti bhuvi mānavaḥ?

BHĪṢMA uvāca:

atra te vartayiṣyāmi pṛcchato, Bharata'|ṛṣabha,
Ugrasenasya saṃvādaṃ Nārade Keśavasya ca.

UGRASENA uvāca:

yasya saṃkalpate loko Nāradasya prakīrtane,
manye sa guṇa|saṃpanno. brūhi tan mama pṛcchataḥ.

VĀSUDEVA uvāca:

Kukur'|âdhipa, yān manye, śṛṇu tān me vivakṣataḥ,
Nāradasya guṇān sādhūn saṃkṣepeṇa, nar'|âdhipa.
230.5 na cāritra|nimitto 'sy' âhaṃ|kāro deha|tāpanaḥ.
a|bhinna|śruta|cāritras, tasmāt sarvatra pūjitaḥ.
a|ratiḥ† krodha|cāpalye, bhayaṃ—n' âitāni Nārade.
a|dīrgha|sūtraḥ, śūraś ca, tasmāt sarvatra pūjitaḥ.
upāsyo Nārado bāḍhaṃ, vāci n' âsya vyatikramaḥ
kāmato yadi vā lobhāt. tasmāt sarvatra pūjitaḥ.
adhyātma|vidhi|tattva|jñaḥ, kṣāntaḥ, śakto, jit'|êndriyaḥ,
ṛjuś ca, satya|vādī ca. tasmāt sarvatra pūjitaḥ.

YUDHI·SHTHIRA said:

WHAT MAN ON this earth is loved by the whole world —the one who gladdens all creatures and is endowed with all qualities? 230.1

BHISHMA said:

Since you have asked about this matter, bullish Bhárata, I will outline the dialogue between Ugra·sena and Késhava about Nárada.

UGRA·SENA said:

The world is eager to praise Nárada, whom I think is endowed with all qualities. Please explain this matter to me, since I ask.

VASUDÉVA said:

Listen, Kúkura chief, ruler of men, to what I think are, in brief, the good qualities of Nárada, since I wish to discuss them.

His conduct does not induce the self-consciousness that torments the body. His learning and conduct is in no way deficient, and so he is revered everywhere. 230.5

Nárada is devoid of displeasure, anger, agitation and fear. He does not procrastinate and is heroic, and so is revered everywhere.

Nárada certainly ought to be venerated, for he commits no transgression in what he says, whether because of desire or greed. Therefore he is revered everywhere.

He knows the truth about the supreme self and the way to realize it, and is patient, able, a master of his senses, honest, and a speaker of truth. Therefore he is revered everywhere.

tejasā, yaśasā, buddhyā, jñānena vinayena ca,
janmanā, tapasā vṛddhas, tasmāt sarvatra pūjitaḥ.

230.10 su|śīlaḥ, sukha|saṃveśaḥ, su|bhojaḥ, sv|ādaraḥ, śuciḥ,
su|vākyaś c' âpy, an|īrṣyaś ca, tasmāt sarvatra pūjitaḥ.

kalyānaṃ kurute bāḍhaṃ: pāpam asmin na vidyate.
na prīyate par'|ân|arthais, tasmāt sarvatra pūjitaḥ.

veda|śrutibhir ākhyānair arthān abhijigīṣati;
titikṣur, an|avajñātas, tasmāt sarvatra pūjitaḥ.

samatvāc ca priyo n' âsti, n' â|priyaś ca kathaṃ cana.
mano|'nukūla|vādī ca, tasmāt sarvatra pūjitaḥ.

bahu|śrutaś, citra|kathaḥ, paṇḍito '|lālaso, '|śaṭhaḥ,
a|dīno, '|krodhano, '|lubdhas. tasmāt sarvatra pūjitaḥ.

230.15 n' ârthe, dhane vā, kāme vā bhūta|pūrvo 'sya vigrahaḥ.
doṣāś c' âsya samucchinnās, tasmāt sarvatra pūjitaḥ.

dṛḍha|bhaktir, a|nindy'|ātmā, śrutavān, a|nṛśaṃsavān,
vīta|saṃmoha|doṣaś ca. tasmāt sarvatra pūjitaḥ.

a|saktaḥ sarva|saṅgeṣu, sakt'|ātm" êva ca lakṣyate.
a|dīrgha|saṃśayo, vāgmī, tasmāt sarvatra pūjitaḥ.

He is steeped in power, reputation, intelligence, knowledge, discipline, birth and asceticism, and so is revered everywhere.

His habits are virtuous, he sleeps blissfully and eats gra- 230.10
ciously; he is very considerate, pure, eloquent and lacking in envy, and so is revered everywhere.

He certainly does what is good: no evil is found within him. He finds no pleasure in the misfortunes of others, and so is revered everywhere.

He only wishes to acquire wealth though Vedic learning and narrating legends; patient and not despised, he is revered everywhere.

Because of his impartiality nothing is dear to him, and he finds nothing disagreeable in any way whatsoever. He speaks what is pleasing to the mind, and so is revered everywhere.

He is very learned and a brilliant speaker; he is wise, noble-minded and free from longing, deceit, anger and greed. Therefore he is revered everywhere.

He has never quarreled over wealth, riches or pleasures. 230.15
He has eradicated sin, and so is revered everywhere.

Resolute in his piety, he is blameless, learned, benevolent and free from the faults such as delusion. Therefore he is revered everywhere.

He is not attached to any object of attachment, unlike an attached person. He speaks eloquently with little hesitation, and so is revered everywhere.

samādhir n' âsya kām'|ārthe, n' ātmānaṃ stauti karhi cit.
an|īrṣur, mṛdu|saṃvādas, tasmāt sarvatra pūjitaḥ.
lokasya vividhaṃ cittaṃ prekṣate c' âpy a|kutsayan.
saṃsarga|vidyā|kuśalas, tasmāt sarvatra pūjitaḥ.
230.20 n' âsūyaty āgamaṃ kaṃ cit, sva|naye n' ôpajīvati.
a|vandhya|kālo, vaśy'|ātmā, tasmāt sarvatra pūjitaḥ.
kṛta|śramaḥ, kṛta|prajño, na ca tṛptaḥ samādhitaḥ.
nitya|yukto '|pramattaś ca, tasmāt sarvatra pūjitaḥ.
n'|âpatrapaś ca yuktaś ca niyuktaḥ śreyase paraiḥ.
a|bhettā para|guhyānāṃ, tasmāt sarvatra pūjitaḥ.
na hṛṣyaty artha|lābheṣu, n' â|lābhe tu vyathaty api.
sthira|buddhir, a|sakt'|ātmā, tasmāt sarvatra pūjitaḥ.
taṃ sarva|guṇa|sampannaṃ, dakṣaṃ, śucim, an|āmayam,
kāla|jñaṃ ca, priya|jñaṃ ca kaḥ priyaṃ na kariṣyati?

He has no interest in an object of desire, and does not brag to anyone. He is free from envy and speaks softly, and so is revered everywhere.

Viewing the various minds of men without condemnation, he is skilled in the science of human intercourse and so is revered everywhere.

He is not disgruntled by any religious teaching and does 230.20
not profit from his own doctrine. Because he never wastes his time and is self-controlled, he is revered everywhere.

Austere and wise, he practices concentration eagerly. Ever disciplined and diligent, he is revered everywhere.

He is confident and diligent when set on a worthy task by others. He does not divulge secrets, and so is revered everywhere.

Acquiring wealth does not excite him, failing to acquire it does not distress him. He is detached, with a steadfast understanding, and so is revered everywhere.

Endowed with all good qualities, he is industrious, pure and free from disease. He understands circumstances and what is best for a person. Who would not love him?

NOTES

Bold *references are to the English text;* ***bold italic*** *references are to the Sanskrit text. An asterisk (*) in the body of the text marks the word or passage being annotated.*

174.1 **Laws that govern the duties of kings**: Nīlakaṇṭha comments *dharmā āpaddharmā uktāḥ*, implying that the laws referred to are those the king should follow in a crisis, i.e. those found in the second of the three books of 'Peace.' But it is just as likely that this verse refers to the laws mentioned in books one and two of 'Peace.'

174.19 A parallel to this verse is found in the early Buddhist literature in the *Indriya Jātaka* (no. 423 v. 2ab).

174.21 Similar versions of this verse are found at 201.21 and 206.4.

174.22 On this verse see 224.7.

174.24 A similar version of this verse is found at 211.9.

174.45 The first half of this verse is identical to the first half of 177.48.

174.62 A Buddhist parallel to this verse is found in the *Sīlavīmaṃsaka Jātaka* v. 3.

175.7–9 Buddhist parallels to these verses can be found at *Suttanipāta* verse 581, *Saṃyutta Nikāya* I verses 213 and 215, and *Theragāthā* verse 448.

175.13 A Buddhist parallel to this verse is found in the *Dhammapada* at v. 47.

175.18 A parallel to this verse in found in the *Dhammapada* at v. 47

175.32 The **sacrifice to** *brahman* (*brahma/yajña*) consists of private Vedic recitation. This "sacrifice" was originally one aspect of the five so-called "great sacrifices," the other four being a fire offering to the gods, an oblation of food and water to the ancestors, hospitality to human beings and a *bali* offering of scraps of food to spirits and various kinds of semi-divine beings. On these sacrifices, see Olivelle (1993: 53–55). This verse seems to show that Vedic recitation was separated from the five great sacrifices and seen by some as a valid ascetic path in its own right. On the practice of Vedic recitation alone as an ascetic path, see cantos 196–200.

176.3–4 The Sanskrit text does not include the words *brāhmaṇa uvāca* between 176.3 and 176.4. The failure to indicate a new speaker is common in the *Mokṣadharma*, but is confusing in long didactic tracts. To make the translation clearer, I occasionally indicate such changes of speaker without altering the Sanskrit text.

176.12 In the "Rig Veda," the *dasyus* are enemies of the Aryans. The term also denotes an enemy of the gods and an outcaste.

176.18 **These three motives**: Nīlakaṇṭha does not note what these things might be, although they are probably "splendrous things" (176.16, *śrī*), physical appearance (176.17, *rūpa*) and "wealth" (176.17, *dhana*).

177.18 The vocative *kāma* (desire) found in 177.23–25, 177.37, 177.39, 177.42, 177.44 and the vocative *kāmuka* (lustful one) found in 177.18–20 indicate that 177.18–44 is a dialogue between *kāma*, the personalization of Manki's desire, and the person they inflict, i.e. Manki. It would appear that hypermetrical remarks attributing verses to desire or Manki have been lost.

177.39 According to Hindu mythology the **Patála hell** is one of the seven regions under the earth and is occupied by serpents and demons.

177.48 For the first half of this verse see 174.45.

177.51 This verse is a repetition of 174.46.

178.1 **On this subject people relate the ancient tradition**: it is unusual for this formula to begin a canto. But in the Critical Edition 'The Song of Bodhya' is not separated from 'The Song of

Manki,' and so the "subject" mentioned here is instantly recognizable as the indifference (*nirveda*) mentioned at the end of canto 177.

178.2 The tradition of King Jánaka's indifference to the burning down of Míthila is also referred to at 219.50.

178.8 For this verse see 174.62.

179.2 In Hindu mythology, **Prahráda**, or Prahláda, was king of a class of demons known as *daityas*, who are similar or identical to the *dánavas* and *ásuras*. Thus in 179.15 Aja·gara calls Prahráda "*ásura* king," and in 179.16 "supreme *dánava*." Prahráda also appears in canto 222 of the present volume.

179.6 **Religion** (*dharma*), **pleasure** (*kāma*) and **material gain** (*artha*) are the three aims of life in Hinduism, to which was added a fourth aim: that of *mokṣa*, liberation.

179.31 **Observing that snakes eat only what comes by:** the word *ājagara* means "in the manner of a large snake." Ganguly (1999: 16) notes that "it is believed that such snakes, without moving, lie in the same place in expectation of prey, eating when anything comes near, famishing when there is nothing."

180.3 **Manki** and **Prahráda** have already appeared, in cantos 177 and 179 respectively. Like Prahráda, **Námuchi** and **Bali** are the names of prominent demons in Hindu mythology. Námuchi was slain by Indra, Bali was humiliated by Vishnu. In the present volume both feature in important dialogues with Indra, the former in cantos 226 and the latter in cantos 223–225 and 227.

180.49 **He will become a jackal just like me**: it is hardly likely that a disguised Indra would be made to speak of his former existence as a heretic. This statement indicates that the jackal of this dialogue was not originally thought to be Indra.

181.1 Apart from a number of divergent readings, this canto is identical to CSL XII.322.

181.5 *hastād vāmena*: K, B1, B2, Dn1 and Dn4 all read *hast'|âvāpena*, although this makes little sense. Nīlakaṇṭha interprets *hast'|âvāpena* as follows: *hast'|âvāpo hasta|nigaḍas tena nigaḍitāḥ*, "*hast'|âvāpo* means they are bound by an iron chain around the hands." He states that this refers to the expulsion of heretics from a kingdom, whereupon they wander the wilderness in fear due to their hands being bound (*sranto nāstikāḥ rāṣṭrād dūrī|kṛtāḥ vyāl'|ādimatsu vaneṣu gacchanti, nigaḍita|hastatvāc ca vyāl'|ādīn vārayitum a|śaktāḥ atyantam udvegaṃ prāpnuvant' îtyarthaḥ*). I have followed a variant reading recorded by Nīlakaṇṭha (and found in the apparatus to the Critical Edition rather than the edition of KINJAWADEKAR): *hastād vāmen' êti vā pāṭhaḥ. hastād vāma|pathen' êti*: "by the left hand means by the left-handed path." The commentator Arjunamiśra records a similar variant (*hasta|vāmen' êti vā pāṭhaḥ*), and two Bengali manuscript read something similar (*hasta(|ā)|vāmena*). A contrast with *hasta|dakṣiṇaṃ* "the right-handed (path)" of 181.6 is probably intended. In Brahminic thought, anything "left-handed" is considered deviant.

182.5 In Hindu mythology both **Bharad·vaja** and **Bhrigu** are seers, the latter being the ancestor of the Bhrigus (a mythical race of beings and/or one of the ancient Brahminical families). Bharad·vaja is believed to have authored a number of hymns in the Rig Veda.

182.13 VAN BUITENEN (1957: 15–25) has pointed out that in early theistic circles the term ***ahaṃ|kāra*** indicated the first utterance "I!" (*aham*) or "I am!" (*aham asmi*) of Brahma upon awakening from his cosmic slumber. This utterance of is thought to initiate world creation, whereas during Brahma's sleep the world remains in an unmanifest and uncreated form. The principle that creation depends on speech is also found in the ancient Brahminic principle that name and form are inseparable.

182.16 **Known by the name "the utterance I!:"** the term *ahaṃ|kāra* has already been mentioned in the latter half of 182.13, and its second appearance in this creation tract creates some confusion. According to the apparatus of the Critical Edition,

182.13*cd* is found in only a minority of manuscripts. This indicates that 182.13*cd*, in which the "absolute" ejaculates the utterance "I!" was probably a later addition to an original tract. If so, in the original theistic tract "space" was the first creation of the absolute *brahman*, and was soon followed by the emergence of the four other material elements (water, fire, wind and earth). These elements provided the material substratum necessary for the appearance of the personal god Brahma, who is said to be identical to the Vedas (182.15). The redactor who inserted 182.13*cd* was probably confused by the phrase *sarva/bhūta/dharaḥ prabhuḥ* in 182.14*ab*, thinking that this was a description of a personal deity rather than an epithet of the deity described in 182.11–13*ab*.

184.19 This does not necessarily disagree with the statement that the five elements are found in animate and inanimate beings (184.5), although the failure to mention inanimate things (*sthāvara*) here suggests that this is a separate tract from 184.5ff. Indeed a different understanding seems to be shown in the following discussion of the five elements and their derivatives in animate creatures. This discussion that beings at 184.19 connects well with the content of 184.1–4, which deal with the great elements and the human body. It is likely that 184.5–18, on the sentience of trees, constitute an interpolation into a tract that was originally concerned with the five elements and their derivatives in the human body.

184.29 Verse 184.29*cd*, found in nine northern and one southern manuscript, is a variant on 184.26*cd*. The Critical Edition omits 184.29*cd* but reads it at 184.26*cd* in place of its variant. It is likely that some northern editors or scribes knew both versions of this half verse and did not wish to choose one at the expense of the other. In order to preserve both readings in the text, one was included at 184.29*cd* although it is clearly out of place there.

184.32 **Fire has three perceptible qualities: sound, touch and visible form**: similar to this statement are those made in 184.35

("Wind has two perceptible qualities, sound and touch") and 184.38 ("space has only one perceptible quality, which is thought to be sound"). These statements reflect a doctrine according to which different combinations of the five elements are found in more than one perceptible object: fire is found in sounds, tactile objects and visible forms; wind is found in sounds and tactile objects; and space is found in sounds alone. This idea is probably based on the notion that each element is thought to include within it the essence of the element from which it is derived. If we assume that this passage is based on a cosmogony in which the elements are created in the order "space—wind—fire—water—earth," it means that wind is derived from space and contains within it the essence of space. Thus space and the perceptible quality particular to it (sound) must be contained within wind, as well as the perceptible quality particular to wind (tactility). This would explain why 184.35 states that wind has two perceptible qualities: sound and touch. By the same reasoning, if fire contains within itself something of the nature of wind and space, it must have the perceptible qualities of sound and touch besides the quality usually associated with fire (visibility). This doctrine, which Erich Frauwallner (1973: 99–101) has called the "accumulation theory," is contrary to statements made in 184.29, 184.32, 184.35 and 184.36, where it seems that smell, taste, vision and touch are the only perceptible qualities of earth, water, fire and wind respectively; this is the standard doctrine found in early Brahminic tracts on world creation. Because the portions of verses suggesting the "accumulation theory" contradict what is stated earlier on, it is likely that they are later interpolations into this canto.

184.34 **Iridescent blue:** the dictionaries render the compound *nīl'|âruṇa* "dark red," although I have followed Nīlakaṇṭha who interprets it *mayūra|picch'|ādeḥ*, i.e. similar to the color of a peacock's tail. The critical edition does not contain a compound at this point: it reads *nīlaḥ pīto 'ruṇas* for *pīto nīl'|âruṇas*.

184.35 Seventeen sorts of visible form are in fact enumerated. However, the six sorts of material objects outlined in 184.34*cd* are tactile qualities rather than visible qualities. It is likely that this half verse, which is only included at this point in six manuscripts of the Critical Edition's apparatus, has been moved from an original position where it described touch. In the Critical Edition (XII.177.34*ab*) it is used to enumerate the different sorts of physical sensation that are derived from wind. It seems that an original passage on the qualities of visible form had been displaced in the texts on which Nilakantha based his edition of the "Maha·bhárata."

184.39 *shadja*, *ríshabha*, *gandhára*, *mádhyama*, *dháivata*, *pánchama* **and** *nishháda*: these are the seven primary notes of the Indian musical scale, although *pánchama* is usually placed before *dháivata*.

185.4 On the term **world self** see the notes to 194.7 and 201.1. For other occurrences of this term, see 203.7, 204.5, 207.8 and 209.31. Its mention here is unusual but the verse is probably an interpolation, a fact that might be suggested by the appearance of *ahaṃ/kāra* in a list of psychological functions (hence the translation "self-consciousness") rather than as a cosmic principle as in 182.13 and 182.16. It would also be unusual to connect the subject of 185.4 with the pronoun *sa* in 185.5*a*, for that would suggest that the "cosmic self" is "circulated to all parts of the body." The pronoun *sa* in 185.5*a* probably picks up the word *prāṇo* in 185.3*c*.

187.2 On the belief that fire exists after it has been extinguished, see 192.6.

187.23 This verse is is omitted from the Critical Edition, being found in only thirteen of its Northern manuscripts. Furthermore, 187.23–26 have nothing to do with Bharad·vaja's question about the existence of the soul, and 187.23 is the only place in the entire dialogue between Bhrigu and Bharad·vaja in which a material source of creation ("evolvents of *primeval matter*") different from the absolute *brahman* is mentioned. This, as well as the reference in 187.25 to the three "states of the soul" (*guṇa*), probably indicates that this section of the dialogue was added later by a dualistic school of Samkhya. On early Samkhya thought, see note to 205.22.

187.28 A variant on this verse is found in the *Kaṭha Upaniṣad* at III.12.

189.2 The **six acts** are a brahmin's duties, and consist ofVedic recitation, instructing others in the Veda, offering sacrifices, performing sacrifices for others, offering gifts and accepting gifts.

190.8 In Hindu mythology **Rahu** was a demon (*daitya*) who disguised himself as a god when the gods were churning the ocean for the nectar of immortality. Immediately after drinking a portion of this aṃbrosia, the sun and moon revealed his identity to Vishnu who then cut off Rahu's head. Because Rahu had not swallowed the nectar, his head became immortal whereas the rest of his body did not. His head is thus thought to circulate in space, and a solar or lunar eclipse is explained as the swallowing of the sun and moon by Rahu's head.

Shiva ... obliterated the love god Kama by depriving him of a body: according to Hindu mythology Párvati, daughter of the Himalayas, was in love with Shiva and served him as his attendant, despite Shiva's disinterest and devotion to asceticism. But when Brahma predicted that the son of Shiva and Párvati would lead the gods to victory over the demons, Indra requested the help of Kama, god of love, to distract Shiva from his religious observations. Just as Kama was preparing to fire one of his arrows at Shiva, as Párvati approached him, Shiva became aware of the presence of Kama and incinerated him with a flame from his eye. Kama survived, but in a bodiless form.

191.8 According to OLIVELLE (1993: 154), the following discourse on the four religious paths (191.9–192.6) is "undoubtedly a remnant of an old *Dharmasūtra*."

192.1 On *bali* **oblations**, see the note to 175.32.

192.6 On the metaphor of the extinguished fire see 187.2. A fire was thought to reenter its essence in the ether when extinguished, rather than simply cease to exist. In the same way a liberated person was thought to be absorbed into *brahman* at death, rather than cease to exist. For more details on this simile and its Buddhist adaptation, see ALEXANDER WYNNE (2007: 95–98).

193.13 *saṃkasuka*, «unsteady, irresolute,» is sometimes written as *saṃkusuka* or *śaṃkusuka*; this is evidently what is meant by *śaṅkuśuko* here.

194.7 The term *bhūt'/ātmā* probably means "self of (all) beings," i.e. the **world self**. For other occurrences of this term, see 201.1, 203.7, 204.5, 207.8 and 209.31.

194.16 This verse is out of place. A slightly different rendering of it is found at 194.56, where it fits the context much better. It is likely that the ancient transmitters of this passage were aware of two versions of this verse, and so included both rather than lose one. They probably inserted it here because some sort of connection can be made between the words *buddhvā* and *buddhyā* of 194.16*a*, and the tract on the faculty of intelligence (*buddhi*) that follows from 194.17–36. If so, it probably means that 194.15*cd* originally preceded 194.17.

194.20 The statement that the **mind** is involved with **desire** differs from the statement that the mind "ponders things" in 194.13. While these two capacities are not mutually exclusive, separate but divergent definitions of the mind's functions probably indicate different strata in canto 194. Indeed the passage as far as 194.14 describes how the "world self" creates and destroys the material elements, and how this "creator" (194.8) pervades the whole world (194.14). Contrary to this, 194.15–44, while probably not unitary, anticipates some of the themes of the later dualistic variety of Samkhya thought. Thus the faculty of intelligence is said to comprise "the entire world" (194.18, which contradicts 194.14) and have three psychosomatic states; this is followed by a short passage on the dualism between spirit and matter (194.38–44). The text from

194.45 onwards refers to meditative ideas and is probably a continuation of the earlier creative tract: 194.49 it likens world creation to the action of a spider emitting its web, a monistic creation simile found in other early Brahminic texts (such as *Bṛhadāraṇyaka Upaniṣad* II.1.20) and *Śvetāśvatara Upaniṣad* (VI.10), and this agrees with the monistic outlook of 194.18. For a more detailed analysis of canto 194, see: VAN BUITENEN (1956: 153–57); FRAUWALLNER (1973: 227ff); BAKKER AND BISSCHOP (1999).

194.31–36 A different treatment of these verses is found at 219.26–31, where they form part of the Samkhya teaching of Pancha·shikha.

194.45 On the notion of the senses emitting rays, see 206.12–14.

196.6 **Yama** is the Hindu god who presides over the spirits of the dead. The story of the encounter between the brahmin and Yama does not begin until canto 199, however. The intervening verses are probably interpolations, the intention of which was to say more about the practice of quiet Vedic recitation (*japa*).

196.7 The term **Vedanta** means "the end of the Veda" and here refers to the early Upanishads and the speculation contained within them.

198.5 The god **Shukra** is Venus, and Brihas·pati is Jupiter.

198.7 Nilakantha interprets **the two** as pleasure and pain (*priy'|āpriya*); the three as the three psychosomatic states of purity, passion and darkness; the eight as material elements (1), senses (2), mind (3), intelligence (4), karmic impressions (5), *karma* (6), the bodily winds (7) and ignorance (8), and the three again as the object of cognition, the subject of cognition and cognition itself (*jñeya|jñāna|jñātṛ|bhāvāḥ*).

199.1 **Please tell me about that**: this comment refers to the beginning of the dialogue (199.6), where Bhishma informs Yudhi·shthira of a dialogue between Yama, Time and a brahmin.

199.2 **Ikshváku** is a legendary king and son of Manu, the father of the human race.

199.4 The father of Vishva·mitra and founder of a mythical royal lineage.

199.5 The **six Vedic disciplines** are phonetics (*śikṣā*), meter (*chandas*), grammar (*vyākaraṇa*), etymology (*nirukta*), astronomy (*jyotiṣa*), and ritual exegesis (*kalpa*).

199.39 On the six duties of a brahmin, see the note to 189.2.

199.68 **Sarásvati** is traditionally held to be the Hindu goddess of eloquence and learning.

199.98 Víkrita's reluctance to receive the merit offered by Virúpa implies a belief in the idea that when a giver receives a gift from a person, it cancels out the merit gained from offering that person a gift earlier on. The notion that the merit gained by offering a donation is canceled out when the donor receives a gift explains why King Ikshváku hesitated to receive a gift offered by the Brahminic ascetic: he thought that the reversal of the usual donative order—according to which kshatriyas always offer donations to brahmins—would cancel out the merit he had gained by offering gifts.

201.1 **World self:** on this term see the note to 194.7; also see 185.4, 203.7, 204.5, 207.8 and 209.31. The sense "self of all beings" is not clear in this verse. The term could mean "self of a single being," i.e. the individual self, as it seems to at 203.7 and 204.5.

201.2 In Hindu mythology **Manu** is the first man and father of the human race, whereas **Brihas·pati** is the chief priest of the gods.

01.12–13 These verses are omitted from the Critical Edition. Although the manuscript evidence is confused at this point, thirty of the Critical Edition's manuscripts read these six *pāda*s in some form.

201.21 For similar versions of this verse, see 174.21 and 206.4.

203.4 The first half of this verse is similar to the first half of 202.16.

203.7 On the term **individual self** (*bhūt'/ātmā*) see the notes to 194.7 and 201.1. For other occurrences of this term, see 185.4, 204.5, 207.8 and 209.31.

203.8 **Marks in the moon ... the hare they resemble:** it is an old Indian belief that the marks in the moon resemble a hare or rabbit.

203.22 On **Rahu** see note to 190.8.

204.5 On the term **individual self** (*bhūt'/ātmā*) see the notes to 194.7 and 201.1. For other occurrences of this term, see 185.4, 203.7, 207.8 and 209.31.

204.7 A virtually identical version of this verse is found at 206.21.

204.16 This verse is found in the "Bhagavad Gita" at II.59 (CSL VI.26.59); for its position in the Clay Sanskrit Library edition of the "Maha·bhárata," see CHERNIAK (2008: 190–91).

205.10 A similar version of the first half of this verse is found at 204.17.

205.22 The word *prakṛti*, which I have translated as **primordial matter**, is also found in 205.23, 205.24 and 205.26, whereas its equivalent, *pradhāna* ("unmanifest matter") is found in 205.25. In the dualistic tradition of Samkhya thought "primordial/unmanifest matter" and "spirit" (*púrusha*) are the two unchanging and ultimately distinct principles of the universe: whereas matter evolves and devolves, spirit stands aloof as its passive spectator. This understanding is not found in the dialogue between Manu and Brihas·pati before this point. Indeed a cosmology lacking any principle of primordial/unmanifest matter is referred to at 204.10–12. Given the late appearance of dualistic Samkhya thought in canto 205, and its divergence from the earlier part of the dialogue in general, it is probably an interpolation of a later redactor. See also 203.3 and 206.7 for other likely dualistic interpolations.

206.4 Similar versions of this verse are found at 174.21 and 201.21.

206.6 All critical edition manuscripts similarly read an extra syllable in *pāda c*.

5.12–13 These verses are probably late Vaishnavite interpolations: no mention of Vishnu is made in the dialogue between Manu and Brihas·pati before this point.

206.21 A virtually identical version of this verse is found at 204.7.

207.4 Both **Jamad·agni** and **Nárada** are mythical Hindu seers; **Krishna Dvaipáyana** is a name of Vyasa, the mythical compiler of the "Maha·bhárata;" **Ásita Dévala** is a Vedic seer believed to have composed a number of hymns from the Rig Veda. **Valmíki** is the compiler of the "Ramáyana," and **Markandéya** is an ancient sage said who is said to have authored the *Mārkaṇḍeyapurāna.*

207.8 On the term **world self** see the notes to 194.7 and 201.1. For other occurrences of this term, see 185.4, 203.7, 204.5 and 209.31.

207.10 According to later tradition, **Bala·deva** or Sankárshana is the second of the four forms of Vishnu, the supreme spirit. Since Sankárshana is the first manifestation of Vishnu here, this text must precede the established tradition.

7.12–13 These verses, describing the manifestation of the god Brahma, make the manifestation of Bala·deva superfluous to the myth of Vishnu's destruction of Madhu. Moreover, the statement that "Bala·deva supports all creatures" (207.11) conflicts with the statement that Brahma is the "grandfather of all living beings" (207.13). It is possible that 207.12–13 are a later "Brahmaistic" interpolation. The same is probably true of 207.17–28: although they describe Brahma's creation of all creatures, they disrupt the account of the creative acts of Vishnu in canto 207. Indeed 207.16 is closely connected to 207.29, and both are integral to canto 207, whereas the intervening verses are self-contained and have nothing to do with the rest of the canto. Proof that 207.12–13 and 207.17–28 are connected seems to be provided by 207.34, which refers to Vishnu's creation of Brahma. Canto 208 gives a fuller account of Brahma's creation of all living beings, and it is possible that this canto was appended to canto 207 to expand upon the latter's Brahmaistic interpolations.

207.16 **Madhu·súdana** means "slayer of Madhu" and is an epithet of Vishnu.

207.26 This verse references the myth of Vishnu's fifth incarnation as a dwarf (*vāmana*). After Indra had been defeated by the demon Bali, Vishnu—disguised as a poor brahmin dwarf—requested a piece of land from him. When Bali assented to this request and allowed the dwarf as much land as he wished, the latter insisted on as much as could be covered in three steps but grew to gigantic proportions and in three steps crossed the universe. With the first step he traversed the earth, with his second he encompassed the heavens and with his third he stepped on Bali's head and consigned him to the underworld.

207.34 According to Hindu mythology there are usually seven **divine mothers** (occasionally eight, nine or sixteen), and they are closely connected with Shiva. Alternatively, the word *gaṇa* in the compound *bhūta|mātṛ|gaṇ'|âdhyakṣaṃ* could be read alone to refer to the demi-gods who are believed to attend Shiva.

208.4 **Maríchi, Atri...**: this list is slightly different from the list in the previous canto, in which the seven sons of Brahma are said to be Daksha, Maríchi, Atri, Ángiras, Pulástya, Púlaha and Kratu (207.17). It seems that cantos 207 and 208 record different early Brahminic traditions.

208.10 **Áryaman** belongs to a class of gods known as Adítyas.

208.11 **Shasha·bindu** is a name of the moon.

208.17 **Martánda** and **Vivásvat** are both names of the sun.

208.19–20 The text is most probably corrupt at this point. The twelve gods named in these verses are not Vasus, and the eight Vasus have not been named in this passage. Moreover, although most of the gods listed here are not traditionally classified as *rudras*, six of this list (Ajáikapad, Ahir·budhnya, Hara, Bahu·rupa, Tryámbaka and Aparájita) are contained in the list of *rudras* found in the *Harivánsha* (I.3.49–51). An extra line that appears after 208.20*ab* in six Southern and one Northern manuscript used by the Critical Edition (*ekādaś' âite kathitā Rudrās tri/bhuvan'/ēśvarāḥ*: "these eleven *rudras* are said to be the lords of the triple world.") was probably added later on in order to solve this old problem, as was an extra verse listing the eight Vasus found in three other Southern Manuscripts (*Dharo, Dhruvaś ca, Somaś ca, Āpaś c' âiv', Ânilo, 'nalaḥ, Pratyūṣaś ca mahā/bhāgaḥ, Sāvitraś c' âṣṭamaḥ smṛtaḥ*: "Dhara, Dhruva, Soma, Apa, Ánila, Pratyúsha and Savítra, who is believed to be the eighth").

208.32 The great seers **Ékata, Dvita and Trita** usually make up a class of water deities called *aptyas*, and so seem out of place in a list of the seers of the Western skies.

209.31 On the term **world self** see the notes to 194.7 and 201.1. For other occurrences of this term, see 185.4, 203.7, 204.5 and 207.8.

ɔ.26–46 The rest of canto 210 appears to be conform to an early tradition of Samkhya thought. Similar Samkhya notions are found throughout the remainder of this dialogue: all are, arguably, later interpolations.

210.27 On the word *ahaṃ/kāra* see note to 182.13.

210.35 This verse seems to use the word *avyakta* as an epithet of *brahman*. If so, it is in disagreement with 210.27–28, where *avyakta* is synonymous with *prakṛti* ("primordial matter") and means "unmanifest matter." The text at this point seems corrupt—the verse following 210.35 has no connection with it, and it appears that part of the text has been lost (perhaps a text on the three psychosomatic states).

211.9 A similar version of this verse is found at 174.24.

214.13 The **'Agha·márshana'** is a poem of the "Rig Veda" (x.190). It is a Hindu belief that by reciting it three times whilst immersed in water, one can expiate one's sin.

214.23 **Three seeds:** according to Nīlakaṇṭha these are chyle (*anna/rasa*), the *mano/vahā* channel and intention (*saṃkalpa*).

215.7 *Pādas ab* are found in sixteen Northern manuscripts, and seem to have been moved from their original place at 215.8*cd*.

216.5 **Hari** is an epithet of Vishnu.

216.13 *Pādas cd* makes little sense in this position, but virtually the same half verse is found at 216.15*cd*. The Critical Edition includes the half verse at 216.15*cd* rather than 216.13*cd*, since only a minority of manuscripts (fifteen) insert it at 216.13*cd* (four of these manuscripts do not repeat it at 216.15 *cd*). 216.15*cd* is probably the original position of this half-verse.

217.1 Nīlakaṇṭha explains the **set of four** as the states of dream (*svapna*), dreamless sleep (*suṣupti*), the state of *brahman* that possesses qualities (*sa/guṇa/brahma*) and the state of *brahman* devoid of qualities (*nir/guṇa/brahma*). A different explanation of the "set of four" is found in his notes on 217.13.

217.6–13 These verses have little to do with the rest of the canto, and are probably a later interpolation from a Samkhya perspective.

217.13 According to Nīlakaṇṭha the **set of four** is spirit (*puṃs*), unmanifest matter (*pradhāna*), the soul (*jīva*) and the personal god (*īśvara*).

218.11–12 Verse 218.11*cd*–12*ab* appears in only eight of the Northern manuscripts utilized by the Critical Edition. Moreover, this verse appears at this point in canto 218 in only two of these manuscript besides Dn1 and Dn4: in two other manuscripts it appears after 218.16, in one it appears after 218.19 and in another it is found after 218.20. This gloss on Pancha·shikha's name is is undoubtedly a later addition to canto 218.

218.27 This verse is very obscure. Verses 218.23–26 seem to be an argument against the various ways in which the Vedic tradition asserts the belief a transcendent reality (218.23: *param*). Pancha·shikha's argument against these Vedic positions is based on the fact that they are disproved by "direct perception" (*pratyakṣa*). If so, the final statement may concern the fact that some Vedic practices are based upon perception—the point is perhaps that unless perception is taken as an authority above scripture, some Vedic practices would be pointless. After this argument against Vedic beliefs, Pancha·shikha seems to refute materialists (218.23–31), Buddhists (218.32–38) and fatalists (218.39–42, although this section may be a continuation of the materialist doctrine). For a different interpretation of this passage, see BRONKHORST (2007: 309–28).

219.2 This question is based on the statement of the Upanishadic sage Yajnaválkya in the *Bṛhadāraṇyaka Upaniṣad* that "after death there is no awareness" (*na pretya saṃjñāstīty are bravīmi*) (II.4.12, IV.5.13).

9.26–31 These verses occur in a slightly different form at 194.31–36. According to MOTEGI (1999: 528–29), the version in canto 194 was interpolated into canto 219 in order to adapt Pancha·shikha's teachings on sensation (*vedanā*: the threefold explanation at 219.11 is identical to the early Buddhist analysis) to the standard Samkhya view.

220.1 An expanded version of this canto appears in the "Maha·bhárata" at CSL XII.160 (CE XII.154).

222.3 **Prahráda** or Prahláda is the king of a class of Hindu demons called *daityas*.

224.7 For a different version of this verse see 174.22.

225.1 The term *śata/kratu* (**one hundred sacrifices**) refers to the fact that Indra is thought to have performed one hundred horse sacrifices.

228.40 Something has probably been lost in the text at this point. The active participles in the genitive plural case of 228.39*cd* and 228.40*cd* require a subject in the nominative case. After 228.40, six Southern manuscripts read *kālo yātaḥ sukhe c' âiva dharma/mārge ca vartatām*: "Time passed for them engaged in the pleasant path of religion," i.e. "The *dánavas* passed their time engaged in the path of religion, taking pleasure in giving and distributing gifts...” This extra verse was probably added at a later date to solve the problem that 228.39*cd*–40 lack a subject.

228.75 The *shraddha* is a daily ceremony in which water and balls of rice are offered to nourish one's ancestors in the afterlife.

228.86 **Slayer of Vritra**: according to Vedic mythology, after drinking a large volume of the intoxicating drink *soma* Indra defeated Vritra, a serpent-demon by whom the waters of the world had been withheld.

174.38 *ālasyaṃ* Dn1 : *ālakṣya* K B1 B2 Dn4. Nīlakaṇṭha reads *ālakṣya* but records the alternate reading *ālasyaṃ*.

174.51 *prasīdati* B2 Dn1 Dn4 : *prapaśyati* K B1. The reading *prapaśyati* in K and B1 is rare, being found in only two Devanāgarī manuscripts in the apparatus of the Critical Edition.

175.6 *putrān* B1 B2 Dn1 Dn4 : *putrāt* K.

175.31 *amartyavat* B1 B2 Dn1 Dn4 : *amatyavat* K

175.33 *kṣatrayajñaiḥ* Nīlakaṇṭha CE : *kṣetrayajñaiḥ.* K B1 B2 Dn1 Dn4. I have followed the reading of Nilakantha's commentary.

177.2 *anāyāsaḥ* B1 B2 Dn1 Dn4 : *anāyāsaṃ* K.

177.13 *upapadyeta* B1 B2 Dn1 Dn4 : *upadyeta* K.

177.23 *vidīryate* B1 B2 Dn1 Dn4 : *vidāyate* K.

177.27 *eva* B1 B2 Dn1 Dn4 : *evaṃ* K.

177.37 *kāma* Dn1 : *kāmaṃ* K B1 B2 Dn1 Dn4.

179.6 *prajāsv avimanā* B2 : *prajāsu vimanā* K Dn1 Dn4 B1. The reading *avimanā* is attested in Nīlakaṇṭha's commentary.

180.6 *tyaktvā* B1 B2 Dn1 Dn4 : *yaktvā* K.

180.28 *rundh' êndriya/grāmaṃ* CE : *buddh'/îndriya/grāmaṃ* K B1 B2 Dn1 Dn4.

181.10 *samācitam* Dn1 Dn4 : *samīhitam* K B1 B2.

183.16 *ākāśe* Dn1 Dn4 : *ākāśaṃ* K B1 B2.

184.37 *ekādaśavidho* B2 Dn4 : *dvādaśadhā sparśo* K B1 Dn1. Only eleven sorts of touch are outlined. But if the six sorts of visible form wrongly placed in 184.34*cd* are understood in place of the five sorts of touch mentioned in 184.37*ab*, then touch would indeed be twelvefold. It is possible that 184.34*cd* was originally situated at 184.37*ab*. When it was removed to its present position, either by accident or on purpose (by Nīlakaṇṭha or another scribe of the northern tradition), an extra half *pāda* was invented to replace it in 184.37*ab*. Although this new half verse only included five kinds of touch, 184.37*cd* was left unaltered.

185.11 *guda* B1 B2 Dn1 Dn4 : *gada* K.

185.13 *prati°* B1 B2 Dn1 Dn4 : *prīta°* K.

186.2 *c' âiva* CE : *c' âitat* K B1 B2 Dn1 Dn4. All Nīlakaṇṭha sources read *c' âitat*, but the Critical Edition reads *c' âiva* on the basis of all available manuscripts. The latter reading makes better sense, although Nīlakaṇṭha's interpretation of *etat* as *annam* is plausible.

186.9 *vyādhivraṇaparikleśair* CE : *vyādhivarṇaparikleśair* K. K, B1, B2, Dn1 and Dn4 all read *varṇa*, but this is probably a misreading of *vraṇa*, "wound," which is found in the Critical Edition.

188.17 *purā* CE : *paraṃ* K B1 B2 Dn1 Dn4.

189.6 *vāṇijyā* Dn1 : *vaṇijyā* K. B2 and Dn4 read *viśaty āśu paśubhyaś ca* for *pāda a*.

189.12 *sa ca* Dn1 Dn4 : *ca sa* K B1 B2.

191.10 *sadācārāṇāṃ* B1 B2 Dn1 Dn4 : *sadācārāṇā* K.

193.27 *chādayanty* Dn1 : *chādayaty* K B1 B2 Dn4.

194.17 *guṇān* CE : *guṇair* K B1 B2 Dn1 Dn4. The reading *guṇān* in the Critical Edition makes better sense, for this section of 194 appears to state a doctrine in which intelligence is the creative principle in the world. It is possible that the intensive form *nenīyate* ("to lead as a captive, have in one's power, rule, govern") was misunderstood in a passive sense because of the *ātmanepada* ending *-te*, and that this brought about the reading *guṇair* to give a logical subject of the verb. But the verb is not passive: it is active and requires an object in the accusative case. Although the same reading *guṇair* is confirmed when this verse is repeated at 285.18, when it is repeated at 247.16 the reading is *guṇān*.

194.40 *matsyo* B1 B2 Dn1 Dn4 : *matsyau* K.

194.53 *śuddhiṃ* Dn1 Dn4 : *siddhiṃ* K B1 B2.

194.59 *bhaved* B1 B2 Dn1 Dn4 : *bhavad* K.

194.60 *viduṣāṃ* B1 B2 Dn1 Dn4 : *viduṣā* K.

194.63 *nirāviśaṃs* B2 : *nirāvaśaṃs* K B1 : *virāviṇas* CE Dn1 Dn4.

199.3 *yathā* B1 B2 Dn1 Dn4 : *prathā* K.

199.87 *parīkṣa* Dn1 : *parīksya* K B1 B2 Dn4.

199.127 *niḥspṛhaḥ* Dn1 Dn4 : *nispṛhaḥ* K B1 B2.

201.12 *na paraṃ* Dn1 Dn4 : *nirayaṃ* K B1 B2.

202.7 *vāpy abhūd* Dn1 Dn4 B1 B2 Nīlakaṇṭha : *vyāpyabhūd* K.

202.7 *param'|ârtha|kārī* B2 Dn4 : *param'|ātma|kārī* K B1 Dn1.

202.13 *budhaḥ* B2 Dn1 Dn4 : *buddhiṃ* K B1.

202.14 *sa|manāḥ* Dn1 Dn4 Nīlakaṇṭha : *su|manāḥ* K B1 : *su|mahān* B2.

202.14 *sa|buddhir* B1 B2 Dn1 Dn4 Nīlakaṇṭha : *su|buddhir* K.

203.12 *evaṃ* Dn1 Dn4 : *eva* K B1 B2.

203.19 *vyayato* CE : *vayasā* K B1 B2 Dn1 Dn4.

205.7 *c' âpy* B9, D5-7 : *v" âpy* K B1 B2 Dn1 Dn4. This verse is not included in the Critical Edition. The reading *cāpy* is attested in no Nīlakaṇṭha source, although it is found in one Bengali and three Devanāgarī manuscripts. Fourteen other Northern manuscripts, including Dn1 and Dn4 read *vāpy*.

205.23 *sargaṃ n' âiv' ôpayānti ca* CE : *svargaṃ c' âiv' ôpayānti ca* K B1 B2 Dn1 Dn4.

207.12 *mahā|bāho* Dn1 Dn4 : *mahā|bāhau* K B1 B2.

207.14 *mahā|bāho* Dn1 Dn4 : *mahā|bāhau* K B1 B2.

207.17 *Atry|Aṅgirasau* CE : *Atry|Aṅgirasaṃ* K B1 B2 Dn1 Dn4.

207.29 *ânvakalpayat* CE : *ânukalpayat* K B1 B2 Dn1 Dn4.

208.12 *śataṃ* CE : *daśa* K B1 B2 Dn1 Dn4.

210.10 *sarga* CE : *svarga* K B1 B2 Dn1 Dn4.

210.16 *pralaye* CE : *pralayaṃ* K B1 B2 Dn1 Dn4.

210.30 *karmaṇām* CE : *karmaṇī* K.

211.1 *Guru* CE : *Bhīṣma* K B1 B2 Dn1 Dn4. The remainder of this dialogue is attributed to Bhishma rather than the *guru* of canto 210, although it is clearly the latter who is speaking. I have followed this reading of the Critical Edition in the remainder of the dialogue.

212.2 *prayojanamahatvāt* B2 Dn1 Dn4 : *prayojanaṃ mahattvāt* K B1.

212.11 *'yaṃ* B1 B2 Dn1 Dn4 : *'rtha* K.

213.5 *snehasaṃbandhaḥ* CE : *snehasaṃbandhāt* K Dn1 Dn4 B1 B2.

213.5 *janmājanmakṛtakṣaṇāḥ* B1 B2 Dn1 Dn4 Nīlakaṇṭha : *janmāj janmakṛtakṣaṇāḥ* K.

213.6 *purīṣamūtravikleda* CE : *purīṣamūtravikledaṃ* K Dn1 Dn4 B1 B2.

213.8 *etāviśeṣeṇa* B2 Dn1 Dn4 : *evāviśeṣeṇa* K B1.

213.8 *na cābhīyur vipaścitaḥ* B1 B2 Dn4 : *naro 'tīyād viśaṣataḥ (sic. viśeṣataḥ)* K Dn1.

214.1 *tadvijñānāc* Dn4 B2 CE : *tattvajñānāc* K B1 : *tadd hi jñānāc* Dn1.

214.12 *dur/balān āviśed* Dn1 : *dur/balānāṃ viśed* K B1 B2 Dn4.

214.16 *kaphān* B2 Dn4 : *kaphād* K B1 Dn1.

215.5 *vāgbuddhikarmabhiḥ* Dn1 Dn4 : *vā buddhikarmabhiḥ* K B1 B2.

215.14 *bhāro* CE : *bhāraṃ* K B1 B2 Dn1 Dn4.

215.19 *saṃprakāśante* Dn4 : *tat prakāśante* K B1 B2 Dn1.

215.20 *etaiś cāpagataiḥ* B2 Dn1 Dn4 : *śanaiś cāpagate* K B1.

216.5 *upapannārthaṃ* B1 B2 Dn1 Dn4 : *upapannāthe* K.

216.7 *manogatam* B1 B2 Dn1 Dn4 : *manāgatam* K.

216.8 *sa ved' ôttama/pūruṣaḥ* B1 : *veda s' ôttama/pūruṣaḥ* B2 Dn1 Dn4 : *sa ved' ôktama/pūruṣaḥ* K.

216.9 *yad yat tat* CE : *yady etat* K B1 B2 Dn1 Dn4.

216.14 *mānasam* CE : *mānuṣam* K B1 B2 Dn1 Dn4.

216.15 *prasādāt* Dn4 : *prasādaṃ* K B1 B2 Dn1.

217.23 *prabhavāprajñā* B2 Dn4 : *prabhavaprajñā* K B1 Dn1.

217.26 *yukto dhāraṇayā kaś cit* CE : *yuktaṃ dhāraṇayā samyak* K B1 B2 Dn1 Dn4. Thirteen manuscripts in the apparatus of the Critical Edition read *vidyā*; twenty-one read *vidyut*, as do all the Nilakantha sources.

217.26 *vidyā* K7, Ds, D7, T, G1.2, M1, M5-7 : *vidyut* K B1 B2 Dn1 Dn4. Thirteen manuscripts in the apparatus of the Critical Edition read *vidyā*; twenty-one read *vidyut*, as do all the Nilakantha sources.

218.4 *nānā/pāṣaṇḍa/nivādinaḥ* CE : *nān"/āśrama/nivāsinaḥ* K B1 B2 Dn1 Dn4.

218.12 *nibodhayat* CE : *nyavedayat* K B1 B2 Dn1 Dn4.

218.22 *tad* CE : *tam* K B1 B2 Dn1 Dn4.

218.32 *°tṛṣṇānāṃ* B2 Dn1 Dn4 : *°ceṣṭānāṃ* K B1.

218.34 *vyūḍhe* CE : *gūḍhe* K B1 B2 Dn1 : *mūḍhe* Dn4.

218.34 *citte* CE : *bhinne* K B1 B2 Dn1 Dn4.

218.35 *eva* B2 Dn1 Dn4 : *evaṃ* K B1.

218.35 *saṃbandhaḥ* CE B2 : *sarvaṃ vā* K B1 Dn1 Dn4.

218.39 *tithyaḥ* CE : *tiṣyaḥ* K B1 B2 Dn1 Dn4.

218.46 *tathātyanta* K Dn1 Dn4 B1 : *vitta* B2.

219.7 *pañcadhā toyaṃ* B2 Dn1 Dn4 : *pañcabhūteṣu* K B1.

219.11 *vedanā* CE : *cetanā* K B1 B2 Dn1 Dn4.

219.42 *na ca svatāṃ* CE : *nadāś ca tā* K B1 B2 Dn1 Dn4.

219.43 *pratisaṃmiśrite jīve* B2 Dn1 Dn4 : *jīve ca pratisaṃyukte* K B1.

219.46 *mahadd hy* CE : *mahaty* K B1 B2 Dn1 Dn4.

220.10 *na mānitā* CE : *'bhimānitā* K B1 B2 Dn1 Dn4.

220.11 *pratyayo nṛṣu* Nīlakaṇṭha : *pratyayeṣu ca* K B1 B2 Dn1 Dn4.

221.2 *vrata|luptā* Dn4 : *vrata|lubdhā* K B1 B2 Dn1 Dn4.

222.5 *vidita|prabhav'|âpyayam* Dn1 : *vidita|prabhav'|âvyayam* K B1 B2 Dn4.

222.7 *ātma|niḥśreyasi* CE : *ātma niḥśreyasi* K B1 B2 Dn1 Dn4.

222.7 *niścitaniścayam* B1 B2 Dn1 Dn4 : *niścitaniścitam* K.

223.29 *carddhiṣu* B1 B2 Dn1 Dn4 : *cardhiṣu* K.

223.30 *syās* K Dn1 Dn4 B1 : *syāt* B2.

224.40 *dānav'|ēśvaram ūrjitam* CE : *dānav'|ēśvara|pūjitam* K B1 B2 Dn1 Dn4.

224.46 *āhur* Dn1 : *āyur* K Dn4 B1 B2.

226.9 *jānāmi śreyo na tu tat karomi* CE : *jñānāc chreyo, na tu tad vai karomi* K B1 B2 Dn1 Dn4.

226.14 *kān āpado* Ś1, K1.2.4, Da4, T2, G3.6, M7 : *kān n' āpado* K B1 B2 Dn1 Dn4. Nine of the Critical Edition's manuscripts, including the old Śāradī manuscript Ś1, read *kān āpado*. The Critical Edition agrees with the reading in K.

226.17 *praṇuden* CE : *praṇudan* K B1 B2 Dn1 Dn4.

226.17 *saṃtāpam āyāsa|karaṃ* CE : *saṃtāpayām āsa karaṃ* K B1 B2 Dn1 Dn4.

226.18 *tat sadaḥ* CE : *na tat sadaḥ* K B1 B2 Dn1 Dn4.

226.18 *sabhā|sadaḥ* CE : *sabhā ca sā* K B1 B2 Dn1 Dn4.

226.18 *yo* Dn1 Dn4 : *yāṃ* K B1 B2.

227.5 *yaś* B1 B2 Dn1 Dn4 : *yac* K.

227.15 *hīnaḥ* B1 Dn1 Dn4 : *hīna* K B2.

227.66 *atītānāgataṃ* B1 B2 Dn1 Dn4 : *atītānāgata* K.

227.75 *vikatthase* CE : *kiṃ katthase* B1 B2 Dn1 Dn4.

227.103 *budhyase* Dn1 Dn4 : *budhyate* K B1 B2.

snuṣā Dn4 : *snuṣāṃ* K B1 B2 Dn1.

228.76 *śiṣyānuprahitās* Dn1 Dn4 : *śiṣyān aprahitās* K B1 B2.

228.77 *°bhijalpatī* Dn1 : *°bhijalpati* K B1 B2 : *abhijalpatā* Dn4.

228.86 *devavartmasu* B1 B2 Dn1 Dn4 : *devavatmasu* K.

228.89 *śriy" ôpapannaḥ* Dn1 : *striy" ôpapannaḥ* K B1 B2 Dn4.

229.22 *vadhyate* Dn1 Dn4 : *budhyate* K B1 B2.

230.6 *a/ratiḥ* Dn1 Dn4 : *a/rati* K B1 B2.

TECHNICAL GLOSSARY

ĀTMAN "Self" or "Soul." In early Brahminic thought the *ātman* is the most essential part of a person that is reincarnated in another body after death. The *ātman* is also believed to be identical with the sacred essence that pervades the cosmos, *brahman*. Once a person realises his *ātman* (usually in a state of *dhyāna* through the practice of *yoga*), he will identify with *brahman* and merge into a death rather than be reborn.

BRAHMAN The non-dual, sacred essence that pervades the world. A common theme of the *Mokṣadharma* is that *brahman* is the source from which the cosmos periodically emerges and into which it subsequently devolves. It is thus thought that *brahman* is responsible for world-creation and imbues it with its sacred essence, but yet remains beyond it in an unmanifest state.

BHĀVA "Psychosomatic state." Various philosophical texts in the *Mokṣadharma* refer to the three psychosomatic states of *sattva*, *rajas* and *tamas*. These three states indicate qualities that are found in sense objects as well as the states of body and mind that a person experiences. In later Samkhya thought, the three states of *sattva*, *rajas* and *tamas* are thought to be the essential qualities that make up the world of matter.

DHARMA "Religion, Law, Duty, Custom, Righteousness." One of the most ambiguous terms in Sanskrit literature. At the simplest level *dharma* means "religious law" and refers to those practices and duties prescribed by sacred tradition (the Dharma Sutras and the exegetical works that followed) and distinguished in terms of a person's class (*varṇa*) and religious path (*āśrama*). Thus the word can refer to individual deeds, the religious laws that determine those deeds and the karmic merit that these deeds create. On a more abstract level *dharma* refers to the inviolable religious order of the cosmos, i.e. a natural law of righteousness from which particular laws of this world derive.

DHYĀNA "Meditation." Derived from the verb √*dhyai* ("to think, contemplate, meditate"), this word refers to the practice of one-pointed concentration as well as the states of inner concentration that this practice effects. In the former sense *dhyāna* is synonymous with the word *yoga*. In the *Mokṣadharma*, meditation is the most common spiritual by which a person can realise the *ātman*.

JHĀNA the Middle Indic form of *dhyāna* used in early Buddhist texts.

KARMA "Action." An important preoccupation of early Indian thinkers. In earlier Brahminism, *karma* refers to religious acts and duties, and especially to the ritual acts enjoined by the Veda. But the concept underwent an ethical transformation in the period of the early Upanishads, and so in the *Mokṣadharma* refers to good and bad deeds as well as the subsequent merit and demerit they cause, this merit or demerit in turn causing good and bad experiences. A general belief of early Indian thinkers was that *karma* causes future reincarnation, and thus that salvation from reincarnation coincides or is effected by the cessation of *karma*.

KṢETRAJÑA Field-knower. An important term in early Brahminic thought that is usually synoymous with the term *ātman*. But whereas the term *ātman* is usually connected with the nondualistic understanding that *brahman* pervades the world, in some passages of the *Mokṣadharma* the *kṣetrajña* is described as "spirit" that stands apart from and observes matter (*pradhāna*, *prakṛti*).

NIRVANA The ultimate goal of Buddhism, where it denotes the cessation or "blowing out" (*nir-√vā*) of the three "fires" of greed, hatred and delusion. Appears in the *Mokṣadharma* in the Buddhist-influenced canto 195, where it simply denotes the religious goal.

PRĀṆA "Breath." A person's inner breaths or winds were an important subject of speculation in early Brahminism. It was believed that a person has five breaths that are responsible for all the vital functions of the body and without which it would not work. In the singular, *prāṇa* refers to a person's "lifebreath."

RAJAS "Passion," one of the three *bhāva*s, i.e. a quality that when sensed in an object causes various states of bodily and mental passion.

SATTVA "Purity," one of the three *bhāva*s and so a quality that when

when sensed in an object causes various states of bodily and mental purity.

SĀṂKHYA An important school of thought. The classical Samkhya thought contained in Īśvarakṛṣṇa's *Sāṃkhyakārikas* expresses a basic duality between spirit and matter, the latter consisting of the three qualities of *sattva*, *rajas* and *tamas*. Although traces of this dualistic understanding are found throughout this first volume of the *Mokṣadharma*, they are not always stated to be ideas related in particular to Samkhya thought. Moreover, the early Samkhya teachings of Pancha·shikha found in cantos 218 and 219 even seem to express a nondualistic understanding.

TAMAS "Darkness," one of the three *bhāva*s and so a quality that when sensed in an object causes various states of bodily and mental darkness.

UPANIṢADS A corpus of sacred texts that conclude the Vedas. The *Bṛhadāraṇyaka* and *Chāndogya Upaniṣad*s, generally thought to be the oldest texts of this type, set the predominant intellectual concerns that were worked out in other early Upanishads and texts of the *Mokṣadharma*.

UPĀSANA "Veneration." This term refers to the esoteric knowledge of Upanishadic masters that is the main subject of the early Upanishads. According to the magical world-view of these thinkers, hidden connections (*upaniṣad*, *bandhu*) link the human being to the external world and the sphere of ritual action. It is the task of the Upanishadic master to know these hidden connections, i.e. to "venerate" one thing as another, and thus attain control of the world.

VEDAS The most sacred texts of Hinduism that are split into four books: the Rig, Yajur, Sama and Atharva Vedas. These works contain the sacred hymns and formulae to be uttered at rituals and sacrifices, although they contain lengthy works of ritual exposition, the Bráhmanas, and are concluded by the more speculative Arányakas and Upanishads.

YOGA "Means, method, work." Although in earlier parts of the "Maha·bhárata" yoga can refer to the practice of asceticism, in the *Mokṣa-dharma* it refers to the "method" or "work" of inner meditation, *dhyāna*. The basic spiritual practice referred to in the *Mokṣa-dharma*, and so a general practice of the renunciant schools of early Brahminism. In later times a "Yoga" school of philosophy emerged based on the *Yogasūtras* of Patánjali, although the dualistic understanding of this work differs from the nondualistic *yoga* passages of the *Mokṣadharma*.

MOKṢA "Liberation," i.e. release or spiritual salvation. The basic concept of liberation in the *Mokṣadharma* is that a person escapes from reincarnation through realising his true nature (the *ātman*). The liberated condition that such a person achieves after death is the unmanifest state of *brahman*.

PROPER NAMES AND EPITHETS

ÁDITI Daughter of Daksha, wife of Káshyapa, and mother of the gods known as Adítyas.

ADÍTYAS Class of Hindu gods born from Áditi.

AGÁSTYA A famous sage who reputedly composed some Vedic hymns.

AILA Name of Purúravas, mythological king who is believed to have instituted the three sacrificial fires.

AJA·GARA Name of sage known elsewhere in Hindu mythology as a demon (*ásura*).

ÁMITA·DHVAJA Son of Dharma·dhvaja, an ancient king of Benares.

ÁNDHRAKA Name of a people from South India, cf. modern day Andhra Pradesh.

ÁNGIRAS Born from Brahma's mouth, a divine seer named as the composer of hymns, laws and a treatise on astronomy.

ASHVINS Name of two Hindu gods who are twins.

ATRÉYA Descendent of Atri.

ATRI A Vedic seer believed to have authored a number of Vedic hymns.

BALA One of a class of gods known as "Vishve Deva."

BHARATA Prototypical ruler of North India; ancestor of most of the characters in the "Maha·bhárata." In the plural, the Bharatas are the descendants of Bharata.

BHÁRATA Descendant of Bharata.

BHISHMA Son of King Shántanu and the Ganges river. He is renowned for his wisdom and fidelity, and fights for the sons of Dhrita·rashtra. He is also known as Gangéya, Shántanava, Deva·vrata, and simply the "grandfather," a label which he shares with the god Brahma.

BHÚRIHAN Name of sage known elsewhere in Hindu mythology as a demon (*ásura*).

BRAHMA The progenitor of all creatures, personification of brahman.

BRAHMAN Divine principle by which the universe is pervaded.

BRIHAS·PATI The god of prayer or devotion and so priest of the gods; the name given to Jupiter in Hindu astronomy.

DHARMA The divine personification of the religious order (*dharma*) and Yudhi·shthira's genitor.

DHAUMYA Ancient seer and also family priest of the Pándavas.

GANDHÁRVA Class of divine beings renowned as celestial musicians or heavenly singers.

GOVÍNDA Krishna.

HÁSTINA·PURA City of the Kurus.

HIRÁNYA·KÁSHIPU A demon king noted for his impiety.

IKSHVÁKU First king of the royal dynasty (sometimes called "solar") based in Ayódhya

INDRA King of the gods. Also known as Shakra, Vásava, and Mágha-vat.

KAILÁSA Mountain on which Kubéra and Shiva dwell.

KÁITABHA A demon who tried to kill Brahma but was killed by Vishnu instead.

KAKSHÍVAT A Vedic seer who authored several hymns of the Rig Veda.

KALI Personification of misfortune and the name of the final and worst cosmic age.

KANVA A Vedic seer who authored several hymns of the Rig Veda.

KÁPILA An ancient sage believed to be the founder of the Sankhya philosophy.

KÁVASHA A Vedic seer who authored several hymns in the tenth book of the Rig Veda.

KÍNNARAS Mythical beings with a human body and the head of a horse, or else a horse's body and the head of a man.

KRISHNA An avatar of the god Vishnu who is allied to the Pándavas. He is also known as Vasudéva, Madhu·súdana, Govínda, Hari,

Pundarikáksha, Hrishikésha and Késhava.

KUBÉRA Lord of riches, leader of the *yakshas*.

KÚKURA Name of a people who descended from prince Kukura.

KUNTI Wife of Pandu; mother of the three eldest Pándava brothers including Yudhi·shthira.

KURU Ancestor of the heroes of the "Maha·bhárata."

LAKSHMI Goddess of good fortune and wife of Vishnu.

MÁGHAVAT A name for Indra. Literally, "bountiful."

MANU The first man, progenitor of the human race.

MARÍCHI Chief of the Maruts.

MEDHÁTITHI Descendent of Kanva, and author of some Vedic hymns.

MERU The mountain at the center of the cosmos.

MÍTHILA Ancient capital of Videha.

NÁHUSHA Ancient king who was briefly ruler of the gods.

NÁIRRITI Demons descended from Nírriti, a goddess of death.

NÁRADA A semidivine figure who circulates widely amongst the inhabitants of the cosmos, telling tales and often making mischief.

NÁRAKA Demon who lives in Prag·jyótisha and personifies hell.

NARÁYANA Supreme deity often identified with Vishnu.

PAKA A Daitya killed by Indra.

PARTHA Son of Pritha = Yudhi·shthira, Bhima, Árjuna, Nákula and Saha·deva (the latter four are not named in this volume of 'Liberation.'

PÁRVATA A seer associated with Narada and composer of a number of Vedic hymns; also believed to be a messenger of the gods.

PIPPALÁDA An ancient teacher of the Atharva Veda.

PISHÁCHAS A class of ogre-like demons.

PRAJA·PATI "Lord of creatures," either the supreme god who created all creatures or else a minor god or "progenitor" who created some classes of creatures.

PRATIRÚPA A demon.

PULÓMAN A demon destroyed by Indra.

PURAN·DARA Epithet of Indra meaning "destroyer of fortresses."

PÚSHPAVAT A demon.

RÁKSHASAS A class of demons.

RASÁTALA One of the seven hells beneath the earth.

REBHA A seer cast into a well by the demons and then rescued by the Ashvins.

SANKÓCHA A demon.

SARÁSVATA A seer believed to have been born from the sacred Sarásvati river.

SATVAT Name of a people (also called Yádava since they descended from king Yadu) who lived in the area of Máthura.

SHÁBARA A wild tribe of the Deccan.

SHAKRA Epithet of Indra meaning "strong" or "powerful."

SHÁMBARA A demon killed by Indra.

SHIVA Supreme deity, often associated with asceticism and/or destruction.

SHRI Epithet of Lakshmi.

SIDDHAS Literally "accomplished ones," these are semi-divine class of beings that inhabit the sky or space and are thought to possess miraculous powers.

SOMA 1. The deified drink of victory. 2. The moon (occasionally identified as a Bhárata ancestor).

SVASTY·ATRÉYA Seer who composed a number of Vedic hymns.

UGRA·SENA Father of Kansa whom Krishna reestablished as king of Máthura.

VARAHÁSHVA A demon.

VÁSAVA Indra indicating his leadership of a class of gods known as Vasus.

VASÍSHTHA A sage and traditional rival of Vishva·mitra.

VASUDÉVA Epithet of Krishna.

VIDÉHA Name of a country in modern Tirhut, in Bihar.

VIDHÍTSA Epithet of Lakshmi.

VIRÚPAKA A demon.

VÍSHKARA A demon.

VISHNU One of the supreme deities in the Hindu tradition.

VISHVA·DANSHTRA A demon.

VISHVA·MITRA Celebrated seer born of the royal Kushika lineage.

VÍSHVAJIT A demon.

VRISHA A demon.

VRISHÁNDA A demon.

VRISHNI A tribe from whom Krishna was descended.

YAMA The god who rules over the spirits of the dead.

YAKSHAS A class of semi-divine spirits.

YUDHI·SHTHIRA Eldest of the Pándavas. Known as Bhárata, Partha, best of the Kurus, the king of righteousness, and Ajáta·shatru.

THE CLAY SANSKRIT LIBRARY

The volumes in the series are listed here in order of publication.
Titles marked with an asterisk* are also available in the
Digital Clay Sanskrit Library (eCSL).
For further information visit www.claysanskritlibrary.org

1. The Emperor of the Sorcerers (*Bṛhatkathāślokasaṃgraha*) (vol. 1 of 2) by *Budhasvāmin*. Sir James Mallinson
2. Heavenly Exploits (*Divyāvadāna*). Joel Tatelman
3. Maha·bhárata III: The Forest (*Vanaparvan*) (vol. 4 of 4)* William J. Johnson
4. Much Ado about Religion (*Āgamaḍambara*) by *Bhaṭṭa Jayanta*. Csaba Dezső
5. The Birth of Kumára (*Kumārasaṃbhava*) by *Kālidāsa*. David Smith
6. Ramáyana I: Boyhood (*Bālakāṇḍa*) by *Vālmīki*. Robert P. Goldman
7. The Epitome of Queen Lilávati (*Līlāvatīsāra*) (vol. 1 of 2) by *Jinaratna*. R.C.C. Fynes
8. Ramáyana II: Ayódhya (*Ayodhyākāṇḍa*) by *Vālmīki*. Sheldon I. Pollock
9. Love Lyrics (*Amaruśataka, Śatakatraya & Caurapañcāśikā*) by *Amaru, Bhartṛhari & Bilhaṇa*. Greg Bailey & Richard Gombrich
10. What Ten Young Men Did (*Daśakumāracarita*) by *Daṇḍin*. Isabelle Onians
11. Three Satires (*Kaliviḍambana, Kalāvilāsa & Bhallaṭaśataka*) by *Nīlakaṇṭha, Kṣemendra & Bhallaṭa*. Somadeva Vasudeva
12. Ramáyana IV: Kishkíndha (*Kiṣkindhākāṇḍa*) by *Vālmīki*. Rosalind Lefeber
13. The Emperor of the Sorcerers (*Bṛhatkathāślokasaṃgraha*) (vol. 2 of 2) by *Budhasvāmin*. Sir James Mallinson
14. Maha·bhárata IX: Shalya (*Śalyaparvan*) (vol. 1 of 2)* Justin Meiland

15. Rákshasa's Ring (*Mudrārākṣasa*)*
by *Viśākhadatta*. MICHAEL COULSON

16. Messenger Poems (*Meghadūta, Pavanadūta & Haṃsadūta*)
by *Kālidāsa, Dhoyī & Rūpa Gosvāmin*. SIR JAMES MALLINSON

17. Ramáyana III: The Forest (*Araṇyakāṇḍa*)
by *Vālmīki*. SHELDON I. POLLOCK

18. The Epitome of Queen Lilávati (*Līlāvatīsāra*) (vol. 2 of 2)
by *Jinaratna*. R.C.C. FYNES

19. Five Discourses on Worldly Wisdom (*Pañcatantra*)*
by *Viṣṇuśarman*. PATRICK OLIVELLE

20. Ramáyana V: Súndara (*Sundarakāṇḍa*) by *Vālmīki*.
ROBERT P. GOLDMAN & SALLY J. SUTHERLAND GOLDMAN

21. Maha·bhárata II: The Great Hall (*Sabhāparvan*)
PAUL WILMOT

22. The Recognition of Shakúntala (*Abhijñānaśākuntala*) (Kashmir Recension) by *Kālidāsa*. SOMADEVA VASUDEVA

23. Maha·bhárata VII: Drona (*Droṇaparvan*) (vol. 1 of 4)*
VAUGHAN PILIKIAN

24. Rama Beyond Price (*Anargharāghava*)
by *Murāri*. JUDIT TÖRZSÖK

25. Maha·bhárata IV: Viráta (*Virāṭaparvan*)
KATHLEEN GARBUTT

26. Maha·bhárata VIII: Karna (*Karṇaparvan*) (vol. 1 of 2)
ADAM BOWLES

27. "The Lady of the Jewel Necklace" & "The Lady who Shows her Love" (*Ratnāvalī & Priyadarśikā*) by *Harṣa*.*
WENDY DONIGER

28. The Ocean of the Rivers of Story (*Kathāsaritsāgara*) (vol. 1 of 7)
by *Somadeva*. SIR JAMES MALLINSON

29. Handsome Nanda (*Saundarananda*)*
by *Aśvaghoṣa*. LINDA COVILL

30. Maha·bhárata IX: Shalya (*Śalyaparvan*) (vol. 2 of 2)*
JUSTIN MEILAND

31. Rama's Last Act (*Uttararāmacarita*) by *Bhavabhūti*.
SHELDON POLLOCK. Foreword by GIRISH KARNAD

32. "Friendly Advice" (*Hitopadeśa*) by *Nārāyaṇa* &
"King Víkrama's Adventures" (*Vikramacarita*). JUDIT TÖRZSÖK
33. Life of the Buddha (*Buddhacarita*)
by *Aśvaghoṣa*. PATRICK OLIVELLE
34. Maha·bhárata V: Preparations for War (*Udyogaparvan*) (vol. 1 of 2)
KATHLEEN GARBUTT. Foreword by GURCHARAN DAS
35. Maha·bhárata VIII: Karna (*Karṇaparvan*) (vol. 2 of 2)
ADAM BOWLES
36. Maha·bhárata V: Preparations for War (*Udyogaparvan*) (vol. 2 of 2)
KATHLEEN GARBUTT
37. Maha·bhárata VI: Bhishma (*Bhīṣmaparvan*) (vol. 1 of 2)*
Including the "Bhagavad Gita" in Context
ALEX CHERNIAK. Foreword by RANAJIT GUHA
38. The Ocean of the Rivers of Story (*Kathāsaritsāgara*) (vol. 2 of 7)
by *Somadeva*. SIR JAMES MALLINSON
39. "How the Nagas were Pleased" (*Nāgānanda*) by *Harṣa* &
"The Shattered Thighs" (*Ūrubhaṅga*) by *Bhāsa*.*
ANDREW SKILTON
40. Gita·govínda: Love Songs of Radha and Krishna (*Gītagovinda*)*
by *Jayadeva*. LEE SIEGEL. Foreword by SUDIPTA KAVIRAJ
41. "Bouquet of Rasa" & "River of Rasa" (*Rasamañjarī & Rasataraṅgiṇī*) by *Bhānudatta*. SHELDON POLLOCK
42. Garland of the Buddha's Past Lives (*Jātakamālā*) (vol. 1 of 2)*
by *Āryaśūra*. JUSTIN MEILAND
43. Maha·bhárata XII: Peace (*Śāntiparvan*) (vol. 3 of 5)*
"The Book of Liberation" (*Mokṣadharma*). ALEXANDER WYNNE
44. The Little Clay Cart (*Mṛcchakaṭikā*) by *Śūdraka*.
DIWAKAR ACHARYA. Foreword by PARTHA CHATTERJEE
45. Bhatti's Poem: The Death of Rávana (*Bhaṭṭikāvya*)*
by *Bhaṭṭi*. OLIVER FALLON

46. "Self-Surrender," "Peace," "Compassion," and "The Mission of the Goose": Poems and Prayers from South India (*Ātmārpaṇastuti, Śāntivilāsa, Dayāśataka & Haṃsasaṃdeśa*) by *Appayya Dīkṣita, Nīlakaṇṭha Dīkṣita & Vedānta Deśika.* YIGAL BRONNER & DAVID SHULMAN
Foreword by GIEVE PATEL
47. Maha·bhárata VI: Bhishma (*Bhīṣmaparvan*) (vol. 2 of 2)* ALEX CHERNIAK
48. How Úrvashi Was Won (*Vikramorvaśīya*) by *Kālidāsa* VELCHERU NARAYANA RAO & DAVID SHULMAN
49. The Quartet of Causeries (*Caturbhāṇī*) by *Śūdraka, Śyāmilaka, Vararuci & Īśvaradatta.* CSABA DEZSŐ & SOMADEVA VASUDEVA
50. Garland of the Buddha's Past Lives (*Jātakamālā*) (vol. 2 of 2)* by *Āryaśūra.* JUSTIN MEILAND
51. Princess Kadámbari (*Kādambarī*) (vol. 1 of 3) by *Bāṇa.* DAVID SMITH
52. The Rise of Wisdom Moon (*Prabodhacandrodaya*)* by *Kṛṣṇamiśra.* MATTHEW T. KAPSTEIN
Foreword by J.N. MOHANTY
53. Maha·bhárata VII: Drona (*Droṇaparvan*) (vol. 2 of 4)* VAUGHAN PILIKIAN
54. Maha·bhárata X & XI: Dead of Night & The Women (*Sauptikaparvan & Strīparvan*).* KATE CROSBY
55. Seven Hundred Elegant Verses (*Āryāsaptaśatī*)* by *Govardhana.* FRIEDHELM HARDY
56. Málavika and Agni·mitra (*Mālavikāgnimitram*) by *Kālidāsa.* DÁNIEL BALOGH & ESZTER SOMOGYI